NATO

Facts and Figures

NATO INFORMATION SERVICE
BRUSSELS

Enquiries concerning this and other NATO Publications
should be addressed to:

NATO INFORMATION SERVICE
1110 BRUSSELS
Tel: (02) 241.00.40   241.44.00   241.44.90
Telex: 23867 OTAN/NATO

January 1976

Table of Contents

PART 3 The structure of NATO

PART 4

APPENDICES

Maps Charts and Statistical Tables

The Secretaries General of NATO

Lord ISMAY
1952–1957

Paul-Henri SPAAK
1957–1961

Manlio BROSIO
1964–1971

Dirk U. STIKKER
1961–1964

Joseph M. LUNS
Oct. 1971–

Preface

No one volume can be sufficient to describe in detail both the evolution of the Atlantic Alliance since 1949 and its wide range and scale of activities to-day. This book, however, contains the essence of what should be known about NATO by all those who wish to keep themselves fully informed about the Alliance which has provided the main basis for the stability and peace in Europe for over twenty-five years.

This edition covers the period from the origins of the Alliance until the end of 1975. When the Treaty was signed in 1949 there was a great sense of insecurity in Europe and contacts between East and West were almost non-existent. To-day the situation is very different.

The well-organized defensive system which has been created by the Allies has provided a basis of stability and confidence from which the Allies could undertake their many initiatives to work with the countries of Eastern Europe for a more stable relationship in which the underlying political issues can be solved. These initiatives led to the opening of important bilateral and multilateral East–West negotiations.

The Atlantic Alliance has two main functions. Firstly, by

maintaining adequate military strength to deter aggression – and to defend members if aggression should occur. Secondly, in the climate of stability, security and confidence created by a balance of forces, to work constructively for detente and the solution of political issues. This book describes not only the military side of the Alliance but its activities in many other fields, including political consultation and co-operation – particularly important during a period of East-West negotiations – as well as work in numerous other areas, notably economics, science and ecology.

Brussels
December 1975

Joseph Luns
Secretary General of NATO

PART 1

Origins and evolution of the Alliance

CHAPTER 1

Origins of the Alliance

In the closing phase of the Second World War, seven weeks after the capitulation of Nazi Germany and six weeks before the Hiroshima bomb, representatives of fifty nations signed the United Nations Charter in San Francisco. The date was June 26, 1945, and the world hoped it had at last learned how to keep the peace. Within four years, ten European countries found themselves faced by a threat the nature of which necessitated some more specific protection than that afforded by the United Nations Charter. Indeed, the latter contained a provision stipulating the right of its members, individually or collectively, to defend themselves against possible armed attack. The Europeans turned to the United States and Canada to under-write their pledge of mutual security and, on April 4, 1949, the North Atlantic Treaty was signed.[1]

What had happened, in the space of three years and not quite nine months, to convince those twelve countries of the need for a regional defence alliance?

The defeat of the two great military and industrial powers, Germany and Japan, had left an immense vacuum to the east and west of the Soviet Union. Taking advantage of such exceptionally favourable circumstances, the Soviet Union made full use of the combined strength of the Red Army and world Communism to conduct an expansionist policy which was soon to threaten peace and collective security. Even in 1945 the most confirmed optimist could not claim that the international sky was unclouded. The British Prime Minister, Sir Winston Churchill, in his telegram of May 12 addressed to President Truman, expressed his anxiety in the following

1. This historical chapter is, for the most part, taken from Lord Ismay's book: NATO – *The First Five Years.*

11

terms: 'What will be the position in a year or two when the British and American armies have melted, and the French have not yet been formed on any major scale, and when Russia may choose to keep 200 or 300 divisions on active service?' and he added: 'An iron curtain is drawn down upon their front (Russia). We do not know what is going on behind. . . .' This, it may be noted, was the first occasion on which this subsequently familiar metaphor was used.

Demobilization of forces

On the morrow of the German surrender, the Western democracies, true to their wartime pledges and to popular demand, began to demobilize. The United States and the United Kingdom quickly withdrew the bulk of their armed forces from Europe. They demobilized most of their troops, with the exception of occupation forces and units committed in other parts of the world. As for the nations of Europe, they addressed themselves to the complex tasks of reconstruction.

The armed strength of the Allied forces in Europe at the time of the surrender of Germany was about five million men. One year later, following demobilization, their armed strength amounted to no more than 880,000 men. The following table, moreover, shows the exact strengths after demobilization:

	1945	1946
United States	3,100,000 men	391,000 men
United Kingdom	1,321,000 ,,	488,000 ,,
Canada	299,000 ,,	0 ,,

The Soviet Union, on the other hand, continued to keep its armed forces on a wartime footing; in 1945 their strength amounted to more than four million men. It also kept its war industries going at full blast.

On the political side, the Western Powers went to the furthest limits of conciliation. They made every effort to reach agreement with the Soviet Government and to make the United Nations an effective instrument for peace. They met with nothing but obstruction.

Problems of peace treaties

At San Francisco in 1945, Poland was not represented at the conference table because the USSR and the Western Powers were unable to agree on the composition of a Polish provisional government.

At the London Conference of Foreign Ministers (September, 1945), Mr. Molotov blocked any discussion of the United Kingdom's proposals for the opening of an impartial enquiry into the situation in Rumania and Bulgaria.

It was only after making concessions that the representatives of the Western Powers were able, in November 1945, to obtain Soviet agreement on a procedure for framing peace treaties with Italy, Finland and Germany's former satellites in the Balkans. The Peace Conference opened in Paris on July 29, 1946, and the peace treaties with Italy, Finland, Bulgaria, Hungary and Rumania were not signed until February 10, 1947.

In March, 1947, the Foreign Ministers met in Moscow to discuss the drafting of peace treaties with Germany and Austria. They were unable to agree on what Germany's fate should be.

A new Foreign Ministers' Conference was held in London in November, 1947, but it did no more than confirm the impossibility of agreement. Shortly afterwards, the Soviet representatives ceased to take part in the Allied Control Council in Berlin. The Foreign Ministers met once more in Paris in May, 1949, to discuss anew the problem of Germany and Austria and, in 1951, their deputies spent 109 days at the Palais Rose Conference in Paris vainly trying to draw up an agenda for a new meeting at ministerial level.

For all practical purposes, the stalemate at the 1947 Moscow Conference put an end to the co-operation which had developed between the USSR and the Western democratic countries during the war. The signing of the United Nations Charter on June 26, 1945, had raised the hopes of the peoples of the Western countries. But the Soviet Union abused the right of veto at the Security Council.

In the case of Greece, to take an example, where incidents had taken place between her and certain neighbouring states – Albania and Bulgaria – a commission of enquiry was appointed in 1947 by the Security Council of the United Nations. Although the report prepared by this commission established the responsibility of both Albania and Bulgaria, all draft resolutions recommending United Nations action encountered the systematic veto of the Soviet Union.

Since then, the Soviet Union vetoed a decision taken by the Security Council on more than one hundred different occasions.

Soviet expansion

Soviet territorial expansion under Stalin had already begun during the war by the annexation of Estonia, Latvia and Lithuania, together with certain parts of Finland, Poland, Rumania, North-Eastern Germany and Eastern Czechoslovakia, a total of about 180,000 square miles of territory occupied by more than 23 million inhabitants. It was this that moved Mr. Paul-Henri Spaak, who was at the time the Belgian Prime Minister and Minister of Foreign Affairs, to state in the General Assembly of the United Nations in 1948: 'There is but one Great Power that emerged from the war having conquered other territories, and that Power is the USSR'.

This territorial expansion continued after the defeat of Germany and was supplemented by a policy of control over the countries of Eastern

Europe. The presence of the victorious Soviet armies in the heart of Europe, coupled with Communist infiltration into 'popular front' governments, effectively compelled Albania, Bulgaria, Rumania, Eastern Germany, Poland, Hungary and Czechoslovakia to fall within the sphere of Soviet domination (an area of about 390,000 square miles and a population of over 90 million non-Russian inhabitants).

Here are the highlights of the 'conquest without war':

In Hungary, from the beginning of 1947, the Communist Party opened a violent campaign against the Smallholders Party, and as a result of its denunciations many arrests were made. The Nagy government had to resign on May 29; new elections did not produce, however, a majority for the Communist Party which was the largest group in Parliament. The Communists quickly formed a new government and formally dissolved the opposition parties on November 21, 1947.

Soviet political pressure

In Bulgaria, the operation was carried out along similar lines. Nicolas Petkov, leader of the Agrarian Party and the opposition, was accused of plotting a military coup d'état, sentenced to death on August 16, 1947, and hanged on September 23. On August 26, the Peasant Party was dissolved as 'fascist' and on November 22, the national administration was organized along Soviet lines. On December 11, 1947, Dimitrov, former Secretary of the Comintern, assumed leadership and formed a predominantly Communist cabinet.

In Rumania, after elections which were regarded as invalid by the Anglo-Saxon countries, the members of the opposition were accused of plotting the overthrow of the democratic regime. The Peasant Party was dissolved on October 10, 1947, and its leader, Dr. Maniu, was sentenced to life imprisonment on October 29. Mrs. Anna Pauker, who had served in Moscow during the war as adviser to the Soviet Government on Rumanian affairs, succeeded Mr. Tataresco, and King Michael had to abdicate on January 1, 1948.

In Poland, Mr. Mikolajczyk, head of the Peasant Party, was compelled to leave the country in November, 1947, in the face of constant threats to his life. His party had to relinquish its role as opposition and was finally dissolved on November 21, 1947. In Czechoslovakia, Soviet interference steadily increased. The Prague government, which had favoured participation in the Marshall Plan, was obliged to revise its views and reverse its decision after a hasty visit by Mr. Gottwald and Mr. Masaryk to Moscow in July, 1947.

In addition, the Communists, by means of a campaign of denunciation, secured the arrest and trial of many members of the democratic party which held an absolute majority. In February 1948, Mr. Zorin, Moscow's special envoy, engineered the resignation of President Benes (May, 1948). A Communist government was then formed.

On March 10, 1948, Mr. Jan Masaryk, Foreign Minister in the Gottwald Government, was found dead on the pavement beneath the windows of his home. . . .

In less than a year, Moscow had thus succeeded in gaining control over the governments in Budapest, Bucharest, Sofia, Warsaw and Prague. The Communist parties ruled alone, or nearly alone, in each of these capitals, from which all opposition had been swept.

It only remained to co-ordinate the activities of these governments on the international level and thus establish a bloc of satellite nations.

The Soviet Union also exerted heavy pressure, directly or indirectly, in various parts of the world:

— in Northern Iran, where the Soviet armies vainly sought a foothold after the war, in spite of the provisions of the Treaty of Teheran and the protests of the United Nations;

— in Turkey, where both government and people resisted all attempts at intimidation, territorial claims on Kars and Ardahan, and demands for the granting of bases in the Straits;

— in Greece, where the guerilla campaign which began in 1944 took on the aspect of real war in 1946, when the rebels received reinforcement from bases in neighbouring states:

— in Asia, where the Soviet Union considerably extended its influence by occupying the greater part of Manchuria and Northern Korea in 1945.

In addition, Communist agitation was intensified throughout the whole of South-East Asia:

— in Indochina, where France and the Associated States were engaged in extensive operations against a Communist-directed rebellion;

— in Malaya, where substantial British Forces were tied down by Communist-inspired guerillas;

— in Burma, where Communist parties fomented strikes and unrest;

— in the Philippines, where armed Hukbalahaps (Communists) engaged in constant guerilla warfare.

Cominform set up

In September, 1947, the Cominform, the Communist answer to the Marshall Plan, was set up. Its members were the leaders of the Communist parties in the USSR, Poland, Bulgaria, Czechoslovakia, Rumania, Hungary, Yugoslavia, France, Italy, and later, the Netherlands.

At the end of 1947, directions for agitation and orders to strike sup-

15

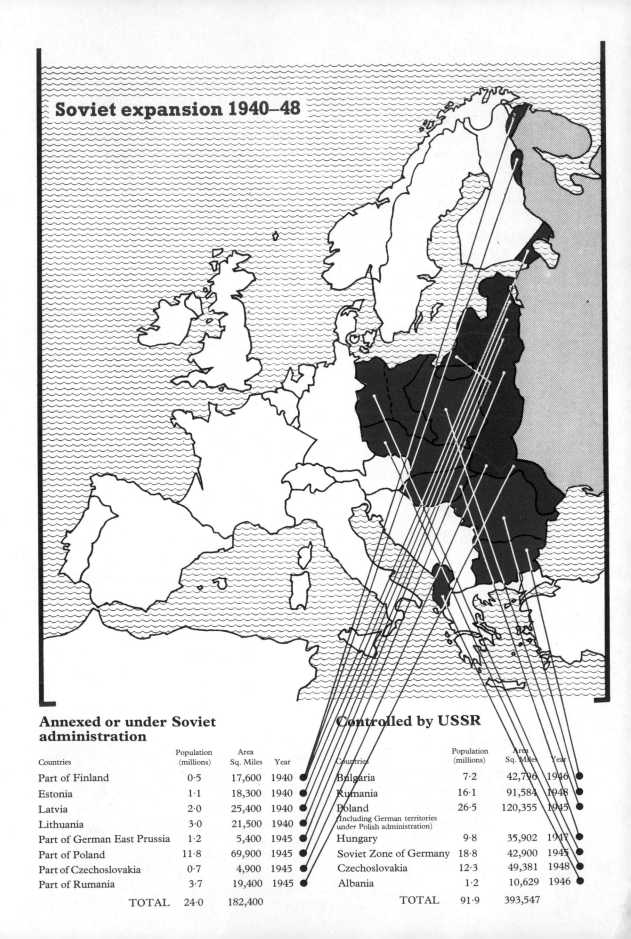

Soviet expansion 1940–48

Annexed or under Soviet administration

Countries	Population (millions)	Area Sq. Miles	Year
Part of Finland	0·5	17,600	1940
Estonia	1·1	18,300	1940
Latvia	2·0	25,400	1940
Lithuania	3·0	21,500	1940
Part of German East Prussia	1·2	5,400	1945
Part of Poland	11·8	69,900	1945
Part of Czechoslovakia	0·7	4,900	1945
Part of Rumania	3·7	19,400	1945
TOTAL	24·0	182,400	

Controlled by USSR

Countries	Population (millions)	Area Sq. Miles	Year
Bulgaria	7·2	42,796	1946
Rumania	16·1	91,584	1948
Poland (Including German territories under Polish administration)	26·5	120,355	1945
Hungary	9·8	35,902	1947
Soviet Zone of Germany	18·8	42,900	1945
Czechoslovakia	12·3	49,381	1948
Albania	1·2	10,629	1946
TOTAL	91·9	393,547	

ported a concerted and virulent campaign of opposition throughout the whole of Western Europe. The struggle continued with persistent attempts to infiltrate into all branches of activity in the Western countries, notably into the trade unions, in France and Italy in particular.

Faced with Soviet expansion, the free countries of Europe, gravely threatened, understandably recognized the need to seek the means of guaranteeing their freedom and security. It was natural that, sooner or later, they should turn towards the United States who alone was powerful enough to impress the USSR. The United States reaction was prompt and decisive.

Truman doctrine

On March 12, 1947, President Truman told Congress: 'It must be the policy of the United States of America to support free peoples who are resisting attempted subjugation by armed minorities, or by outside pressure'. Following that statement, which became known as the 'Truman doctrine' the Congress of the United States authorized the appropriation of $400 million for aid to Greece and Turkey up to June, 1948. It was, indeed, on these countries that Soviet pressure had been brought hardest to bear. Congress also authorized the despatch to these countries of American civilian and military missions.

The 'Truman doctrine' was designed to deal with the specific threat to Greece and Turkey. But the situation in Western Europe generally was no less alarming. In spite of the aid received by the free countries of Europe from the United States to relieve post-war shortages, the mechanism of European economy remained badly jammed and Western Europe would have found itself on the brink of economic collapse. On June 5, 1947, in a speech at Harvard University, the then Secretary of State of the United States, General George C. Marshall, initiated the idea of a Programme for European Recovery. He proposed that the United States should come to the help of Europe and suggested that the European countries should agree on their requirements and draw up a common programme agreed by a number, if not all, of the European nations. He added that this policy was 'directed not against any country or doctrine but against hunger, poverty, desperation and chaos'.

Marshall Plan

This offer of economic assistance, which, in the next few years, contributed largely to the economic recovery of the Western countries, was also open to the Soviet Union and the countries behind the Iron Curtain. Stalin refused all American aid for the USSR and, despite initial interest on the part of both Czechoslovakia and Poland, forced satellite governments to do likewise. Finally, he set up the Cominform, whose allotted aim was to fight the Marshall Plan as 'an instrument of American imperialism'.

17

The world thus found itself split into two blocs. The nature and extent of the Soviet intentions were henceforth clearly perceived. As regards the free countries of Europe, the only way they could begin to re-establish a balance of forces was to come together. A number of statesmen, particularly Sir Winston Churchill, the former British Prime Minister, and Mr. Louis St. Laurent, the Canadian Secretary of State for External Affairs, had already contemplated in 1946 the idea of a defensive alliance within the framework of the United Nations.

On January 22, 1948, Mr. Ernest Bevin, the United Kingdom Foreign Secretary, suggested a formula for Western Union consisting of a network of bilateral agreements on the lines of the Dunkirk Treaty.

This Treaty had been signed on March 4, 1947 by France and the United Kingdom. It was a 'Treaty of alliance and mutual assistance' of 50 years' duration, according to which the two countries would unite in the event of any renewed attempt at aggression by Germany. Under its terms they were also bound, by means of continuing consultation on problems bearing on their economic relations, to take all measures necessary to increase their prosperity and economic stability and thus enable them to make a more effective contribution to the economic and social aims of the United Nations. Although the idea was warmly welcomed it was felt that, as the Dunkirk Treaty had been aimed expressly against a renewed German aggression, it might be preferable to take the Rio Treaty as a model. This Treaty had been signed on September 2, 1947, by the United States and the Latin American countries, with the exception of Nicaragua and Ecuador. It was essentially a collective, defensive alliance against any aggression and provided an example of 'regional grouping' within the framework of the United Nations Charter.

While these problems were under discussion, the Prague coup d'état, in February 1948, drew Czechoslovakia into the Soviet orbit and came as a sharp reminder to the Western Allies that common defensive action was needed.

Brussels Treaty

On March 4, 1948, representatives of Belgium, France, Luxembourg, the Netherlands and the United Kingdom met in Brussels to consider the terms of a treaty of mutual assistance. Their efforts soon met with success. The Brussels Treaty was signed on March 17, 1948 by Belgium, France, Luxembourg, the Netherlands and the United Kingdom. These countries pledged themselves to build up a common defence system and to strengthen their economic and cultural ties.

Article IV of the Brussels Treaty states that should any of the contracting Parties be the object of an 'armed aggression in Europe', the other signatories to the Treaty would afford the attacked Party 'all the military aid and assistance in their power'. The Treaty, with a duration of 50 years, provided for the creation of a supreme body in Western Union, known as the Consultative Council, consisting of the five Foreign Ministers. Under it was a Western Defence Committee consisting of the Defence Ministers.

Berlin blockade

The Brussels Treaty was scarcely signed when the Russians started the blockade of West Berlin (June, 1948). It was to last for 323 days and was only countered by the organization of an air-lift by the Western Powers. The Berlin blockade hastened the setting up of Western defence.

On April 30, 1948, the Defence Ministers and Chiefs-of-Staff of the five Brussels Treaty signatory Powers met in London to discuss their countries' military equipment needs, to see how far they could be met from their own production resources, and how much additional aid would have to be requested from the United States. From July, 1948, onwards, United States and Canadian experts attended these meetings as observers.

Western Union Defence Organization

In September, 1948, a military body was created within the Brussels Treaty known as the Western Union Defence Organization. Field Marshal Montgomery was appointed Chairman of the Commanders-in-Chief Committee and set up his Headquarters at Fontainebleau, France. Commanders-in-Chief were appointed: General de Lattre de Tassigny (France) for the Land Forces; Air Chief Marshal Sir James Robb (United Kingdom) for the Air Forces; Vice Admiral Jaujard (France) for Naval Forces.

The creation of a defence organization by the free countries in Europe could not fail to awaken a response from the United States.

On April 11, 1948, the United States Secretary of State, General George C. Marshall and the Under-Secretary, Mr. Robert M. Lovett, opened preliminary talks with Senators Arthur H. Vandenberg and Tom Connally on the problems of security in the North Atlantic area.

Vandenberg Resolution

On April 28, 1948, the idea of a single mutual defence system, including and superseding the Brussels Treaty, was publicly put forward by Mr. St. Laurent in the Canadian House of Commons. It was warmly welcomed one week later by Mr. Ernest Bevin. But it was essential that the United States should be able, constitutionally, to join the Atlantic Alliance. To this end, in consultation with the State Department, Senator Vandenberg drew up a Resolution[1] which recommended, in particular, 'the association of the United States, by constitutional process, with such regional and

1. For text of the Vandenberg Resolution, see 'NATO Basic Documents' published by NATO Information Service.

19

other collective arrangements as are based on continuous and effective self-help and mutual aid' and its 'contribution to the maintenance of peace by making clear its determination to exercise the right of individual or collective self-defence under Article 51 (of the United Nations Charter) should any armed attack occur affecting its national security'.

This Resolution, thanks to the timely initiative of Senators Vandenberg and Connally, was adopted on June 11, 1948, by the United States Senate. The road was now clear. Preliminary talks opened in Washington on July 6, 1948, between the State Department and the Ambassadors of Canada and of the Western Union Powers. They ended on September 9, 1948, with a report to governments. This report having been favourably received by governments, the Consultative Council of the Brussels Treaty was able, at the end of October, 1948, to announce complete identity of views on the principle of a defensive pact for the North Atlantic area.

The text of the Treaty was published on March 18, 1949. Even before that, on March 15, 1949, the Brussels Treaty signatory Powers, Canada and the United States, officially invited Denmark, Iceland, Italy, Norway and Portugal to accede to the Treaty.

April 4, 1949 – Signature of North Atlantic Treaty

On April 4, 1949, in spite of the pressure brought to bear by the Soviet Union on the Parties to the Treaty (notably a memorandum addressed to the twelve original signatories alleging the hostile nature of their action), the North Atlantic Treaty was signed in Washington.[1]

The Parliaments of the member countries ratified the Treaty within five months thereafter.

Subsequently, three other countries joined the twelve original signatories.

Greece and Turkey were invited to join the Alliance in September, 1951; they formally acceded to the Treaty on February 18, 1952.[2]

The Federal Republic of Germany was invited to accede to the Treaty following the signature of the Paris Agreements in October, 1954, and officially became a member of the North Atlantic Treaty Organization on May 9, 1955.[3]

---

1. See Appendix 2, page 300, for the text of the North Atlantic Treaty.
2. See Appendix 3, page 304, for the Protocol of Accession of Greece and Turkey.
3. See Appendix 4, page 306, for the Protocol of Accession of the Federal Republic of Germany.
For text of the Paris Agreements see 'NATO Basic Documents' published by the NATO Information Service.

CHAPTER 2

Analysis of the North Atlantic Treaty

Essentially the North Atlantic Treaty is the framework for wide co-operation among its signatories. More than a military alliance formed to prevent aggression, or to repel it should need arise, it also provides for continuing joint action in the political, economic and social fields.

The signatory countries undertake, in conformity with the provisions of the Charter of the United Nations, to preserve peace and international security and to promote stability and well-being in the North Atlantic area. They also undertake to eliminate incompatibilities in their economic policies and to encourage economic co-operation among themselves.

Thus the Treaty is dual in nature. It proclaims the importance of economic and social progress and, at the same time, reaffirms a security policy based on nations' inherent right to collective self-defence.

The Treaty consists of a preamble and fourteen articles.

The preamble outlines the Treaty's main features. It is a treaty of alliance, within the framework of the United Nations Charter, for the defence of a way of life not only by military means but also through co-operation in political, economic, social and cultural fields.

Article 1 defines the basic principles to be followed by member countries in the conduct of their international relations in order to avoid endangering peace and world security. It refers expressly to the United Nations Charter and is, indeed, an almost literal repetition of paragraphs 3 and 4 of Article 2 of the Charter.

Article 2 defines the aims to be followed by the member countries in their international relations and indicates broadly how these aims should be fulfilled. It is inspired by Article 1 of the United Nations Charter, which defines as the aims of the U.N.: preservation of peace, development of friendly relations among nations, achievement of international co-operation in solving international problems of an economic and social character.

Obligations of signatories

The obligations undertaken by the signatories are as much external (the bringing about of better understanding of the principles upon which Western civilization is founded) as internal (the strengthening of their free institutions and the elimination of disputes or conflicts within the Alliance in the economic and social fields). This article is the clear authority for all co-operation of a non-military character within the Alliance, that is, for co-operation beyond that called for in pursuance of the Treaty's military aims. It underlines the fact that the alliance was brought into being to defend a way of life.

Article 3 deals with ways and means of maintaining and increasing the individual and collective capacity of members to resist armed attack. They must develop this capacity through joint action and through mutual assistance.

From this article stem, among other things, the co-ordination of military instruction and training, joint production programmes for equipment, the infrastructure programme and all the varied forms of military assistance provided by the United States.

Article 4 lays down the obligations incumbent on member countries in the event of a threat to one of them. The only explicitly expressed requirement is that signatories should consult together if the territorial integrity or political independence of any member is endangered.

Such consultation, which may be requested by any member country and not necessarily the one threatened, would in practice take place at a meeting of the North Atlantic Council in Brussels, which can be called at an hour's notice.

It should be remembered, however, that, as stipulated in Article 7 of the Treaty, primary responsibility for the preservation of peace and international security remains with the United Nations Security Council.

Collective defence

Article 5 contains one of the Treaty's most important provisions: 'The Parties agree that an armed attack against one or more of them in Europe or North America shall be considered an attack against them all. . . .' It serves warning on a would-be aggressor that he cannot hope to attain even a limited military objective.

Having stated this principle, the Article goes on to define the obligations of countries in the event of armed attack. They must at once, individually and in concert with the other members, take such action, including the use of armed force, as each deems necessary.

Each country is free, therefore, to take whatever action it judges necessary. Every armed attack does not of necessity call for an automatic declaration of general war. Moreover, all Parties to the Treaty would not necessarily be required to provide the same type of assistance.

Any such joint action would be justified by the inherent right to self-defence recognized by Article 51 of the United Nations Charter. But the exercise of this right in no way detracts from the responsibility of the Security Council. Article 5 ends with the stipulation that action taken in conformity with its provisions shall be reported to the Security Council and terminated when that body has taken what measures are necessary.

Article 6 defines the area within which the provisions of Article 5 are applicable. This article was amended after the accession of Greece and Turkey.[1]

The definition of a geographical area for the purposes of Article 5 in no way precludes discussion by the Council of events which may occur outside that area. On the contrary. The maintenance of peace and security in any part of the world is dependent upon the international situation as a whole and the Council as a matter of normal practice exchanges information and views on major world events wherever they occur.

Compatibility with UN Charter

Article 7 states the Treaty's compatibility with the United Nations Charter.

In *Article 8* the Parties confirm the compatibility of the Treaty with their other international commitments, and undertake not to enter into any commitments in the future which may conflict with the Treaty.

Creation of the Council

Article 9 calls for the creation of the North Atlantic Council and provides for the setting up of whatever additional bodies may be needed to implement the preceding Articles.

This is the legal basis for the existence of the specialized committees and groups set up by the Council, the International Secretariat which services them, the major and subordinate military commands and the various military and civilian agencies.

Article 10 stipulates that the Parties may, by unanimous decision, invite any other European State in a position to further the principles of the Treaty to accede to it. This was the authority for the invitations to Greece and Turkey in 1951 and the Federal Republic of Germany in 1955.

---

1. See Appendix 3, page 304, Protocol of Accession of Greece and Turkey, for the new definition of the NATO area.

Article 11 deals with arrangements for ratification of the Treaty and its entry into force.

Articles 12 and 13 provide for the possibility of revisions to the Treaty or withdrawals from it. After the Treaty has been in force for ten years the Parties may agree to revise it. After twenty years any Party may put an end to his own participation, giving one year's notice of denunciation. It follows that, as from August 24, 1969, the 20th anniversary of the Treaty's entry into force, any Party may give one year's notice of withdrawal.

Revision of the Treaty

It may be noted that the question of revising the Treaty has never so far been raised, although there have been exercises such as the 'Three Wise Men's' Report in 1956 and the more recent 'Harmel Report', which have given fresh meaning to some of its provisions. Even the French Government's decision to withdraw from the integrated military commands did not necessitate any alterations to the original Treaty since it proved possible by negotiation to relate this decision to existing arrangements. Since the Treaty is of unlimited duration it will in any case remain in force for as long as it is considered useful irrespective of any decision by any individual member to withdraw.

Finally, *Article 14* deals with arrangements for depositing the Treaty document.

3

The Atlantic Alliance from 1949 to 1975

The evolution of the Atlantic Alliance has been characterised by successive phases, each one contributing to its policies and activities a fresh aspect. The immediate task following the Treaty's signature in April 1949 was the construction of an effective system of collective defence. The Allies have, from the outset, consulted together with regard to political issues but in the early years they directed their main effort towards defence problems including their economic and financial consequences. This period saw also the enlargement of the Alliance; in 1952 the twelve original signatories were joined by Greece and Turkey and in 1955 by the Federal Republic of Germany.

A second phase began in 1956 with the adoption by the Council of the Report on Non-Military Co-operation in NATO, better known as the Report of the Committee of Three. In the previous period the Soviet challenge was limited to Europe and essentially military in nature; by 1956 it was apparent that the Soviets were extending their influence all around the world and that the challenge now appeared in a variety of forms. By adopting the Three Wise Men's Report[1] the Council gave a new impulse to their political consultation, with the result that today it covers practically every subject of common interest, for the most part in the formative stages of the elaboration of national policies.

The third phase is associated with the Council's approval, in December 1967, of the Report on the Future Tasks of the Alliance, or Harmel Report. Although the members of the Alliance have consistently declared themselves to favour, both individually and collectively, the relaxation of tension

1. The Committee of Three – Dr. Gaetano Martino (Italy), Mr. Halvard Lange (Norway), and Mr. Lester Pearson (Canada) – became known as the 'Three Wise Men'.

in Europe, in adopting the Harmel Report the fifteen member governments undertook to pursue a positive policy of seeking realistic solutions aimed at furthering East-West détente. In consequence, studies in the field of disarmament and practical armaments control measures were intensified. From 1969 a particularly active period ensued with, on the one hand, the preparation and co-ordination of multilateral East–West negotiations in the framework of the Conference on Security and Co-operation in Europe and, on the other, further work in connection with mutual and balanced force reductions.

Since 1969 the Council, following an initiative by President Nixon, have also concerned themselves with the urgent challenge made to mankind by problems of the human environment. Without doubt, other issues will arise in the future which the Alliance, without abandoning its dual mission of defence and détente, will attempt to tackle in the same spirit as in the past.

First results

Far from leading to increased tension between East and West, as implied by the Soviet Union's memorandum on the eve of signature, the creation of the North Atlantic Treaty on April 4, 1949, was followed by a slight easing of the situation. In May, 1949, the USSR raised the Berlin blockade. On May 23, 1949, the French, British, American and Soviet Foreign Ministers, meeting in Paris, achieved positive agreement on a limited number of practical problems arising in respect to Germany and Berlin and notably to commercial relationships with other countries, as well as on the question of a peace treaty with Austria. Finally, the halting, in October, 1949, of Albanian and Bulgarian-based assistance for the Communist insurrection in Greece brought peace to that country.

Ratification by member governments having been completed, the Treaty came into force on August 24, 1949. The signatory countries were faced with two immediate tasks, that of creating a structure capable of implementing the Treaty and that of working out a common defence policy.

First Council meetings

Meeting for the first time, in Washington on September 17 and 19, 1949, the North Atlantic Council began to build a civilian and military framework. The Council itself, composed of Foreign Ministers of member countries would, it decided, normally meet annually in ordinary session, but could be convened more frequently should this prove desirable. Furthermore, an extraordinary session could be convened at any time in the event that any member were to invoke Article 4 or Article 5 of the Treaty.

In accordance with Article 9 of the Treaty, the Council created a

Defence Committee composed of the Defence Ministers of member
countries, responsible for drawing up co-ordinated defence plans for the
North Atlantic area. It was agreed that this Committee would meet at least
once a year.

A number of permanent military bodies were set up: a Military Com-
mittee, consisting of Chiefs-of-Staff of member countries and responsible
for advising the Council in military matters; a Standing Group,[1] the
Military Committee's executive body, composed of representatives of
France, the United Kingdom and the United States and responsible for
strategic guidance in areas in which NATO forces operated; and five
Regional Planning Groups, for Northern Europe[2] (Denmark, Norway,
U.K.), Western Europe (Belgium, France, Luxembourg, Netherlands,
U.K.), Southern Europe/Western Mediterranean[3] (France, Italy, U.K.),
Canada/United States, and the North Atlantic Ocean (all countries except
Italy and Luxembourg). These groups were to develop defence plans for
their areas. At its first session the Council had recognized that such
questions as military production and supply and the economic and financial repercussions of the defence effort required detailed study. Meeting
again, in Washington on November 18, 1949, it decided to set up two
further bodies to carry out this task.

Civil and military bodies

The Defence Financial and Economic Committee, composed of Finance
Ministers of member countries, was to develop, in co-operation with the
Military Committee and the Standing Group, overall financial and
economic guidance for defence programmes and to fix the limits both of
these programmes and of military production in relation to the economic
and financial resources of member countries. It was also to appraise the
financial and economic impact on member countries of major defence
projects formulated by the Military Production and Supply Board or the
Military Committee, to recommend financial arrangements for military
defence plans and, particularly, to make recommendations on the interchange of military equipment among Treaty countries. Finally, it was to
study ways of meeting foreign exchange costs for materials and equipment
imported from non-member countries for the defence programmes.

The Military Production and Supply Board was to promote co-ordinated
production, standardization and technical research in the field of armaments, reporting to the Defence Committee.

Some ten weeks after its creation the Defence Committee, meeting in
Paris on December 1, 1949, agreed upon a strategic concept for the in-

1. Dissolved in 1966.
2. Dissolved 1st August 1951.
3. Dissolved 10th April 1952.

tegrated defence of the North Atlantic area as well as on methods of working out a programme for the production and supply of arms and equipment. Both recommendations were approved by the Council during a meeting in Washington on January 16, 1950.

Meeting again, at the Hague on April 1, 1950, the Defence Committee approved the first draft of a four-year defence plan, the 'medium term defence plan'.

The control and supervision of the civilian and military agencies of the Alliance could no longer effectively be undertaken by the Council in the course of its infrequent meetings. The Council therefore decided, at its meeting in London of May 15 to 18, 1950, to set up a civilian body to execute its directives, co-ordinate the work of the Alliance's civilian and military bodies and act as a forum for regular political exchanges between member governments.

Council Deputies

The Council Deputies as the new body was named, was composed of deputies to the Foreign Ministers of each member country, and was to meet in continuous session in London. In addition to co-ordinating the work of the NATO agencies, the Deputies had to study the relationship between different defence plans, suggest measures to be undertaken by governments in pursuit of those plans, hold political discussions, seek ways and means of implementing Article 2 of the Treaty (calling for co-operation in other than military fields), and encourage efforts to bring the Alliance to the attention of the public in member countries.

The Foreign Ministers also directed that the questions of adequate forces and of their financing should be tackled as a single problem rather than separately. They noted that the combined resources of the member countries were sufficient to achieve the progressive and rapid development of adequate defences without impairing social and economic progress. They urged governments to concentrate on setting up balanced collective forces for the overall defence.

The Korean war

Soon after this Council session there occurred an event which had a far-reaching effect on the evolution of NATO, the Communist attack upon South Korea. The Security Council, denouncing North Korea for the aggression, decided upon economic and military sanctions. All member countries of the United Nations were requested to go to the assistance of the South Korean Republic.

When the Council met again, in New York on September 15 to 18, 1950, its discussions centred on the problem of how to defend the NATO area against an aggression similar to that in Korea. It was unanimously agreed that a Forward Strategy must be adopted for Europe, that is to say that any aggression must be resisted as far to the East as possible in order to ensure the defence of all the European member countries. Such a strategy, however, demanded forces far exceeding those available to NATO at the time (approximately fourteen divisions on the European continent as against some 210 Soviet divisions). Military strength would have to be built up and defence plans revised. The Council accordingly requested the Defence Committee as a matter of urgency to plan for the creation of an integrated force under centralized command, adequate to deter aggression. The Standing Group was to be responsible for strategic direction of the force, which was to be placed under a supreme commander appointed by NATO.

The session was then adjourned to enable Ministers to consult their governments. On reconvening, on September 26, 1950, the Council, recognizing that a forward strategy implied the defence of Europe on German soil, decided to study the problem of the political and military participation of the Federal Republic. Germany's participation raised difficulties of principle for some member countries and for France in particular, and it was four years before a final solution was found to this problem.

The principle of German participation in the common defence was established when the Council, meeting again in Brussels on December 18, 1950, recognized that such participation 'would strengthen the defence of Europe without altering in any way the purely defensive character of the North Atlantic Treaty Organization'. The Ministers then invited the three Occupation Powers in Germany, France, the United Kingdom and the United States, to explore, in co-operation with the Federal Republic itself, ways of achieving this participation.

First Supreme Allied Commander December 1950

At Brussels the Council also took important decisions on military matters. It approved the Defence Committee's recommendations for the creation of an integrated European defence force, for the establishment of a Supreme Headquarters in Europe and for the reorganization of the NATO military structure. It also decided that the Supreme Headquarters should be placed under an American officer and requested President Truman to designate General Dwight D. Eisenhower as Supreme Allied Commander (SACEUR). The President agreed, and on December 19, 1950, the Council officially announced the appointment.

On December 29, 1950, the Standing Group issued the first Terms of Reference to General Eisenhower. These directed that the NATO forces made available by member nations for the defence of Western Europe would, in the event of an emergency, be organized, equipped, trained and ready to implement agreed plans. It was agreed to establish a Supreme Headquarters in Europe early in 1951 and that SACEUR would be supported by an international staff drawn from the nations contributing to the integrated force. General Eisenhower's Command, Allied Command Europe (ACE), and the Supreme Headquarters Allied Powers Europe (SHAPE), were set up at Rocquencourt near Paris, France, on April 2, 1951.

Also at the December meeting in Brussels the Council approved a Defence Committee recommendation to replace the Military Production and Supply Board by a Defence Production Board, with wider powers than its predecessor. This new Board was given the task of increasing production and facilitating the joint use of industrial installations in the member countries.

In May, 1951, the Council Deputies in London announced important developments in the evolution of the NATO structure. The Defence Committee and Defence Financial and Economic Board were abolished, leaving the North Atlantic Council as the Alliance's one Ministerial body. A Financial and Economic Board was established in Paris, where the Organization for European Economic Co-operation (OEEC) could provide it with assistance. (The OEEC had been set up in 1948 to channel Marshall Plan aid.) The task of this Board was to advise both the Council Deputies and the other NATO agencies under their control on the economic and financial aspects of the defence programme. It could, in certain specific cases, also approach member governments direct.

New structure of NATO

One result of the reorganization was to increase the status of the Council Deputies. Governments could now be represented on the Council itself by their Foreign Ministers, or their Defence Ministers, or both, or by other interested Ministers and in particular Finance Ministers or Ministers for Economic Affairs. Heads of Government could also attend meetings of the Council. The Deputies, therefore, now represented all Ministers in their government concerned with NATO matters, where previously they had represented Foreign Ministers alone. They thus became in effect the permanent working organization of the North Atlantic Council, and, to service their needs, an International Staff, paid for out of a budget to which all member countries contributed, was set up under the direction of their Chairman, Charles M. Spofford (United States).

The Council Deputies now tackled certain legal and financial problems arising out of the establishment of the new civil and military bodies. On June 19, 1951, an 'Agreement between the Parties to the North Atlantic Treaty regarding the Status of their Forces'[1] was signed, which determined

1. These Agreements are contained in 'NATO Basic Documents' published by NATO Information Service.

the legal status of military personnel of one member country called upon
to serve under NATO command in another. A protocol to this agreement
defined the status of military headquarters. A further 'Agreement on the
Status of the North Atlantic Treaty Organization, National Representatives
and International Staff'[1] was signed in September, 1951, covering the
civilian side of the Organization. The Deputies also settled the question of
the joint financing of military headquarters and, in August, 1951, a cost-
sharing formula was agreed for SHAPE and its subordinate headquarters.

While the efforts made since the creation of the Alliance had reduced
the danger of aggression in Europe, continued tension between East and
West, the wars in Korea and Indo-China and the United Nations dead-
lock on disarmament and the control of atomic energy made it clear the
NATO countries could not discontinue their defence preparations. But their
attention was increasingly to be occupied by the economic and financial
problems involved in a sustained military effort.

Temporary Council Committee

At the Council meeting held in Ottawa from September 15 to 20, 1951,
Foreign Ministers were joined by Defence and Finance Ministers. The
Alliance's military needs as assessed by the Military Committee called for
financial contributions far greater than those which the member states
considered themselves able to make. The effectiveness of the defence effort
was further threatened by rising prices, the danger of inflation, imbalance
of payments, and difficulties in the distribution of raw materials. The
Ministers accordingly set up a Temporary Council Committee (TCC) whose
task it was to reconcile requirements of collective security with the political
and economic capabilities of the member countries. The TCC, in fact, had
to decide whether the military authorities were asking too much or whether
the governments were offering too little. To enable it to do so it was empowered to seek information, assistance and advice from all member
governments as well as from the military and civilian agencies of NATO.

The Council at Ottawa was informed by the three Occupying Powers of
progress in negotiations to establish a formula for Germany's participation
in Western defence. France, the United Kingdom and the United States
announced their support for a plan for a European Defence Community to
include the Federal Republic.

Accession of Greece and Turkey

Also at Ottawa, the Council formally recommended to member governments that Greece and Turkey should be invited to accede to the Treaty.
It also determined to examine the possibility of extending NATO's non-
military activities, and established a Ministerial Committee composed of

1. These Agreements are contained in 'NATO Basic Documents' published by NATO Information
Service.

31

representatives of Belgium, Canada, Italy, the Netherlands and Norway to consider means of strengthening the Atlantic Community and implementing Article 2 of the Treaty.

The Temporary Council Committee started work immediately after the Ottawa meeting. Consisting of representatives of the twelve member countries, its detailed work was delegated to a three-man Executive Board, Mr. Averell Harriman (United States), the Committee's Chairman, Mr. Jean Monnet (France) and Sir Edwin Plowden (United Kingdom). The report submitted by the TCC on December 18, 1951, was in the nature of a first comprehensive review of the military capacity of the member countries under peacetime conditions. It was the forerunner of the procedures subsequently adopted for determining the contributions individual member countries could and should make to the common defence effort.

Sharing the defence burden

Based on the principle that the burden of defending the West should be shared equitably among the member countries, it recognized that the defence build-up must rest on a foundation of social and economic stability and that the latter demanded expanded production through concerted action. In the light of these considerations, and of the Committee's assessment of the capabilities of individual countries, the report indicated the maximum force build-up the Alliance could realistically plan for and ways and means of attaining it.

Specifically, in the latter context, there were recommendations for relieving balance of payments difficulties and on the different forms of American participation in Europe's military expenditures via, notably, contributions to common infrastructure costs and offshore procurement (a procedure whereby the United States purchased from one or another European member equipment to be given to it or to another member as aid under the Mutual Defence Assistance Programme).

The TCC set the pattern for a continuing process of appraising defence programmes in the light of economic and political development, the Annual – later the Triennial – Review.

Meanwhile the Council had held a further meeting, in Rome from November 24 to 28, 1951, where it received progress reports on tasks initiated at Ottawa, including the work of the TCC. A statement was also made by General Eisenhower summarising progress made by SHAPE in formulating military strategy.

The Council called for an immediate study of what the relationship should be between NATO and the proposed European Defence Community. It also examined an interim report by the Atlantic Community Committee and instructed that certain proposals, notably those concerning availability of manpower, be examined in detail. The Rome meeting was, in effect, a prologue to the Council's next session, in Lisbon, which polished off important items of unfinished business and, in the process, substantially altered and added to the Alliance's still evolving civilian and military structure.

The Lisbon decisions – February 1952

At the top of the agenda when the Council met in Lisbon from February 20 to 25, 1952, was the Temporary Council Committee's detailed analysis of the defence capabilities of each member country. The Ministers adopted the firm force goals proposed by the TCC, a total of 50 divisions, 4,000 aircraft and strong naval forces by the end of 1952, as well as their provisional estimates for 1953 and 1954.

Endorsing the plans then under negotiation in Paris for the establishment of a European Defence Community, Ministers recommended that a protocol should be added to the North Atlantic Treaty, specifying the guarantees to be given to members of the proposed Community, and to be signed at the same time as the EDC Treaty, then due for signature in May, 1952.

Stressing that the Alliance aimed not only to protect its members but also to ensure lasting progress and a more closely knit Atlantic Community, the Council adopted a report by the Atlantic Community Committee which emphasized the importance of economic co-operation, advocated expansion and liberalization of trade and called for closer collaboration with other international bodies, in particular the OEEC.[1]

At this meeting, the Council formally welcomed the accession of Greece and Turkey who had meanwhile signed and ratified the Treaty.

Also in Lisbon, in response to recommendations by the Council Deputies and the Temporary Council Committee, the Council drastically reorganized the Alliance's civilian agencies, starting with itself. While continuing to be a council of governments, represented by Foreign, Defence, Finance and/or other competent Ministers according to the requirements of its agenda, the North Atlantic Council was to become a permanent body with headquarters in Paris. To enable it to function continuously, with effective powers of decision irrespective of the presence or otherwise of Ministers, each government would appoint a permanent representative who was to head a national delegation of advisers and experts.[2]

Permanent Council and First Secretary General

The Permanent Council was to take over the tasks of the Council Deputies, Defence Production Board and Financial and Economic Board, which were to be dissolved. Its chairmanship was entrusted to a newly appointed vice-

1. Now the OECD.
2. See Appendix 10, page 352 for list of Permanent Representatives to the Council.

33

chairman[1] of the Ministerial Council who was also to serve as Secretary General of the North Atlantic Treaty Organization. He was to be an international civil servant rather than a member of any one delegation and was both to organize the work of the Council and to direct the activities of an International Staff. The task of the latter would be to prepare matters for Council action and to implement Council decisions.

The Council was in future to work more closely with the military agencies. This would be facilitated by the move from London to Paris which put the civilian headquarters at an easy commuting distance from the Supreme Command. The responsibilities of the Standing Group and of General Eisenhower were increased, particularly with respect to setting priorities for the equipment of forces and to planning for their logistic support.

Creation of new commands – 1952

The military structure was rounded out by the setting up of two new commands, Atlantic Command, established at Norfolk, Virginia (United States), in January, 1952, and Channel Command, established at Portsmouth, United Kingdom, the following month. The former was made responsible to the Standing Group, the latter to a Channel Committee consisting originally of the Naval Chiefs-of-Staff of Belgium, France, the Netherlands and the United Kingdom. Vice-Admiral Lynde D. McCormick (United States) was appointed the first Supreme Allied Commander Atlantic (SACLANT) and Admiral Sir Arthur John Power (United Kingdom) became the first Commander-in-Chief Channel.[2]

The remainder of the year 1952 was largely occupied by putting into effect the organizational decisions reached in Lisbon. On March 12, 1952, Lord Ismay, Secretary of State for Commonwealth Relations in the United Kingdom Government, was appointed Vice-Chairman of the Council and Secretary General of NATO. The International Staff of the Organization was installed in Paris where it was joined by all the Permanent Representatives and their national delegations.

Holding its first meeting on April 28, 1952, the Permanent Council appointed General Mathew B. Ridgway to the post of Supreme Allied Commander in replacement of General Eisenhower who had asked to be released in order to enter United States politics. It also decided to continue the study instituted the previous autumn by the Temporary Council Committee in the form of an Annual Review of the defence effort undertaken by member countries. Finally, in the context of its decision to work more closely with the military, the Council instituted the practice of attending international manoeuvres.

1. See Appendix 9, page 350 for list of Chairmen.
2. See Appendix 12, page 358 for list of major NATO Commanders.

Lord Ismay's first report

At a Ministerial meeting in Paris, December 15 to 18, 1952, the Secretary General submitted his first report on the progress of work in NATO. In adopting it, the Council voted a resolution for further detailed economic study with a view to promoting social progress in application of Article 2 of the Treaty, and invited member governments to seek solutions to the problems of balance of payments, increased production, internal financial stability and manpower, with a view to strengthening their countries both politically and economically. The Military Committee also reported on progress achieved, in particular in the force build-up and in inter-unit co-operation.

This meeting was the occasion for the Council's first Resolution on the international situation outside the NATO area. It stated that the campaign then being waged in Indo-China by the forces of the French Union deserved the support of the NATO governments.

Rejection of the EDC

At a Ministerial meeting, April 23 to 25, 1953, the Council adopted short and long-term goals for NATO forces and agreed to a £250 million 3-year cost-sharing formula for infrastructure expenditures. It also worked out a method of preparing co-ordinated production programmes with the assistance of United States offshore purchases.

At a further Ministerial meeting, December 14 to 16, 1953, the Council concentrated on the preparation of long-term defence plans and on improving the quality of the NATO forces. It also emphasized the importance of co-ordinating national civil defence plans as well as plans for the allocation and control of supplies and transport in wartime.

The main task for 1954 was to settle the question of German participation in Western defence. The formula approved at the Lisbon Conference was invalidated when, on August 29, 1954, the French National Assembly refused to ratify the Treaty establishing the European Defence Community. After a period of intense diplomatic activity an alternative solution was found.

At the suggestion of the British Government, the London Conference, held from September 28 to October 3, 1954, brought together the Foreign Ministers of the five Brussels Treaty powers and of Germany, Italy, the United States and Canada. The conference formulated a series of decisions to form part of a general settlement which concerned, directly or indirectly, all the NATO powers. It also recorded the view of all governments represented 'that the North Atlantic Treaty should be regarded as being of indefinite duration'.

These decisions were approved at a further meeting held in Paris from October 20 to 22, 1954, and the Paris Agreements were signed on

October 23, 1954.[1] Concluded nearly 10 years after the end of hostilities with Germany, and with no early prospect of agreement with the USSR on a final peace settlement, the Agreements regularized relations between the NATO allies and the Federal German Republic, brought the latter into the Western alliance framework and supplied guarantees concerning European force and armament levels.

Briefly, the provisions of the Paris agreements were as follows:

The Paris Agreements October 1954

– France, the United Kingdom and the United States terminated the occupation regime in the Federal Republic of Germany and recognized it as a sovereign State. The Federal Republic undertook to authorize the maintenance on its territory of foreign forces at least at the strength obtaining at the date the Agreements came into force.

– The Federal Republic and Italy acceded to the Brussels Treaty and the Western Union became the Western European Union (WEU). There was to be extremely close co-operation between the WEU and NATO.

– The Federal German Republic was invited to join NATO, contributing a national army to be integrated into the forces of the Alliance. Machinery was set up to limit the strength of forces and quantities of armaments which could be created within the WEU.

– The United States and United Kingdom (the latter with certain reservation in case of overseas emergency or financial difficulties) undertook to maintain for as long as necessary their forces on the European continent. (President Eisenhower publicly confirmed this undertaking on March 5, 1955.) A unified military formation was to be established by assigning to the Supreme Allied Commander Europe all member countries' forces, with certain exceptions, stationed within the area of his command.

Accession of the Federal Republic of Germany

The accession of the Federal Republic of Germany to the North Atlantic Treaty became effective on May 5, 1955.[2] Two days later the USSR denounced its treaties with France and the United Kingdom. On May 14, 1955, by way of reply to the Paris Agreements, the USSR concluded the Warsaw Pact with its European satellites.

On May 15, 1955, the Austrian State Treaty was signed, ending the Four-Power occupation regime in that country. The moment appeared ripe for a fresh attempt at resolving the problem of Germany. On June 7, 1955, the Governments of the United States, France and the United Kingdom sent a joint invitation to the USSR to attend a Four-Power Con-

1. The Paris Agreements are contained in 'NATO Basic Documents' published by the NATO Information Service.
2. See Appendix 4, page 306.

ference of Heads of Government to be held in Geneva from July 18 to 21. On June 14, the Soviet Government agreed to attend this meeting which, it was anticipated, would decide a broad course of action the details of which would subsequently be worked out in a longer conference of the four Foreign Ministers. On July 16, a Ministerial Meeting of the North Atlantic Council was held to enable the NATO allies to exchange views prior to the Geneva meeting.

Geneva Summit Conference

The 'Summit' Conference, as it came to be known, ended on July 21 without any agreement of substance having been reached. But the Heads of Government instructed their Foreign Ministers to continue to study the problems at issue. Again, before the Second Geneva Conference, which convened on October 27, the NATO Council held a Ministerial Meeting to discuss the proposals the Foreign Ministers of the United States, France and the United Kingdom were to put forward. Their position was that Germany's reunification should take place under terms permitting her to remain in the Western Alliance. The Soviet Union rejected this view, and the Foreign Ministers concluded their talks on November 11 without results. Throughout this conference, as during the first, the governments of all the NATO countries were continuously informed and consulted in the North Atlantic Council.

Hungarian uprising and Suez intervention

At a Ministerial Meeting, December 1955, the Council declared that the negative outcome of the Geneva Conference had in no way halted the efforts of the North Atlantic Powers to secure the reunification of Germany in freedom. It urged the importance of further consultation within NATO on this question and on that of Berlin. Approving force goals for 1956, 1957 and 1958, it also took a major decision regarding defence planning. All member governments having expressed the firm intention of seeing the Atlantic forces equipped with the most modern weapons, the Council noted that substantial progress could be achieved in this respect with the assistance of the United States, the United Kingdom and Canada. The Council also devoted attention to improving arrangements for air defence and warning in Europe, and agreed on re-organization and closer co-ordination in order to integrate further NATO activities in this field.

While the Geneva Conference produced no result, it had demonstrated that East and West could meet and exchange views in a civilized manner. This was one effect of the Soviet adoption of the policy of peaceful co-existence which was cautiously welcomed by the Atlantic powers to the extent that it involved a certain easing of tension. But this was to be short-lived. The year 1956 witnessed the stamping out by Russia of the

Hungarian people's rebellion and a systematic campaign to replace
Western influence in the Middle East. The latter progressed through
Czechoslovakia's arms sales to Egypt, and the USSR taking over financing of
the Aswan Dam and culminated in President Nasser's nationalization of
the Suez Canal and the Franco-British military intervention. The end of
the year saw a return to the cold war. Meanwhile, at a Ministerial Meeting
in May 1956, the NATO Council had recognized that progress towards a
final European settlement could only be achieved on the basis of the unity,
solidarity and co-operation of peoples sharing common ideals. In this
connection they considered it timely to endeavour to extend their activities
in the non-military field, as called for by Article 2 of the Treaty. In
particular they appointed a committee of three Foreign Ministers to
recommend ways in which the Council could better perform its task as a
forum for consultation.

The Committee of Three

The three Ministers – Dr. Gaetano Martino of Italy, Mr. Halvard Lange
of Norway and Mr. Lester B. Pearson of Canada – submitted their report[1]
to the Ministerial Meeting in December 1956, at which the Council approved their recommendations, chief among which were: Member
governments were to inform the North Atlantic Council of any development significantly affecting the Alliance in order that effective political
consultation could be held on the action to be taken; each Spring the
Foreign Ministers were to make an appraisal of the political progress of the
Alliance, based on a review prepared by the Secretary General; disputes
among members not capable of direct settlement as called for in Article 1
of the Treaty should be submitted to good offices procedures within NATO
and the Secretary General was empowered, with the consent of the parties
to initiate procedures to settle such disputes.

At the same meeting, the Council approved a directive for future
military plans based on an assessment of the continued rise in Soviet
capabilities and the various types of new weapons available for NATO
defence. It reaffirmed the concept of forward defence in NATO strategy.

Lord Ismay retires – Mr. Spaak appointed

At this time, Lord Ismay announced his desire to retire in the spring of
1957 as Secretary General and the Council appointed Mr. Paul-Henri
Spaak, Foreign Minister of Belgium, to succeed him. Mr. Spaak took
office on May 15, 1957. In November 1956, General Lauris Norstad
(United States) succeeded General Gruenther as Supreme Commander,
Allied Forces in Europe.

1. See Appendix 5, page 308.

38

One recommendation of the Committee of Three had been that the Council should meet from time to time in different member capitals, and the Ministerial Meeting in May, 1957, was held in Bonn. NATO's defence policy was one of the main subjects discussed. The Soviet leaders had launched a campaign aimed at inducing public opinion in various member countries to oppose the modernization of Western defence forces. The Council agreed that one object of this campaign was to ensure for Soviet forces a monopoly of nuclear weapons on the European continent and that in the face of this threat the Atlantic Alliance must be in a position to meet any attack which might be launched against it. No power, it stated, could claim the right to deny the Alliance the modern arms needed for its defence. At this meeting a question was raised which was to occupy the military planners for many years to come. This was the correct balance between nuclear and conventional arms. The Council stated that there was a continuing need for a powerful shield of land, sea and air forces to protect the territory of member states.

Ministers also determined to intensify their efforts for German re-unification through free elections, since the prolonged division of Germany and anomalous situation in Berlin constituted a continuing threat to world peace.

Defence and disarmament problems

At the Bonn meeting ministers had pointed out that a remedy existed for fears professed by the Soviet Union with regard to the availability to NATO's defence forces of nuclear weapons. This remedy was the acceptance of a general disarmament agreement embodying effective measures of control and inspection. Disarmament was frequently discussed by the Council in the following months, during which the United Nations Disarmament Sub-Committee was meeting in London with the participation of four NATO countries – Canada, France, the United Kingdom and the United States. These four countries made a habit of consulting their NATO partners about any proposals they intended submitting to the Sub-Committee and informing them on the progress of the London talks. In addition to such routine consultation, Mr. Harold Stassen and Mr. Jules Moch, the respective representatives of the United States and France at the talks, on two occasions reported personally to the Council.

The Western proposals put forward to the London Conference on August 29, 1957, were based on advice given by the military authorities of the Alliance and reflected a viewpoint common to all the NATO partners. The Western proposals comprised measures to be carried out under international control. These were: reduction of all types of armaments and military forces; cessation of production of fissionable material for military purposes; reduction of existing stocks of nuclear weapons; suspension of

39

nuclear weapon tests; and adoption of protective measures against the risk of surprise attack. These proposals were rejected by the USSR, but later approved by a considerable majority of the General Assembly of the United Nations. Subsequently the General Assembly set up a new disarmament commission which the USSR announced it would boycott.

First sputnik launched

Other factors contributed to the increased international tensions brought about by this boycott. Firstly, the launching of the first sputnik, on October 4, 1957, heralded the Soviet Union's emergence as a nuclear power with a capability matching that of the United States. Further, it implied future military superiority, particularly in the field of long-range missiles. Then, Western fears that Syria, with its strategic control over the pipeline outlet from the Iraqi oil fields, was in process of becoming a Russian satellite appeared to be confirmed by a sudden Soviet move. Moscow claimed that Turkey, backed up by the United States and United Kingdom, was preparing to invade Syria.

Meeting of Heads of Government December 1957

In October 1957, President Eisenhower and Prime Minister Macmillan of the United Kingdom met in Washington to consider action to be taken to combat the new aspects of the Soviet threat. The Secretary General of NATO, Mr. Spaak, was invited to join them for part of these talks, at the close of which the President of the United States and the Prime Minister of the United Kingdom issued a declaration of common purpose. This stressed, in particular, the fact that the countries of the free world were interdependent and must increase their co-operation, pool their resources and share tasks essential to their security and well-being. Following the Washington talks it was decided, in order to mark with particular solemnity the unity of the Alliance, that the North Atlantic Council would meet for the first time at the level of Heads of Government.

The heads of Government met in Paris from December 16 to 19, 1957. In a solemn declaration the Council re-dedicated itself to the principles and purposes of the Alliance, and reaffirmed the common position of its members regarding the maintenance of peace and security.

In the field of defence, the Council stressed that NATO must possess the most effective military defensive strength, taking into account recent developments in weapons and techniques. To this end, it was necessary to establish stocks of nuclear warheads readily available for the defence of the Alliance in case of need. In view of Soviet policies in the field of new weapons, the Council also decided that intermediate-range ballistic missiles should be put at the disposal of the Supreme Allied Commander Europe. The deployment of these stocks as well as arrangements for their use were to be decided in agreement with the countries directly concerned.

Political and military recommendations

Recognizing the growing interdependence of the nations of the free world, the Council recommended closer co-ordination in the organization of forces to enable each NATO country to make the most effective contribution to the requirements of the Alliance. It also pointed out that better use of the Alliance's resources and greater efficiency for its forces would be obtained through as high a degree of standardization and integration as possible.

In the political field, the Heads of Government recognized the need for fuller consultation and for a broad co-ordination of policies.

They reaffirmed their unity regarding the problem of German reunification and of the security and freedom of Berlin. In the field of disarmament, they emphasized the need for adequate international control and agreed to establish a technical group to advise on problems of arms control arising out of new technical developments. They stated their willingness to promote any negotiations with the USSR which would lead to the controlled reduction of armaments within the limits imposed by security. They proclaimed that they were prepared to examine any proposal, from whatever source, for general or partial disarmament.

Scientific affairs

In the course of this same Ministerial Meeting, moreover, the foundations were laid for co-operation in the field of scientific and technical matters.

Recognizing that progress in this field depended on vigorous action within each member country and also in the co-operation of teachers and scientists, the Heads of Government stressed their desire to increase the effectiveness of national efforts by pooling scientific facilities and information and by sharing out the tasks. They therefore decided to establish immediately a science committee on which all NATO countries would be represented by experts who could speak authoritatively on scientific policy. They also recommended the appointment of an outstanding scientist as Science Adviser to the Secretary General of NATO.

The Heads of Government reaffirmed the need for closer economic association between the countries within the Atlantic Community and in the free world as a whole. They decided that the North Atlantic Council should, from time to time, in the spirit of Article 2 of the Treaty and without duplicating the work of other agencies, review economic trends, assess economic progress and make suggestions for improvements.

41

Soviet reactions

Before the Heads of Government Meeting began in Paris, the Soviet Union launched a diplomatic offensive which continued long after the Ministerial session. It took the form of an avalanche of letters to the various member governments; most of them were signed by Mr. Bulganin, at that time Soviet Prime Minister. These messages raised a number of issues such as the calling of a summit meeting, the suspension of nuclear tests, the renunciation of the use of nuclear weapons, the institution of a de-nuclearized zone in Europe, the installation of launching ramps for missiles, the signing of a non-aggression pact, etc. The messages were clearly aimed at creating dissension, which could then be exploited with a view to persuading the countries of the Alliance to negotiate separately with the Soviet Union.

The NATO partners found in political consultation the answer to this attack. By agreeing to discuss within the Council both the contents of the Soviet letters and the draft replies prepared by each of the governments, the members of NATO were able to achieve a remarkable degree of harmony in their views. As regards Soviet proposals for a summit meeting, studies were carried out by the Council on procedural questions and a possible agenda, in order to agree on a common Western position. In accordance with the decisions taken on defence questions in December 1957, by the Heads of Government, the Defence Ministers of the Alliance met in Paris from April 15 to 17, 1958.

They agreed on measures aimed at achieving greater co-ordination and widening co-operation among member countries in the fields of defence research, the development of production and the organization of forces. They also confirmed their support of the basic NATO defensive strategy, which continued to be founded on the concept of a strong deterrent, comprising the 'Shield' with its conventional and nuclear elements, and the nuclear retaliatory forces.

East–West relations

Russia's achievement of the status of a great military power in nuclear terms as well as conventional brought home afresh to the West the need to find a peaceful solution to the potentially explosive situation created by the continued division of Germany. While continuing the long-term defence build-up in conformity with the decisions of the Heads of Government and Defence Ministers, the Alliance now directed considerable effort towards the organization of a Summit Conference to discuss a European settlement with the USSR. In preparation for such a meeting the member countries intensified political consultation and co-operation amongst themselves.

The Council held its spring Ministerial Meeting at the level of Foreign

Ministers in Copenhagen from May 5 to 7, 1958. Its discussions centred chiefly on political and economic co-operation within the Alliance.

A political report prepared by the Secretary General figured on the agenda for the first time, in accordance with the recommendations of the Committee of Three. This document emphasized the very real progress made by the Alliance in the field of political co-operation.

Regarding a possible summit conference, the Council adopted a positive attitude, with the proviso that such a meeting should offer prospects of reaching settlements on important questions; it should, in other words, be properly prepared and take place in a favourable atmosphere. The Foreign Ministers emphasized that the questions of German reunification and controlled disarmament should be discussed.

With regard to the latter point, the Council demonstrated its willingness to negotiate by proposing partial measures which could serve as test cases and might later be applied on a wider scale. It pointed out that agreement on measures which might, for example, prevent surprise attacks or detect nuclear explosions would go far towards demonstrating the possibility of agreement on disarmament.

Negotiations for a summit conference continued during the summer of 1958, but the USSR, when it failed to obtain agreement to a conference on its own terms, appeared to lose interest in a summit meeting.

The North Atlantic Council, however, continued to be the forum for Western consultation on matters involving relations with the Soviet Union, including the suspension of nuclear weapons tests and the prevention of surprise attacks.

Declaration on Berlin – December 1958

The Secretary General of NATO played an active role during this period in efforts to settle disputes between member countries such as those concerning fishing rights off Iceland, and the future of Cyprus.

Towards the end of 1958 it was the question of Germany's future, and that of Berlin in particular, which dominated the scene. On November 10, 1958, Mr. Khrushchev declared that the USSR wished to terminate the present status of Berlin and on November 27, 1958, the Soviet Government confirmed this intention. It announced that it proposed to transfer to the Pankow Authorities, within six months, all the powers it exercised in East Berlin by virtue of the 1945 agreements, as well as the control of communications between Western Germany and Berlin.

The North Atlantic Council held its regular Ministerial session in Paris from December 16 to 18, 1958. It gave special attention to the question of Berlin and associated itself fully with the views previously expressed on the subject by the Governments of the United States, the United Kingdom, France and the Federal Republic of Germany. It stressed in particular that the NATO countries could not approve a solution of the Berlin question which would jeopardize the right of the three Western Powers to remain there as long as their responsibilities so required, and which would not assure freedom of access and communication between Berlin and the free world. It emphasized that the Soviet Union would be held responsible for any action which would have the effect of hampering free access and communication. The Council stated that the question of Berlin could only be settled in the context of an agreement with the USSR on Germany as a whole. It recalled that the Western powers had always been and still were ready to discuss this problem, as well as those of European security and disarmament.

Improvements in political consultation

The Council also examined a report submitted by the Secretary General of NATO on political co-operation in the Alliance. The Ministers agreed that the existing machinery of NATO was well suited to the needs of the Alliance, but that political consultation could be improved by more systematic study of long-term political questions.

The Council reaffirmed the importance it attached to the measures taken both individually and collectively by member countries to stimulate economic activity and to ensure continued expansion without inflation.

Examining the military situation of the Alliance, the Council emphasized the vital need, in view of the continuing increase in Soviet armaments, to sustain member countries' efforts to improve the Alliance's defensive power. It reaffirmed NATO's defensive strategy as continuing to be based on the existence of effective Shield forces and on the firm will to use nuclear retaliatory forces to repel aggression.

The Ministers approved the conclusions of the report on the 1958 Annual Review noting that plans agreed in December 1957, by the Heads of Governments were being actively implemented. They suggested measures for accelerating their realization. The Council decided to hold its next Ministerial Meeting in Washington in order to celebrate, on April 4, 1959, the Tenth Anniversary of the signing of the North Atlantic Treaty.

Within two weeks of this meeting, and the unanimously firm stand taken by the Alliance as a whole in face of the new threat to Germany, the three Western Governments chiefly concerned sent formal replies to the Russian Notes on November 27. They reaffirmed their intention to stand their ground in Berlin and rejected the proclaimed Russian decision to transfer to the East German régime Moscow's responsibility for Berlin and the access routes. The Soviet bluff had failed. During the first three months of 1959 Mr. Khrushchev set about a strategic withdrawal from the apparently unyielding position he had adopted. A détente, based on

44

'peaceful co-existence', which he himself had defined as 'the continuation of the struggle between the two social systems, but by peaceful means', suggested itself as a more fruitful course than threats of nuclear conflict.

Possibilities of détente

On March 5, Mr. Khrushchev said in a speech at Leipzig that there was no question of an ultimatum over Berlin or of regarding May 27 as an irrevocable deadline for the transfer of Soviet control to the German Democratic Republic. That date could be moved to June, July or even later. A few days later, speaking in East Berlin, he announced that the Soviet Union was prepared to accept maintenance by the Western Governments of troops in West Berlin. And on March 19, Mr. Khrushchev said at a press conference that the United States, Britain and France had a legal right to remain in Berlin. The threat to that city was thus lifted – albeit temporarily – and the stage set for a form of détente.

The Western powers examined the prospects of genuine agreement which such a détente might offer. In February 1959, personal contact was again made between the Soviet and Western leaders when Mr. Macmillan, the British Prime Minister, visited Moscow. In August, Mr. Nixon, the United States Vice-President, also went there. In February 1960, Mr. Gronchi, President of Italy, made an official visit to the USSR. Mr. Khrushchev, on his side, accepted the invitation of the United States Government in September 1959 and that of the French Government in March 1960 to visit their respective countries. Meanwhile, the French, United Kingdom and United States Governments were reaching agreement with the Soviet Government on the principle of a conference of the four Foreign Ministers to deal primarily with the German question. The re-opening of negotiations on a question which affected the basic interests of the Alliance called for detailed consultation between the member countries to ensure that they were all in agreement on the position to be defended by the three Western Powers.

Tenth anniversary

The Ministerial Meeting in Washington afforded the opportunity for such consultation, and the Council made a point of recalling that the unity of action and policy rendered possible by the Alliance was the best guarantee of success in negotiations with the Soviet Government and the finding of genuine solutions to the problems which divided the East and the West.

At this meeting the Council received a report from the Powers with special responsibilities for the German question and fully discussed the viewpoints they intended to put forward at the forthcoming negotiations with the Soviet Union.

The Four-Power meeting of Foreign Ministers (France, the United Kingdom, the United States and the USSR) opened in Geneva on May 11. It continued until June 19, when it adjourned until July 13 and finally adjourned on August 5. Throughout this period close liaison was maintained in the NATO Council between the negotiating powers and the other Allies. In addition to the routine consultations and progress reports, both the French and the British Foreign Ministers, Mr. Couve de Murville and Mr. Selwyn Lloyd, who participated in the Conference reported personally to the Council.

Towards a summit conference

These negotiations had revealed that the Western and Soviet positions concerning Germany were still irreconcilable. However, the discussions between President Eisenhower and Mr. Khrushchev shortly afterwards at Camp David opened the door to further negotiation, undertaken this time at the level of Heads of Government. The 'summit conference' now appearing on the horizon, was to take first place in the Council's work for some time.

The Ministerial Meeting, held from December 15 to 22, opening with the inauguration of the new NATO Headquarters, was largely devoted to the forthcoming negotiations between the East and the West. The Ministers initiated a procedure for consultation and the exchange of information with a view to continuing the preparation for the summit conference.

Whilst continuing to prepare this conference, the Permanent Council was kept constantly informed of developments in the disarmament negotiations, re-opened in Geneva since March 15, 1960, within the framework of the Ten-Power Committee.[1] On May 2, when the Ministerial Meeting opened in Istanbul – it was to end on May 4 – the Summit Conference was very near. The Council was able to note that all member countries were in agreement with 'the common position of the United States, France and the United Kingdom as worked out in consultation with their allies'.

The Council re-stated the Western position on Germany – reunification on the basis of self-determination – and Berlin; it declared itself in favour of 'general and complete disarmament, to be achieved by stages under effective international control'; it denounced the efforts of Soviet propaganda to discredit the Federal Republic of Germany and certain other NATO countries as 'inconsistent with a real improvement of international relations' since 'détente, like peace, is indivisible'.

1. Participants included five Western countries: Canada, France, Italy, United Kingdom, United States; five Eastern countries: Bulgaria, Czechoslovakia, Poland, Rumania, USSR.

Breakdown of summit

The day after the Istanbul meeting there occurred an incident which was to undo all the careful planning for the Summit Conference. Mr. Khrushchev announced that an American plane had been shot down over Soviet territory. This was one of the U-2s, or high altitude reconnaissance planes used by the United States to obtain the kind of strategic data which Soviet intelligence, operating in open Western societies, could gather without resorting to such methods. President Eisenhower acknowledged the facts of the situation and assumed personal responsibility for it. Moscow had been aware all along that the U-2 flights were taking place but they flew too high and too fast for her to be able to do anything about them. Now she had tangible evidence, the plane and its pilot, and as soon as the Summit Conference opened, on May 16, Mr. Khrushchev announced he would go ahead with the meeting only on condition the United States condemned the action of the United States Air Force and punished those directly responsible. President Eisenhower replied that the flights had been suspended and were not to be resumed. But this did not satisfy Mr. Khrushchev, who promptly broke up the meeting.

On May 19, the Foreign Ministers of France, the United Kingdom and the United States reported to the Permanent Council on what had occurred. The ensuing discussion showed that member countries were in agreement with the positions taken by the three Heads of State and Government.

'Peaceful co-existence'

A few weeks later, on June 27, the Communist bloc countries suddenly left the Geneva Disarmament Conference, claiming that the disarmament talks could only be usefully continued within a wider framework.[1] The only surprising factor in the cessation of the talks was its suddenness. It was, in fact, a logical step in the hardening of Soviet policy noted since the abortive conference of May 16. Moreover, it was the forerunner of a spectacular initiative by Mr. Khrushchev who personally attended the General Assembly of the United Nations at New York in September and succeeded in inflaming the debates by his vehement interventions and extravagant behaviour. In November, a secret meeting took place in Moscow which was attended by representatives of the 81 Communist Parties in the world. This conference ended with the publication of a voluminous document from which it was clear – so far as international politics were concerned – that Mr. Khrushchev's views on peaceful co-existence had finally been approved unanimously by the delegates.

From December 16 to 18, the North Atlantic Council held its

---

1. Discussions on this subject were taken up on March 15, 1962 within the Conference of the Committee on Disarmament.

Ministerial Meeting in Paris. As announced by the Secretary General, it was a transition meeting, for the Kennedy Administration was in the process of taking over in the United States.

Resignation of Mr. Spaak – appointment of Mr. Stikker

The Ministers made their usual broad study of the international situation from the political, military and economic angles. They also examined the question of long-term planning on the basis of a progress report from the Secretary General and suggestions put forward by governments. In the military sector, the Ministers considered that the Alliance should be able to respond to any attack with whatever force might be appropriate. They decided to study a United States suggestion that a multilateral medium-range ballistic missile force be set up.

On February 1, 1961, the Secretary General, Mr. Paul-Henri Spaak, informed the Council of his decision to resume political life in his own country. He left office on March 5 and on April 21, Mr. Dirk U. Stikker, the Netherlands Permanent Representative to the North Atlantic Council, took office in his place.

The Council met in Ministerial session from May 8 to 10 in Oslo. It expressed regret at lack of progress on the reunification of Germany. Referring to 'the often repeated threat by the Soviet Union to sign a separate peace treaty', the Ministers reaffirmed their view that denunciation by the former of the interallied agreements on Berlin would in no way deprive the other parties of their rights to relieve the Soviet Union of its obligations. The Council expressed the hope that the recently initiated consultations between the United States and the USSR on a procedure for disarmament negotiations would allow the prompt resumption of those negotiations. It agreed that members participating in such discussions should develop their positions in close consultation with the NATO Council. Ministers regretted the negative attitude of the Soviet Union with regard to the comprehensive draft treaty prepared by the United States and the United Kingdom for an agreement on the suspension of nuclear tests.

Aid to Greece and Turkey

The Ministers noted the large volume of aid to the world's less developed areas being furnished by the Free World, and reaffirmed its determination to increase these efforts. Furthermore the Council devoted special attention to the economic problems of Greece and Turkey. It considered ways of assisting the two countries to speed up their development programmes and improve the living standards of their peoples.

Soviet ultimatum on Berlin

President Kennedy visited the North Atlantic Council in Paris on June 1. On June 2 and 3, 1961, he met Mr. Khrushchev in Vienna to establish personal contact and exchange views. It was not anticipated this meeting would have immediate results and, in fact, it brought out the divergent views separating East and West, particularly on the subject of Berlin. These differences were promptly confirmed when, on June 15, Mr. Khrushchev delivered an address in Moscow. As in November 1958, he issued an ultimatum to the West. The Soviet Union would conclude a separate peace treaty with East Germany by the end of the year. This would terminate the West's rights of access to Berlin. The crisis built up rapidly. On July 8, Mr. Khrushchev announced Russia was abandoning a projected reduction in its armed forces and increasing its defence expenditures by over a third. On July 25, President Kennedy called for a substantial build-up of NATO forces. 'We cannot and will not permit the Communists to drive us out of Berlin, either gradually or by force', he said.

Berlin wall

On August 7, Mr. Khrushchev threatened to increase the strength of the Red Army on the Western frontiers and call up reserves. The mounting crisis prompted increasing numbers of East Germans to escape to West Germany. (During the first six months of the year over 103,000 had fled to the West.) But during the night of August 13, the Pankow régime barricaded the Eastern sector of Berlin and, despite the protest of the three Allied Powers, commenced the building of the Berlin Wall.

Soviet nuclear tests

By tacit agreement, the United States, Britain and Russia had, since November 1958, discontinued nuclear test explosions. On August 31, 1961, however, claiming that the United States was threatening war as a countermeasure to the proposed separate peace treaty with East Germany, the Soviet Union resumed nuclear testing on an unprecedented scale. Within two months she had produced some 50 nuclear explosions, culminating, on October 30, with a 50 megaton bomb.

22nd Soviet Communist Party Conference

The West continued to show a unitedly firm front and, just when the tension appeared to be reaching its height, Mr. Khrushchev once again raised his ultimatum. Speaking at the 22nd Soviet Communist Party Congress, which had opened on October 17, he said the question of time-limits was less important than the willingness of the West to solve the German problem. The USSR would not insist on signing a treaty with East Germany before December 31. In all other respects, however, the Soviet position remained unchanged. The Allies nevertheless continued to believe that a peaceful solution to the problem might be negotiated if such a negotiation could be carried out under reasonable conditions. This problem was the object of detailed study in the weeks preceding the next Ministerial Meeting, which took place in Paris on December 13, 14 and 15, 1961.

In a communiqué issued after the session, the Ministers deplored the Soviet Government's continued refusal to accept effective international controls for disarmament. They also expressed regret over the Soviets' refusal to hold serious discussions and their obstruction, for over three years, of the nuclear test ban talks while at the same time they were secretly preparing for the longest series of tests ever held, topped off by the most powerful explosion yet set off.

The Ministers once again reaffirmed their conviction that a just and peaceful solution to the German problem, including that of Berlin, must be based on the principle of self-determination. The Council heard statements on Berlin by the Foreign Ministers of the countries most directly concerned, and was informed of the intention to resume diplomatic contacts with the Soviet Union 'in the hope that these contacts might serve to determine whether a basis for negotiation could be found'.

Mobile force created

In the military field, the Ministers noted the improvements made by member countries in their force contributions, particularly in response to the aggravation of the military threat arising from the deterioration of the Berlin situation. A mobile force had been created from units supplied by six different countries. It consisted at that time of a multinational land element of five air-transportable battalions and a multinational air element of four fighter bomber attack squadrons. The role of the force, which remains unchanged, was to demonstrate NATO solidarity and unity of purpose in any threatened area. There had also been advances in co-operative programmes for defence research and production, as well as in communications and infrastructure. In the economic field, the Council noted that a mission of high ranking personalities had been set up to study ways and means of assisting Greek and Turkish efforts to speed up their development programmes.

The early months of 1962 brought no particular indication of a relaxation of tensions. The problems of Berlin and disarmament remained unsolved, while in South-East Asia the situation showed signs of deteriorating.

Hence, at the regular spring Ministerial session of the North Atlantic Council, held in Athens from May 4 to 6, 1962, Foreign and Defence Ministers could only reaffirm once again their positions with regard both to the Berlin question and to the Geneva Disarmament Conference, and recall the principles upon which they were founded.

Nuclear defence – Athens guidelines

At the same time, the Ministers adopted the 'Athens Guidelines', setting out certain broad assumptions regarding the circumstances in which NATO might be forced to have recourse to nuclear weapons in self-defence and the extent to which political consultation would be possible in the various circumstances. The United States confirmed their determination to continue to make available for the Alliance the nuclear weapons necessary for NATO defence and, with the United Kingdom, gave firm assurances that their strategic nuclear forces would continue to provide defence against threats to the Alliance beyond the capability of NATO committed forces.

Finally, the Ministers decided to institute procedures for the exchange of information among all members concerning the rôle of nuclear weapons in NATO's defence. In addition, the Ministers considered the questions of accelerating scientific co-operation among the NATO countries and of intensifying the efforts undertaken to encourage the economic development of Greece and Turkey. In this connection they invited member countries to consider the establishment of consortia to co-ordinate the measures to be undertaken in order to secure such development.

Finally, Defence Ministers, at a special meeting on May 3, reviewed progress in military co-operation.

Cuba crisis

The second half of 1962 was overshadowed by the grave dispute between the United States and the Soviet Union in the Caribbean. Cuba, it is true, is outside the NATO area, but the events which took place on the island confirmed the fact that through the commitments of certain of its members, the Alliance is inevitably involved in the consequences of political events occurring outside its territory. Hence, well before the second half of October, that is before the United States became certain of the presence of Soviet missiles in Cuba, the situation there had become the subject of consultation within NATO.

Throughout the crisis, the entire Alliance gave unwavering support to the United States' position, and at the Ministerial Meeting in Paris in December 1962, an extensive exchange of views took place regarding the implications of the Cuban affair. The Ministers considered that the Soviet action in Cuba had brought the world to the verge of war, and that the peril had only been averted by the firmness and restraint of the United States, supported by the Alliance and other free nations. Regarding Berlin – where, despite fears to the contrary, no crisis had developed in 1962 – the Ministers re-affirmed the policy set out in their Declaration of December 16, 1958.

51

Need to increase conventional forces

Furthermore, the Ministers considered that, in view of the failure to reach a positive solution to the disarmament problem, no progress could be made in settling international disputes if the Alliance did not maintain its defensive strength. In this connection they stressed the need to increase the effectiveness of the Alliance's conventional forces.

Assignment of nuclear forces

In addition, the proposals contained in the Communiqué published following the meeting in Nassau on December 21, 1962, of President Kennedy and Prime Minister Macmillan introduced fresh and highly important elements into NATO's defence policy: on the one hand, the United States and the United Kingdom proposed in effect to set up a NATO nuclear force to which they would commit a part of their strategic nuclear forces; on the other, they proposed the creation of a NATO multilateral nuclear force to which would be assigned submarines armed with Polaris missiles.

The Permanent Council undertook the study of these proposals at the beginning of 1963 and, after discussing the matter on numerous occasions, reached certain conclusions which were studied by Ministers at Ottawa during the meeting held in the Canadian capital from May 22 to 24, 1963. At this session Ministers again affirmed their unanimity with respect to the Cuba and Berlin problems as well as the disarmament question. It was, however, to the organization of the Alliance's nuclear forces that their attention was principally directed. Important decisions were reached, notably for the assignment to SACEUR of the United Kingdom v-bomber force as well as three United States Polaris submarines, and for the establishment by SACEUR on his staff of a Deputy responsible to him for nuclear affairs.[1] Ministers also decided upon measures both to permit broader participation by officers of NATO member countries in nuclear activities in Allied Command Europe and in co-ordination of operational planning at Omaha, and also to facilitate the provision of fuller information to national authorities, both political and military. Recognizing equally the need to achieve a satisfactory balance between nuclear and conventional arms, the Ministers directed the Council in permanent session to under-take, with the advice of the NATO military authorities, further studies of the inter-related questions of strategy, force requirements and the resources available to meet them.

A few weeks later President Kennedy went to Europe and, in a speech at Frankfurt, Germany, on June 25, renewed his country's pledge to Europe and reaffirmed the principle of equal partnership within the Alliance.

1. This post was discontinued in September 1968.

Test Ban Treaty

At about this time, intensive diplomatic activity took place which was to lead to two conciliatory measures, the first a US-Soviet agreement, signed in Geneva on June 20, for the installation of a 'red telephone' between Washington and Moscow, the second a US-UK-Soviet agreement for the banning of nuclear tests in the atmosphere, in space and under water. The treaty embodying this agreement was signed at the Kremlin on August 5 and all countries who wished to support it were invited to add their signatures.

Sino-Soviet discord

This treaty led to a further deterioration in relations between China and the USSR. On September 21, the latter country denounced China's determination at all costs to obtain nuclear weapons for itself, and, furthermore, accused the Chinese of more than 5,000 violations of the Soviet frontier.

One month later the United States, anxious to demonstrate their ability in case of need to deliver reinforcements rapidly to the NATO Command in Europe, carried out a large scale airborne exercise entitled 'Big Lift'.

Assassination of President Kennedy

It was beginning to look as if the year 1963 would run its course without any fresh elements emerging in East–West problems when, on November 22, a dramatic event took place: the assassination in Dallas, Texas, of President Kennedy. The tragic death of the American President was a blow to public opinion the world over, bringing fears of repercussions at the international level. On November 25, the North Atlantic Council paid solemn homage to his memory and three weeks later the new American President, Mr. Johnson, sent to the North Atlantic Council, meeting in Ministerial session on December 16 and 17, a message reaffirming the United States' loyal support for NATO.

This session also gave Ministers an opportunity to take fresh stock of a situation which, despite some persistent dark spots, did present certain positive aspects. No major crisis had developed since the confrontation over Cuba, and Ministers emphasized that the unity and military strength of the Alliance had largely contributed to this result and to the international atmosphere then prevailing, which gave them grounds for hope that further progress could be achieved. In addition, the Council reviewed progress during the year in every field of the Alliance's activity: political consultation, defence, co-operation in research, economic affairs, etc. While no relaxation of the collective effort was yet justified, the reckoning was on balance satisfactory.

Discord in Cyprus

The beginning of 1964 was marked by serious disorder among the Greek and Turkish communities in Cyprus, which had the natural effect of straining relations between Greece and Turkey. In face of this disquieting situation, the North Atlantic Council, rightly anxious to preserve friendship between these two members of the Alliance, spared no effort to this end. At its Ministerial Meeting in The Hague in May 1964 the Council entrusted Secretary General Stikker with a 'Watching Brief' on Greek/Turkish Relations which was passed on to his successor Mr. Brosio. (It was under this 'Watching Brief' that the latter, in November 1967, visited Athens and Ankara in the interest, together with the United States and the United Nations, of improving relations between the two states following certain incidents in Cyprus). On March 4, the Security Council decided to send a peace-keeping force to the island. Although feelings on the subject to some extent quietened down, the problem was still far from solution and the North Atlantic Council, while giving full support to the United Nations in its mediating rôle, continued throughout the year to follow developments closely.

Departure of Mr. Stikker and appointment of Mr. Brosio

At the beginning of April, NATO's Secretary General, Mr. Dirk U. Stikker, informed the Council of his intention for health reasons to relinquish his functions during the summer. Meeting in Ministerial session from May 12 to 14 at The Hague, Netherlands, the Council paid tribute to Mr. Stikker's untiring efforts and expressed their gratitude to him. Their choice for his successor was Mr. Manlio Brosio, at that time Italian Ambassador in Paris. In addition, the Council reaffirmed its position with regard to such major world problems as disarmament, Berlin, the reunification of Germany, Cyprus, and aid to developing countries. On July 29, 1964, Mr. Stikker bade farewell to the North Atlantic Council and on August 1, Mr. Manlio Brosio took up his appointment.

Eviction of Mr. Khrushchev and China's first atom bomb

The summer went by without any major crisis developing. In South-East Asia, the situation continued to be disquieting while relations between China and the Soviet Union were still strained, without however giving rise to any specific friction.

Two events, occurring one on top of the other, brought the news of the day back into prominence: on October 15, Mr. Nikita Khrushchev was deprived of his office and replaced, as head of the government, by Mr. Alexis Kosygin, and as Secretary General of the Communist Party by Mr. Leonid Brezhnev; on October 16 China exploded its first atomic bomb. This latter event did not come entirely as a surprise, but the former occurred with startling suddenness and for a time remained shrouded in mystery. The two events were bound, sooner or later, to have repercussions on the international situation and were consequently made the subject of exchanges of view within the North Atlantic Council.

At the opening of the Council's meeting in Ministerial session in Paris on December 15, 1964 (it was to continue until the 17th), little light had been thrown on the situation so far as it concerned future relations with the Chinese communist leaders and the new team in power in the Kremlin. Ministers noted cautiously that both the eviction of Mr. Khrushchev and the explosion of the Chinese atomic bomb had increased the uncertainties with which the Alliance was faced, and consequently stressed the importance of maintaining the cohesion of member states in the strategic as well as the political field. In the Council's view this implied the continued examination of the important and complex problems confronting NATO in the field of conventional and nuclear weapons; perseverance, also, in the study of the various formulae already proposed, or which might be advanced in the future, in an effort to find a solution, in particular, to the problem of sharing nuclear responsibilities within the Alliance. In this respect, the December 1964 session constituted a logical follow-up to the Ottawa session, where an approach to these problems had already been made. For the rest, Ministers reaffirmed positions which by that time had become traditional, particularly stressing the need to speed up the economic development of Greece and Turkey. They also established a procedure aimed at contributing to the solution of the special defence problems of Greece and Turkey in 1965.

The year 1965 brought very few new developments in the solution of outstanding problems. It was a year which saw no major crisis in Europe but in which the Soviet Union continued to oppose a settlement of the cardinal issues between East and West and to devote an increasing share of its economic and technical resources to military purposes. This naturally strengthened the determination of member countries to maintain the unity of the Alliance and to tighten their defence system still further, particularly through broader allied participation in nuclear force planning.

Independence of Malta

The presence of NATO establishments and forces in Malta had raised a problem for the Alliance when the island attained independence on September 21, 1964. The Council adopted in 1965 a resolution confirming the agreement of the Government of Malta for the continued legal status of the installations pending further discussions and also confirming the interest of NATO member countries in the island's security. In August 1968 an open-ended Working Group was created under the authority of the Council, in accordance with the Resolution of 1965, to proceed with consultations and discussions concerning relations with Malta. The Government of Malta appointed its diplomatic representative in Brussels to represent Maltese interests in relations with NATO.

Allied participation in nuclear planning

The development by both East and West of an invulnerable nuclear second strike capability and the availability to the Major NATO Commanders of strategic and tactical nuclear weapons had raised highly complex political and technical problems. Among these were the need to frame a nuclear policy for the Alliance, to associate non-nuclear members of NATO as closely as possible with nuclear planning, and to develop appropriate procedures for consultation and decision-making. As has been mentioned previously, various proposals for the establishment of a specifically allied force equipped with nuclear weapons had been put forward. Chief among these was an American proposal for the creation of a multilateral nuclear force (MLF), several versions of which, along with a British alternative proposal for an Atlantic nuclear force (ANF), were for a while under study by a number of member governments. However, neither of these projects reached the stage of actual implementation. A decisive step towards the improvement of allied cooperation in nuclear affairs was taken in the spring of 1965 when an ad hoc Special Committee of Defence Ministers was established under whose aegis three working groups conducted studies on exchange of intelligence, information and other data; communications; and nuclear planning.

New procedures for defence plans

At their meeting in Paris on May 31st and June 1st, the Ministers of Defence laid stress on the need to secure a closer alignment between NATO military requirements and national force plans within the agreed strategic concept of a forward defence posture. In this respect, the Ministerial Meeting of December 1965 confirmed that progress had been made, for Ministers accepted in principle the introduction of new procedures which, by projecting Alliance force goals and country plans five years ahead each year, were designed to enhance the capacity of the Alliance to adapt its defence plans to changes both in military technology and in the international situation.

At the general political level, on the other hand, Ministers could only note with regret that no real progress had been made towards overcoming the division of Germany or towards disarmament. Only the efforts to promote contacts and exchanges with the Soviet Union and the countries of Eastern Europe had met with some degree of response, mainly in the sphere of bilateral relations. Furthermore, in view of the renewed tension over Cyprus, the Council reaffirmed its determination to contribute to bringing about a peaceful, agreed and equitable solution of the problem in accordance with the principles of the United Nations Charter. It was agreed that the next Ministerial Session of the Council would be held in Brussels on the invitation of the Belgian Government. In the meantime, however, events occurred which were to have serious implications for the work and structure of the Organization.

Withdrawal of French forces – 1966

In March 1966, in a series of aide-memoires to the Governments of the fourteen other NATO member countries, the French Government announced that it intended to withdraw French personnel from the NATO integrated Military Headquarters, terminate the assignment of French forces to the international commands and request the transfer from French territory of the International Headquarters, allied units and installations or bases not falling under the control of the French Authorities. These memoranda were not entirely unexpected since the President of the French Republic had already given some indication of his intentions in his speeches.

The French decisions made it necessary for negotiations to be held between the French Government on the one hand, and its fourteen allies on the other hand. As early as March 1966, the 'fourteen' accordingly held meetings as a group set up under the Chairmanship of Mr. André de Staercke, the Belgian Permanent Representative and Doyen of the Council, to work out a common basis for negotiations with France. These meetings were held less and less frequently as problems were gradually solved.

Brussels decisions – June 1966

By the time the Council met in Ministerial Session on June 7th and 8th in Brussels, a number of solutions acceptable to all concerned had already been worked out, and the Ministers took several important decisions. They decided to transfer the Military Headquarters of NATO from France, invited the Benelux countries to provide a new site for SHAPE, and agreed that some simplification of the Command structure should be carried out. The Council also decided that the Standing Group should be abolished and replaced by an appropriate alternative body. Furthermore, it extended an invitation to Italy to provide a new home for the NATO Defence College.

The remaining related problems, such as the tasks of French forces in Germany and French participation in NATO infrastructure projects, were referred to the Council in Permanent Session for discussion.

Having made these arrangements, the Council then turned to its customary review of the international situation. There had been little change since December 1965. No progress had been made on the German problem, East–West relations, disarmament or Greek–Turkish relations over the Cyprus issue. Ministers could therefore only reaffirm their position on each of these problems. On the other hand, as regards co-operation between member countries in the spirit of Article 2 of the Treaty, they acknowledged the need to join efforts in order to narrow the gap in technological achievement between Europe and North America.

This session was followed several weeks later by a meeting of the Defence Ministers in Paris on July 25th.

Their discussions centred mainly on the new defence planning procedures adopted at the December 1965 meeting and on ways of improving them.

During the following months, Permanent Representatives were extremely active in tackling the numerous new tasks devolving upon them by reason of the events which had occurred inside the Alliance itself. Since France, while remaining a member of the Alliance, did not take part in NATO military discussions, the Council was obliged to find a forum in which to discuss these questions.

Defence Planning Committee

The answer was found in meetings of the Council as the Defence Planning Committee (DPC). This had been established in 1963, and France was, of course, a member like any other NATO country, but the new departure was that since 1966 France did not exercise the right to sit. Whether at Ministerial or at Permanent Representative level the Committee meets under the Chairmanship of the Secretary General; it has become the organ of co-ordination and decision for all questions concerning the integrated defence system in which fourteen countries take part. It should be noted that France maintains a military liaison mission with the Military Committee and with Major NATO Commanders.

Many military problems had arisen, particularly owing to the transfer of the two Headquarters. Belgium had offered a site for the Supreme Headquarters Allied Powers Europe at Casteau on the outskirts of Mons, and the Netherlands had decided to accommodate the re-organized Central Europe Command at Brunssum. The difficulties to which these transfers gave rise were complicated by a problem of communications between the Military Authorities and the Council in the event the latter remained in Paris, a point on which no decision had yet been taken. In addition, there was still the wider problem of allied participation in the formulation of NATO's nuclear strategy. Finally, there were unmistakable signs of uneasiness within the Alliance which were not due solely to the French actions.

The Alliance and public opinion

This feeling stemmed also from the general pattern of developments, from the impression that the danger of aggression had receded and from the coming of age of a generation which had not known the war and its aftermath and was therefore less receptive to the lessons of that experience. In short, it reflected the reasons which were causing public opinion to question the need for the Alliance. In these circumstances, it is not surprising that the winter Ministerial Session of the Council, which was held in Paris on December 15th and 16th 1966, should have taken on special significance.

All the unresolved issues were discussed by the Ministers, as can be seen from the unusually long communiqué issued after the meeting.

With reference to the general political situation, Ministers, after reaffirming their position on a number of outstanding questions and on Agenda items such as the draft treaty on the peaceful use of outer space and the multilateral tariff negotiations (Kennedy round), associated themselves with the views expressed in the Declaration on Germany by the Governments of France, the United Kingdom and the United States, in which these countries confirmed that they would continue to be responsible for the security of Berlin.

The Council also adopted a resolution on international technological co-operation. This question had been the subject of an exchange of views held on the initiative of the Italian Government.

'Harmel exercise'

Furthermore, the Council approved a second resolution whose implementation was to prove particularly fruitful for the Alliance. On the proposal of the Belgian Government and recalling the initiative taken by Canada in December 1964, the Council resolved 'to undertake a broad analysis of international developments since the signing of the North Atlantic Treaty in 1949', so as 'to determine the influence of such developments on the Alliance and to identify the tasks which lie before it, in order to strengthen the Alliance as a factor for a durable peace'. This study was later to be known as the 'Harmel Exercise' and reference is made to it further on.

Nuclear planning arrangements

The decisions taken in the military sphere were no less important. Meeting as the Defence Planning Committee, the Council approved recommendations of the Special Committee of NATO Defence Ministers (see page 56) calling for the establishment of two permanent bodies for nuclear planning: the Nuclear Defence Affairs Committee, open to all member countries, and a smaller Nuclear Planning Group of seven countries[1] drawn from the larger membership of the Nuclear Defence

1. Since January 1, 1970, membership varies between seven and eight countries.

Affairs Committee. The composition of the Nuclear Planning Group rotates periodically so that all interested countries may participate actively in its work. The Council also approved in principle the establishment of a NATO-wide communications scheme and agreed to study whether a NATO satellite communication programme should be established which would provide for a co-operative effort by member nations in the new and developing field of space technology.

The last, but not the least, of the Council's decisions of immediate practical significance was to transfer the NATO Permanent Headquarters to Brussels. This city was also to be the new home of the Military Committee which had been located in Washington since its creation.

Relocation

From the material point of view, 1967 was for the Atlantic Alliance primarily a year of moving out and settling in. The flags of the fifteen NATO member countries were lowered at SHAPE – Rocquencourt on March 30th, and on March 31st General Lemnitzer and his staff officially took possession of their new Headquarters at Casteau Mons in Belgium. The Central Europe Command moved to Brunssum in the Netherlands, and for several weeks long lines of military lorries evacuated the Allied bases from France. During the summer, the NATO Air Defence Ground Environment Organization (NADGE) was transferred to Brussels and in October the Council, the Military Committee and the International Staff moved into the temporary Headquarters which had been built for them in six months on the outskirts of the Belgian capital.

In spite of all this, the North Atlantic Council neither interrupted nor slowed down its work.

Meeting as the Defence Planning Committee on May 9th, 1967, Ministers gave political, strategic and economic guidance to the Military Authorities with a view to the adoption in December of NATO's first five-year force plan covering the period up to the end of 1972. Indirectly, this was an indication of their common resolve not to invoke Article 13 of the Treaty under which countries could cease to be a party to the Treaty after it had been in force twenty years, i.e. in August 1969.

Luxembourg Meeting

One month later, on June 14th, the North Atlantic Council held its regular spring Ministerial Meeting in Luxembourg. By then, however, the outlook had suddenly darkened in international affairs. Between the two meetings of the Council, hostilities had broken out in the Middle East between Israel and the Arab countries and a cease-fire had only just taken place. It was therefore natural that Ministers should partly devote their exchange of views to a review of the situation in this area. They stressed the urgency of humanitarian efforts to alleviate the sufferings caused by the war and expressed their support of all efforts to establish a lasting peace in this troubled area of the world. Although hostilities had ceased, their explosive violence had suddenly made public opinion more keenly aware of the potential dangers of an international situation in which too many problems were left unsolved. Just such a situation existed over Cyprus, where the deterioration of Greek–Turkish relations was giving cause for concern. Against this background, the non-proliferation of nuclear weapons and disarmament – questions closely linked with European security – stood out in stronger relief. In this connection, Ministers made a new proposal which was later to assume considerable importance. They suggested that, if conditions permitted, a balanced reduction of forces by the East and West should be made, adding that a contribution on the part of the Soviet Union and the Eastern European countries towards a reduction of forces would be welcomed as a gesture of peaceful intent.

The studies on the future tasks of the Alliance had been initiated in accordance with the Ministerial resolution of December 22nd, 1966. As early as January 1967, work had started on this broad analysis which, as already stated, was called the 'Harmel Exercise' after the Foreign Minister of Belgium who had suggested it. Four sub-groups had been set up, each working on a basic subject of interest to the Alliance: East-West Relations, Inter-Allied Relations, General Defence Policy and Relations with other Countries. These sub-groups were chaired by rapporteurs of repute drawn from the political and academic world in member countries. The reports were drawn up during the summer and submitted to governments.

Nuclear Planning Group

In the meantime, the seven Ministers composing the NATO Nuclear Planning Group had held their first meeting in Washington in April and they met again in Ankara in September.

Their agenda included matters of strategic defence and of the possible tactical use of nuclear weapons in certain regions of Allied Command Europe. Mr. McNamara, the then United States Secretary of State for Defense, gave a status report on the efforts made by his country to open discussions with the USSR on a limitation of the nuclear arms race.

Ministerial Meeting Brussels December 1967

The first Ministerial Meeting of the North Atlantic Council to be held at the new Brussels Headquarters opened on 12th December. The fact that the relocation operations had scarcely disturbed the activities of the Alliance gave reason for satisfaction. Furthermore, the crisis in the relations between Greece and Turkey over Cyprus, which had recently gone through an acute phase, was now gradually receding, largely thanks to the important rôle played by the Secretary General of NATO in reducing tension. This Ministerial Meeting therefore took place in an atmosphere to which internal calm had, in large measure, been restored. While all the usual questions were examined – Germany, disarmament, non-proliferation of nuclear weapons, technological co-operation – it was in the specifically political and military spheres that the major decisions were taken.

Revised strategic concept

Sitting as the Defence Planning Committee, Ministers adopted a revised strategic concept resulting from the first comprehensive review of NATO's strategy to be undertaken by the Military Committee since 1956. This concept, which adapts NATO's strategy to current political, military and technological developments, is based upon a flexible and balanced range of responses, conventional and nuclear, to all levels of aggression or threats of aggression. Ministers also adopted for the first time a five-year force plan, covering the period 1968–1972.

Harmel Report

From the point of view of the future of the Alliance, the political decisions taken by Ministers at this meeting were of the highest importance. After exchanging comments on the extensive studies undertaken in connection with the 'Harmel Exercise', the fifteen Governments agreed on a document which outlines certain basic principles and lists a number of tasks with which the Alliance could be entrusted in the future. This report is entitled 'Report of the Council on the Future Tasks of the Alliance', and a copy was attached to the communiqué. It is also known as the 'Harmel Report'.[1] In the history of the Atlantic Alliance, this document is in the tradition of the 1955 'Report by the Committee of Three' although it is much shorter and, in certain respects, less exhaustive. Like all diplomatic documents, the Report is the outcome of much compromise and conciliation, but it lays the emphasis on the continuing relevance of the twin political and military functions of the Alliance and the latter's ability to adapt itself to changing conditions. The Report sets the Alliance a general goal: the establishment of a more stable international relationship, which is essential if the underlying political issues are to be solved, the ultimate purpose being to achieve a just and lasting peaceful order in Europe. It also describes the method to be adopted, namely a common approach to problems through greater consultation.

Finally, it defines two specific tasks, one of them of a military nature, namely the defence of the exposed areas and particularly the Mediter-

1. See Appendix 6, page 336 for the full text of the Harmel Report.

ranean, where events in the Middle East had led to an expansion of Soviet activity, and the other mainly political, although bearing on a military problem, namely the formulation of proposals for balanced force reductions in East and West, a suggestion which had been advanced earlier at the Luxembourg meeting. The Harmel Report presented the Alliance with a realistic programme of work which could be time-phased over what would probably be a prolonged period. From the beginning of 1968, the Council got down to implementing this programme.

Reykjavik Meeting 1968 – Declaration on MBFR

At the next Ministerial Meeting, which was held for the first time in Reykjavik, Iceland, on June 24 and 25, the Council examined the progress achieved up to then in carrying out the main tasks set by the Harmel Report for the Alliance in the years ahead. In a Declaration appended to the Communiqué, the Foreign Ministers and Representatives of countries participating in the NATO Defence Programme affirmed their readiness to explore with other interested States specific and practical steps in the field of arms control. They invited the USSR and other Eastern European countries to study the problem of mutual and balanced force reductions (MBFR) and called on them 'to join in this search for progress towards peace'. This historic Declaration became known as the 'Reykjavik Signal'.

Nuclear planning 1968

During 1968, the Defence Ministers of the Nuclear Planning Group held two more meetings, at The Hague in April and at Bonn in October. The Ministers continued to focus their attention on the possible tactical use of nuclear weapons in defence of NATO. They also concluded that, in the light of existing and foreseeable technological circumstances, the deployment of anti-ballistic missiles (ABMS) in NATO Europe was not warranted at that time.

Invasion of Czechoslovakia

Two months after Reykjavik the efforts of NATO Ministers to further a détente in East-West relations were to receive a serious setback. On August 20th, 1968, armed forces of the Soviet Union and four other Warsaw Pact countries invaded Czechoslovakia. During the days which followed the North Atlantic Council, setting aside its regular business, kept the situation under continuous close review. The unanimous conviction of member governments was that the military intervention of the Warsaw Pact countries was a clear violation of the U.N. Charter and of international law. At the same time they were careful to avoid any action which might be considered to exacerbate the situation. On September 4th, the Defence Planning Committee issued a statement re-affirming 'the necessity of maintaining NATO'S military capability and of taking into account the implications of recent developments in Eastern Europe in the planning of their national forces'.

The Council immediately initiated a series of studies analysing the political, military and economic implications of the event and those on the technical side of crisis management.

Whilst these studies were still under consideration the Council decided to advance the date of the normal year-end Ministerial Meeting by a month.

Advanced Ministerial Meeting

Accordingly, it took place on November 15th and 16th 1968 at the Brussels headquarters. The Ministers in their communiqué reaffirmed the inviolability of the principle that all nations are independent and that consequently any intervention by one state in the affairs of another is un-lawful. In the case of Czechoslovakia they noted that this principle had been deliberately violated by the Soviet leaders and four of their allies. They also underlined the dangers of the Soviet contention that a right exists for intervention in the affairs of other states deemed to be within a so-called 'Socialist Commonwealth' as this runs counter to the basic principles of the United Nations Charter. The Ministers considered that grave uncertainty about the situation and the calculations and intentions of the USSR had been created by this use of force and that great vigilance was now required on the part of the Allies, particularly with regard to Berlin and the access routes to that city, and to the situation in the Mediterranean.

Warning to the USSR

Addressing a warning to the USSR, the Ministers made it clear that any Soviet intervention directly or indirectly affecting the situation in Europe or in the Mediterranean would create an international crisis with grave consequences. Following this, and after stating that recent events had obliged the Allies participating in NATO's integrated defence programme to re-assess the state of their defences, the Ministers announced a number of measures calculated to improve the overall NATO defence posture. Finally, whilst regretting the severe setback to possibilities of further measures of détente as foreseen at the June 1968 Ministerial Meeting in Reykjavik, the Ministers reaffirmed that NATO's ultimate objective remains the establishment of secure, peaceful, and mutually beneficial relations between East and West and that, towards this end, the Atlantic Alliance would continue to stand as the indispensable guarantor of security and the essential foundation for the pursuit of European reconciliation.

DPC Meeting Brussels January 1969

Two months later, on January 16, 1969 the Defence Planning Committee met in Ministerial Session and Ministers announced that they had taken certain measures designed to strengthen the conventional capability of NATO and that they had adopted a NATO force plan for 1969–1973. Ministers had also approved the concept of an Allied naval force capable of being assembled on call in the Mediterranean; a special command located in Naples had already been activated (on November 21, 1968) for the purpose of co-ordinating the maritime air reconnaissance operations of a number of Allied countries in the Mediterranean area.

20th Anniversary

The year 1969 marked the twentieth anniversary of the signing of the North Atlantic Treaty. Commemorating the event during the Council's meeting on April 10 and 11 in Washington, Ministers expressed their satisfaction at the decisive contribution the Alliance had made to the maintenance of peace and to the security of all its members. The Alliance, they recalled, was established to safeguard the freedom of all its peoples and also in response to a common fear that without an effective security system another war might break out in a divided Europe. The Alliance, they concluded, would continue as the expression of the common purposes and aspirations of the member countries.

East–West relations

Some time earlier, in February 1969, President Nixon, on a visit to NATO Headquarters had voiced his hope that the period of confrontation was over and that an era of negotiation with the USSR was about to start. This hope was shared by the other member governments who were seeking the means of recreating a climate of détente along the lines of their earlier efforts. The declaration by the Warsaw Pact countries in Budapest in March 1969, which advocated the holding of an early Conference on European Security, thus came at a timely moment. Although this declaration contained proposals which had already been made previously, its tone was more moderate.

Washington Ministerial Meeting April 10–11 1969

This was a particularly opportune meeting inasmuch as the Council considered the extent to which this situation could contribute to the relaxation of tension. The Ministers set themselves the task of exploring with the Warsaw Pact countries what specific issues could best lend themselves to fruitful negotiation and early resolution. They instructed the Council in Permanent Session to draw up a list of these issues and to study how a useful process of negotiation could, in due course, be initiated.

Improvement in East–West relations

This new departure in East-West relations was henceforward to take
precedence over all the other issues with which the Alliance was concerned. A searching study of its implications was carried out. As a result
of this study and the diplomatic contacts with all the countries concerned,
together with the additional proposals for a draft agenda put forward by
the Warsaw Pact countries in October 1969 and May 1970, Ministers were
able at ensuing meetings to spell out their ideas concerning the form and
content of such negotiations.

Problems of environment

It was likewise at this meeting that President Nixon formulated his idea
that member countries should act jointly to tackle the problems of
environment, a suggestion which was to be taken up rapidly, as will be
seen later.[1]

DPC Meeting Brussels May 28, 1969

Shortly after the Washington Meeting, the Defence Planning Committee in
Ministerial Session met in Brussels on May 28, 1969 and reaffirmed the
continuing validity of the NATO strategy based on deterrence, flexibility
in response and forward defence. Ministers also reaffirmed their determination to make appropriate contributions on a collective basis to support
this strategy and to ensure that the overall military capability of NATO
should not be reduced except as part of a pattern of mutual force reductions balanced in scope and timing.

They gave political and economic guidance to the NATO Military
Authorities for the next planning period; and they approved the actual
establishment of the naval on-call force for the Mediterranean.

DPC Meeting Brussels December 3, 1969

Ministers discussed arrangements for the reinforcement, in times of
tension, of NATO's ready forces. They noted a preliminary report on a
comprehensive study of the relative capabilities of the forces of NATO and
the Warsaw Pact. They took note of the outcome of consultations with the
Canadian Authorities concerning their forces for NATO, and endorsed a
number of consequential remedial measures taken, or under consideration,
by other member countries in order to maintain adequate forces in
Central Europe.

Brussels Ministerial Meeting December 4–5, 1969

At their meeting in Brussels on December 4 and 5, 1969, Ministers recalled that the policy of the Alliance was directed wholly towards the

1. See, in particular, the detailed Chapter on this subject, page 179.

establishment of a just and lasting peace. This must be the ultimate aim of any negotiations which, in the first instance, must be concerned with the source of tensions, namely the fundamental problems of European security. In addition, the negotiation must be carefully prepared if it was to have any reasonable chance of success. To avoid the risk of disillusion, moreover, an undertaking of this magnitude could only be embarked on if the parties had from the outset given tangible signs of their sincerity and of their determination to reach a satisfactory settlement. In this connection, the attitude of the USSR and the other East European countries in the negotiations, particularly those on Germany and Berlin, which were about to begin, would show whether those countries were ready to contribute to the creation of a favourable climate, the absence of which would bode ill for the success of all subsequent talks. As for the procedure for negotiation, consideration could be given to all constructive possibilities, including a general conference, or a series of conferences, on European security provided that they were not designed to ratify the present division of Europe. After defining their attitude towards the future development of East–West relations, Ministers indicated that, on this basis, they would continue and intensify their contacts, discussions or negotiations through all appropriate channels, both bilateral and multilateral.

Ministers also examined the increasing Soviet presence in the Mediterranean and agreed to study this further at their Spring 1970 meeting. They agreed that NATO's defence posture continued to be an essential stabilizing factor in support of the search for a meaningful détente, and reaffirmed the principle that NATO would continue to ensure that there was no reduction in its overall military capability.

East–West negotiations

Members of the Alliance took the initiative of starting important bilateral talks, the progress of which could be indicative of the chances of making headway in other areas of East–West relations. Talks between the United States and the USSR on strategic arms limitations were begun in November 1969, and have since continued either in Helsinki or in Vienna. At each of their meetings, Ministers stressed the importance of these talks for security in Europe and the future of mankind. Soon after, in December 1969, the Federal Republic of Germany embarked on negotiations with the Soviet Union which led to the signature, on August 12, 1970, of the German-Soviet Treaty. While these negotiations with the Soviet Government were still going on, the Government of the Federal Republic also began talks with Poland, in February 1970, with a view to normalizing relations between the two countries. These talks culminated in the signature, on December 7, 1970, of the German-Polish Treaty. As part of its Ostpolitik, designed to improve its relations with its Eastern neighbours,

the Government of the Federal Republic likewise set itself the task of
establishing a modus vivendi with the German Democratic Republic and to
this end began talks on March 19, 1970. Ministers assured the Federal
Republic that all these initiatives had their sympathetic support.

In the past, Ministers had consistently stressed the need for improving
the position of Berlin and access to that city, pointing out that a satisfactory settlement would be a major factor in the evaluation of overall
prospects for East–West negotiations. The three Allied powers (United
States, United Kingdom and France) acting in pursuance of their special
responsibilities for Germany and Berlin as a whole, began talks with the
Soviet Union to this effect on March 26, 1970.

The progress of all these talks and the results of bilateral contacts made
by other member countries became the subject of continuing consultations
within the Alliance.

Nuclear planning 1969

The Defence Ministers of the Nuclear Planning Group, for their part, had
continued their deliberations on fundamental nuclear issues of interest to
the Alliance, meeting in London in May and in Warrington, Virginia, in
November. Principal agenda subjects included consideration of strategic
aspects of NATO's nuclear defence, tactical use of nuclear weapons, and
consultation arrangements. This work led to the formulation of some
general guidelines on consultation procedure and some political guidelines
for the possible initial defensive tactical use of nuclear weapons in defence
of the Treaty area which were endorsed by the Nuclear Defence Affairs
Committee and approved by the Defence Planning Committee in
Ministerial session in December 1969.

Proposals for multilateral exploratory contacts
(Council Meeting Rome, May 1970)

The Ministerial meeting held in Rome on May 26 and 27, 1970 was of
outstanding importance in the context of East–West relations. Ministers
declared their willingness, in so far as progress was recorded as a result of
their above-mentioned talks and the talks in progress at the time, in
particular on Germany and Berlin, to enter into multilateral contacts of
an exploratory nature with all the governments concerned. The purpose
of these contacts would be to establish when it would be possible to
convene a conference or series of conferences on European security and
co-operation. The establishment of a permanent body could be envisaged
as one means, among others, of embarking upon multilateral negotiations
in due course. Ministers emphasized, in this connection, that it was not
sufficient to discuss European security in the abstract. Among the subjects
which could be discussed within the framework of the multilateral contacts

proposed were the principles which should govern relations between States, including the renunciation of force. Another subject which could be discussed concurrently was the development of international relations with a view to contributing to the freer movement of people, ideas and information and to developing co-operation in the cultural, economic, technical and scientific fields of human environment.

To underline the importance which they attached to their proposals, Ministers decided that for the first time the Rome Communiqué, together with the Declaration on Mutual and Balanced Force Reductions, should be forwarded through the Foreign Minister of Italy to all other interested parties including neutral and non-aligned governments. They further agreed that member governments would seek the reactions of other governments to the initiation of the comprehensive programme of exploration and negotiation which they envisaged.

At the same meeting in Rome, Ministers expressed their continued concern about the increased Soviet presence in the Mediterranean. As regards disarmament, they re-emphasized the importance of limiting the spread of nuclear weapons and welcomed the coming into force of the Non-Proliferation Treaty.

Rome declaration on mutual and balanced force reductions

Despite the absence of any meaningful reaction from the Warsaw Pact countries, the Allies nevertheless went ahead with studies designed to explore further the ways and means of examining the possibility of mutual and balanced force reductions. In view of the new developments in East–West relations, it was obvious that efforts to reduce the level of armed confrontation in Europe must be given priority in Western preparations. It was in this spirit that the Declaration appended to the Communiqué on the Rome meeting invited the Warsaw Pact countries and the other countries concerned to join in exploratory talks with a view to identifying the criteria which could serve as a starting point for fruitful negotiation.

DPC Meeting Brussels June 1970
Review of Allied defence problems

When the Defence Planning Committee met in Brussels on June 11, 1970, Ministers expressed concern at the continuing growth of the armed forces of the Warsaw Pact countries. They reaffirmed the determination of NATO countries to maintain the overall military capability of the Alliance. They also reviewed the status of various on-going Alliance defence planning studies, including measures to strengthen the defence of the flanks and the report on the study of the relative force capabilities of NATO and the Warsaw Pact. They noted recent steps taken in support of NATO's strategy of flexible response, namely the approval of a new five-year infrastructure programme, methods of improving co-operation in research, development and production and the successful launching and testing of the first NATO communications satellite, which marked the implementation of the programme approved in 1966. Another important decision was taken at the meeting: it was agreed that a comprehensive review should be undertaken of the defence problems the Alliance would have to overcome during the next decade and that a report on the outcome of this study should be submitted to Ministers at their next meeting.

DPC Meeting Brussels December 2, 1970

Ministers agreed that East–West negotiations can be expected to succeed only if NATO maintains an effective deterrent and defensive posture. They noted the continuous rise in Soviet defence and defence-related expenditure and the evidence that the USSR is continuing to strengthen still further its military establishment, including that in the maritime field, where its power and the range of its activity have markedly increased. They therefore emphasized particularly the need for improvements in NATO's conventional deterrent. They underlined the special military and political role of North American forces present in Europe as an irreplaceable contribution to the common defence. In parallel they welcomed the important decision of certain European member nations[1] to make an increased common European effort to strengthen the defence capability of the Alliance in areas identified as having special importance. They invited the DPC in Permanent Session to prepare a programme for following up the recommendations of the study.

Brussels Ministerial Meeting December 4–5, 1970

The Ministerial Meeting held in Brussels on December 3 and 4, 1970, was of special significance as Ministers took stock of the developments in East–West relations over the preceding months. As a result of Allied initiatives 1970 had been a year of intensive diplomatic activity. In the course of their customary review of the international situation, Ministers noted the existence of both positive and negative factors.

The treaties between the Federal Republic of Germany and the USSR and the Federal Republic and Poland were held to be a major contribution to détente in Europe. The exchange of views between the Federal Republic of Germany and the German Democratic Republic would, it was hoped, pave the way for genuine negotiations which would necessarily take account of the special features of the situation in Germany. Ministers noted, however, that no solution had as yet been found, within the framework of the quadripartite talks, to the problem of Berlin which was a

1. The EUROGROUP – an informal grouping of 10 member countries co-ordinating their defence efforts within the framework of NATO.

potential source of trouble and thus had a decisive effect on the political climate of Europe. They also noted that the talks between the Soviet Union and the United States on strategic arms limitation had not so far produced any tangible results. In conclusion to their discussion, Ministers issued an important statement in which they declared that as soon as the talks on Berlin had reached a satisfactory conclusion and insofar as the other talks under way proceeded favourably, their governments would be ready to enter into multilateral contacts with all interested countries to explore when it would be possible to convene a conference, or a series of conferences, on security and co-operation in Europe. In this event, the Council would give immediate attention to the matter. As for the issues which might be discussed within the framework of exploratory multilateral talks, Ministers referred to their earlier proposals.

Mediterranean issues

As regards the situation in the Mediterranean, it should be recalled that since the Ministerial Meeting held in Reykjavik on June 24 and 25, 1968, Ministers were increasingly concerned with the expansion of Soviet military power and political influence in the Mediterranean area. Soviet penetration, in terms of a growing naval presence in the Mediterranean, poses a potential threat to the southern flank of the Alliance.

The Soviet Union's significant role as military adviser and supplier of arms to the Arab states in their confrontation with Israel increasingly affects existing Western political and economic interests in the area, among which the considerable dependence of Western Europe upon oil supplies from the Middle East deserves special mention.

Against the background of these considerations, Ministers have expressed, on the occasion of their meetings since June 1968, their concern at these developments which require constant vigilance on the part of the Alliance. In these conditions, Ministers repeatedly stressed the importance of full and frequent consultation among the Allies and instructed the Council in Permanent Session to continue its close review of the developing situation in the Mediterranean. In the framework of measures studied at the Reykjavik Meeting, Ministers of the countries participating in NATO's integrated defence programme subsequently approved, in May 1969, the establishment of the naval on-call force for the Mediterranean which had been approved in principle in January 1969.

Allied defence in the seventies

Sitting as the Defence Planning Committee, Ministers concentrated their discussion on the comprehensive study ('Alliance Defence in the Seventies') which was commissioned in May 1970, on the defence problems which the Alliance will face in this decade. Ministers affirmed that NATO's approach to security in the 1970's would continue to be based on the twin concepts of defence and détente. They reaffirmed the principle that the overall military capability should not be reduced except, as they had stipulated at a previous meeting, 'as part of a pattern of mutual force reductions balanced in scope and timing'. Allied strategic nuclear capability will in any event remain a key element in the security of the West during the 1970s. At the present time, adequate nuclear forces exist and it will be essential to ensure that this capability, which includes the continued commitment of theatre nuclear forces, is maintained. The situation in the field of conventional forces – Ministers stated – is less satisfactory in view of certain imbalances between NATO and Warsaw Pact capabilities. Careful attention therefore needs to be paid to priorities in improving NATO's conventional strength in the 1970s. The study underlined the special military and political role of North American forces present in Europe. Their replacement by European forces would be no substitute. At the same time, their significance is closely related to an effective and improved European defence effort.

European Defence Improvement Programme

It was with this in mind that ten European countries (the EUROGROUP) had decided to adopt a special European Defence Improvement Programme going well beyond previously existing plans and designed to improve Alliance capability in specific fields identified as of particular importance in the AD 70 study. Ministers expressed their profound satisfaction with a statement from President Nixon which pledged that, given a similar approach by the other Allies, the United States would maintain and improve its own forces in Europe and would not reduce them except in the context of reciprocal East–West action.

Nuclear planning 1970

On the specific question of nuclear planning, two meetings of the Nuclear Planning Group Defence Ministers were held in 1970; in Venice in June and in Ottawa in October. Culminating several years of study and discussion, they reached agreement on proposed political guidelines for the possible use of atomic demolition munitions in NATO's defence and they completed the drafting of policy proposals concerning the role of theatre nuclear strike forces. These guidelines and proposals were approved by the Defence Planning Committee at Ministerial level in December 1970.

Defence Planning Committee Meeting – May 1971

In May 1971, Ministers sitting as the Defence Planning Committee welcomed the substantial and concrete progress reported in the development and implementation of the European Defence Improvement Programme announced in December 1970, both as regards the Infrastructure element – protection of aircraft on bases, and the integrated communications system – and the national force improvements and intra-alliance aid.

Lisbon Ministerial Meeting 1971

Meeting in Lisbon on June 3 and 4 for the first time since 1952, the NATO Foreign Ministers, during their customary review of the international situation welcomed the joint statement to the effect that the United States and the USSR had reached agreement regarding the framework for further negotiations on strategic arms limitation. Noting that the talks on Berlin had made headway, Ministers expressed the view that progress in the talks between German Authorities would make an important contribution to a relaxation of tension in Europe. They noted with interest that the Kremlin had now for the first time reacted positively to the proposals on Mutual and Balanced Force Reductions (MBFR) originally put forward by the Allied countries at the Reykjavik meeting in Spring, 1968. Although this reaction had been slow to materialize and was couched in very general language, they felt that it was an encouraging sign in the lengthy history of East–West relations.

East–West relations

On the basis of these considerations, Ministers pointed out that an agreement on Berlin would greatly assist in improving the political climate in Europe. They expressed the hope that before their next meeting the negotiations on Berlin would be on the point of reaching a successful conclusion; the Council as a whole expressed its full support for the efforts of the Western Governments taking part in these negotiations. The Members of the Alliance also expressed their determination to contribute to the reduction of tension in Europe and stated that they proposed to take part – to the extent that this was likely to be productive – in the preparatory negotiations for a Conference on European Security (CES); in this spirit, they would continue their policy of engaging in frequent exchanges of views with the countries which would be concerned should an international meeting of this kind take place.

Mutual and balanced force reductions

As regards force reductions, the Kremlin had so far confined itself to statements of intention. These did not provide an adequate basis, in terms of hard facts, for getting to grips with this question round a table in an effort to reach a solution. The members of NATO therefore expressed their willingness to intensify, at the bilateral level, all contacts with the East European countries which would assist in clarifying the position of the Soviet Union and its allies on this question. They also indicated that they proposed to move on to negotiations as soon as this was practicable. In order to save time and improve their readiness for such negotiations, Ministers instructed the Council in Permanent Session to undertake any consultations and studies likely to facilitate the meeting of Deputy Foreign Ministers or high officials which, they agreed, should be held at an early date to review the results of the exploratory contacts and to consult on substantive and procedural approaches to Mutual and Balanced Force Reductions (MBFR). The NATO Foreign Ministers reiterated their concern at the situation in the Mediterranean. They likewise drew attention to the importance of making progress in all disarmament negotiations. In this connection, they welcomed the recent conclusion of a treaty banning the emplacement of weapons of mass destruction on the sea bed and ocean floor.

Committee on the Challenges of Modern Society (CCMS)

The Council warmly congratulated the Committee on the Challenges of Modern Society on its work and drew attention to the impressive progress that had been achieved in the development of road safety and in combating the pollution of the seas by oil. In this connection, it was pointed out that NATO's efforts to assist in improving the environment not only benefited the countries of the Alliance but complemented and contributed to the success of the work going on in other international organizations.

Resignation of Mr. Brosio and appointment of Mr. Luns

At the same Council Meeting in Lisbon, Ministers expressed their regret at the impending departure of Mr. Brosio, who had informed them of his intention to resign as Secretary General of NATO. In their tributes to Mr. Brosio, Ministers dwelt on his outstanding stewardship and expressed to him their deep appreciation of the services he had rendered to the Alliance and to peace in the past seven years.

The Council invited Mr. Joseph Luns, Foreign Minister of the Netherlands to succeed Mr. Brosio as from October 1, 1971 and he accepted.

NAVSOUTH leaves Malta

In July 1971 a narrow switch in the parliamentary election caused a change in Malta's international policy. Although not a member of the Alliance, Malta had been host to a NATO military headquarters for many years (since the time when the island was a dependency of the UK) and given military facilities for British and other NATO forces.

The NATO presence was never the subject of formal or definite commitment by any Maltese Government, and accordingly, after full consultation between all parties concerned, NATO acceded to the Maltese request to withdraw NAVSOUTH from Malta. Following an invitation by the Italian Government, NAVSOUTH was transferred to Naples.

Agreement on Berlin

After eighteen months of patient and intensive diplomacy, the four-Power negotiations on Berlin, which began on March 26, 1970, resulted on September 3, 1971 in the signing of the first stage of a quadripartite agreement between France, the United Kingdom, United States and the Soviet Union. This was the first written agreement on Berlin reached by the four Powers since 1949.

The agreement, which would not come into effect until completed by the conclusion of the intra-German arrangements and the signature of the final quadripartite protocol, reaffirms four-Power responsibility for Berlin and is designed to ensure unimpeded civilian access between the Western sectors and the areas under the authority of the German Democratic Republic. The talks between the authorities of the Federal Republic and East Germany began on September 6.

Increasing East–West contacts

As had been repeatedly forecast by Ministers, the impending agreement on Berlin paved the way for multilateral East–West talks to gauge the prospects for a conference on security and co-operation in Europe (CSCE). Within this context, there was an increase in bilateral contacts between the Allied countries on the one hand and the Eastern countries and neutrals on the other. On the strength of these developments Ministers, at their meeting on December 9 and 10, 1971 in Brussels, renewed their instructions to the Council in Permanent Session to carry on with the preparation in depth of those issues which they had already indicated as being suitable for discussion at a conference. At this same meeting, they expressed their regret that the Soviet Union and its allies had not responded to their proposals for mutual and balanced force reductions (MBFR) and in particular to their suggestion, made in October 1971, that Mr. Brosio be asked to conduct an exploratory mission. A series of events in the Spring of 1972 provided evidence that the USSR and its allies seemed willing to adopt a co-operative stance. Within the framework of the first phase of the 'Ostpolitik', the Federal Republic of Germany (FRG) had ratified treaties with the Soviet Union and with Poland. Negotiations between the Federal Republic and the German Democratic Republic (GDR) were in progress and had borne fruit in the shape of a treaty on access and arrangements supplementing the quadripartite agreement on Berlin. This being so, the Four Powers agreed to sign the final protocol to this quadripartite agreement in June 1972. Other important events were the first official visits made by the President of the United States to Peking and Moscow.

First SALT agreements

It was on May 26, 1972, during this visit to Moscow, that agreements were signed recording the positive outcome of the first series of strategic arms limitation talks (SALT) begun in November 1968. These agreements, which had been reached after particularly arduous negotiations reflecting the complexity of the problems at issue, consisted on the one hand of a treaty of unlimited duration on the limitation of anti-ballistic missile systems and, on the other hand, of an interim, five-year, agreement on certain measures relating to the limitation of offensive strategic weapons. These agreements had been preceded by the conclusion, during the previous autumn, of agreements to reduce the risk of accidental nuclear war and to improve communication arrangements between the United States and the Soviet Union. Further negotiations between the two parties were resumed in Geneva on November 21, 1972 for the purpose of working out more detailed means of limiting offensive strategic weapons (SALT II). The SALT negotiations have, from the beginning, been the subject of intensive consultation within the Alliance thereby providing the opportunity for other member countries to be fully informed of developments and to voice their particular points of view.

The events just described were evidence of a new climate in international relations which was reflected in the world balance of forces. They were, moreover, consistent with Allied efforts to achieve a rapprochement and to establish constructive and more broadly based contacts with the East. At a time when the preliminary conditions for such a move seemed to have been met, it was only fair to recall that this encouraging move towards the relaxation of tension was entirely due to the initiatives and to the perseverance of the West. It was equally important to realize that all these diplomatic efforts were interconnected, designed as they were to gauge, in different spheres, the willingness of the Eastern countries to co-operate with a view to achieving tangible improvements in East–West relations based on balanced concessions. The essential part played by the Alliance in the preparation and co-ordination of the Western negotiating positions also needed to be underlined.

Bonn Ministerial Meeting – May 30–31, 1972

It was against this background that the Spring Ministerial Meeting took place in Bonn on May 30 and 31, 1972. It was a particularly important meeting since it gave the green light for a new phase in East–West relations. Noting with satisfaction the progress made in a number of important fields since their last meeting, Ministers agreed to enter into multilateral conversations concerned with the preparations for a Conference on Security and Co-operation in Europe (CSCE) and accepted the proposal of the Finnish government that such talks be held in Helsinki at the level of heads of mission. At the same time they made it plain that the aim of the Allied Governments at the multilateral preparatory talks (MPT) would be two-fold: on the one hand to ensure that their proposals for the strengthening of security and co-operation in Europe would be fully considered at a Conference and on the other hand to establish that enough common ground existed among the participants to warrant reasonable expectations that a Conference would produce satisfactory results. In other words, there was no question at that stage of dealing with the substance of the problems dividing East and West but of identifying them and of ensuring that they were examined. Ministers noted the progress of studies made on possible issues for negotiation which had been undertaken on their instructions. They also expressed the opinion that, in the interests of security, the examination at a CSCE of appropriate measures, including certain military measures, aimed at strengthening confidence and increasing stability would contribute to the process of reducing the dangers of military confrontation. As regards MBFR, and while expressing their regret on the lack of response from the Eastern countries, Ministers proposed that multilateral exploratory talks should start as soon as practicable, either before or in parallel with multilateral preparatory talks on a CSCE.

Agreement on military facilities in Malta

The negotiations between the United Kingdom and Malta which had followed the withdrawal of NAVSOUTH at the request of the Valetta government, led to the signing on March 26, 1972 of a seven-year agreement on the use of certain military facilities on the island. The preparation of these negotiations, in which the Secretary General played a significant role, formed the subject of particularly frequent consultation within the Council.

Inter-German relations and Four Power Declaration on Berlin – November 9, 1972

The negotiations which had begun on March 19, 1970 and which were designed to take account of the special situation in Germany, ended on November 8, 1972 with the initialling of a Treaty on the basis of relations between the Federal Republic of Germany (FRG) and the German Democratic Republic (GDR) (the Treaty was signed on December 21, 1972). This was followed, on the next day, by a declaration of the Four Powers. In this declaration the Four Powers recorded their agreement that they would support the applications for membership of the United Nations when submitted by the FRG and the GDR, it being understood that these applications would be submitted simultaneously. The Four Powers affirmed in this connection that such membership must in no way affect their rights and responsibilities in Berlin and the corresponding related quadripartite agreement, decisions and practices.

Multilateral preparatory talks in Helsinki

Multilateral preparatory talks on a possible CSCE, attended by representatives from 35 countries – all the European countries (excepting Albania), the United States and Canada, opened in Helsinki on November 22, 1972. Although the Allied countries brought with them their own national proposals, these had none the less been carefully co-ordinated within the framework of NATO.

Brussels Ministerial Meeting – December 7–8, 1972

These events inevitably dominated the Ministerial Meeting which took place in Brussels on December 7 and 8, 1972. Welcoming the initialling of the treaty between the FRG and the GDR, Ministers noted the Four Power declaration of November 9, 1972 and indicated that their governments would consider the possibility of negotiations with the GDR with a view to establishing bilateral relations. The member countries of the Atlantic Alliance, they added, would continue to support the policy of the Federal Republic of Germany to work towards a state of peace in Europe in which the German people would regain their unity through free self-determination. At this same meeting in Brussels, Ministers, referring to the opening of the multilateral preparatory talks in Helsinki, recalled that these were designed to establish whether such a Conference could produce constructive results, and noted that the latter could be achieved only through the process of detailed negotiation without artificial time-limits.

MBFR exploratory talks in Vienna – January 31, 1973

It was likewise at the Brussels winter Ministerial meeting that significant progress was recorded in the efforts which the Allied countries had unceasingly pursued since 1968 to lower the level of military confrontation through constructive negotiations with the East. More specifically Ministers of the countries concerned noted the invitation extended by the NATO countries to the Warsaw Pact countries to join them in exploratory talks, beginning on January 31, 1973, on the question of mutual and balanced force reductions in Central Europe.[1] After expressing the hope that these talks would make it possible to commence negotiations in the autumn of 1973 – and thus in parallel with CSCE – they pointed out that while it would be inappropriate to establish specific links between the two sets of negotiations, progress in one would have a favourable effect on the other. Ministers took note of the work already carried out within the

1. The direct participants in these talks and in the negotiations which followed are: Belgium, Canada, the Federal Republic of Germany, Luxembourg, the Netherlands, the United Kingdom and the United States, on the NATO side; Czechoslovakia, the German Democratic Republic, Poland and the Soviet Union on the Warsaw Pact side. The other NATO participants are: Denmark, Greece, Norway, Italy and Turkey, while Bulgaria and Romania make up the remaining Warsaw Pact delegations. The position of Hungary is under discussion.

Alliance and in view of the new developments, instructed the Council in Permanent Session to continue consultations in preparation for eventual negotiations. They took the opportunity to recall the general principles governing negotiations which they had defined, inter alia, at their Rome meeting in 1970 and which are intended primarily to ensure undiminished security at a lower level of forces. They emphasised in particular that force reductions in Central Europe should not operate to the military disadvantage of any one side and that since the security of the Alliance is indivisible, they should not diminish security in other parts of Europe.

End of multilateral preparatory talks in Helsinki

The multilateral preparatory talks ended in Helsinki on June 8, 1973, with the adoption of a series of final recommendations to governments. These were concerned primarily with the conference agenda which was divided into three major chapters: (i) questions relating to security in Europe, inter alia, principles governing relations between States and confidence-building measures; (ii) co-operation in the fields of economics, science and technology, and of the environment; (iii) co-operation in humanitarian fields, more especially human contacts, information, and co-operation and exchanges in the field of culture and education. It was also agreed that, depending on the progress made during the conference, consideration would also be given to any follow-up procedures which might be required. As for the conference itself, it was suggested that this should take place in three stages, the first at the level of Foreign Ministers of participating countries who would be required to approve and implement the recommendations as a whole.

Start of Conference on Security and Co-operation in Europe – Helsinki, July 3, 1973

The progress of the preparatory talks in Helsinki provided ample proof that careful preparation by the Allies and the co-ordination of member countries' national positions had been well worthwhile in terms of protecting Allied interests and negotiating aims. Thus, at their Spring meeting on June 14 and 15, 1973, in Copenhagen, Ministers, after considering the outcome of these talks were able to note with satisfaction that it had been possible to agree on arrangements to ensure their proposals would be examined fully and in depth at a conference. While stressing that constructive and specific results could only be achieved through a process of detailed and serious negotiations without artificial time-limits, the Ministers expressed their willingness to begin the first stage of the conference. During this first stage, which took place in Helsinki from July 3 to 7, 1973, the Ministers of all participating States adopted the programme of work submitted to them and issued instructions to the

Committees and sub-Committees for the preparation, during the second main working stage, of definite proposals concerning the various agenda items. The Ministers also set up a co-ordinating committee to harmonize the activities of the various conference committees. The level of representation at which the CSCE would meet for its last stage would be decided before the end of the second main working stage on the basis of the recommendations made by the Co-ordinating Committee.

Atlantic relations

The passage from a period of confrontation in East–West relations, to an era of negotiation meant that it was more than ever necessary to preserve the cohesion between the member countries of the Alliance – a cohesion based on frequent consultation and on the support of public opinion in the West. It was clear that the prospects for a relaxation of tension would have a bearing on efforts to safeguard new Allied security. It was the NATO method of consultation which had enabled member countries to bring about an improvement in East–West relations. If, however, these encouraging developments were to continue it would have to be realized that maintenance of the defence effort and the affirmation of Western solidarity were the essential twin requisites of any further progress in the implementation of a policy of détente. On the other hand, it had to be recognized that while the principles and objectives of the Alliance remained as valid as they had ever been, profound changes had taken place in every field of international activity in recent years. Solidarity of purpose, which had withstood the test of time, was being exposed to a fluid situation which favoured centrifugal tendencies. Problems which had been unforeseeable a generation ago had suddenly appeared, calling for new forms of action and co-operation by the West. To mention only the most outstanding developments which had had a direct impact on Allied policy, there was firstly the realization that Europe, now prosperous again, would have to make a larger contribution to the common defence effort, in order to relieve the United States of part of the burden. Secondly, the fact that the USSR had more or less achieved strategic nuclear parity with the Americans could not fail to have a bearing on the defence of the European continent. It was not, however, the first time that the Alliance was faced with the need to adapt itself to a changing international scene. It had done so successfully in the past with the adoption in December 1956, of the Report of the Committee of Three and, later, when it had endorsed the conclusions of the Report on the Future Tasks of the Alliance in December 1967. For these reasons Ministers decided, at their Copenhagen meeting, that the time had come, without prejudice to ongoing negotiations in other fora, for member governments to examine in a spirit of solidarity and common effort their relationships in the light of these changes. Accordingly, they entrusted the Council in Permanent Session to undertake this task.

Arab-Israeli War – October 1973

On October 6, 1973 hostilities flared up again in the Middle East between Israel on the one side and Syria and Egypt on the other, ending with a ceasefire on the field on October 24. The Soviet attitude compelled the United States to activate some of its forces on the following day. This situation provided clear evidence that the danger of a sudden crisis was still a very real one and that it was consequently important to preserve the means of dealing with it. This being so, there was a need for a guarded approach to the process of détente, the present limits of which were suddenly apparent. These developments provided justification for the Allies' determination not to relax their defence efforts. They bore out the wisdom of the concept repeatedly proclaimed by the West, namely, that détente and security are indivisible. Moreover it could not be ignored that the Soviet Union was continuing its steady military build-up, in particular the reinforcement of its naval power. The new crisis in the Middle East highlighted the necessity of keeping a close watch on events in this area and of continuing the practice of frequent and timely consultation to enable the Allies to compare their evaluations.

Ministerial Meeting Brussels – December 10–11, 1973

It was against this disturbing background and the repercussions of the selective embargo on certain Allied countries enforced in the autumn by the oil-exporting countries that the winter Ministerial Meeting was held in Brussels on December 10 and 11, 1973. In their review of world developments, Ministers recognized that international peace remained fragile and they stressed once again the importance for the Alliance of maintaining to the full its defensive and deterrent military capability. Turning to the situation in the Middle East, they expressed their overriding concern to see a just and lasting settlement in that area and reaffirmed the support of all member governments for the relevant resolutions of the United Nations Security Council. In the same context, they took note of the half-yearly report by the Council on the situation in the Mediterranean. This situation had been kept under continuing review by the Council in Permanent Session in accordance with instructions first issued by Ministers in Reykjavik in June 1968. These reports, which reflected Allied concern over the continuous Soviet naval build-up, acquired heightened relevance with the renewed tension generated by the resumption of Arab-Israeli hostilities. As regards East–West relations, there had been a number of positive developments in the previous months, particularly the recognition of the GDR by the Allied countries, the admission of the two Germanies to the

United Nations in September, the normalization of the relations between the Federal Republic and Czechoslovakia, Bulgaria and Hungary, as well as Mr. Brezhnev's visits, to Berlin in May and to Washington in June. This last visit was a particularly important one since it included the signature on June 21, 1973 within the framework of SALT II, of a declaration which crowned the United States efforts to reach a permanent agreement on the limitation of strategic offensive arms. This was the Declaration of Basic Principles of Negotiations on the Further Limitation of Strategic Offensive Arms, including in particular the recognition of each side's equal security interests, of which Ministers took note. As regards the CSCE, the second stage of which had begun in Geneva on September 18, 1973 they took stock of the progress of the committee set up by the Foreign Ministers of participating States in accordance with the programme established for the detailed examination of the various Agenda items.

In a different sphere, namely, internal relations between their governments, Ministers noted that substantial progress had been made towards agreement on a joint declaration on Atlantic Relations and gave instructions that this important work should be pursued to a successful conclusion.

Start of MBFR negotiations – Vienna, October 30, 1973

The MBFR negotiations proposed by the Allies opened in Vienna as planned. Ministers of the countries concerned considered a report by the Allied negotiators and reaffirmed the principles which they would continue to uphold during the course of these talks. It was within this context at the Brussels winter meeting that ministers reported the proposal they had made in Vienna to establish approximate parity between the two sides in the form of a common manpower ceiling for overall ground forces on each side in the area in which reductions would take place, having regard to combat capability. They also proposed a first phase agreement providing for reductions of Soviet and US ground forces in the area.

Cost-sharing

Allied governments had repeatedly indicated the value which they attached to the special role played by the US forces in Europe as a means of preserving a credible deterrent based on a satisfactory balance of forces. It had been their constant conviction, since the policy of détente had first been conceived that any reduction in Allied defence capabilities should take place only in the context of MBFR. The European countries had welcomed the renewed assurances of the United States government in this respect. It was clear to all the Allied countries however that the maintenance of US forces in Europe at their present levels called for a common effort on the part of the Allies to achieve a solution to the financial problems of the us. In the course of 1974, a number of steps were taken to meet this aim, among them the bilateral offset agreements (e.g. between the United States and Germany) and the measures taken within the Eurogroup as well as real improvements in NATO-assigned European forces.

25th Anniversary (Declaration on Atlantic relations)

As far as Allied internal relations were concerned, the principal feature of the Spring Ministerial Meeting which was held in Ottawa on June 18 and 19, 1974 – and which marked the 25th Anniversary of the Alliance – was the adoption by Ministers of a Declaration on Atlantic Relations which had been the subject of thorough discussion in the Council for over a year.[1] This important document reaffirms the commitment of all members to the Alliance, and sets its course in the light of new perspectives and challenges of a rapidly changing world. It is built around certain guiding principles. The Alliance is the indispensable basis for the security of the member countries and thus makes possible the pursuit of détente; the common defence is one and indivisible. Given that the strategic relationship between the Soviet Union and the United States has reached a point of near equilibrium, the Alliance's problems in the defence of Europe have assumed a different and more distinct character; however, the essential elements have not changed; the us nuclear forces and the presence of North American forces in Europe remain indispensable to the security of the entire Alliance; on their side the European members undertake to make the necessary contribution to maintain the common defence; all necessary forces would be used to deny to a potential adversary the objectives he seeks to attain through an armed conflict; fulfilment of the common aims requires the maintenance of close consultation and co-operation on matters relating to the common interests of the members of the Alliance, it being borne in mind that those interests can be affected by events in other areas of the world; in particular they will work to remove all sources of conflict between their economic policies and encourage economic co-operation with one another. Finally, the members recall their dedication to the principles of the Alliance and their responsibilities towards the world at large. To underline the importance of the event, the Allied Heads of Government – for only the second time in the history of the Alliance – met in Brussels on June 26, 1974 for the solemn signing of the Declaration after a meeting devoted to consultation on East–West relations during which the United States President referred, inter alia, to his forthcoming visit to Moscow.

1. See Appendix 7, page 340 for the full text of this Declaration.

83

Current East–West negotiations

The Ottawa Ministerial meeting also provided an opportunity to take stock of current East–West negotiations. The harmonization of Allied views had continued to bear fruit at the CSCE. Despite the very moderate proposals put forward by the Allied countries, however, progress had been slow and unequal. Ministers, in noting this state of affairs, added that much work remained to be done on such key questions as the improvement of human contacts, the freer flow of information, confidence-building measures and essential aspects of the principles guiding relations between States. As regards MBFR, the Vienna negotiations had undoubtedly enabled both sides to circumscribe the general objective more closely but there was still a big gap between the respective viewpoints. The Ministers concerned re-iterated their proposals for a common ceiling for ground force manpower which had been referred to at the previous meeting in Brussels, adding that a first phase agreement providing for the reduction of United States and Soviet ground forces would be an important initial step. In their customary review of the international situation, Ministers likewise welcomed the evolution towards the establishment of a democratic and representative government in Portugal as well as the diplomatic efforts being made to restore peace to the Middle East which had resulted in the conclusion of agreements for a disengagement in the field. They discussed the experience gained in the application of the quadripartite agreement on Berlin of September 3, 1971 the strict observance of which remained a prerequisite for lasting détente.

Revision of the Iceland-United States defence agreement

At the request of the Icelandic Government, the Council put forward recommendations concerning the renewal of the agreement of May 5, 1951 between Iceland and the United States for the use, on behalf of NATO, of the Keflavik facilities. The issue was complicated by a dispute between the United Kingdom and Iceland on fishing limits but this was finally resolved, partly through the efforts of the Secretary General. On the defence agreement the United States and Iceland reached an understanding on October 22, 1974 under which US forces were to continue to be stationed at the base, subject to various adjustments to be made in the operation of the agreement.

The Cyprus crisis

In mid-July there was a coup d'etat against President Makarios in Cyprus. This was followed by a Turkish decision to take military action on the island. After the failure of conciliatory attempts in Geneva, with the help of the United Kingdom, a guarantor power, to achieve a compromise between Greece and Turkey, the Ankara Government then ordered its troops to occupy more territory on the island. This led to a serious crisis in Greek–Turkish relations. The new regime which had meanwhile restored legality in Greece announced its decision to withdraw from the NATO integrated military structure. While the solution to the Cyprus problem as such is a matter for the United Nations, the Council, which was concerned to safeguard Allied cohesion, had from the start of the crisis and in the course of intensive consultations redoubled its efforts to bring about a reconciliation between the two member countries concerned. The Secretary General, in his personal capacity, also worked towards this end by virtue of the Watching Brief for Greek–Turkish relations which dates back to the May 1964 Ministerial Meeting in The Hague.

World economic developments

The effects of the energy crisis generated by the events in the Middle East in October 1973 became increasingly pronounced as the year went by. The four-fold increase in the exported price of oil coincided with a shortage of certain raw materials and with a consequent leap in prices. This provoked a build-up in inflationary pressures on the Western economies and, inevitably, a threat of recession.

Ministerial Meeting of the Council – December 12–13, 1974

It was with these economic problems very much in mind that Ministers foregathered for their winter meeting which took place in Brussels on December 12 and 13, 1974. Ministers had a broad discussion on the implications of the economic situation for the maintenance of Allied defence and reaffirmed their determination to seek appropriate solutions to the difficulties confronting the economies of the Allied countries in a spirit of co-operation. Turning to other international events, Ministers expressed their concern about the situation in the Middle East which could have dangerous consequences for world peace and thus for the security of the members of the Alliance. They reaffirmed the importance they attached to progress towards the restoration of peace in this area.

In their review of East–West relations, Ministers again noted that progress towards détente had remained uneven in the preceding months. At the CSCE, there had been enough progress to show that substantial results were possible but there were important questions still to be resolved.

As for MBFR, the Ministers concerned, after reaffirming their positions, noted that the Vienna negotiations had not so far produced results and expressed the hope that a constructive response to the Allied proposals would soon be forthcoming. The impact of events in Cyprus on Greek–Turkish relations was referred to by the Secretary General in a report on his Watching Brief. Ministers also heard a report from their United States colleague, within the context of the United States-Soviet SALT II negotiations, on the prospects which had emerged from the Vladivostok meeting between Mr. Ford and Mr. Brezhnev on November 24, 1974 for the conclusion of a permanent agreement on the limitation of strategic offensive arms.

Summit Meeting, May 29–30, 1975

The Spring meeting of the Council was held in Brussels at the level of Heads of State and Government. This summit meeting, following the Ottawa Ministerial session of 1974, at which the Declaration on Atlantic Relations had been approved (and subsequently signed by the Heads of Government in Brussels on June 26) emphasized the concern of the member countries to take the measure of an international situation complicated by increasingly severe economic problems and to manifest their solidarity in the face of such exceptional events. Recalling that the security provided by the Alliance is an essential condition for détente and peace, the Heads of State and Government reaffirmed their commitment to the North Atlantic Treaty, in particular Article 5, which provides for collective defence.

End of the Conference on Security and Co-operation in Europe, Helsinki, August 1, 1975

The second phase of the CSCE took place at Geneva from September 18, 1973 to July 21, 1975. During this time, the Commissions completed drafting the proposals relating to various items of the agenda previously approved by the Ministers of the participating countries. The third and final phase took place at Helsinki on July 31 and August 1, 1975 at the level of Heads of State and Government, who signed the Final Act of the Conference. With regard to follow-up action, it was decided that a first meeting of participating countries should be held at Belgrade in 1977 to examine the implementation of the Final Act.

Allied initiative towards Mutual and Balanced Force Reductions (MBFR)

In the months which followed the substantial progress hoped for in East–West relations failed to materialize. Whilst it was certainly too early to expect any results from the Helsinki agreements it was disappointing to find no forward movement in the MBFR negotiations, already in progress for more than two years. In addition, in another context, the joint discussions between the US and the USSR within the framework of SALT II had not produced a satisfactory agreement on a new limitation of strategic weapons.

It was against this background that the usual winter Ministerial meetings to review the state of the Alliance took place in Brussels. Of particular note in these Ministerial discussions was an important Allied initiative in the field of MBFR. Ministers of the participating countries took important decisions which envisage the inclusion of US nuclear armaments in the Allied proposals. These new negotiating proposals were presented to the Eastern negotiators in Vienna on December 16, 1975.

The Ministers also expressed their strong hopes for the full implementation of the measures contained in the Final Act of Helsinki by all signatory states during the coming months. In conjunction with this appeal the Ministers also emphasized their view that in the political sphere the maintenance of détente requires the natural contest of opposing ideologies to be conducted in a manner compatible with the letter and spirit of the Final Act.

CHAPTER 4

Warsaw Pact military capabilities

The Warsaw Pact, dominated by the Soviet Union and her political objectives, continues to improve its military capabilities in quantity as well as in quality.

The Soviet Armed Forces, which continue to be developed carefully and systematically, are a modern and formidable, well-balanced, organized and trained force capable of conducting both defensive and offensive operations, ranging from conventional to nuclear warfare.

The Armed Forces of the Non-Soviet Warsaw Pact (NSWP) countries also have been improved qualitatively to a considerable degree and they are largely equipped with Soviet-designed weapons. These forces most likely would be employed as part of an overall Warsaw Pact Force.

Warsaw Pact forces maintain a state of readiness which presents a serious threat to NATO countries. A large proportion of the Soviet and Non-Soviet Warsaw Pact countries budget is spent annually on defence and defence-related research and development.

Warsaw Pact armed forces

The total strength of the Warsaw Pact forces is now estimated to be over 5 million men, of which approximately 3.9 million are Soviet.

Soviet strategic missile forces

The Soviet Strategic Missile Forces have approximately 1,600 operational intercontinental ballistic missiles (ICBMs) and about 600 intermediate range/medium range ballistic missiles (IRBMs/MRBMs) with launchers. Their personnel strength is about 380,000 men. The missiles constitute the main strategic threat to NATO. ICBMs can reach the most distant targets, including those in the United States and Canada, while IRBMs/MRBMs are primarily directed against targets in Western Europe. The force is being improved qualitatively towards increased effectiveness and accuracy. The Soviets have recently tested new variants including three with multiple independently targetable re-entry vehicle (MIRV) capability. Other variants may permit a land-mobile deployment of ICBMs. Furthermore, a new additional anti-ballistic missile (ABM) system may become operational.

The Naval ballistic missile capability has been greatly enhanced with continued construction of the DELTA class nuclear powered submarine, capable of submerged launching of missiles with ranges of over 4,000 nautical miles.

Soviet ground forces

The Soviet ground forces have an estimated strength of 2.7 million men, organized in higher command elements, combat and logistic support units and about 170 tank, motorized rifle and airborne divisions. About 95 of these divisions are oriented against Allied Command Europe, 31 of which are stationed in other Warsaw Pact member countries (20 in the German Democratic Republic; 2 in Poland; 5 in Czechoslovakia and 4 in Hungary). These 31 divisions in Eastern Europe are ready to conduct combat operations almost immediately after notification. Most of the other divisions stationed in the USSR vary widely in combat readiness, however the airborne divisions are considered to be fully combat ready. Nevertheless, all these divisions can be assembled and can achieve sufficient unit integrity to begin movement within 72 hours after orders are issued. Approximately 45 additional divisions are in the Sino-Soviet border area, including 2 divisions in the People's Republic of Mongolia. In addition, the remaining divisions stationed in Central USSR are considered as strategic reserves.

The Soviets place particular emphasis on increased mobility, cross-country and river-crossing capabilities. One of the most important aspects of the ground forces modernization has been the increase in conventional artillery and the equipping of these forces with a variety of tactical nuclear weapons.

The number of tanks assigned to the motorized rifle division (MRD) has been increased, and a new medium tank may be entering service.

A new airborne armoured combat vehicle has been observed and may be replacing older equipment in the airborne forces. Self-propelled artillery pieces also are thought to have been developed. Anti-tank guided missiles are being fitted to helicopters, and helicopter-equipped regiments have been noted in forward areas.

In general, the Soviet ground forces are kept at a high level of proficiency. They are able to operate efficiently in both small and large-scale manoeuvres. These facts make the Soviet Army a modern, well-equipped and efficient fighting force.

Ground forces of NSWP countries

The Non-Soviet Warsaw Pact ground forces have an estimated strength of 760,000 men. They are generally organized along Soviet lines, and they have approximately 60 motorized rifle, tank, airborne and sea landing divisions. There are about 6 East German, 15 Polish, 10 Czechoslovak, 6 Hungarian, 10 Romanian and 13 Bulgarian divisions. They vary widely in terms of peacetime personnel strength and levels of equipment. The GDR divisions are manned and equipped at levels comparable to full strength standard Soviet divisions. The other NSWP divisions are maintained at less than full strength. In some situations, the reliability of some NSWP forces might be questionable.

Soviet air forces

The Soviet air forces are organized into five major components: Air Defence, Long Range, Frontal, Military Transport and Naval Aviation, and have approximately 850,000 men of which some 320,000 are in ground force elements of air defence.

The estimated strength of the Soviet aircraft is about 7,000 fighters, 2,900 light, medium and heavy bombers and 2,700 transport and other aircraft, or a total of approximately 12,500 aircraft. About three-quarters of these aircraft include some 2,500 air defence fighter aircraft and are likely to be of direct concern to NATO. A further 3,500 multi-seat and combat type training aircraft are used at training establishments.

The quality of the aircraft is high and generally compatible with Western standards. A large proportion of the Soviet Air Force has been equipped with aircraft of modern design and high performance capability. Developments of particular note include the addition of a swing-wing bomber, which is expected to be operational this year, and a multi-role fighter, the FLOGGER, is assigned to Frontal Aviation units. A new fighter bomber is expected to be in service this year and a new helicopter has been observed in service configured as an armed troop-carrying assault vehicle.

A large number of well protected airfields are available, providing the Soviet Air Force with a rapid redeployment capability and thus improving their flexibility, mobility, and survivability.

Airlift capability continues to improve. In addition, Soviet civil aviation could conceivably double military aircraft capability.

Air forces of NSWP countries

The NSWP countries have tactical air and air defence forces. These air forces comprise a total of some 2,700 combat aircraft and transports, most

of which are Soviet fighters and bomber types. The air force personnel
strength is about 140,000 men. It can be assumed that tactical air forces of
NSWP countries augment the Soviet air force capabilities in Eastern
Europe and the air defence of those countries is integrated in the Soviet
air defence system.

Soviet navy

The Soviet navy consists of four fleets, the Northern, Baltic, Black Sea and
Pacific Fleets. The estimated personnel strength of the Soviet Naval Forces
is about 480,000 men including naval aviation and naval infantry. The
Baltic and Black Sea Fleets share the problem of limited and difficult
access to the open sea in wartime. Since 1967, the Soviets have established
a greatly increased presence in the Mediterranean. The Soviet Mediterranean Squadron (SOVMEDRON), normally consists of a total of some 50–60
ships of various types.

The Northern Fleet, with direct access to the Atlantic Ocean, forms the
main threat against the sea lines of communication between North
America and Europe.

The Soviet submarine fleet numbers about 320 submarines, of which
some 125 are nuclear powered submarines. Three-quarters are long-range,
ocean-going types, capable of operations almost anywhere in the world.
This impressive Soviet submarine force, like the rest of the fleet, is under-
going extensive modernization and has been improved significantly in
recent years. The nuclear powered submarine strength continues to grow.
Deactivation of diesel powered submarines will decrease total numbers, but
the newer type nuclear powered submarines add to overall capability. The
largest number of Soviet submarines belong to the Northern Fleet, with
easy access to areas of vital importance to NATO.

The pride of the Soviet surface fleet is now the cruiser-destroyer force,
estimated at approximately 110 ships, including two helicopter cruisers.
Construction of newer classes of cruisers, destroyers and destroyer escorts
as well as amphibious and support ships is continuing. Most of these are
armed with the latest missile systems, detection devices and communication equipment. The tendency to equip newly constructed ships with
missiles rather than guns is also evident in quite small classes of vessels
such as in missile patrol craft with surface-to-surface missiles.

Of significance will be the entry into service of the first Soviet aircraft
carrier, of the KURIL class, expected in 1975. It appears that a second aircraft carrier may also be under construction.

Each of the Soviet fleets is backed up by its own Fleet Air Force
consisting of strike/reconnaissance and anti-submarine aircraft, with a
number of transport aircraft in support. Nearly all Soviet medium-range

naval aircraft can carry anti-ship missiles with ranges of about 100 nautical miles.

Soviet merchant fleet and intelligence collecting vessels

Also of concern is the continued growth of the Soviet merchant and fishing fleets. From very modest beginnings, both have grown spectacularly in recent years. The Soviet 'fish factory' ships and trawlers now range over the world's oceans and it is significant that a high proportion of them are equipped for intelligence gathering. They carry comprehensive monitoring equipment and highly sophisticated electronic gear. It is not unusual for such a trawler to attach itself to NATO formations during exercises as an uninvited and extremely persistent observer. The Soviet merchant fleet is made up of about 2,700 ships of all types, over 100 gross register tons; it includes dry cargo, tankers, passenger and coastal ships and is the sixth largest in the world in terms of tonnage.

Other Warsaw Pact navies

The non-Soviet Warsaw Pact navies are small and mainly equipped to assume responsibility for the defence of home waters and for amphibious operations. The total personnel strength is about 58,000 men. They include a naval infantry force of one sea landing division and about two assault landing regiments. Combined Warsaw Pact exercises have been carried out in both the Baltic and Black Seas and an improved operational capability has been demonstrated.

Conclusions

Although a military balance still exists between East and West when their military potential is viewed as a whole, the Warsaw Pact maintains a clear superiority of conventional forces in the European region.

This advantage may be assumed to be offset by NATO's numerical superiority in tactical nuclear weapons. Strategic nuclear parity or even superiority appears to be a Soviet objective; should they reach this goal, the balance between NATO and the Warsaw Pact could swing in favour of the latter, thus enabling the USSR to be more venturesome in trying to impose their will not only on their allies but on NATO countries and the rest of the world.

Finally, Soviet leaders still consider military strength the best guarantee for their security and the backbone for great power policy. As long as the power relationship between the Warsaw Pact and NATO remains as it is now, with NATO maintaining a cohesive and credible defence posture, an act of military aggression by the Soviet Union against NATO is assessed as being unlikely.

PART 2

Activities of the Council

Diplomatic workshop

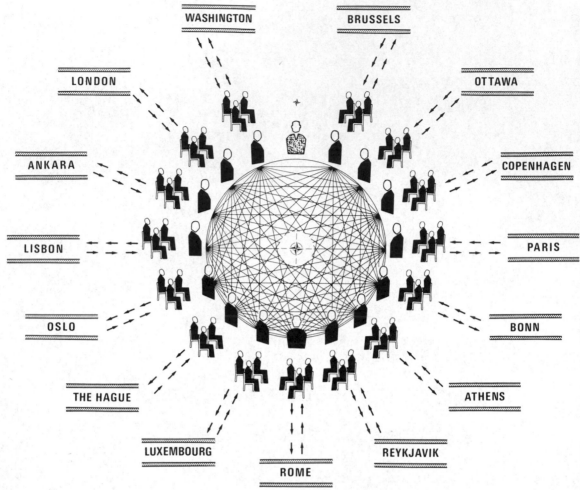

WASHINGTON BRUSSELS
LONDON OTTAWA
ANKARA COPENHAGEN
LISBON PARIS
OSLO BONN
THE HAGUE ATHENS
LUXEMBOURG REYKJAVIK
ROME

Permanent
Representative

National
Delegation

Chairman and
Secretary General

National
Government

NORTH ATLANTIC COUNCIL

The North Atlantic Council provides a unique forum for confidential and constant intergovernmental consultation on all topics as well as providing the highest level of decision making machinery within NATO. There is no supranational element in the Organization and all the fifteen sovereign member countries have an equal right to express their views round the Council table. Political consultation ranges over the whole field of foreign affairs and is not limited to NATO's geographical area. The only topics excluded are those relating to the purely internal affairs of member countries. Each national delegation is headed by a Permanent Representative with the rank of Ambassador supported by staffs which vary in size. All act on instructions from their capitals. Thus the Council provides a unique type of 'Diplomatic Workshop' under the Chairmanship of the Secretary General. To attain such a high degree of constant consultation between the fifteen by the customary method of bilateral diplomatic exchanges would be quite impracticable – in fact each meeting of the Council represents the equivalent of over 100 bilateral exchanges as shown by the lines in the diagram above.

CHAPTER 5

Political consultation

During the first five years of its existence, the North Atlantic Council concentrated its attention on implementing co-ordinated defence plans. But from the very beginning, it also practised political consultation. While there is still room for improvement, political consultation in the Council and its Committees has since then never ceased to grow, both in scope and importance.

The creation of NATO made it clear to the Soviets that open aggression in Europe would entail serious consequences. So, without abandoning the objective which they could no longer hope to achieve by military pressure alone, and while maintaining their armed forces along the Iron Curtain boundaries, the Soviets changed the focus and nature of their threat. Their course of action became one of harrassment directed to fighting the West on far broader fronts. This policy encompassed virtually every field of human activity and extended geographically over the whole world.[1]

In other words, instead of concentrating on a military threat against Western Europe as had been the case under Stalin, the USSR relied increasingly on political, economic and cultural penetration and tried to

1. Historical Footnote: In the early 'fifties the Soviets tried through a world-wide propaganda campaign to induce the West to relinquish voluntarily its superiority in nuclear weapons, deliberately ignoring the fact that such superiority did much to balance the Western inferiority in the field of conventional weapons. They conducted a campaign against the presence of British, Canadian and American troops in Europe and tried to intimidate certain countries into refusing to allow the establishment of missile launching sites on their territory, such sites having become an integral part of the Western defence system. They proposed plans for the de-nuclearization of certain areas of Europe, the effect of which would have been to neutralize these areas and render them defenceless. In the political field the Soviets continued to paralyse the United Nations through systematic abuse of the veto in the Security Council. They sought to divide the NATO countries by taking advantages of incidents (such as the Suez Affair), on occasion provoking them and by hindering, in those years, the work of the United Nations Disarmament Committee. They refused to discuss the problem of the

undermine the positions of the free world not only in Europe, but also in Asia, Africa and Latin America.

The change in Soviet tactics did not, of course, occur overnight. Nor was NATO's reaction immediate although its members quickly realized that its policy and practices of the early 'fifties needed adaptation to meet the new situation. It rapidly became apparent that the new danger called for a new form of joint action. The obvious answer was closer co-operation between NATO members in every sphere, and particularly in the political field where it was essential to achieve harmony of views and action. This was to prove a gradual process, complicated by the very nature of the Alliance and its structure.

National sovereignty

Above all, NATO is an international, not a supranational organization. It is composed of sovereign nations which have relinquished none of their independence in the field of foreign policy. Decisions in the Council are not taken by majority vote, but by common consent. And the process of achieving common consent among a number of parties, each of which brings to any given problem its individual experience and outlook, necessarily demands patience and time.

Nations react to a large extent in the light of their immediate or future interests, but the force of their past also exerts strong pressures. Inevitably, an alliance of fifteen nations whose respective histories reflect so many divergencies must sooner or later encounter differences of opinion when dealing with its problems. While all NATO allies have equal rights and each has one vote at the Council table, the member countries vary in size, population and territory. The larger countries have world-wide responsibilities which do not exist for some of the smaller ones. If all are freely to agree, the first requirement is therefore that they fully understand one another's positions.

Hence close political co-operation among the Allies depends first and foremost on all member governments being fully informed of each other's policies and of the underlying considerations which give rise to them. Secondly, if there is to be any co-ordination of foreign policies, there must

reunification of Germany, despite their acceptance at Geneva, in 1955, of a solution based on free elections. They did their utmost to disturb the 1957 NATO Heads of Government Conference with a pressure campaign on Western public opinion. Mr. Khrushchev walked out of the Paris Summit Conference (1959), followed by his outburst at the United Nations General Assembly. In 1962 the Soviets attempted to install missiles in Cuba aimed at the heart of the United States.

The Communists bitterly opposed all efforts to unify Europe, attacking the European Coal and Steel Community, the European Economic Community, Euratom and the Free Trade Area, thus trying to block all moves to strengthen Europe politically and economically.

This account of some of the facts in the struggle between East and West is far from complete. It does, however, indicate that the contest had assumed proportions far exceeding those of a localized military threat in Europe.

be continuing consultation among member countries regarding their respective questions. These two aims are separate but linked.

Informing member governments

Keeping the other member governments informed consists of the regular exchange of information on events of interest to the Alliance as a whole, and of the notification of decisions before they are made public. In practice such an exchange of information was in the first instance little more than a gesture of courtesy. But it has come to be established as the highly import-ant first stage of a recognized procedure for political co-operation. Political consultation, however, if it is to be more than information, should consist of governments exchanging views before taking any decision, i.e. during the policy-making stage. Clearly this is more desirable and more likely to open the way to genuinely co-ordinated policies than mere information.

Necessity for political co-operation

Political consultation started as a systematic exercise in NATO when the Council Deputies first met in May 1950. One of their tasks was to exchange views on political problems of common interest within the scope of the Treaty. In this context the member countries co-ordinated their view-points, in particular with respect to how Germany might best contribute to the defence of the West, and to the question of Greek and Turkish association with NATO. They also exchanged views and information on the policies of the Communist bloc countries.

Next, the Council began to meet in permanent session, in April, 1952, and extended the field of political consultation in the light of recommenda-tions adopted that year at the Lisbon Conference. The Council's powers in this field were further increased by a resolution approved in April, 1954. Member countries were urged to submit to the Council all political information likely to be of interest to other members. It was during this period (starting in 1953) that the Council discussed the replies drafted by the three Western occupying powers to various notes on Germany from the Soviet Union. It also took part in negotiation of the Paris and London agreements, approved in October, 1954, and the preparatory work for the Geneva Summit Conference during the summer of 1955, and for the Geneva Foreign Ministers' Conference which followed in the autumn of the same year. Political events within the NATO framework and the growing conviction that the Organization should become more closely knit, led to the establishment, at the Ministerial session of May, 1956, of the Commit-tee on Non-Military Co-operation.

This Committee – more frequently referred to as the 'Committee of Three' or the 'Three Wise Men' – was instructed 'to advise the Council on ways and means to improve and extend NATO co-operation in non-military fields and to develop greater unity within the Atlantic Community'. It was this Committee's report and recommendations, approved by the Council on December 13, 1956, shortly after the Suez crisis, that highlighted for the first time the vital importance of NATO political consultation and did much to spur its development. In summary form, the main points of its conclusions and recommendations were as follows.[1]

Report of 'Committee of Three'

The Committee emphasized that NATO could only fulfil its deterrent task under certain conditions and in particular if there were close political and economic relations between its members. 'An Alliance in which the members ignore each other's interests, or engage in political or economic conflict, or harbour suspicions of each other cannot be effective either for deterrence or defence'. In this way they made clear their conviction that the two aspects of security – political and military – cannot be considered separately; NATO must 'do enough to bring about that close and continuous contact between its civil and military sides which is essential if it is to be strong and enduring'. The Committee specifically recommended expanded co-operation and consultation in the political field, 'in the early stages of policy formation and before national positions became fixed', noting that 'at best it will result in collective decisions on matters of common interest affecting the Alliance', at least, 'it will ensure that no action is taken by one member without a knowledge of the views of the others'.

The Committee foresaw difficulties and problems in applying these principles once they were agreed. They nevertheless thought it worthwhile to set down a number of suggestions to serve as guidelines for future development. They were:

– members should inform the Council of any development significantly affecting the Alliance. They should do this not as a formality but as a preliminary to effective political consultation;

– both individual member governments and the Secretary General should have the right to raise in the Council any subject which is of common NATO interest and not of a purely domestic character;

– a member government should not, without adequate advance consultation, adopt firm policies or make major political pronouncements on matters which significantly affect the Alliance or any of its members, unless circumstances make such prior consultation obviously and demonstrably impossible;

– in developing their national policies, members should take into consideration the interests and views of other governments, particularly

1. For the full text of the Report on Non-military Co-operation see Appendix 5, page 308.

those most directly concerned, as expressed in NATO consultation, even where no community of view or concensus has been reached in the Council;

– where a concensus has been reached, it should be reflected in the formation of national policies. When for national reasons the consensus is not followed, the government concerned should offer an explanation to the Council.

It is even more important that when an agreed and formal recommendation has emerged from the Council's discussions, governments should give it full weight in any national action or policies related to the subject of that recommendation.

Specific recommendations

These were the general guidelines. With regard to practices for strengthening procedure the Committee drew up a number of more specific recommendations, including the following:

– to strengthen the process of consultation, the Foreign Ministers, at each Spring meeting, should take stock of the political progress of the Alliance based largely on an annual political appraisal to be submitted by the Secretary General;

– to assist the Permanent Representatives and the Secretary General in discharging their responsibilities for political consultation, a Committee of Political Advisers should be constituted under the Council;

– any dispute between member countries which has not proved capable of direct settlement should be submitted to good offices procedures within the NATO framework before resorting to any other international agency (except for disputes of a legal or an economic character for which attempts at settlement might best be made initially in the appropriate specialized organizations). The Secretary General should be empowered to offer his good offices to the countries in dispute and with their consent to initiate or facilitate procedures of enquiry, mediation, conciliation or arbitration.

These general guidelines and practical recommendations of the Committee of Three still form the basis of political consultation to-day. They have given new impetus to this particular feature of NATO's work which, alongside the co-operation in the military field, is considered an indispensable activity of the Alliance.

Political consultation

The main forum for political consultation is the Council where, under the chairmanship of the Secretary General, the Permanent Representatives of member countries raise any political problems which their Governments, or they themselves, consider merit discussion. These meetings of the Council take place with a minimum of formality; discussion is frank and direct. The Secretary General may also initiate the discussion of questions and, by virtue of his Chairmanship, plays an important part in the deliberations of the Council.

Because of the multiplicity of its tasks, the Council requires the assistance of the Political Committee. The latter (originally named 'Committee of Political Advisers') was set up in 1957, pursuant to a recommendation of the Committee of Three. It is chaired by the Assistant Secretary General for Political Affairs. As a result of the increased political activities of the Alliance (especially since the adoption of the 'Harmel Report'), the Committee now meets twice a week, either on the level of Deputy Permanent Representatives or on that of political counsellors of Delegations. Besides keeping abreast of political trends and developments of interest to NATO in all areas of the world, the Committee prepares studies of political problems for discussion by the Council and submits reports to it on subjects to be debated. Moreover, it has the task of following up and implementing Council decisions.

Political consultation is also carried out within a number of Ad Hoc Political Working Groups dealing with specific themes; furthermore groups of national experts study specific world regions in preparation of the bi-annual discussions of the international situation by Foreign Ministers.

Atlantic Policy Advisory Group

Another development in consultation has been the creation, within the Alliance and subordinate to the Council, of the Atlantic Policy Advisory Group (APAG), composed of senior Foreign Office officials from NATO countries. APAG's main function is, without committing governments, to discuss long-term political problems. The Group reports, through its Chairman, the Assistant Secretary General for Political Affairs, directly to the Council.

Future tasks of the Alliance

The recommendations on Political Consultation by the Committee of Three which continue to provide a main source for NATO's political activity, were redefined by the 'Report on the Future Tasks of the Alliance' (the 'Harmel Report') which was unanimously approved by the Council of Ministers in December 1967.[1] The Report stated in particular:

'As sovereign states, the Allies are not obliged to subordinate their policies to collective decision. The Alliance affords an effective forum

1. See Appendix 6, page 336 for full text of the 'Harmel Report'.

and clearing house for the exchange of information and views; thus each Ally can decide its policy in the light of close knowledge of the problems and objectives of the others. To this end, the practice of frank and timely consultations needs to be deepened and improved . . .'

The ultimate political purpose of the Alliance is described as the achievement of 'a just and lasting peaceful order in Europe accompanied by appropriate security guarantees'. Furthermore, it defines the role of the Allies – and of their consultation – in promoting an improvement in relations with the Soviet Union and the countries of Eastern Europe.

Five elements of consultation

Thus, there are five distinct elements in the mechanism of political consultation: the Council, the Political Committee, Regional Experts Committees, Ad Hoc Political Working Groups and the Atlantic Policy Advisory Group. Their activities are assisted by the International Staff. As a rule the working papers and reports for political consultation are based on information supplied by national Delegations and prepared by the Political Affairs Division.

East–West negotiations

Political consultation based on these principles already extended in practice to all international political issues. It entered a particularly active phase as a result of the opening of broadly-based negotiations on East–West relations, to which reference is made in Chapter 3. This consultation was largely concerned with the co-ordination at Council level of the Allied negotiating positions on Mutual and Balanced Force Reductions and the Conference on Security and Co-operation in Europe.

Mutual and Balanced Force Reductions (MBFR)

In the case of the negotiations on Mutual and Balanced Force Reductions (MBFR), the Alliance has taken a major step beyond simple consultation and has assumed a management role. Prior to the start of the negotiations, the Allied nations which participate in MBFR decided to negotiate on the basis of NATO-agreed positions on all questions of policy and strategy. These common positions are elaborated in Brussels on the basis of national instructions by the Council in Permanent Session, assisted by the Political Committee at Senior Level. They are then transmitted as binding guidance to the Ad Hoc Group of Allied negotiators in Vienna. Only in the case of day-to-day negotiating tactics is Council guidance not required. This is the first time in the history of the Alliance that a negotiation has been managed by the North Atlantic Council. It is indicative of both the closeness of intra-Alliance consultations on major questions and the increased role of NATO in recent years in the areas of disarmament and détente.

Disarmament and arms control

The Alliance pays very special attention to the vital question of disarmament and arms control and extensive consultations on all aspects in this field are carried out within the Council with a view to achieving maximum harmonization and co-ordination of national positions.

Thanks to these consultations, member countries are better able to pave the way for negotiations at the Conference of the Committee on Disarmament, some of which have culminated in the conclusion of treaties such as the 1963 partial test ban treaty, the 1968 treaty on the non-proliferation of nuclear weapons, the 1971 treaty on the prohibition of the emplacement of nuclear weapons and other weapons of mass destruction on the sea-bed and the 1972 convention of the prohibition of the development, production and stock-piling of biological weapons.

The Soviet-United States strategic arms limitation talks (SALT I and II), which led to the Moscow agreement of May 26, 1972, and the Vladivostok agreement of November 24, 1974, although bilateral negotiations, are also the subject of very thorough discussions, especially the aspects of these talks which affect more specifically the Alliance as a whole and its European members.

Conference on Security and Co-operation in Europe (CSCE)

The question of holding a conference on security and co-operation in Europe and of what the conference should deal with were discussed extensively within the Alliance. The member countries went into every aspect of the problem thoroughly and agreed on joint positions and aims for the preparatory conference held in Helsinki in 1972–73 and for the subsequent conferences in Helsinki in July 1973 and then in Geneva. Not only were major problems examined by the Council and other NATO committees in Brussels but, through negotiations, there was the closest possible day-to-day co-ordination of positions between the delegations of the Alliance countries at the conference itself.

Declaration on Atlantic Relations approved in Ottawa on June 19, 1974

This declaration[1] gave fresh impetus to political consultation within the Alliance. Paragraph 11 states that 'The Allies are convinced that the fulfilment of their common aims requires the maintenance of close consultation, co-operation and mutual trust, thus fostering the conditions necessary for defence and favourable for détente, which are complemen-

---

1. See Appendix 7, page 340 for full text of Declaration on Atlantic Relations.

tary. In the spirit of the friendship, equality and solidarity which characterise their relationship, they are firmly resolved to keep each other fully informed and to strengthen the practice of frank and timely consultations by all means which may be appropriate on matters relating to their common interests as members of the Alliance, bearing in mind that these interests can be affected by events in other areas of the world.

North Atlantic Assembly

This over-all picture of political consultation within NATO would be incomplete without a brief reference to the activities of the 'North Atlantic Assembly'. This body is the inter-parliamentary organization of member countries of the Alliance, and as such it provides a forum where North American and European parliamentarians meet frequently to discuss wide-ranging problems of common concern.

The Assembly, which was founded in 1955, has as its aims to strengthen co-operation among the countries of the Alliance, to help governments understand the Alliance viewpoint when framing legislation and particularly to encourage a common feeling of Atlantic solidarity in national parliaments.

Although the Assembly is completely independent of NATO, it constitutes a link between member parliamentarians and the Alliance. The highest military and civilian authorities of the Alliance address the Assembly at their Annual sessions and at meetings of the Assembly's committees during the year, when the range of Alliance policies and activities are examined and discussed in detail.

The Secretary General of NATO usually attends the Assembly's Annual Session to comment on the state of the Alliance and to answer questions from members. He also answers written questions during the year from Assembly parliamentarians on various aspects of NATO activity.

The North Atlantic Assembly has 172 members who are appointed by their respective parliaments according to national procedures. Each country's representation is determined according to its population, e.g. United States has 36 seats while Iceland and Luxembourg have 3 each.

The Assembly operates through five committees which cover the wide range of its activities – namely Economic, Education, Cultural Affairs and Information, Military, Political, and Scientific and Technical.

The Committee meet regularly in the spring and in the autumn, prior to the Plenary Session, to consider current problems affecting the Atlantic Community and they often form sub-committees or working groups to analyse specific subjects in greater depth. Recent examples of sub-committees' interests include European Defence Co-operation, the problems of the Southern Flank, Energy Supplies, Economic Relations between member Alliance countries and the Free Flow of Information between East and West. These sub-committees, which meet frequently during the year, give a continuous element to the work of the Assembly.

The North Atlantic Assembly meets in Plenary Session every autumn to debate and vote those issues which it feels are of immediate concern and interest to the Alliance and which are the subject of the reports, recommendations and resolutions tabled by its Committees.

Recommendations are addressed to the Secretary General of NATO, who after consultation with the North Atlantic Council comments on them. Resolutions are sent to member governments or parliaments and to relevant international organizations.

The Assembly organizes study tours in Europe and North America for parliamentarians of member countries. The purpose of these tours, which are mainly of military installations, is to give parliamentarians a first-hand view of the problems particularly associated with Atlantic defence.

The contribution of the North Atlantic Assembly to the effective functioning of the North Atlantic Alliance was acknowledged in the Declaration on Atlantic Relations signed by the heads of NATO Governments in Brussels, in June 1974. Paragraph 13 said: 'They (the members of the North Atlantic Alliance) recognize that the cohesion of the Alliance has found expression not only in co-operation among their governments, but also in the free exchange of views among the elected representatives of the peoples of the Alliance. Accordingly, they declare their support for the strengthening of links among parliamentarians'.

Further information on the North Atlantic Assembly may be obtained from the International Secretariat – Place du Petit Sablon 3 – 1000 Brussels. Tel: (02) 513.28.65.

6

Defence planning and policy

Defence policy

From its inception the defence policy of the Alliance has been essentially deterrent in nature. Designed to persuade any potential aggressor that war will not pay, the concept of deterrence has successfully kept the peace in Europe for over 25 years and is still valid today.

In the early days of the Alliance NATO's strategy to realize this basic objective rested to a very considerable degree on the overwhelming nuclear superiority of the United States. In view of the very marked inferiority of NATO conventional strength in Europe, an allied strategy that threatened immediate retaliation against any form of attack against NATO territory with the full force of US nuclear might seemed to be the only one available. It was from this situation that the strategy of 'massive nuclear retaliation' evolved. But the importance of having a 'conventional option', and of building up the forces to make it possible, was always recognized.

Under the protective umbrella of the US nuclear forces, the most urgent task facing the Alliance immediately after the decision to set up integrated commands at the beginning of 1951 was that of building in the shortest possible time well equipped and well trained forces in Europe capable of defending NATO territory against aggression. In that year the United States agreed to place its units in Germany under SACEUR's command. France, the United Kingdom and other members followed suit. In May 1952, the military targets (the Lisbon Force Goals) proposed by the Temporary Council Committee for the period up to 1954 had been accepted; machinery for co-ordinating the military efforts of member countries had been set up; the command structure had been considerably improved; the forces of Greece and Turkey had been incorporated into Allied Command

Europe; the strategic concept had been further developed; and the effectiveness of the armed forces had increased.

In the next four years further substantial progress was made. In particular, with the accession of the Federal Republic of Germany, it had become possible to plan for the forward defence of Europe much closer to the eastern frontier.

Revised strategic concept – 1957

It had speedily become apparent that the goals for conventional forces established at the 1952 Lisbon meeting were unrealistically high. At the same time technological advances both in the West and in the Soviet bloc had changed the premises on which the strategy had been based. In particular Russia's newly acquired capacity to deliver a nuclear strike made a reappraisal of Western defence policy imperative. The strategic concept of massive retaliation was further evolved, on the assumption that it would be necessary to use both strategic and tactical nuclear weapons at a relatively early stage in response to any aggression that was not of a minor character. SACEUR was requested by the North Atlantic Council to base his forward planning on the assumption that a large variety of nuclear weapons would gradually be introduced into the forces both of the NATO countries and of the Soviet bloc. At the same time he was required to take account of a levelling off of the defence expenditures of member countries.

These developments were dramatized by the launching of the first Russian sputnik. The Heads of Governments of the NATO countries meeting soon afterwards in Paris (December 1957) decided that NATO's defensive strength should take account of recent developments in weapons and techniques; that to this end it was necessary to establish stocks of nuclear warheads readily available for the defence of the Alliance in case of need; and that intermediate range ballistic missiles should be put at the disposal of the Supreme Allied Commander Europe. The deployment of the stocks of nuclear warheads, and arrangements for their use, were to be decided in agreement with the countries directly concerned.

Since that time, the importance of nuclear weapons for NATO's defence and the increasing stockpile of such weapons in Europe have kept nuclear problems in the forefront of Ministerial consideration.

Athens Guidelines – 1962

A major action in this regard was taken at Athens in 1962, where the Ministers adopted the 'Athens Guidelines'. These outlined in general terms the situations in which it might be necessary to use nuclear weapons in NATO's defence and the degree to which political consultation on such use might be possible. Both the United Kingdom and the United

States specifically committed themselves to consult with their allies, time and circumstances permitting, before releasing their weapons for use.

Assignment of nuclear forces

At the beginning of 1963 the nuclear forces available to NATO Commanders were strengthened by the assignment to SACEUR of the United Kingdom's V-bomber force and of three United States POLARIS submarines. These latter replaced the Jupiter IRBM missiles which had been stationed in Italy and Turkey in conformity with the decision of the Heads of Government in December 1957 and which were by this time becoming obsolete. At the same time, in May 1963, the North Atlantic Council at its Ottawa meeting approved the measures taken to organize the tactical nuclear strike forces assigned to SACEUR. These measures included arrangements for broader participation by officers of non-nuclear member countries in the nuclear activities of Allied Command Europe and in the co-ordination of operational planning at the Headquarters of the United States Strategic Air Command at Omaha.

Review of defence policy

As the 1960s progressed there came the realization that a large-scale attack on NATO, although certainly the most deadly danger and one against which NATO must continue to be prepared, was nevertheless not the only possibility or perhaps the most likely one. Increasing account began to be taken of the possibility and the implications of aggression with relatively limited objectives, and of attacks of a minor or probing kind which might begin through miscalculation of NATO's will to resist but which could very rapidly expand or escalate. Moreover, it was noticeable that the Soviet Union was developing types of forces designed to enable it to deploy a significant military capability in any part of the world. In particular the increasing Russian penetration of the Mediterranean area posed a potential threat to NATO's Southern flank.

Secondly, the development of the inter-continental ballistic missile (ICBM) as the principal means of delivering a nuclear warhead and the construction of hardened launching sites produced a capability to survive a surprise nuclear attack and retaliate within a matter of minutes. This capability was further enhanced by the development of the even less vulnerable weapon system represented by the nuclear-propelled ballistic missile submarine. Each side was thus in a position to destroy important areas of the potential enemy's territory and to annihilate a large proportion of his population even after itself being hit first. These developments reinforced the doubts about the assumption that a major nuclear war was the most likely form of conflict, and also about the credibility of a strategy of massive retaliation in circumstances other than a major nuclear attack.

A new and more flexible strategic concept was accordingly developed and adopted by Ministers in December 1967.

Strategic concept of flexibility in response

The basis of this concept is that NATO should be able to deter, and (if deterrence fails) to counter, military aggression of any kind; and that this can be secured only through a wide range of forces equipped with a well-balanced mixture of conventional, tactical nuclear, and strategic nuclear weapons. The purpose of this balance of forces, while retaining the principle of forward defence, is to permit a flexible range of responses combining two main capabilities: to meet any aggression by direct defence at a level judged to be appropriate to defeat the attack, and to be able to 'escalate' the level, deliberately under political control, if defence at the level first selected is not effective. An aggressor must be convinced of NATO's readiness to use nuclear weapons if necessary; but he must be uncertain regarding the timing or the circumstances in which they would be used. In this connection, however, selective and limited tactical use of nuclear weapons could not be deferred until NATO's conventional defences were completely defeated; first, it would probably be neither feasible nor effective to use the nuclear weapons; the enemy would already have advanced too far and there would be a danger of hitting friendly troops or the civilian population. And secondly, our own forces would be in no condition to exploit and drive home the advantage gained by the use of the weapons. Under the new strategic concept of flexibility in response, with its increased emphasis on the need to be prepared for attacks of varying scales in any region of the NATO area, the aim is that NATO should have available a considerable sea, land, and air conventional combat potential, supported by nuclear weapons for tactical use, over and above the strategic nuclear forces. All these forces must be well organized and prepared for immediate employment. NATO's readiness posture and its capacity to reinforce, deploy, and mobilize in time of tension and crisis are the foundations of 'controlled escalation'.

Multinational NATO forces

In 1960 the first elements of a Mobile Force for Allied Command Europe were constituted. Various member countries assigned to SACEUR well-equipped land and air units immediately available for despatch to any threatened area, particularly on the flanks of Europe. Though capable of giving a good account of itself if attacked, this multinational force is primarily intended to demonstrate the solidarity of the Alliance in times of crisis or tension and to deter any enemy who might be tempted to launch an aggression with limited objectives in the hope of facing the Alliance with a 'fait accompli' situation. Confronted with this force, he must realize with special clarity that in attacking it he would be attacking the NATO Alliance rather than the forces of one country. The ACE Mobile Force has held numerous exercises in both the Northern and Southern flanks of Allied Command Europe.

Somewhat similarly, a Standing Naval Force Atlantic (STANAVFORLANT) has been established under SACLANT since 1967. Composed of destroyer class ships drawn from the navies of member countries, this force, which flies the NATO flag, carries out in peacetime a programme of scheduled exercises, manœuvres, and port visits. By rotating the ships composing the unit, the national naval forces contributing to STANAVFORLANT gain useful experience in working as a multinational team, in command and control procedures, communications, surveillance, as well as tactics and operations. In times of crisis or tension this naval force has a capability for rapid deployment to a threatened area.

In keeping with this concept, a Standing Naval Force Channel (STANAVFORCHAN) was commissioned in May 1973, consisting of mine counter measure vessels and operating under the command of the Allied Commander-in-Chief Channel Command. This force consists of units from Belgium, the Netherlands and United Kingdom with other countries participating on a temporary basis. Its activities are confined to mine-sweeping and minehunting.

In addition, an On-Call Naval Force for the Mediterranean was created in 1969. Similar in purpose to STANAVFORLANT, this naval force, as its name implies, is not permanently in being but assembles only when called upon, the ships remaining under national command in between exercises.

Nuclear planning

Allied nuclear planning and policy

The important role assumed by the nuclear weapons in NATO's strategy and the ever increasing complexity of political and technical problems raised by the availability of nuclear weapons led to a need for the association of non-nuclear members of NATO with allied nuclear planning. This in turn led to the formation of the Nuclear Defence Affairs Committee and the Nuclear Planning Group in 1967.

Nuclear Defence Affairs Committee

The Nuclear Defence Affairs Committee (NDAC) is a committee of the Council/DPC. Membership is open to any interested NATO country. It meets under the Chairmanship of the Secretary General, normally at Ministerial level. Its task is to propose to the Council/DPC general policy on the nuclear affairs of the Alliance.

Nuclear Planning Group

A second body, subordinate to the NDAC, is the Nuclear Planning Group (NPG) consisting of seven or eight countries drawn from the membership of the NDAC. The composition of the NPG changes on an eighteen-month cycle so as to provide full opportunity for all NDAC countries to participate in its work. The NPG meets at the level either of Defence Ministers or Permanent Representatives. Its task is to undertake the detailed work required as a basis for the preparation of policy and to formulate policy proposals for submission to the NDAC for endorsement and final approval by the Council/DPC. The NPG's activities span the full range of the various uses of nuclear weapons, and associated problems. In this connection, at their various meetings, the Ministers of the NPG receive briefings by the United States Secretary of Defense on the balance of strategic forces and hold discussions on specific aspects of current or prospective future developments.

In keeping with the objective of enhancing the participation of all members, including the non-nuclear countries, in the nuclear defence affairs of the Alliance, the major part of the NDAC/NPG effort has been carried directly by Ministries in national capitals and country delegations in Brussels. To support this work, a small Nuclear Planning Directorate was created in the International Staff in 1966 under the supervision of the Assistant Secretary General for Defence Planning and Policy.

One of the first accomplishments of the NPG was the elaboration, in collaboration with the Military Committee, of recommendations for the improvement of national participation in military operational nuclear planning at the levels of the Military Committee, the major NATO Commands and lower Allied Commands. At about the same time the NPG agreed that the deployment of anti-ballistic missiles in NATO Europe was not at present warranted.

During this introductory Phase (1967–1970), the NPG generated four basic nuclear policy documents which were approved by the DPC, and issued as policy guidance for national initiatives and directives to the NATO Military Authorities. These concerned the initial defensive tactical use of nuclear weapons, general guidelines for a procedure to be followed during consultations on an actual use, a concept for the role of theatre nuclear strike forces, and a special political guidance concerning the possible use of ADMs (Atomic Demolition Munitions).

After this introductory Phase there began a period of more detailed and specific examinations when the NPG looked into a number of studies. Such studies dealt with several hypothetical situations in connection with initial defensive use of nuclear weapons in various contingencies. Another series of studies was oriented towards defining politico-military problems in connection with the possible defensive employment of nuclear weapons by

NATO in cases where initial defensive use would not achieve its purpose. This study programme is to be continued in a final phase designed to consolidate NATO's nuclear employment policies. Furthermore, the NPG has embarked on examining the political and military implications of recent technological improvements which might affect NATO's deterrent posture. United States' initiatives in the field of force posture modernization (particularly in connection with the so-called NUNN Amendment) are also designed to align Alliance strategy with the necessities which have been brought about by the changing realities in the world-wide strategic balance.

Consultation arrangements

The importance of timely and effective decisions in a time of crisis is greater than ever under the present concept. With the co-location of the Military Committee with the Council in Brussels, the machinery for consultation and decision-making, a vital aspect of crisis management, has been improved and a NATO-wide communications system far more rapid and comprehensive than anything that has gone before has been established.

Force planning

NATO's force planning, which must continuously be adapted to keep pace with changing circumstances and technological developments, is based on an evaluation of the relative force capabilities of NATO and Warsaw Pact countries.

This comparative study is continuously extended and updated by an effort of close co-ordination between the International Staff, Defence Planning and Policy Division, the International Military Staff and the NATO Military Authorities. The foundation for this study and indeed for all NATO force planning studies is the data base on NATO and Warsaw Pact forces which is regularly updated under the general oversight of the Defence Review Committee.

In determining the size and nature of their contribution to the common defence, member countries have full independence of action. Nevertheless, the collective nature of NATO's defences demands that in reaching their decisions governments take account of the force structure recommended by the NATO military authorities and of the long-term military plans of their partners. NATO's procedures for common force planning must take into account such factors as the military requirements which have to be met, the best use of the available resources, advances in science and technology, a rational division of effort among member countries, and the need for force plans to be within the countries economic and financial capabilities.

Resources for defence

The provision of adequate forces for implementing the agreed strategic concept involves inter-related questions of strategy, force requirements and the resources available to meet them. The achievement of the appropriate balance between these three elements demands that full weight be given in defence planning to economic considerations. Economic and financial studies undertaken in this context have three main objectives: to ensure that adequate resources are applied to the fulfilment of agreed defence programmes; to contribute to the most rational use of available resources, in particular through long-term planning and through encouraging such concepts as cost effectiveness; and to progress, as far as possible, towards an equitable distribution of the economic and financial burden of the common defence.

These objectives are not easy to reach in an Alliance whose members differ widely from the economic viewpoint, and particularly in their population and stage of economic development. Those countries whose per capita income is still low must ensure that their defence effort does not hamper economic progress. At the same time, members of the Alliance must take account of developments in Warsaw Pact countries and, not least, of Warsaw Pact defence expenditures. For example, the rate of increase of military expenditures of the Soviet Union is expected to accelerate to 3% or 5% annually for the next year or two as conventional weapons are replaced or modernized and a new generation of strategic arms are brought into service. (The predicted increase for the Warsaw Pact as a whole falls within the same range.) This is part of a cyclical development that is expected to result in a longer term trend in Soviet military spending of the order of 3% yearly in real terms.

Annual Review

The first attempt at reconciling NATO's military requirements with the economic and financial resources of member countries dates back to 1951. The report, prepared by 'Three Wise Men' – Mr. Averell Harriman, Sir Edwin Plowden and M. Jean Monnet – for the Ministerial Meeting at Lisbon in 1952, was founded on the principle that defence must be built on a sound economic and social basis and that no country should be called on to shoulder a defence burden beyond its means. This was the basic premise of the 'Annual Review' examinations of countries' defence efforts carried out between 1952 and 1961 and of the 'Triennial Review' procedure adopted in 1961. This latter was designed to improve the effectiveness of the annual review and to simplify a process which, because of the many different elements which must be taken into consideration, was necessarily very complex.

Current planning procedures

Meeting in Ottawa in May 1963, Ministers instructed the Council, with the help of the NATO military authorities, to study the inter-related questions of strategy, force requirements, and available resources. This exercise was completed in 1966, when a NATO force plan for the period 1966–1970 was adopted. It was recognized that there was a continuing need for such studies, and procedures for NATO defence planning reviews were approved in the same year. The procedures to a considerable extent reflect those introduced in the United States by Mr. Robert McNamara during his term as Secretary of Defense, which have also, with suitable modifications, been adopted by a number of other member countries. These procedures, by which NATO's force plans are reviewed and projected each year for a period of five years ahead, should make it possible to modify future force plans to meet changing circumstances, and also provide a firm basis on which countries can plan their force contributions.

Military appreciation

In the context of the current procedures for the NATO Defence Planning Review, NATO 'force goals' represent the target which the Alliance sets itself for the six years ahead as part of the process in the development of NATO five-year force plans. The process of drawing up NATO Force Goals begins with the Military Committee appreciation of the situation as it may face the Alliance for the period of the five-year planning review and a little beyond it. This appreciation attempts to identify all military factors and considerations likely to affect force structures, deployments, and equipment both in NATO and in the Soviet bloc during the period under review. It may also deal with the implications of technological and demographic developments.

Ministerial guidance

Ministers take full account of the Military Committee's appreciation and also the Economic appreciation in the Guidance they issue to the NATO Military Authorities for the preparation of Force Proposals for the relevant planning period; the Guidance also adds in the political factors affecting the development of NATO forces over the period and assesses the likely impact of all these factors on the current strategic concept of the Alliance

113

generally, and on the preparation of the next set of Force Proposals in particular. The Ministerial Guidance of 1975 outlined a Long Range Defence Concept which places increased emphasis on co-operative resources within the Alliance and the establishment of rigorous priorities. The principal features of this Guidance are given in full at Appendix 8, page 344.

Force Proposals

The Force Proposals are now prepared by the Major NATO Commanders, setting out country by country what the Commanders propose should be the contribution of each one in the planning period. These proposals are co-ordinated and reviewed by the Military Committee before being forwarded to the Defence Planning Committee with a statement of the reasons underlying the Force Proposals and any risks which might be associated with them. The Defence Review Committee (DRC), then conducts a searching examination of the Force Proposals on behalf of the Defence Planning Committee, in particular as regards the financial, economic, and political implications. The Defence Review Committee must satisfy itself as to the compatibility of the Force Proposals with the guidance given by Ministers. It must seek to ensure that there is an element of challenge in the Goals which each country is being asked to accept: a reasonable and realistic challenge in all the circumstances, but still a challenge which goes somewhat beyond the countries' supposed intentions, in the interests of collective defence planning for the Alliance. The Defence Review Committee then reports to the Defence Planning Committee on its examination of the Force Proposals, on any adjustments which it believes necessary for economic or any other reasons, and on the associated risks as assessed by the Military Committee.

Adoption of Force Goals

In the light of the reports by the Military Committee and the Defence Review Committee, the Defence Planning Committee approves a set of forces for adoption as NATO Force Goals, which countries are to use as the basis of their Force Plans for the five-year period under consideration. These Country Force and Financial Plans are duly formulated and forwarded to NATO, where they are analysed by both the NATO Military Authorities and the International Staff. When differences occur between the Plans and the Goals a first joint attempt is made to reconcile them by the International Civil and Military Staffs, and the Major NATO Commanders' Representatives; these 'trilateral' discussions are reported to the Defence Review Committee, which conducts a further critical 'multilateral' examination of countries' Plans, particularly directed at eliminating, as far as possible, any remaining differences between country Force Plans and NATO Force Goals. On the basis of these multilateral examinations, the Defence Review Committee reports to the Defence Planning Committee how far countries have been able to meet the Force Goals, and why they have fallen short if indeed they have. At the same time, the Military Committee reports on the military suitability of the emerging Alliance-wide five-year Force Plan and on the degree of risk associated with it. In the light of these reports, the Defence Planning Committee is in a position to recommend a five-year Force Plan to Ministers.

Adoption of a five-year NATO Force Plan

Ministers consider the Defence Planning Committee's report and recommendations for the NATO Force Plan from the viewpoint of its overall balance, feasibility, and acceptability, taking account also of the Military Committee's advice regarding the military suitability of the Plan and the associated degree of risk. This NATO five-year Force Plan is then adopted as a basis for national defence planning over the whole period and as a firm commitment of forces by each country for the first year. The 1974 Force Plans gave major emphasis to the strengthening of NATO's conventional forces.

Significance of the NATO force planning procedures

NATO's force planning procedures are thus the machinery for determining the forces required for the defence of the Alliance, co-ordinating national defence plans, and drawing them towards the agreed Goals in the best interests of the Alliance as a whole, while also monitoring countries' actions in respect of the recommendations of studies – some of which may be undertaken independently of the procedures but can be introduced into the process at an appropriate stage when ready for implementation. It may be added that such collective consideration of countries' defence efforts and the attempt to harmonize them from an Alliance-wide point of view have contributed considerably to mutual understanding; they have provided the means for reaching agreement on what is both desirable and practicable, and in many cases have led to co-operative efforts for solving problems. It is significant that to enable this to be done, for over 25 years the countries of the Alliance have agreed to the systematic exchange of detailed and precise information on their military, economic, and financial programmes on a scale previously unprecedented in peace or even in war, and have submitted these programmes to the examination and criticism of their partners.

115

Comparative Defence Figures for 1974   October 1975

Rank	Defence Expenditures as % of GNP		Defence Expenditures per head $		GNP per head $		Defence Personnel (military and civilian as % of labour force)	
1	Portugal	8·1	United States	405	United States	6,069	Portugal	8·4
2	United States	6·7	F.R. Germany	230	F.R. Germany	5,478	Greece	6·2
3	United Kingdom	5·9	France	190	Luxembourg	5,476	Turkey	4·0
4	Greece	4·4	Norway	179	Canada	5,458	United States	3·4
5	France	4·3	Netherlands	176	Denmark	5,241	France	3·2
6	F.R. Germany	4·1	United Kingdom	175	Norway	4,993	Italy	3·1
7	Turkey	4·1	Belgium	151	Belgium	4,969	Norway	3·0
8	Netherlands	3·8	Denmark[1]	144	Netherlands	4,631	Netherlands	2·9
9	Norway	3·6	Canada	130	France	4,408	Belgium	2·8
10	Italy	3·1	Portugal	112	United Kingdom	2,947	United Kingdom	2·6
11	Belgium	3·0	Greece	90	Italy	2,582	F.R. Germany	2·4
12	Denmark	2·8	Italy	79	Greece	2,021	Denmark	1·8
13	Canada	2·4	Luxembourg	51	Portugal	1,388	Canada	1·3
14	Luxembourg	0·9	Turkey	28	Turkey	696	Luxembourg	0·8

1. This estimate is from latest information received, $140 are shown in the Chapter.
Source: Figures as reported in the Country Chapters for the NATO Defence Planning Review 1975–1979 series of documents.

Civil emergency planning

Nowadays defence is not a matter for the armed forces alone. Civil preparedness is complementary to, and in some cases a pre-requisite for, effective military preparedness. All the civil resources and power of a nation have therefore to be capable of being rapidly mobilized in support of the total defence effort, if and when required.

Thus the scope of civil emergency planning is extremely wide. It embraces such matters as the maintenance of the machinery of government and law and order, and the mobilization and use of national resources including manpower, industry, food, agriculture, fuels, transport, and so on, as well as the civil defence measures designed to warn the public of impending attack and protect them as far as possible against the consequences of enemy action.

Planning assumptions

But civil emergency planning not only covers a very wide variety of subjects; it also has to provide for a wide range of contingencies related to an appreciation of the various types of attack which could be delivered against the Alliance, the likely target areas and the general effects which modern weapons might be expected to have, from nuclear attack to a large variety of contingency situations short of nuclear war.

The task at NATO level

Whatever the contingency, however, there is a need to provide for consultation and co-ordination between member nations at NATO level in order:

a. in peacetime, to further national planning by providing for the exchange of experience and opinions on matters of common interest; and to develop arrangements for dealing with those things which would have to be handled, in one way or another, at NATO level during an emergency because they would call for international co-operation or would have international implications or repercussions;

b. in a period of rising tension, to facilitate crisis management arrangements within the Alliance so that the North Atlantic Council could be properly and regularly informed of the state of civil preparedness of member nations and the latter could act in harmony when advancing their state of readiness;

c. in war, to provide for international co-operation in such matters as the protection of populations and population movements and, particularly, the co-ordination of the use of vital resources for essential civil and military defence purposes; and

d. after a general nuclear attack, to ensure the continued survival of the survivors and the recovery and rehabilitation of national economies.

Civil Emergency Planning Committee

The policy direction and general co-ordination of civil emergency planning at NATO level is undertaken on behalf of the Council by the Civil Emergency Planning Committee supported by an International Staff element, the Civil Emergency Planning Directorate of the Defence Planning and Policy Division. In plenary session, the Committee is chaired by the Secretary General, or the Assistant Secretary General for Defence Planning and Policy, and the members are the national representatives from the 15 NATO nations who are responsible for civil emergency planning in their own countries. The plenary session convenes once or twice a year. In between, the Committee meets, normally once a month, in permanent session under the chairmanship of the Director of Civil Emergency Planning; the representatives are drawn from the national delegations to NATO.

Planning boards and committees

The CEP Committee directs and supervises the activities of eight planning boards and committees each of which covers a specific field in civil emergency planning. The importance of the co-ordinated use of resources to the defence of the Alliance has already been mentioned. Civil preparedness as a whole is a national responsibility and resources management is no exception. Although, however, control over their own resources in times of crisis and war would remain a matter for individual member nations, national economies are nowadays so entwined and interdependent that it is perhaps not surprising that six out of the eight planning boards and committees deal with resources of one sort or another. They are:

in the field of supplies:

– the Food and Agriculture Planning Committee;

– the Industrial Planning Committee;

– the Petroleum Planning Committee;

in the field of transport:

– the Planning Board for Ocean Shipping;

– the Planning Board for European Inland Surface Transport;

– the Civil Aviation Planning Committee.

NATO civil wartime agencies

These planning boards and committees consist of representatives with specialized knowledge appointed by the various member nations. Under the overall guidance of the CEP Committee they have evolved plans for setting up NATO civil wartime agencies (NCWAS) which would be activated in times of emergency. These NCWAS, which would operate broadly in the fields covered by their parent planning boards or committees, would consist of a directing body, in which all participating member nations would be represented, and an international staff of experts.

Communications

The Civil Communications Planning Committee is concerned with the problems of maintaining civil communications in an emergency.

Civil Defence

The Civil Defence Committee is composed of members who are senior officials with responsibility for civil defence arrangements in their own countries. When necessary, the Committee appoints sub-committees or working groups, as do the other planning boards and committees, to study special problems.

Effective, well-organized civil defence is an essential part of civil preparedness and is especially important in the face of the threat of general nuclear war.

In most NATO countries reliance is placed on volunteers who are trained to form the cadres for civil defence teams in an emergency. The emphasis is on local defence although most NATO countries also have mobile civil defence columns which could be deployed to stricken areas.

To a considerable extent, however, civil defence is a matter of self-help and this pre-supposes a well-informed public who would understand the risks and what they had to do in an emergency to remain at work as long as possible, to lay in stocks of food and water, prepare domestic shelters and so on. The majority of NATO countries have prepared material for distribution to the public in time of emergency and have plans to reinforce this by radio and television broadcasts at the time.

The arrangements for shelter provision vary throughout the Alliance but it is generally agreed that a combination of public and domestic shelters, combined with effective evacuation or dispersal plans in the case of likely target areas, offers the best solution to a difficult problem.

Refugees

The Civil Defence Committee has also planned to set up a NATO Refugee Agency which would advise and assist governments on refugee matters.

Training

The plans and procedures for all the NATO civil wartime agencies are tested in exercises and training sessions and are subject to continuous review and improvement.

7

Machinery for crisis management

The growing importance of nuclear defence planning in NATO has been accompanied by correspondingly increased recognition of the Council's role as a forum for consultation within the framework of crisis management of the Alliance. This has created a requirement for improved facilities for the exchange of information, intelligence and other data within NATO at Council level and correspondingly with national capitals and Major NATO Commanders. The co-location of the Council and Military Committee in Brussels and the move to the new Headquarters provided an opportunity for the construction and operation of a Situation Centre with up-to-date facilities for NATO-wide communications and the display and processing of appropriate, political, military and economic data.

NATO Situation Centre

The Centre is designed specifically to enable the Council, both in peace-time and in a period of rising tension and crisis, to assemble, collate and disseminate all available intelligence and information with regard to developing situations. Consultation can therefore take place on the basis of a current and realistic review of latest developments at every stage of a crisis situation and on a common data base. The Situation Centre, which is manned on a continuous watch basis, follows all developments of interest to NATO and serves as the primary contact point for all elements of the Headquarters after normal working hours and on weekends and holidays. The Secretary General, acting for the Council, has responsibility for the overall policy, general organization and effective functioning of the Centre. The Director of the Office of Council Operations and Communications, on behalf of the Secretary General, is the senior staff official responsible for the development and control of the Situation Centre.

The Situation Centre thus gives the Council the technical facilities necessary for the performance of its task in times of crisis. It provides the means for effective and rapid consultation among Permanent Representatives, and between them and all member capitals, and thus enables them to give guidance to the NATO Military Authorities.

Participation in exercises

The Defence Planning Committee participates in exercises at regular intervals jointly with the Military Committee, national capitals and the Major NATO Commanders, to examine, test and develop procedures associated with their respective roles and responsibilities in a period of tension and crisis. Appropriate committees of the Council/Defence Planning Committee are called upon to provide support to the Defence Planning Committee during such exercises, particularly in the fields of political, economic and civil emergency activities.

Other exercise activity in the Headquarters involves the participation of the Defence Planning Committee in major NATO military exercises and also the conduct of special civil logistic-type exercises involving the civil emergency planning bodies and the NATO Military Authorities.

A Council Operations Directorate has been established to co-ordinate all activities connected with the functioning of the Situation Centre and for the co-ordination of planning and conduct of all types of exercises in which the Council, Defence Planning Committee and the appropriate supporting committees of the Council are engaged. It is also responsible for ensuring that, in peace and in time of crisis, the needs of the Council and the Defence Planning Committee in respect of briefings, compilation of reports and dissemination of information are effectively met.

Council communications

The Council's communication requirements are served by the NATO-Wide Communications Systems (NWCS), which provides secure teleprinter communications between the Council Headquarters in Brussels, the capitals of the member nations, and the Major NATO Commands. Further information related to this System and other communications to serve the Council is contained in Chapter 8.

CHAPTER 8

NATO communications

NATO's communications have grown up with the Alliance. Initially, the requirement was principally for communications to link the various NATO Military Headquarters and to exercise command and control over NATO forces. These services were provided in the main through the facilities of the various PTTs of the member nations.

ACE HIGH system

The first highly modern military communications capability was established in the 1960s when SHAPE installed the 'ACE HIGH' Tropo-scatter system which provided high capacity microwave voice and telegraph circuits throughout the area of Allied Command Europe from the northern tip of Norway, through central Europe and the Mediterranean, to the eastern part of Turkey.

NATO-wide communications

In the late 1960s two additional steps were taken further to improve NATO's communications capability. The first arose from the deliberations of the Special Committee of Defence Ministers in that, in December 1967, a decision was taken to establish, for the first time in NATO, a special communications network for political consultation, for the exchange of intelligence and other data and, if the need were ever to arise, to speed up critical NATO decisions on the use of nuclear weapons. This was called colloquially the 'NATO-Wide Communications System' and provided direct and dedicated telegraph links between NATO Headquarters at Evere, the NATO capitals (except Paris) and the Major NATO Command Head-quarters. The second significant step, taken in the late 1960s, was the

122

adoption by NATO of a United States proposal to enhance the survivability, reliability and speed of NATO's vital communications, and at the same time to take NATO into the very latest area of modern telecommunications technology by entering into the field of satellites.

Satellite communications (SATCOM)

In March 1970 the first of two NATO Phase II communications satellites for a fully operational system was launched, and later in the Spring of the same year, the first of the twelve satellite ground terminals of Phase II of the NATO Satellite Communications Programme was brought into service. The ground stations of this system are established on the territory of each of the member nations (except France, Iceland and Luxembourg). The coverage of the system extends over the whole of the NATO area, providing increased capabilities for reliable telephone conversations and telegraph traffic transmission between the Headquarters in Brussels, each of the member nations and the NATO Military Commands. These capabilities will be greatly enhanced by the planned Phase III, which provides for additional satellite ground terminals and a satellite space segment of greatly increased power. This Phase III system, which will eventually form part of the new NATO Integrated Communications System (NICS), is due to become operational in the latter half of the 1970s.

NICS

In recent years, with the growing emphasis within the Alliance on con-sultation and crisis management during periods short of actual hostilities, it has become increasingly clear that it is no longer possible to have a strict separation between purely 'military' and 'political' (civil) communications. Accordingly, at their meeting in December 1970, NATO Ministers agreed upon the establishment of a new NATO Integrated Communications System (NICS) designed to meet the Alliance's requirements during the 1970s for high-level political consultation and for improving the command and control capability of the NATO Military Authorities.

The NICS will provide a modern automatically switched common-user telephone and telegraph network covering the whole of the NATO area. New communications 'nodal' points and Message Distribution Centres (MDCS) will be established in the various NATO countries, which will enable messages and telephone calls to be automatically and rapidly switched from one point in the system to another. The system will provide, for example, automatic dial telephone facilities through the network which will be comparable to, if not better than, those now available to civil subscribers within and between certain NATO countries. The NATO Phase III SATCOM system, as well as the 'ACE HIGH' and 'NATO-Wide' networks, will form integral parts of the NICS. This new Integrated Communications

System will significantly improve communications facilities available for Alliance consultation and action in times of peace as well as in times of tension and/or hostilities. The full NICS plan will be implemented on an incremental basis through the late 1970s and early 1980s, the first increment of which is scheduled to cost in the order of IAU 80 million. [1]

NICSMA

In order that the NICS can be effectively planned, implemented and managed, the North Atlantic Council established a new communications agency, called the NICS Management Agency (NICSMA). This Agency is located in Brussels and is responsible for the overall planning and implementation of the new system. The staff comprises military officers and civilians drawn largely from existing communications and electronics elements throughout NATO. The policy control for the new NICS and for the Management Agency is exercised by a 'Policy Committee' comprising senior military and civilian officers from each of the participating countries, which acts under the overall authority of the North Atlantic Council.

1. IAU = Infrastructure Accounting Unit used as base for the conversion of different currencies.

CHAPTER 9

Economic co-operation

The authors of the Atlantic Treaty, mindful of all the bitterness and hardship caused by the crisis in the thirties, were insistent that economic rivalry, institutionalized at the level of the nation State, while useful perhaps as a stimulus to competition and growth, must not be allowed to become a source of friction within the Alliance and thus affect its solidarity.

For this reason Article 2 of the North Atlantic Treaty lays down that 'The Parties will seek to eliminate conflict in their international economic policies and will encourage economic collaboration between any or all of them'.

From the start the Atlantic Alliance, while primarily concerned with co-ordinating the common defence effort and promoting political consultation, has been alive to the value of economic consultation which has developed steadily since 1949 and is now an integral part of NATO's activities.

In 1956 a decisive fillip was given to NATO's work in this field when three leading Allied statesmen, Gaetano Martino (Italy), Halvard Lange (Norway) and Lester Pearson (Canada) were commissioned to propose ways in which NATO might extend its activities in non-military fields. Their reports, known as 'Report of the Committee of Three'[1] comprised a number of important recommendations and basic principles as the result of which NATO's rôle in the economic sphere was strengthened and has continued to develop.

The idea running through Chapter 3 of their report, which deals with

1. See Appendix 5, page 308, for full text of 'Report of Committee of Three'.

125

economic co-operation, is that 'political co-operation and economic conflict are not reconcilable'. Consequently, Allied countries recognize that they have common interests in the economic sphere which should induce them, collectively or individually, to do all they can to foster the growth of their economies. This means that NATO countries must keep economic activity at a high level if they are to succeed in improving the standard of living of their peoples, in maintaining full employment, in keeping up a sustained research and development programme, assisting the less developed countries and maintaining and, if necessary, increasing their defence capability.

The report does not say that the implementation of practical measures of economic co-operation must necessarily take place within the NATO framework. It would, indeed, be pointless for the Alliance to undertake tasks which are already carried out by international organizations specifically set up for the purpose. The member countries which play a major rôle in these organizations are in a position to prevent the adoption of economic policies which run counter to the spirit and the interests of the Alliance. However, the report does suggest that consultations might take place within NATO whenever questions arise which are of particular political or strategic importance for the Alliance, especially those which 'affect the economic health of the Atlantic Community as a whole'.

Finally, in their Ottawa Declaration of June 19, 1974 the Allied Governments reaffirmed their wish 'to ensure that their essential security relationship is supported by harmonious political and economic relations. In particular they will work to remove sources of conflict between their economic policies and to encourage economic co-operation with one another.'

The Alliance provides an effective framework where different and interrelated aspects of political, military and economic questions can normally be examined. In this connection the NATO approach and machinery may serve a very useful purpose in facilitating discussion of certain delicate aspects of international economic relations, as is shown by the communiqué issued after the Ministerial Meeting in Brussels on December 12 and 13, 1974.

NATO's economic activities

The Report of the Committee of Three resulted in the creation by the NATO Council in 1957 of an Economic Committee which reports directly to the Council itself and meets under the Chairmanship of the Director of Economic Affairs. All member countries are represented on the Economic Committee.

The Committee has two main functions. First of all, it acts as a clearing-house for the exchange by member countries of information on current economic questions of direct concern to the Alliance and it enables their implications to be discussed. It is a convenient forum for the regular discussion of problems raised by one or other member of the Alliance or by the Council. Consultations of this kind may, where appropriate, result in recommendations which can guide member governments in framing national policies. The Economic Committee, for instance, played an important rôle in forging common views among members during the preparation of the CSCE. Secondly, the Economic Committee regularly prepares a number of reports covering different aspects of the economic and financial relations between East and West as well as studies analysing the economic situation in the various Eastern countries.

Within the NATO International Staff, the Economic Directorate, which forms part of the Political Division, is the body responsible for this work. The Directorate operates at three levels:

(i) it contributes to the activities of the Council and the Economic Committee and, whenever necessary, certain other Committees, such as the Defence Planning Committee, the Political Committee and the Military Committee;

(ii) it provides the Secretary General with any studies or economic analyses he may require;

(iii) it carries on research in various fields and passes on information and statistics concerning NATO. Generally speaking, it maintains contact with the national delegations, NATO bodies, and other international organizations, both governmental and non-governmental, which are concerned with economic matters.

Economic impact of the defence effort

NATO's procedures and its machinery for consultation make it possible to examine the impact of defence spending on the economies of the member countries. At the present juncture, more attention is being given to the economic factors which would allow better use to be made within the Alliance of the resources available for defence.

The problem facing NATO experts is how to spread as fairly as possible the financial and economic burden occasioned by defence, bearing in mind the current economic situation. In its studies the International Staff makes due allowance for a number of indicators, such as the share of GNP going to defence, income per head of population, the balance of payments, labour resources, percentage use of industrial capacity, investment requirements, and the tax burden.

East–West economic relations

The countries of the Alliance have always favoured the expansion of East–West trade not merely because of the resultant economic benefits but also because this is a way of promoting détente. Negotiations at present taking place within the framework of the Conference on Security and Co-operation in Europe should open up new prospects for economic relations between East and West.

It should be borne in mind, however, that trade with the Eastern countries can raise certain problems because their economies are centrally controlled, political aims often outweigh economic considerations, and their foreign trade is run by State monopolies. Despite fairly rapid progress over the decade 1960–69 and further satisfactory growth in the first four years of the present decade, trade with Communist countries still represents only a small share, about 3.8%, of the total foreign trade (exports plus imports) of NATO countries as a whole. The share varies, of course, from one Allied country to another, without reaching a level which would make any or all of them too dependent on trade with the Communist world.

However, East–West trade is quite important for the Eastern countries; 22% of all Soviet imports come from NATO countries, while the corresponding percentage is 40% for China and 33% and 34% for Poland and Romania respectively. In assessing these figures it should be borne in mind that the significance of foreign trade is not the same in the USSR, where its impact on the economy is slight, as in the East European countries where trade is important, and even essential, to economic growth.

Since the end of the sixties efforts have been made to develop East–West economic relations, by means of co-operative agreements between Eastern enterprises and Western firms. These agreements cover various forms of sub-contracting, specialized co-production or manufacturing and are sometimes supplemented by contracts covering common efforts to promote sales in Western, Eastern or Third World countries, the exchange of technical information and co-operation in research in certain sectors. Many of these contracts are linked to Western credits repayable in the form of deliveries of goods produced in Eastern factories, the building or expansion of which has been partly due to these credits. Industrial co-operation is of considerable interest to the Eastern countries as it helps to overcome certain problems inherent in their economic system.

Allied countries regularly carry on consultations and exchange information on economic and commercial relations with the Eastern countries. This approach enables them to work out their position with a full knowledge of the facts.

A better understanding of Communist economies

In order to assess the political and military power of a nation it is essential to understand its economic potential—hence the need to follow as objectively as possible the economic development of the Communist countries. The Allied countries therefore make a point of analysing as accurately as possible the progress made by these countries and the economic resources available to them.

Leaving aside all propaganda considerations, NATO is a useful forum where research can be carried on by all the interested countries in order to hammer out, on the basis of the best available information, a common view of the chief issues which determine the economic development of the Communist countries such as demographic growth, the relative weight of agriculture, economic reform of centralized planning systems, the harnessing of sources of energy, the development and pattern of foreign trade, the assessment of their national product in terms comparable with that of Western countries. Such studies, the results of which are reported to governments, not only foster a better understanding of the current state of these economies but also make possible a more accurate assessment of possible future developments and the share of their resources these countries can allocate to defence.

New activities in a changing scene

The Economic Committee and the Economic Directorate have, in recent years, extended their activities in response to a rapidly changing situation:

- detailed and systematic economic studies have been carried out on COMECON countries;
- studies have been made covering a number of specific fields such as demography, basic products, petrol and energy, credits, balance of payments, indebtedness and the methods of calculating Soviet GNP;
- more attention has been paid to economic problems affecting defence and especially the impact of inflation on resource allocation to defence and trends in defence spending in East and West;
- meetings and symposia have been organized and contact established with academic circles and research workers throughout the Alliance.

Do we stop here? Probably not. It seems likely that political and economic relations within and outside NATO will continue to evolve. In the context of this evolution economic co-operation within the Alliance will doubtless remain in the forefront of NATO's activities.

CHAPTER 10

Defence support and infrastructure

NATO, since it is not a supranational organization, does not possess mandatory powers over national governments. The responsibility for equipping and maintaining forces remains therefore a national one. There is no NATO development and production in the sense of orders being passed by NATO to equipment manufacturers and no centralized NATO logistic system. The rôle of NATO is one of advice and co-ordination. The first attempts to rationalize defence production in NATO were made by the Military Production and Supply Board set up in November 1949, and its successor the Defence Production Board. They had studies prepared by specialists, recommending means of increasing production in fields where deficiencies were greatest. One of the responsibilities of the Temporary Council Committee, set up in 1951, and of the Annual and Triennial Review procedures adopted subsequently, was to submit proposals for the reconciliation of military requirements, including arms and equipment, with the means available to NATO countries for defence.

Early in 1952 a Production and Logistics Division was set up as part of the newly created International Staff. In October 1960, its title was changed to that of Production, Logistics and Infrastructure Division. On September 1, 1967, it became the Defence Support Division as part of the reorganization which took place upon the transfer to Brussels. This broader title now includes Defence Research.

Its main rôle in the Armaments and Logistics field remains to promote the most efficient use of the resources of the Alliance for the equipment and support of its forces.

As a first task in 1952, using the studies already prepared, the Secretariat made plans for correlated production programmes of major items of equipment, including aircraft, artillery, small arms, radar and wireless sets, vehicles, ships and various types of ammunition.

Early difficulties

These programmes were limited in scope. No attempt was made to draw up any overall master plan for the equipment of all NATO forces which would parcel out production to the most efficient or economical sources. Such ideas, canvassed in the early days of NATO, ran into a number of obstacles. National authorities naturally tended to favour home industries and to be reluctant to finance multi-national projects. Member countries were at differing stages of economic and industrial efficiency. There were serious problems in respect of security. Furthermore, large programmes imposed upon industries would have had the effect of smothering incentive and reducing useful competition in the private industrial sector of many of the countries concerned.

Under these circumstances, even limited programmes did not achieve many spectacular results. Indeed, it was usually North American aid in the form of off-shore procurement orders which acted as the spur to increased production.

Joint production planning

The most interesting example of multi-national teamwork was that of fighter aircraft production. Belgium and the Netherlands had already co-operated in 1949 in the joint production under licence of British aircraft and engines. When later a correlated programme for combat aircraft was agreed, covering production of British, French and United States aircraft in five Western European nations, Belgium and the Netherlands continued their co-operation, adopting the Hawker Hunter fighter and agreeing on a joint production programme with supply of components and assembly work divided between them and the United Kingdom, while considerable financial support was given by the United States. This was in a sense the first co-operative production project in NATO. Useful results were also obtained under correlated production programmes for electronic equipment and for ammunition. In the latter case, large United States off-shore orders and grants towards the cost of establishing new plants helped to increase five-fold the overall ammunition production capacity of the European NATO countries.

Defence Production Committee

The Defence Production Committee set up in 1954 took over supervision of correlated production programmes and of other associated activities, in particular work on standardization and the exchange of technical information.

Standardization of equipment, components and spare parts simplifies the logistic support of forces and facilitates co-ordinated production. But there are a number of factors which limit progress in this direction. Differing geographical conditions give rise to differing requirements; large quantities of equipment exist which cannot just be scrapped or discarded; countries have to be persuaded of the merits of new equipment designed by some other nation; and then there are the economic and financial aspects.

Problems of standardization

Some degree of standardization was ensured at an early stage by the extensive range of items of equipment of North American origin received under mutual aid. The need to find sources of spare parts for these items brought countries into close co-operation, and groups of national experts were formed under the aegis of the Defence Production Committee to discuss these and similar problems.

Examples of items or areas for which Standardization Agreements have been promulgated are specifications for explosives of various types, ammunition (notably the 7.62 mm. NATO basic round), vehicle components and attachments, a priority list of electronic valves, impact tests for steels for guns, the adoption of a standard atmosphere for ballistic purposes, and rules for the conversion of dimensions on drawings of United States origin for countries using the metric system. Valuable as these agreements have been, they have been concerned mainly with components and procedures. In recent years the emphasis has been placed increasingly on projects for entire items of equipment. Consequently, although the Standardization Agreement method is still used when need arises, it no longer represents a major part of co-operative efforts in the equipment field.

Both the studies on correlated production and the work involved in standardization necessitated the exchange of much technical information. Groups of qualified technicians from the countries concerned in the particular field or item of equipment under study met, normally at NATO Headquarters, to exchange views and information and try to arrive at a common policy.

Ammunition specifications

One of the most fruitful subjects studied in the early days was ammunition. For example, a special Panel was set up to monitor test centres in order to control proof and inspection of NATO standard small arms ammunition. Various manufacturing techniques were discussed, as well as methods of packaging and storing. One interesting study concerned production methods for steel cartridge cases instead of brass ones. Another

Group started by considering the different types of steel used in the manufacture of weapons, particularly guns, and its activities were later extended to cover other metals. Among other subjects on which information was exchanged were equipment for protection against chemical warfare, ballistics and a broad range of electronics equipment.

Agreement on the Mutual Safeguarding of Secrecy of Inventions

In an effort to promote the free exchange of technical information within the Alliance, a Working Group of highly specialized experts was set up in 1955 to study mainly the means of protecting proprietary technical information belonging to private firms or individuals. Among the important tasks already performed by this Group, the NATO Agreement on the Mutual Safeguarding of Secrecy of Inventions relating to Defence and for which Applications for Patents have been made, should be noted. By committing governments to safeguard the secrecy of such inventions, the Agreement makes it possible for nations to lift the former prohibitions on patent applications in other countries.

Agreement on the Communication of Technical Information for Defence Purposes

The NATO Agreement on the Communication of Technical Information for Defence Purposes which was also prepared by the Group, was signed by the NATO Permanent Representatives. This constitutes an important step forward by the members of the Alliance in their efforts to develop technological co-operation. The purpose of this Agreement is to facilitate further the exchange of technical information by providing safeguards to the owners of such information, who would otherwise be reluctant to release it.

Among the works accomplished by the Group, the following should also be mentioned: The drafting of industrial property clauses applicable to the contracts of employees of the NATO research organizations. 'Guidance on drafting international co-operative research and development agreements' intended for the experts responsible for the preparation of such agreements, as well as 'Guidance for NATO procurement authorities'; both texts have been published in the form of a brochure. The elaboration of several comparative studies one of which, on the recoupment of research and development costs in NATO countries is already edited, while two others, the first on 'Employees' inventions in NATO countries' and the second on 'National practices regarding proprietary rights in co-operative research and development programmes', will be edited in the near future. A glossary of terms used in the field of industrial property has been reviewed for a second time; the latest version will be edited for the intention of NATO organizations and national services interested.

Early efforts in co-operation

The advent of more complicated and costly items of equipment, such as missiles and the more advanced types of aircraft, demands new manufacturing processes and facilities on quite a different scale. The financial and technical resources required to develop and produce these complicated weapon systems were originally available only to the wealthiest countries and this led others to consider more favourably closer co-operation in new projects.

With the gradual abandonment of the correlated programme concept there was tacit agreement that any approach to production should be on the basis of individual projects. Many factors combined – and still combine – to make agreement on specific projects a long and difficult business. In general terms the problem is first to select an item which can serve the needs of forces with varying missions in different geographical locations and, second, to ensure its economical production without prejudice to national industries.

Joint Aircraft Production—the G. 91

The first multi-national venture for development and production within NATO of a totally new major item of equipment began in 1954. The idea of a very light jet fighter for close support of ground troops was conceived by the NATO Military Authorities, and SACEUR took the lead in implementing the NATO lightweight Tactical Reconnaissance Aircraft. After general specifications had been prepared, designs were drawn up and prototypes developed and constructed. Three prototypes were tested, and one design, the Italian FIAT G. 91 with a British Bristol Orpheus engine, was selected for the first generation.

More than 600 aircraft of this type, in its different roles, were produced under a joint programme in Italy and (under licence) in Germany, and are now in service with the air forces of the two nations. A further 40 aircraft are in service with the Portuguese Air Force. A new version of the G. 91, the twin-engined G. 91Y, is now being produced in Italy. A number of useful lessons on how to set about a co-operative venture of this kind were learned from this first experience.

NATO Maritime Patrol Aircraft—the 'Atlantic'

The next multi-national project, the NATO Maritime Patrol Aircraft, started early in 1957. In the course of the 1956 Annual Review, the Alliance's potential deficiencies in modern maritime patrol aircraft were revealed. The NATO Military Authorities formulated basic military requirements, describing the missions for which such an aircraft was required and the characteristics and capabilities considered necessary.

A group of experts set up by the Defence Production Committee

converted these requirements into operational characteristics with a more
detailed description of the type of aircraft and equipment required. After
examining the possibility of finding an existing aircraft to meet these
characteristics it was decided that a completely new aircraft would have to
be designed, and technical specifications were produced and circulated to
aircraft companies in various countries.

The design finally selected was the French Bréguet 1150, given the
name 'ATLANTIC'. Co-operative arrangements were worked out between
the four European producing countries – Belgium, France, the Federal
Republic of Germany and the Netherlands – and the United States
Government.

Design and manufacture were entrusted to a Consortium, headed by
Bréguet in France and including SABCA and Fairey in Belgium, Sud
Aviation in France, Dornier and Siebel in Germany and Fokker in the
Netherlands. Industrial agreements for the Tyne engine were signed
between Rolls-Royce in the United Kingdom, Hispano Suiza in France,
FN in Belgium and MAN in Germany, and for the propellers between De
Havilland in the United Kingdom and Ratier in France. Much of the
electronic equipment is supplied by the United States and built under
licence in the European participating countries. The breakdown in
prototype work among the European countries set the pattern for the
sharing of work and equipment in the production phase.

The first prototype began its tests in late 1961. The production design
was adopted and the procedure for sharing production agreed in early
1962. Eighty seven aircraft have been produced under this programme,
twenty for the German Navy, and forty for the French Navy, nine for the
Netherlands and eighteen for Italy, who joined the project in 1968. To
facilitate training on the aircraft and its weapon system, three simulators
have been built; two for France and one for Germany. An International
Supply and Logistics Centre and an International Warehouse provide for
joint logistics and spare parts for the French, German, Italian and
Netherlands Navies.

Complexities of joint production

These first attempts at co-operative production which were no more than
relatively successful when it came to adoption by the armed forces of the
Alliance, revealed the complexity of the problem. It was clear that the
enormous potential advantages of joint production were dependent upon
the right kind of co-operative planning at the earliest possible stage.
Agreed procedures were needed to cover the entire life of a co-operative
project – from the selection of a particular item of military equipment,
through the formulation of military requirements, operational characteristics and technical specification, the submission and selection of designs,

135

the development, production and testing of prototypes, up to final production of the fully developed item.

In the decade following initiation of the 'Atlantic' project the history of co-operative production in NATO was one of a continuing search for the right procedural framework.

US offer

Towards the end of 1956, the United States, aware from her own experience of the full cost and complexity of planning and producing new weapons, began to make suggestions for co-ordinated efforts and to be more forthcoming with information about her own equipment. At the Heads of Government meeting in December 1957, President Eisenhower offered to make available his country's technical knowledge and experience to further joint European weapons production. The first two projects selected by European nations, in discussion with the International Staff, were a ground-to-air and an air-to-air missile system.

Hawk programme

Early in 1958 Belgium, France, the Federal Republic of Germany, Italy and the Netherlands accepted the offer to use United States government-owned property rights and to facilitate industrial contracts for the manufacture in Europe of the ground-to-air missile system the HAWK. Five European firms combined to form an international company organized under French law and known as SETEL (Société Européenne de Téléguidage) to act as the European prime contractor. At government level the programme was supervised by the NATO HAWK Production and Logistics Organization, with a Board of Directors drawn from the participating countries, and an internationally staffed Management Office. Production was allocated in proportion to the number of complete weapon systems which each nation agreed to buy.

The initial production programme, which included over 4,000 missiles and associated equipment was completed in 1967 at a total cost of $600 million; later on additional orders, to the value of $50 million, were received.

In November, 1967, the participating countries started on an exploratory phase of a new programme, known as HAWK European Limited Improvement Programme which, taking as its basis the American HAWK Improvement Programme would make it possible to adapt the HAWK weapon system to the air environment of the next decade and prolong its use accordingly. This would reduce logistic support costs and improve the very low altitude capabilities of the weapon system and its resistance to electronic counter-measures. During this initial phase, which ended in 1970, the European industry collected technical, operational,

136

industrial and financial data on the Programme, and the Production Organization established the necessary agreements to cover governmental and industrial property rights.

This phase was followed in 1971 by field experiments in Europe with a US HAWK improved battery in order to obtain complementary data aimed at enabling countries to decide on their participation in the Programme. In 1972, Greece was admitted as a NATO HAWK Production and Logistics Organization (NHPLO) member country. Early in 1974, the decision to launch the HAWK European Limited Improvement Programme (HELIP) Production Phase was taken by Denmark, France, Greece, Italy, the Netherlands and the Federal Republic of Germany. Denmark was accordingly admitted as a new member of the NHPLO.

The launching of the Production Phase can be considered as a great achievement in terms of improvement of the basic HAWK System from an operational point of view, in terms of standardization and of introduction of new technology in European industry.

In connection with the common logistic support of the basic HAWK, the transfer of this support and of procurement activities to the NATO Maintenance and Supply Agency (NAMSA) has been completed as of January 1, 1975.

Sidewinder programme

The air-to-air missile SIDEWINDER was the second existing United States missile to be chosen for production in Europe, this time by Belgium, Denmark, the Federal Republic of Germany, Greece, the Netherlands, Norway, Portugal and Turkey. A German firm – Fluggerätewerk – was selected as prime contractor. Production arrangements were agreed by the Council in December 1959, and the first missiles assembled in Europe in November 1961. Most of the flight tests were performed in Europe with the assistance of France, who ordered several hundred missiles. Production, which involved a programme of the order of 10,000 missiles was disbanded in December 1966 and responsibility for logistic support transferred to NAMSA.

Naval torpedo programme

A co-ordinated programme for the production of several hundred American Mark 44 Anti-Submarine Torpedoes in Europe was undertaken in late 1960 by France and Italy with United States co-operation. Production was also undertaken in the United Kingdom and Canada under prior arrangements with the United States.

A Group of Experts was set up to ensure full interchange of information amongst all those involved in the further development and production of this torpedo. In July 1966 this Group organized a series of trials at La

137

Spezia, which demonstrated the reliability and interchangeability of complete torpedoes and major components manufactured by the various countries.

The Starfighter programme

In December 1960 four European countries, Belgium, the Federal Republic of Germany, Italy and the Netherlands, announced that they had agreed to participate in a programme for the co-ordinated production in Europe of the American F104G STARFIGHTER Aircraft. This was a multipurpose aircraft intended to fulfil a number of military roles. In June 1961 the Council approved this as a NATO Programme, and set up a Direction and Control Organization. Production of nearly 1,000 aircraft was completed in 1966, with United States assistance. Canada, who produced similar aircraft for her own forces, was closely associated. The F104G STARFIGHTER was by far the largest integrated production programme hitherto undertaken. The programme was a great step forward for the European aerospace industry.

Bullpup missile programme

Following discussions within NATO, Denmark, Norway, Turkey and the United Kingdom decided to obtain the US BULLPUP air-to-surface missile for their forces from a common European production source. In May 1962, the Council set up the NATO BULLPUP Production Organization, with headquarters in Oslo, to produce BULLPUP missiles on a co-operative basis. The production programme, the amount of which exceeded $38 million, was shared among the participating countries roughly in proportion with their orders. Production of more than 5,000 missiles was completed in 1967 and the liquidation of the production organization and transfer to NAMSA of responsibility for logistic support was completed in 1968.

AS 30 missile programme

In June 1962 the Council set up a NATO Steering Committee for the production of the French-developed AS 30 air-to-surface missile. France, the Federal Republic of Germany and the United Kingdom committed themselves to adopt the missile, and production of nearly 2,000 missiles was completed in 1966. The Steering Committee was disbanded in June 1966 and an agreement made between the interested nations to co-ordinate logistic support.

M-72 Light Anti-Tank Weapon

In July 1963 the Council set up a NATO Steering Committee for the production of the M-72 US Light Anti-Tank Weapon. Canada, the

Netherlands and Norway undertook to adopt the missile and production, involving expenditure of more than $10 million, was completed in 1968.

Armaments Committee

In April 1958, the European countries submitted to a meeting of Defence Ministers proposals for specific items which might be produced jointly, as well as for some reorganization of structure and procedures. The terms of reference of the Defence Production Committee, which now became the Armaments Committee, were extended to permit it to deal with questions of applied research and development. This reflected the recognition that joint action must substantially precede the production stage.

In 1959, a new set of procedures for research, development and production of modern weapons and equipment was agreed. They provided for full co-operation at all stages between countries and between the military and technical sides of both national and international staffs. Designed to be flexible, the procedures could be brought into effect at any stage if a project already embarked upon by one country were selected as meeting a basic military requirement.

The following year, bodies known as Ad Hoc Mixed Working Groups, including military and civilian operational and technical representatives, were formed to seek projects suitable for co-operative effort. As a result, some new common production efforts were set on foot, including an anti-submarine torpedo, a multi-purpose fighter aircraft, two air-to-surface missiles and a light anti-tank weapon.

The need for change

Progress in defining common requirements and equipping NATO forces with modern weapons remained unsatisfactory. It came to be realized that what had been designed as a flexible set of procedures had become a rigid system. The NATO military authorities, in particular, found themselves in a false position in that they were approving NATO Basic Military Requirements (NBMRS) without having responsibility for developing and producing the resulting equipment, and often without adequate scientific and technical advice. In order to help overcome this last difficulty the Council created a Committee of Defence Research Directors. This was set up in early 1964 and began to undertake work in the area of applied research connected with new weapons which had nominally been the responsibility of the Armaments Committee. This brought new life to the research side but created some over-lapping between the armaments and science activities in NATO. Finally it became evident that the whole approach to co-operation needed changing and so in October 1965 an exploratory group was set up by the Council to examine the question thoroughly and propose new solutions. This group prepared a report setting out the principles on which co-operation should be based, the procedures which should be followed and the proposed structure for putting them into effect. This report, approved by the Council in May 1966, has become the standard work of reference on all matters concerning co-operation in research, development and production of military equipment.

New forms of co-operation

The new procedures embody a change in philosophy based on recognition of the fact that countries cannot be compelled to co-operate nor to observe rigid procedural rules. What is needed is to make co-operation as easy and as advantageous as possible. The mandatory aspects of the earlier system were abandoned. The NBMRS were abolished, and it was agreed that co-operative action could start on the basis of proposals from any country or from the NATO military authorities. If at least two countries express interest in a proposal, a Group can be formed to discuss it. Gradually those NATO countries who have no intention of participating in the project or making any commitments drop out. The remainder draw up characteristics and plan the development and production of the equipment, with timing and cost estimates. When they have completed a plan and are ready to make final commitments to proceed, they present a report asking for the project to be designated as a NATO project. From that point on, participating countries make their own arrangements, the only conditions being that they must make an annual report to NATO and that, if other countries wish to join at a later stage, they can do so on reasonable equitable conditions. The body managing the project is called a NATO Project Steering Committee and takes whatever form the participants wish. Projects can start at any point in the research, development and production process but for completely new items of equipment it is preferable to begin as early as possible in the research stage before countries have taken firm decisions on them.

Conference of National Armaments Directors (CNAD)

A certain number of organizational changes were made by the Council to operate the new procedures. The Armaments Committee was disbanded. Four main bodies responsible for promoting co-operation were created by transforming the three Service Advisory Groups into Service Armaments Groups and changing the Committee of Defence Research Directors into the Defence Research Group. A new high-level body entitled the Conference of National Armaments Directors was established to act under the authority of the Council. A new and more economical subsidiary structure was set up, in which very few of the old Ad Hoc Working

140

Groups and other bodies were retained, although their most important unfinished tasks were transferred to the new structure.

This organization under the Conference of National Armaments Directors not only encourages and assists the countries to join together in equipment and research projects, but also provides the means for exchanges of information on operational concepts, national equipment programmes and appropriate technical and logistic matters where co-operation can benefit NATO and the nations, even if no particular project as such is likely to materialize. It further encourages discussions on longer-term research activities with a view to providing guidance on the possibility of meeting future military needs through the application of advanced technology or new scientific discoveries.

The initial experience of the new procedures and organization was most encouraging. There was a new air of freedom and a greater readiness to bring forward proposals for projects and to discuss ways and means of co-operating. The fact that there no longer had to be NATO-wide agreement on requirements helped to encourage proposals as it was realized that if only two countries co-operated to produce a weapon for their forces, this was better than nothing in the hope that one day all countries would agree to develop and produce completely standard items of equipment. In the first years, many of the proposals concerned items which were already at a late stage of development in one country or another. However, once these items had been thoroughly examined, the tendency was to look further ahead, and this encouraged countries to exchange ideas and intentions. This has been and is extremely valuable in helping to harmonize national concepts and practices in a variety of fields, thus making a broader contribution to the cohesion of the Alliance than is revealed by merely totalling up the projects which had so far received the designation 'NATO Project' under the new procedures. The list of these is already impressive in its scope and variety and is made up as follows:

– NATO JAGUAR Tactical and Training Aircraft
– NATO SEASPARROW Point Defence Ship Missile System
– NATO AZORES Fixed Acoustic Range
– NATO FH-70 Towed Howitzer
– NATO SP70 Self-Propelled Howitzer
– NATO Acoustic Communication with Submarines
– NATO PUMA, GAZELLE and LYNX Helicopters
– NATO Multi-Rôle Combat Aircraft
– NATO Combat Vehicle Reconnaissance (Tracked)
– NATO Mark 20 RH202 Rapid-Fire Gun and Anti-Aircraft Field Mount HS 669N

141

- NATO MILAN Anti-Armour System
- NATO FORACS (NATO Naval Forces Sensor & Weapon Accuracy Check Sites in Europe)
- NATO Frigate for the 1970s
- NATO Patrol Boat Hydrofoil (Guided Missile)

The former NATO Project, the NATO USD-501 Surveillance System has passed into the production phase, as a result of the successful co-operation between the participating nations.

In the case of the NATO Multi-Rôle Combat Aircraft Project, the intergovernmental body, which has been set up to manage it, was established by the North Atlantic Council in September 1969 as a NATO Production and Logistics Organization under the title of NATO Multi-Rôle Combat Aircraft Development and Production Management Organization (NAMMO). In addition there is the NATO Atlantic Maritime Patrol Project which, as described earlier, was set up before the new procedures and provided a useful model for later projects.

Redirection of effort

Despite these successes it began to become evident by the end of 1971 that although the Conference of National Armaments Directors (CNAD) and its subsidiary bodies provided an excellent basis for more co-operation in the research, development and production of weapon systems and equipment, nations were not taking sufficient advantage of it. Most of the projects undertaken, excellent though they were, concerned very few nations and did not add greatly to standardization and interoperability, nor meet the most pressing needs of the Alliance defence as a whole. In 1972 therefore the CNAD began to redirect its efforts so as to focus its attention on particular problems of major concern to the Alliance. Priority items for co-operation were identified, and examined in depth with a view to preparing specific proposals for multi-national collaboration. When appropriate, reports were made to Defence Ministers in order to elicit their support. This method is beginning to bear fruit so that in certain major areas even if no single standard NATO equipment is developed and produced, at least the wide proliferation of systems with its waste of scarce resources and inhibiting effect on military flexibility will be reduced.

Following on this redirection of efforts and spurred by the need to obtain a more cost effective use of resources in a period of economic stringency, the whole issue of standardization in its broadest sense is being given a new emphasis. The CNAD is working much more closely with the NATO Military Authorities to identify where the most pressing needs are for interoperability, while the economic aspects of collaboration are being investigated. In the light of the need for credible conventional forces as an integral part of the flexible response policy, the objective is to provide adequate defence at a cost which member nations can support.

One area of major importance in achieving this cut is that of defence industry. Early on in its existence the CNAD found that insufficient account had been taken of the resources or possible contributions of industry to the common effort. Arrangements were therefore made to convene an Experimental Consultative Conference of Industrialists (ECCI) to examine a general approach to the problems existing in the industry/government relationship and advise on the extent to which industry could help to solve some of these and other problems. The Conference took place at the NATO Headquarters in Brussels in May 1968 and was attended by more than 50 leading industrialists from all NATO countries except Iceland and Luxembourg, as well as representatives from governments and international civilian and military staffs. A number of recommendations were prepared, one of which concerned the institution of a permanent consultative body of senior industrialists to assist and advise the CNAD.

NATO Industrial Advisory Group (NIAG)

In June 1968, the CNAD established the NATO Industrial Advisory Group (NIAG); this decision was subsequently endorsed by the North Atlantic Council in October 1968. The objectives of the NIAG are to provide a forum for free exchange of views on the various industrial aspects of NATO armaments questions, to foster a deeper feeling of international involvement in research, development and production, to seek closer co-operation amongst the industries of member countries, and to encourage the timely and efficient exchange of information between member governments and their defence industries.

In view of the complete novelty of NIAG as an institution, there was no precedent to follow and principles and procedures had to be worked out in order to enable it to start its practical work on a suitable basis. For example, the members of NIAG, who are either representatives of industrial groups or members of industrial firms, recognized that a conflict of interest could arise during their discussions on defence projects which would give an insight into the activities or interests of industries in particular countries. It was agreed that a free exchange of ideas could only take place if they had the absolute certainty that nothing said during their discussions could be used against them under existing conditions of competition, and a moral code on this basis was unanimously adopted. Similarly, it was necessary to lay down clearly that NIAG delegations represented their national industries as a whole and not individual firms; furthermore, a national NIAG delegation does not necessarily represent the view of its government.

However, the practice of close liaison between NIAG representatives and their appropriate government departments is growing up.

One of the most difficult procedural problems which had to be settled was that of communication of classified information between NIAG and the CNAD and its subordinate bodies. Arrangements have been made for this to be done within the terms of the NATO security regulations, and procedures have been agreed for the two-way exchange of various types of information. In addition to the organization of this method of work, the NIAG has undertaken discussion on a number of general items which present common problems to both industry and government, and has started work on the study of particular equipment projects or requirements which have been passed to it for advice.

The establishment of such a group of industrialists was greeted with some initial hesitation and even suspicion in some quarters, but the ability and enthusiasm with which it has set about its work has already demonstrated the value of this initiative, and the work which has already been accomplished testifies that NIAG has become a powerful aid in NATO's co-operative equipment endeavours.

Since its inception NIAG, at the request of the CNAD, has organized a dozen technical sub-groups to make prefeasibility studies in particular areas of armaments or offered special industrial management advice on procedures to be followed in international co-operation in industry with the NATO governments. The range of subjects has been very wide and include, among others, Advanced Approach and Landing Systems, Battlefield Surveillance, Compatibility of Command and Control Systems, certain Radar problems, the broad subject of Air Defence and Standardization of protective clauses in Industrial Property Rights.

The most recent prefeasibility study is on a Second Generation Anti-Ship Missile (Sub-Group 8). This was requested urgently by the NATO Naval Armaments Group, based upon their agreed outline operational objective. The study was completed on June 26, 1975, just six months after it began. It is hoped (and expected) that this kind of close co-operation between government groups and the NIAG will become a continuing pattern.

International logistics

The equipping of forces is only part of the story. There is then the maintenance and supplying of them to be considered. In the early days of the Alliance countries were content to maintain and supply their own national forces assigned to NATO without any centralized system. Experience, especially with large-scale military exercises and the growing cost and complexity of equipment, has since caused certain countries to have second thoughts to the extent of wishing to discuss common

144

problems and, in certain areas, to co-operate actively. For reasons both of geography and command structure, future progress in common logistics is likely to take on a regional aspect.

NATO Pipeline System

This has, in fact, already occurred in one case, in that the supply of fuel in the field through the NATO Pipeline System is regionally based. Under the NATO Common Infrastructure Programme (see page 157) networks have been constructed in six regions. The largest of these is in Central Europe where some 3,400 miles (5,400 kilometres) of pipelines have been laid in five countries. It is operated and maintained by an integrated multi-national organization which is described below. The next largest network is in Turkey where there are two separate lines, one in the East and the other in the West of the country. There are networks in Greece, Italy, Denmark (the Jutland system which reaches into North Germany) and Norway. Operation and maintenance of these systems are undertaken by national pipeline organizations acting in consultation with the NATO Military authorities. The host nations are the normal users but other NATO nations can use the systems by arrangement.

In July 1956 the Council set up the NATO Pipeline Committee to act on its behalf, in full consultation with the NATO military authorities and other compctent bodies, on all matters connected with the control, operation and maintenance of the NATO pipeline system. One of the main problems of the Committee is to obtain sufficient use of the system in peacetime to maintain it at the desired state of readiness for emergency or wartime operation. With this in view, the Council agreed, under certain safeguards, to permit limited use of the system for other than NATO military purposes. Some movements of fuel have been undertaken on this basis. In addition products other than the jet fuel and motor spirit for which the system was originally designed can now be moved through it. In particular, with the increasing use of diesel motors in military vehicles, diesel fuel is now not only transported but stored in the System.

The System in Central Europe lies in the territories of Belgium, France, the Federal Republic of Germany, Luxembourg and the Netherlands. In addition, Canada, the United Kingdom and the United States make use of it. It is operated by seven national pipeline divisions and a central co-ordinating and controlling body, the Central Europe Operating Agency (CEOA).

Pipeline Agency

The Agency is a civilian organization under the direction of a general manager who is responsible jointly to two Central European bodies – one military, the Central Europe Pipeline Office, and one political and

financial, the Central Europe Pipeline Policy Committee. The network in
Central Europe has been particularly successful in obtaining revenue from
both military use and the transport of products for civilian companies.
This has enabled it to cover a high proportion of its operating costs in
recent years. To illustrate the flexibility of the system, during one very
hard winter, fresh water was passed through a section of line in the
Netherlands for a few days to assist in an emergency, while heating oil has
been transported on several occasions and there is a regular movement of
crude oil through a section of line in France.

Much of the other co-operative action now being undertaken in
logistics has arisen out of production problems, and it is evident that the
more countries adopt common items of new equipment or even
standardized components, the easier it will be to introduce some form of
common logistic support. Progress in this area is also sought through
rationalization and specialization of defence tasks among the Allied
countries. The need for more coherence in logistics is now being
recognized in view of the improvement it can bring to the defensive
capability of the Alliance and the economies which can be obtained in the
use of resources. Some of the ground work has already been done in
certain directions as the following paragraphs demonstrate.

NATO Codification system

An important factor in logistics management for national armed forces is
the supply problem. Huge stocks with millions of individual items
necessitate a system of handling that is fast, flexible and precise. The NATO
Codification System provides for a uniform method of supply classification
and item identification and is thus an ideal tool for data management. It
also helps inventory managers in the simplification of supply and
procurement procedures and forms a basis for standardization. A particular
asset is the use of one number for one item in NATO projects, regardless of
origin, which is a sine qua non for efficient cross-servicing. The system has
resulted in a reduction in items and stocks; a decrease in management costs
and an improved determination of assets and measures to be taken.

Use of the system is now spreading to the civilian departments of
governments, to international organizations' and to some of the non-NATO
nations. As it is ideally suited to mechanization, its use in the data
management fields other than item identification, which is already
computerized, is under intensive study by many authorities.

The system is managed by a NATO group composed of Directors of
National Codification Agencies and supported by a small NATO
Secretariat. This group, which comes under the Conference of National
Armaments Directors, operates Panels which cover all codification
procedures and methods, and Sub-Groups which supervise the

co-ordination of codification of all joint NATO projects. There are at present four Panels and ten Sub-Groups supporting the day-to-day operations of the 13 national codification bureaux of the NATO nations.

Quality assurance

As soon as NATO countries and Agencies started to implement equipment programmes in which the manufacture of various components was entrusted to industries of different countries, it became clear that requirements for uniform and adequate quality standards could not be satisfactorily met unless the participants in co-operative projects followed common rules and procedures. The task of drawing these up was given to the Group of National Directors for Quality Assurance specially established for this purpose. As a result of its work the basic requirements of the NATO Quality Assurance doctrine and policy have been established and published as NATO Allied Quality Assurance Publications (AQAPs).

The Group is continuing its work in developing quality assurance requirements in those areas related to procurement which most affect the attainment of quality targets: the preparation of technical specifications and technical documentation for the operation, control, maintenance and repair of equipment and the development of the reliability assurance policy. It is to be expected that the scope and impact of NATO quality assurance policy will continue to grow both within the Alliance and beyond, as is the case with Codification.

Safety aspects of storage and transport of ammunition and explosives

A more specialized logistic activity in which considerable success has been achieved on a NATO-wide basis is that of safety aspects of storage and transportation of Ammunition and Explosives. A Group of Experts has provided a comprehensive manual on safety principles for storage, which is the most authoritative work in existence on this important subject. The same group is developing similar publications to cover safety in the various means of transporting explosive material.

NATO Maintenance and Supply Organization (NAMSO)

The problem of supplying spare parts for all equipment of North American origin led the United States in 1957 to propose an entirely new approach – the development of an effective regional system for logistic support which entailed the progressive delegation to a central organization of the functions previously performed by the countries concerned.

In April 1958, the North Atlantic Council approved the establishment of a central organization entitled the NATO Maintenance Supply Services System (NMSSS) which later became known in 1964 as the NATO Maintenance and Supply Organization (NAMSO), being one of the series of

NATO Production and Logistics Organizations. This organization consists of a Board of Directors, subsidiary committees, and an operating element known as the NATO Maintenance and Supply Agency (NAMSA). The Board, which is composed of one member from each participating country (all NATO countries except Iceland), decides on financial matters and establishes policy.

The mission of NAMSO consists mainly in facilitating the supply of spare parts and the provision of maintenance and repair facilities necessary for the support of various weapons systems in the inventories of NATO nations. At the discretion of the Board of Directors, it also embraces the provision of clearly specified and already defined end-items for modern and conventional weapons systems and the assumption of residual responsibilities of other NATO Production and Logistics Organizations, both during and after their liquidation. The objectives of this mission is maximum effectiveness of logistic support to NATO armed forces in both peace and war at minimum cost to NATO nations, both individually and collectively.

The Headquarters of the Agency was established in Paris, mainly as a procurement activity. The development of NAMSO was expanded in March 1960 when the NATO Supply Centre (NSC) was created at Châteauroux, in France, as the first Operational Centre under NAMSA Headquarters' control.

In 1965, a second Operational Centre was activated for the procurement of spare parts for the F 104 aircraft: namely the F 104 Koblenz Procurement Centre (KPC) at Koblenz, in Germany.

Early in 1968, NAMSA Headquarters and the NSC were transferred from Paris and Châteauroux to the Grand-Duchy of Luxembourg.

A third Operational Centre was activated in 1972. In order to increase the efficiency of the support services provided to NATO countries on the Southern Flank, the NAMSA Southern Depot was established at Taranto, in Italy.

Weapons and materiel currently supported by NAMSA are seven missile systems, NIKE, HONEST JOHN, SIDEWINDER, BULLPUP, HAWK, LANCE, TOW, the F 104 aircraft, the FORWARD SCATTER and SATELLITE Communication Stations, NADGE Air Defence System (including EARLY WARNING), NAMFI (NATO Missile Firing Installation), MARK 37/44 Torpedoes and miscellaneous conventional equipment.

NAMSA normally stocks some 81,000 line items worth $60 million. In addition to providing spare parts from stock, however, NAMSA also fills requisitions on a brokerage basis, and by multinational support between nations (mutual emergency support and routine redistribution). Other supply functions performed relate to codification and item identification, preparation of documentation, etc.

In-house maintenance services provided by NAMSA's own technicians and facilities include the following tasks:

Calibration by special calibration vans of the various NATO nations' test equipment used at missile sites, radar and communication stations; repair and recertification of calibration equipment in NAMSA Calibration laboratory; depot level repair and testing of electronic optical equipment for LANCE and TOW missile systems; repair of FORWARD SCATTER communication equipment and in-storage maintenance of material stocked in NAMSA's depots.

Contractual maintenance services are provided via NAMSA from industry and display such features as international competitive bidding, pre-award surveys (to assess technical/financial capabilities of bidding contractors), economic multi-year contracts, consolidation of customer requirements, and quality assurance by governmental authorities.

Technical support provided by NAMSA embraces both technical assistance and configuration management, and is a centralized logistic support field growing in importance. Technical assistance covers on-site assistance, the preparation of technical specifications for maintenance contracts, the monitoring of surveillance programmes, etc. Configuration management covers failure data collection and analysis, technical studies, modification proposals, status accounting and maintenance and updating of technical documentation.

NAMSA does not perform all the above tasks for all the weapons systems and equipment it supports. In consultation with NAMSA, the user countries select those tasks which, on cost-effective grounds, can be shown to be best performed centrally.

For all weapons systems which in the future will be held in common by several nations, NAMSA should be considered as *the* instrument established by the NATO Council to provide centralized supply and maintenance support services most economically and efficiently for the benefit of the entire NATO Community.

NATO Common Infrastructure
Definition

Infrastructure in the NATO context means those fixed installations which are necessary for the deployment and operation of the armed forces, e.g. airfields, signals and telecommunications installations, military head-quarters, fuel pipelines and storage, radar warning and navigational aid stations, port installations, missile installations, etc. Because of the requirements of modern weapons, certain mobile installations, closely associated with the fixed installations referred to above, are classed as an integral part of NATO infrastructure.

National infrastructure, that is installations set up solely for the use of national forces, is paid for out of national budgets. Installations set up at the request of NATO international Commanders for the training of international forces in peacetime and for their operational use in wartime rank as 'common infrastructure'. Such installations are financed collectively by member governments and may be used by each one of them, but acquisition of sites and provision of certain local utilities remain a national responsibility.

Background

Western Union programme

The need for common infrastructure first became apparent in 1950 after the Western Union had been formed under the Brussels Treaty. At that time the forces available were limited and an infrastructure programme of only some £32 million was envisaged. Most of the installations, consisting of airfields and signals networks, were to be set up in France and the Netherlands for the use of the five Brussels Treaty Powers – the United Kingdom, France, Belgium, Luxembourg and the Netherlands. These powers agreed to share the cost of the programme which, when it was inherited by NATO, came to be known as Slice I.

NATO programmes

This principle of cost-sharing in common was adopted by NATO for the following slice which, although it was the first slice to be financed by NATO, was called the 'Second Slice', and for the subsequent programmes.

Up to and including Slice IV, the NATO military authorities submitted annual infrastructure programmes to the Council for approval, and a cost-sharing formula had to be devised for each.

Then, to avoid over-frequent discussions on cost-sharing, the Council requested the submission of rough cost estimates and a general outline of programmes designed to cover several years.

A single cost-sharing formula is applied throughout the duration of these longer-term programmes, although the military authorities continue to submit to the Council detailed programmes and estimates for each annual Slice. The first of the longer-term programmes was drawn up for the three years 1954 to 1956 (Slices V to VII), the second for four years 1957 to 1960 (Slices VIIb[1] to XI).

---

1. Slice VIIb was devoted entirely to works to be carried out in the Federal Republic of Germany which had just joined the Alliance. The Federal Republic has financed 50% of this slice.

In May 1960, the Council agreed on a single cost-sharing formula for Slices II to VII (1951–56) to replace the four formulae previously applied to these Slices. In July 1960, a third programme was approved for the years 1961–64 (Slices XII to XV).

Finally, at the beginning of 1966, the member countries agreed to finance a five-year programme totalling £228 million for the years 1965–69 and agreed on a cost-sharing formula as set out in Table II (page 153). On September 7, 1966, the French Permanent Representative told the Council that his country would not in future take part in either planning or financing the common infrastructure programmes. With respect to the already agreed Slices – up to and including Slice XVII – France would only maintain her participation in respect to those individual projects for which funds had already been authorized. She would withdraw completely from projects in those Slices for which funds had not yet been authorized.

France, however, decided to continue to participate in the NADGE programme (NATO air defence ground environment), which constituted a special case, as well as in certain alert and long-range detection installations, under special agreements for co-operation in these fields.

As a result of the French decision, the programme for Slices XVI–XX had to be reduced by almost the whole of France's share which had originally stood at £30 million.

In February 1970 the Defence Planning Committee approved a new Five Year Plan amounting to IAU 250,000,000[1] for the period 1970–74 (Slices XXI to XXV).

In December 1973, the Defence Planning Committee agreed to an additional amount of IAU 55,000,000 being provided for the financing of Slice XXV, since the funds previously approved were not sufficient to cover the needs beyond the first four slices of this five-year programme.

In December 1974, a new programme of IAU 400 million was envisaged to cover the needs for the period 1975–79. The cost-sharing breakdown has not yet been finally decided at the time of writing. As of now, it is more or less certain that this amount will not be sufficient to cover all the essential needs.

The total cost of NATO Common Infrastructure from 1951 up to date, including the first Slice planned by Western Union and projects in Germany before the latter became a member of NATO is approximately IAU 2,350,000,000 (European Defence Improvement Programme included) (see Chart on page 158).

---

1. IAU = Infrastructure accounting unit used as base for the conversion of different currencies. (Note: 1 IAU = £1 at the rate prevailing before the 1967 revaluation.)

Cost-sharing formulae

Since the 'common installations' can be used by the forces of each member country of the Alliance, the country on whose territory installations are set up (the 'host country') cannot and should not bear alone the cost of these installations. Furthermore, for geographical and strategic reasons, certain member countries are required to act as host to a greater number of installations than others. It would be unfair to impose too heavy a financial burden on them. Contributions from the other countries, some of which may be users of the infrastructure installations, therefore represent the only fair way of paying for these projects. However, the host countries still have to bear a fairly high proportion of the expenditures, including purchasing the land, providing public utilities, etc.

The common financing of the installations is worked out on the basis of a cost-sharing formula drawn up by NATO and agreed by all. This is based on three essential criteria: the contributive capacity of the member countries, the advantage accruing to the user country or countries and the economic benefit to the host country. The contributive capacity of member countries is calculated on the basis of the national product, which is the best available indication of the wealth of a country and of its capacity to pay. The contribution of the user country is proportionate to the extent to which its forces will employ the installations in question. In many cases, the economic benefits to the host country are by no means negligible: influx of foreign exchange, employment for local manpower, improvements to the local transport system, arrangements for facilities (pipelines, telecommunications, etc.) which will subsequently strengthen the host country's general economy.

However, the economic benefit to the host country is counterbalanced by the fact that the host country is obliged to bear expenditure which is not eligible for common financing such as purchases of land and the provision of public utilities.

The following tables show how the cost-sharing has been broken down between the different member countries in the different groups of slices which have been approved at the time of writing.

NATO neither holds nor administers funds allocated to infrastructure. The member countries enter into mutual financial commitments and pay their contributions in advance for each stage of construction, as called for by the host country. Actual payments are made by the host country, using contributions from the other member countries, to which it adds its own. A record is kept of all these transactions by the NATO Secretariat, which keeps track of the account situation of each host country on the basis of advance contributions paid and actual expenditures reported.

The cost-sharing formulas agreed by the member countries for Slices

Infrastructure cost-sharing formula

I. SLICES I TO XV

Country	Slice I	Slices II to VIIa	Slices VIII to XI	Slices XII to XV
	Cost-sharing approved in 1950 (Brussels Treaty Powers)	Cost-sharing approved in June 1960 (Paris)[1]	Cost-sharing approved in February 1957 (Paris)[2]	Cost-sharing approved in February 1961 (Paris)
	%	%	%	%
Belgium	13.18	5.462	4.39	4.24
Canada	—	6.021	6.15	5.15
Denmark	—	2.767	2.63	2.87
France	45.46	15.041	11.87	12.00
Germany	—	—	13.72	20.00
Greece	—	0.750	0.87	0.67
Italy	—	5.681	5.61	5.97
Luxembourg	0.45	0.155	0.17	0.17
Netherlands	13.64	3.889	3.51	3.83
Norway		2.280	2.19	2.37
Portugal	—	0.146	0.28	0.28
Turkey	—	1.371	1.75	1.10
United Kingdom	27.27	12.758	9.88	10.50
United States	—	43.679	36.98	30.85

1. This formula replaces the shares previously applied in Slices II, III, IVa and IVb–VIIa.
2. The expenses up to 50% of cost in Slice VIIb (entirely devoted to Germany) are completely paid by Germany.

II. SLICES XVI TO XX
(in thousands of £s (old rate))

Country	Total
Belgium	10.500
Canada	12.500
Denmark	7.000
France	30.000[1]
Germany	49.850
Greece	1.500
Italy	15.000
Luxembourg	400
Netherlands	9.650
Norway	5.900
Portugal	700
Turkey	2.500
United Kingdom	23.750
United States	58.750

III. SLICES XXI TO XXV
(Programme of IAU 305 million)

Country	%
Belgium	5.3031
Canada	6.3132
Denmark	3.5354
Germany	25.1767
Greece	0.7576
Italy	7.5757
Luxembourg	0.2020
Netherlands	4.8738
Norway	2.9798
Portugal	0.3535
Turkey	1.2626
United Kingdom	11.9950
United States	29.6716
	100.0000

1. This amount is the initial amount. It was revised by decision of September 7, 1966.

I–XV are shown in Table I. In Table II the contributions by countries for Slices XVI to XX are shown not in percentages but in fixed sums agreed by the nations. It should be noted that, following the decision taken by France on September 7, 1966, her initial contribution to Slices XVI to XX of IAU 30 million has actually been less than IAU 1 million. Table III shows the coefficients of the cost-sharing formula agreed in February 1970. The revised ceiling amounts to IAU 305,000,000. In addition to this amount, due to lack of funds to cover the necessary military requirements for this period, certain European nations have agreed to the financing of an additional programme of IAU 150 million (European Defence Improvement Programme (EDIP), which was originally intended to finance the Aircraft Survival Measures programme (ASM) and the first phase of the NATO Integrated Communications System (NICS). In view of the extent of the survival programme and its cost, it has only been possible to cover this latter programme by the EDIP programme.

Programme formulation

The formulation of programmes is initially and principally the responsibility of the military authorities. Once a long-term programme proposed by the NATO military authorities has been accepted by the Council or the Defence Planning Committee, then the most urgent work must be started as soon as possible in the different subordinate command areas.

The first step in formulating a yearly programme, or slice, is for the subordinate commands to inform their Supreme Commander of infrastructure work needed in their respective assigned areas. The Supreme Commanders co-ordinate these requests, after ensuring that the proposed installations are, on the one hand, indispensable to the support of forces and, on the other, that they can be used in common or have a common interest.

Examination of proposals

After a general examination carried out in co-operation with experts from all countries, the Supreme Commanders recommend a proposed infrastructure slice for the years in question. The financial and technical aspects of this proposal are critically examined by the Infrastructure Committee with the assistance of the International Staff, before the Slice is sent to the Council (or the Defence Planning Committee) for approval.

Simultaneously the proposed programme is examined by the Military Committee which, in its turn, makes recommendations to the Council or the Defence Planning Committee from the military point of view.

Once an infrastructure slice has been approved by the Council or the Defence Planning Committee, the execution phase begins. The entire responsibility for implementation of individual projects is assumed by the host country.

The host country must decide, in consultation with the NATO military authorities, upon sites for the works to be carried out. It must acquire the necessary land at its own expense and draw up a plan which is then sent to the relevant Supreme Commander for approval.

After the plan has been approved, the host country authorities prepare a detailed estimate of construction costs which must be approved by the NATO Infrastructure Payments and Progress Committee before any funds can be committed. The host government then invites bids for the contract from firms of participating member countries and notifies national delegations of the opening and closing bid dates.

Progress of works

Once a contractor has been selected and work is under way, experts of the International Staff as well as representatives of the Supreme Commanders and of the user country, or countries, make regular inspection visits to the site and report on progress of work.

The rules adopted in order to ensure an effective control of common infrastructure expenditure have made a remarkable contribution to the solution of new international problems.

Expenditure authority for all approved projects is in the hands of the Infrastructure Payments and Progress Committee (made up of members of the delegations), which has technical assistance from experts on the International Staff. The Committee's terms of reference include close examination of the estimates submitted and, where necessary, suggesting alternative and more economical methods of carrying out the work to the required specifications. These estimates are called 'requests for authorization to commit funds' and they constitute the basis for the amount due to host countries. The Infrastructure Payments and Progress Committee also examines the financial reports submitted by host countries carrying out the works and each quarter endorses the amount of contributions due to host countries by the other participating countries.

International competitive bidding

A system of international competitive bidding has also been introduced, which is restricted to the member countries which participate in the financing of the project and ensures that the work is entrusted to the firm charging the lowest price.

Upon completion, a project is inspected by a team consisting of representatives of the host country, user country (in many cases not the host country) and the military authorities. The team, which is chaired by a member of the International Staff, inspects all the projects and draws up a

155

report for the Infrastructure Payments and Progress Committee recommending that the project be accepted by NATO.

Both throughout execution and on completion of the works, an International Board of Auditors, entirely unconnected with the host countries and responsible only to the Council, examines the financial statements made out by host countries, thus ensuring the correctness of expenditures charged to NATO common funds.

Main elements of the Infrastructure Programme

Airfields

In 1951, General Eisenhower, the first Supreme Allied Commander Europe, had at his disposal only a negligible number of airfields. Consequently for many years half of the infrastructure programme was directly devoted to airfields. At the present time 220 NATO airfields are operational or could be used by the NATO forces in an emergency.

A new airfield costs between 2 and 4 million IAU, depending on geographical situation and installations. But it has been possible in many cases to use existing airfields, modifying them as necessary. The total expenditure on airfields amounts to about IAU 473 million. All comply with standards laid down by the NATO military authorities, are suitable for different types of aircraft, and include such essential installations as fuel storage facilities for jet and other aircraft and electronic devices which permit aircraft to operate night and day in all weather. The EDIP programme, devoted to the survival of the air forces, has been in operation since 1972–73 and has enabled 70% of aircraft at each base to be hardened.

As airfields are completed, communications must be established for full co-ordination between them and the different allied fighter commands.

Communications

At present the signals networks represent an investment of more than IAU 326 million. It is estimated that about 31,000 miles (50,000 kilometres) of landlines, radio links and submarine cables will have been built to supplement existing civilian networks. However, in spite of the considerable number of available circuits, the military authorities were aware that the present system did not provide all the safety measures necessary in time of war, particularly as regards security and speed of transmission. NATO has therefore developed an integrated communications system referred to as NICS. This new communications system introduces the latest techniques, principally to enable the Supreme Command and the political authorities to be informed very rapidly of developments in wartime or of any other situation which may arise, whether it be a nuclear action or otherwise, and so enable them to take the necessary decisions.

Pipeline System

To avoid bottlenecks in the conventional methods of transporting fuel (rail and road tankers, barges, etc.) a vast oil pipeline system started in 1953 has now been completed. Pipelines are used to convey fuel from a number of Atlantic and Mediterranean ports to airfields. They can carry the petrol and diesel fuel required for military vehicles and diesel engines, as well as jet fuel. The NATO Pipeline System comprises about 6,300 miles (10,000 kilometres) of pipe and storage for about 70 million cubic feet (2 million cubic metres) of fuel.

The System is divided up on a regional basis. The major part is an integrated network situated in the Central Europe region, constituting the most complicated and extensive fully operational system of pipelines in the world. The remainder is composed of separate pipelines and associated storage in Denmark, Norway, Italy, Greece and Turkey. For both geographical and financial reasons, these are not interconnected, nor are they linked to the large Central European network. The organization of the operation and maintenance of the system in Central Europe is undertaken by a central co-ordinating and controlling body, the Central Europe Operating Agency (CEOA). For more details of the operation and organization of CEOA see page 145.

NADGE

By far the largest single defence project so far authorized by the Council is concerned with early warning of and response to hostile aircraft and missiles. The project is known as NADGE (NATO Air Defence Ground Environment). NADGE, though not financed and managed in the same manner as the earlier NATO Infrastructure Programmes, is a classic example of international co-operation in common defence.

Excluding Iceland but including France,[1] all countries of the Alliance have taken part in this project. It is now completed and provides the air defence system for the whole of NATO Europe.

This complex system, involving a large number of locating sites, consists primarily of radars, computers and electronic data transmission facilities. It supplements and modernizes air defence elements in nine European NATO countries, following a continuous North-South sweep that runs through Norway, Denmark, Germany, the Netherlands, Belgium, France, Italy, Greece and Turkey.

Besides these main categories of works, other important projects include naval installations, missile sites, etc. which are listed in the following table together with those already mentioned above.

---

1. France is integrated only to the point where reporting ends and the control of retaliatory devices begins.

The Infrastructure Programme (in millions of IAU)

A. SLICES II–XXIV

Airfields Number of airfields: 220	473
Signals Network Landlines, submarine cables, radio links and NICS projects Over 50,000 km. (31,000 miles)	326
Fuel Supply Systems Pipelines: about 10,000 km. 6,300 miles Storage: about 2 million cubic metres or 440 million Imperial gallons	233
Naval Facilities	125
Radar Warning Installations	67
Air Defence Ground Environment	115
Special Ammunition Sites	36
Missile Sites	118
Other Projects Including War Headquarters, training installations, radio navigational aids, etc.	189
	1,682

B. SLICE I–INFRASTRUCTURE IN GERMANY

(*Slices II to VI*) – *Slice XXV and programmes XXVI to XXX*: about	527
C. EDIP (EUROPEAN DEVELOPMENT IMPROVEMENT PROGRAMME)	150
Total	2,359

CHAPTER 11

Scientific co-operation[1]

NATO's role

The report of the Committee of Three, submitted to the Council in December 1956, stated that 'one area of special importance to the Atlantic Community is that of science and technology'. The Committee found that progress in this field 'is so crucial to the future of the Atlantic community that NATO members should ensure that every possibility of fruitful co-operation is examined'. Against the background of the more general need for individual member countries to adopt more positive scientific policies, the Committee of Three specifically pointed to the central and urgent problem of improving recruitment, training and utilization of scientists, engineers and technicians, and recommended that the Council as a first step convene a conference of one or two outstanding authorities of each country to give further advice with regards to NATO's role.

The Council adopted the recommendations and a Task Force on Scientific and Technical Co-operation was appointed in June 1957. The Task Force found that 'the future of the West is dependent to an ever-increasing degree on the rate at which science and technology advance'. While emphasizing that national efforts must continue to form the basis of any general action, the Task Force believed NATO had a constructive role to play. This lay in influencing member governments to carry out national programmes for the development of scientific and technical resources; organizing international activities with a view to economizing national resources and stimulating exchanges; and co-operating with other agencies active in the scientific field.

1. A more comprehensive account of scientific co-operation in NATO is given in the book 'NATO and Science. An Account of the Activities of the NATO Science Committee, 1958–1972', published by NATO Scientific Affairs Division.

159

The Task Force carried out its deliberations with an urgency which was emphasized by the launching of the first Soviet Sputnik in October 1957. The political and scientific implications of this event resulted in the Task Force Report being presented directly to the Heads of Government of the Alliance at their meeting in December 1957. The Heads of Government gave careful consideration to scientific co-operation and adopted two specific recommendations made by the Task Force. A Science Committee was established, composed of national delegates in a position to speak authoritatively on science policy. While the Committee was to develop its own programme in the light of circumstances, it was given the broad responsibility of advising the Council on how NATO could fulfil the role ascribed to it by the Task Force Report. The position of Science Adviser was created on the International Staff. This high-ranking official was to give impetus and direction to the work of the Committee as well as to act as the Secretary General's adviser on scientific questions. The work of the Science Committee rapidly increased in importance and it was not long before the Science Adviser was made Assistant Secretary General for Scientific Affairs, with a staff of scientists forming the Scientific Affairs Division of the International Staff. As the Division also became involved with environmental affairs with the establishment of the Committee on the Challenges of Modern Society,[1] the title was in 1973 changed to Assistant Secretary General for Scientific and Environmental Affairs.

The NATO Science Committee

The NATO Science Committee, which meets three times a year and is chaired by the Assistant Secretary General for Scientific and Environmental Affairs, is composed of national representatives qualified to speak authoritatively on science policy in the name of their respective governments. However, they have consistently insisted upon being considered not only government representatives, but also scientists in pursuit of knowledge. The Science Committee is charged with the overall mission of stimulating and strengthening science within the Atlantic Alliance; the Assistant Secretary General for Scientific and Environmental Affairs, with the aid of his small scientific staff, is responsible for implementing the committee's decisions, administering the various science programmes, and advising the Secretary General of NATO on scientific matters. He is also assisted in this work by groups or panels of individual experts, in the different areas of the science programmes. The willingness of these high-level scientists to put their professional expertise at the disposal of the Scientific Affairs Division, has been of inestimable value in arriving at, and maintaining, a high scientific standard in the NATO Science Programmes.

1. See Chapter 12.

The first meeting of the Science Committee was held in March 1958. During its first year of existence, the Committee examined carefully a large number of proposals for strengthening science in the NATO countries. Three main programmes were established which today remain the backbone of the NATO science activities. These are the Science Fellowships Programme, the Advanced Study Institutes Programme, and the Research Grants Programme. In addition, activities were initiated in several specialized scientific fields in need of special attention or of more immediate short-term interest to the Alliance. These programmes have never been static but have continuously been reassessed both in relation to other activities in NATO and in relation to the wider area of international and national support of science. Nevertheless, their predominant characteristics have remained an emphasis on co-operation and catalysis, and a capacity for rapid response to new developments. Each of the programmes has been consciously designed, and deliberately implemented to improve the exchange of information which is a key requisite for scientific progress.

In addition to the continuous review, the Science Committee, when it seems appropriate, appoints an Ad Hoc Working Group from amongst its members, to make a general review of its programmes. Such a Science Committee Working Group was appointed in 1971. The Working Group found that the Subsidiary Bodies had a great variety of functions, organization and procedure and that no attempt had been made to harmonize the arrangements. Thus, the Working Group first developed a logical framework in which all present and future programmes and the bodies dealing with them, could easily be located in a well-defined complete structure.

The new structure, approved by the Science Committee in May 1972, makes a clear distinction between two types of Subsidiary Bodies:

(i) *Standing Bodies* dealing with basic, programme-oriented activities, characterized by:

– a special type of action in all fields of science;

– indefinite duration.

(ii) *Temporary Bodies* dealing with subject-oriented activities, characterized by:

– all types of actions in a specific field of science;

– definite duration.

In implementing the various science programmes, the Science Committee has a budget which has risen from B.Fr. 57.5 million ($1.15 million) in 1959 to B.Fr. 200 million ($4 million) in 1964. In 1975 the budget is B.Fr. 273 million, shared between the various programmes as follows:

	Million B.F.
Science Fellowships	148.0
Advanced Study Institutes	55.0
Research Grants	36.0
Air-Sea Interaction	3.5
Eco-Sciences	5.0
Human Factors	4.0
Marine Sciences	4.0
Radiometeorology	2.0
Stress Corrosion Cracking	1.0
Systems Science	5.5
Programme Development	9.0

The NATO Science Programme

General

The NATO Science Programme is the only co-operative international effort embodying multilateral government support for advancing the frontiers of modern science through high-level basic research. This activity – in which scientists of both the advanced and the developing nations of the Alliance can and do participate on an equal basis – is of real benefit in strengthening science in all the member countries of NATO. It has shown itself to be an extremely useful vehicle for trans-Atlantic communication, and has perhaps been especially valuable in fostering intra-European co-operation where surprising insularity has been found.

The sheer number of people who have directly participated in these programmes, now totalling over 50,000 individuals of which some thousands come from countries outside the Alliance, including some hundreds from Eastern Europe, cannot but help to rebound both to the credit of NATO and to the strengthening of international scientific co-operation. These participants, members of the international scientific community, are engaged in professional work of immediate concern to the strength of their countries and also play an increasingly significant role in the decision-making élite of their countries. The ties engendered between them, brought out by the close co-operation implicit in the NATO pro-grammes, have undoubtedly endured and grown through the years, adding increased strength to the invisible links which hold our nations together in trust and understanding. Moreover, many tens of thousands of additional scientists have been served by the widely disseminated and highly respected publications which have carried the results achieved through the NATO programmes far beyond their immediate participants.

The NATO Science Fellowship Programme

The need for new scientists to be trained and established scientists to be given the opportunity to further and renew their specialized education and scientific techniques, was recognized by the NATO Heads of Government when in December 1957, they agreed that 'more should be done to increase the supply of trained men in many branches of science and technology'. A training period for young scientists, outside their own countries, is recognized as a normal and effective part of a scientific education. The possibilities for obtaining scholarships for such training were very limited in many countries, and the Science Committee therefore established the NATO Science Fellowships Programme as its first programme. The main purpose of this programme is to stimulate the member countries to enlarge the exchange of post-graduate and post-doctoral students of the pure and applied sciences, and thus help to increase the scientific strength of the NATO Alliance. The Science Committee exercises general supervision over the Programme, but the detailed administration is carried out in each country by a national agency; in many cases the same agency administers national fellowship schemes. The selection of fellows is based entirely on scientific merit and ability, but the criteria vary from one country to another. Some limit the awards to post-doctoral research workers, while others emphasize post-graduate training and research.

The NATO Science Fellowships Programme started in 1959 with a budget of $1 million. No fellowships programme on the same scale as this had previously been undertaken by an international organization. The Fellowships budget has now stabilized at some $3.5 million or 50–60% of the total Science Committee budget. Experience over the past decade has shown that the NATO Programme has favourably stimulated an active national fellowships programme of at least comparable magnitude in most member countries.

During the early 1960s as many as 1,000 Science Fellowships were awarded annually. As the amount of each stipend has increased owing to inflation and the rising standard of living in the member countries, the number of fellowships has now levelled off at about 600 per year. Since the programme started in 1959, well over 10,000 scientists have benefited from NATO Science Fellowships, enabling them to study overseas for periods of about one year or longer. Almost all of the NATO Science fellows now study in a country other than their own. The United States hosts about half of all the fellows, with the United Kingdom, France and Germany being other popular host countries. The fellows study a large number of subjects, with chemistry and physics as the most popular, while biology and engineering also attract a large percentage.

The Advanced Study Institutes Programme

A primary aim of the NATO Science Committee has been to further inter-national collaboration amongst scientists from member countries of the

163

Alliance. A major factor in furthering this goal has been the broad-based, wide-reaching and perhaps most outstandingly successful programme of the Science Committee, the Advanced Study Institutes Programme. Each year the Programme sponsors about 50 Institutes, with from 40 to 130 scientists attending each meeting. The purpose of the Programme is to contribute to the dissemination of advanced knowledge and the formation of contacts among scientists from different countries. A NATO Advanced Study Institute is primarily a high-level teaching activity at which a carefully defined subject is presented in a systematic and coherently structured programme. The subject is treated in considerable depth by lecturers eminent in their field and normally of international standing; the subject is presented to other scientists who will already have specialized in the field or possess an advanced general background. Advanced Study Institutes are aimed at audiences of approximately post-doctoral level; this does not exclude post-graduate students, and it may well include senior scientists of high qualifications and notable achievement in the subject of the Institute or in related fields.

Subjects treated at the Institutes vary as widely as the nationality of participants, and Institutes have been arranged in subjects from mathematics and astronomy through biological and medical topics, to embrace such areas as psychological measurement theory and language programming for computers. Of particular interest are the Institutes organized as an interdisciplinary meeting. In such cases the didactic aspect of the Institute consists of scientists specialized in one field teaching scientists highly qualified in a different area. The role of the lecturer and student will then be interchanged during the meeting as the theme of common interest is developed from the viewpoint of different sciences.

The Advanced Study Institutes Programme seeks to improve the general level of scientific competence throughout the NATO area and provides the extra benefit of high-level scientific exchange in interdisciplinary areas which are rarely found in university curricula. The programme is considered unique and is highly regarded in the scientific community. Since its inception in 1959, the Programme has supported over 650 Advanced Study Institutes in which over 35,000 scientists have participated, many of them leaders in their respective fields. Added benefits of the ASI are the proceedings of which about two-thirds appear in book form. These have been generally recognized as authoritative surveys of their subjects, and have reached a very large audience, both inside and outside the NATO Alliance. In 1973 an agreement was reached with four international publishers to publish a uniform NATO Advanced Study Institutes Proceedings Series, and about 30 books are now published in this series each year.

164

The Research Grants Programme

As a co-ordinator and catalyzer, the NATO Science Committee comes to the fore in its Research Grants Programme. Scientific progress depends upon research and although the Committee believes that research is mainly a matter for national funding, it established a Research Grants Programme in 1960 to stimulate collaboration between scientists in the member countries of the Alliance. The main purpose of the Research Grants Programme is to strengthen scientific research, both fundamental and applied, in universities and research institutions in NATO countries; specifically to promote the flow of ideas and sophistication of experimental and theoretical methods across the frontiers. Financial aid is thus given for research carried out jointly by scientists in institutions in different NATO countries which require funds to pool their expertise. A condition for support is that international collaboration must be essential to the success of the project and that NATO assistance will not duplicate the activities of other national or international organizations. In the past research grants were also given, when deemed necessary, to individual scientists without international collaboration, but this is no longer the case as national funds are now considered sufficient to finance projects of purely national interest. However, this general rule may be disregarded in quite special cases, when there is evidence that national funds are not available and that such a grant will act as a catalyzer of importance for the general build-up of a scientific field in a specific country.

There is no typical project financed by a NATO Research Grant. The projects vary greatly in areas of research, cost, character, and in the number of scientists and countries involved. Support ranges from a grant to pay for travel so that a scientist in one country may test a new theory or process on unique equipment in the laboratory of a scientist in another country, to a multinational research programme involving many scientists. Usually, however, two, three or more scientists in two or three countries will collaborate in a specific research programme. Since the NATO Research Grants Programme was started in 1960, research grants have been awarded for one to three years to over 700 different projects.

The Senior Scientists Programme

The Senior Scientists Programme is concerned with the planning, evaluation and awarding of NATO Science Lectureships, NATO Visiting Professorships and NATO Senior Fellowships. As part of the objective of the NATO Science Committee to further dissemination of information, it established in 1965 the Visiting Lectureships Programme. This programme permits a few outstanding scientists each year to give lectures in other NATO countries in new fields of science having important implications and in which monographs or other advanced texts have not yet

165

appeared. The Lecturers are selected by three members of the Science Committee, and the invitation is given by the Science Committee itself. Invitations are offered only to distinguished members of the scientific community to ensure the highest quality of the lectures. Although only a small number of Lectureships has been awarded, the programme has been well received and has proved to be useful. In 1966 the Science Committee included awards for Visiting Professorships and Senior Research Fellowships to be awarded to highly qualified senior scientists for studies not eligible under other parts of the NATO Science Programme. This Programme is operated with the overhead funds (7%) from the NATO Science Fellowship Programme.

The Science Committee Conference Programme

In this day of exploding science and technology, it is patently unreasonable to expect any individual, or any small group of individuals, no matter how clever or erudite they may be, to be able to assess adequately the many fields of science and engineering endeavour, and to serve as critics of what should be done and the priority which should be assigned to it. A scientific field can hardly be considered without contemplating also its interaction with other scientific and technological areas. When in addition we bear in mind the importance and difficulty of constructing a bridge between basic research and engineering technology and application, then the task of providing research guidelines truly becomes a staggering one. It has therefore been logical for the Science Committee, confronted with the responsibility of providing research guidelines and advice in many scientific fields, to seek techniques by which the capabilities of the Committee members may be supplemented by the efforts of the best collective talent available in restricted fields.

Such a technique is that of the Science Committee Conference, also known as the Research Evaluation Conference. The main purpose of these conferences is to identify particularly fruitful areas for future research and to make recommendations; these recommendations are directed both to those having a responsibility for selecting and supporting research programmes and to the Science Committee itself as a guide for allocation of human and material support. Unlike the other Science Committee Programmes, the Science Committee Conferences are both planned and administered by the Scientific Affairs Division itself. Conferences are held in areas which the Science Committee feel are in special need of development and are limited to one or two a year. The attendance is limited to about 60 experts and a few observers, so that it becomes a working conference, with all participants playing an active, contributory role. The reports from the conferences are published and are given a wide distribution. The programme was started in 1967 and the following Science Committee Conferences have been held:

  (i) High Temperature Materials (August 1967)

  (ii) Software Engineering (October 1968)

  (iii) Software Engineering Techniques (October 1969)

  (iv) The Theory of Stress Corrosion Cracking in Alloys (March–April 1971)

  (v) North Sea Science (November 1971)

  (vi) Catalysis (December 1972)

  (vii) Modelling of Marine Systems (June 1973)

  (viii) Technology of Effective Energy Utilization (October 1973)

  (ix) Eco-Toxicity of Heavy Metals and Organo-Halogen Compounds (May 1974)

  (x) Benthic Boundary Layer (November 1974)

The Oceanographic Research/Marine Sciences Programme

Oceanography is still largely an experimental science where the complexity of the research requires multitudes of ships and expensive equipment, and no one nation can hope to support the scale of exploration deemed necessary by modern science. Only by international collaboration and joint research can the required resources in ships, men and instrumentation be properly mastered. Considering that all but one of the NATO countries have at least part of their boundaries on the ocean, one can readily appreciate the basis for the work of NATO in oceanographic research. Already in 1959, the pressure of the cost of oceanographic research was being felt in Europe where each nation's investment was limited to one, or at best only a very few ocean-going vessels equipped for meaningful modern scientific research. With this in mind, and acting on the policy recommendation on co-operative research from the 'Three Wise Men', the NATO Science Committee in 1959 decided to set up a Sub-Committee on Oceanographic Research. The Sub-Committee was charged with recommending appropriate actions in the field of oceanographic research, preparing specific plans for co-operative activities among the Allies, and initiating direct action to aid joint research projects. It was also to serve as a forum for the establishment of informal co-operative actions between oceanographers as a supplement to existing arrangements, particularly for the areas and problems of great interest to NATO.

The Sub-Committee has been effective in acting as a catalytic centre for combined operations in which manpower and major equipment managed by national institutions, often with inputs from NATO's military oceanographic research centre at La Spezia, Italy, could be brought together for joint experiments at sea, and has planned and/or sponsored a multitude of joint operations at sea. In the field of oceanography, instrumentation has often been the limiting factor for effective research. The Sub-Committee has therefore concentrated much of its effort on making sure that the best instruments available in the member nations of the Alliance are made available for each project; and to encourage developments of new instruments and new methods of measurements, has recommended grants for research and development in this area, especially for current meters. The NATO support has led to the development and construction of fully automatic instruments for surveying the maritime areas of particular interest. Furthermore, buoys have been developed to take measurements over long periods. This very valuable work culminated in the construction of some high-performance measuring devices which will be improved with components used for ocean surveys. The Sub-Committee has also done much to encourage promising young scientists to enter the field of oceanography, and has made funds available for Research Associateships in national oceanographic laboratories. Such visits have aided in the planning of combined co-operative experiments at sea.

It should be noted that the results of the expeditions planned or sponsored by the Sub-Committee, in common with all the work of the Sub-Committee, have been widely disseminated. They are, moreover, the subject of systematic exchanges with thirty or so countries, including countries of the Middle East and Eastern Europe. It should be further noted that these results, which have made substantial contributions to the understanding of the seas, have been obtained by a relatively small catalytic support from NATO while the major part of the expenses has been borne by the different countries involved.

The Sub-Committee was terminated in 1973, and a new Special Programme Panel on Marine Sciences was started in 1974, with the objective to further the understanding of the mechanisms of physical, chemical and biological marine phenomena. During the first year of its existence the Panel has discussed a large number of subjects for possible support, has continued the support of research projects and taken preliminary steps to start a conference programme.

The Meteorology Programme

Meteorology is another important subject where co-operation between the Allied countries is desirable. Thus, the Science Committee in 1959 established an Ad Hoc Advisory Group in Meteorology, 'to review teaching and research facilities in meteorology in the universities of the member countries; to consider possible research projects suitable for collaboration under NATO auspices in the light of facilities available; to explore possibilities with national experts as may be desirable; and to recommend NATO financial support in appropriate cases'.

The Advisory Group has found that there existed relatively poor facilities in most countries for the education of professional meteorologists, and the improvement of these facilities has been a key aim of the Group. In 1965, two new schemes were launched. The first scheme concerns Research Associateship in Meteorology which are intended to enable young research workers to acquire experience in particular fields of research and to encourage recent science graduates to embark on a career in meteorological research, by working in laboratories in other countries. The other scheme concerns visiting lectureships in Meteorology which are intended to enable senior research scientists to present their recent work, with the object of encouraging the more rapid dissemination of knowledge of new advances in meteorological research, and allowing exchanges of information between research groups in different countries of the Alliance. The Advisory Group has also sponsored and initiated a number of Advanced Study Institutes and research projects devoted to meteorological research. The Meteorology Programme was terminated in 1972.

The Human Factors Programme

Human Factors is a short and convenient term for a group of sciences which primarily deal with the scientific study of the behaviour of man either as an individual or in a group. The application of such findings is relevant to most fields of human activity, including military operations, government, education, commerce and industry, and the management of scientific research. The field which may be described as 'behavioural science', includes psychology, applied psychology, social psychology, human engineering (ergonomics) and some aspects of social anthropology.

The Science Committee found at an early stage that there was a need for closer co-operation among the countries of the Alliance in this field, especially in the area of military psychology, and established the Advisory Group on Human Factors in 1960. A special feature of the behavioural sciences in the NATO Alliance was that the nations had very different levels of development in this area. In some countries, psychology was well established as a scientific discipline, in others the subject was only just beginning to emerge as a separate discipline and had hardly yet separated from its origins in philosophy and medicine. Applications could be non-existent and trained professional staff limited to a handful. The Advisory Group held strongly to the view that all countries would benefit from shared experience and that scientists in the less developed countries would be stimulated through meeting their colleagues in the more developed areas and discussing topics of common interest. Thus, at the

169

beginning, the Group was mostly active in organizing conferences and disseminating information.

In 1967, however, recognizing the growing importance of this scientific area and the need for a broader activity, the Advisory Group designed an expanding programme in Human Factors which was approved and put into operation. The programme had three main objectives: first, to assist in the exchange of information through the organization of conferences, symposia and visiting lectureships; secondly, to increase the provision of advanced instruction through the sponsorship of Advanced Study Institutes and the award of study visit grants; thirdly to support co-operative research. During the intervening years, in view of continued development of behavioural studies and the utilization of human factors in educational, social and defence aspects of the NATO nations, more sophisticated and intensive programmes have become possible. The various means available to the group have been used for imparting and exchanging professional and technical knowledge, for the development of guidebooks on human factor principles and for publication of current information. Another major task of the group over the last years has been to establish a common base of understanding and methodology in dealing with the problem areas in today's social and economic world; as human factors are now recognized as basic in dealing with the introduction, appraisal and utilization of new technology and social systems and their effects, as reflected in ecological and social imbalance. In 1973 the Advisory Group was changed to a Special Programme Panel, and the new Panel has continued in line with the work started by the Advisory Group.

The Operational Research/Systems Science Programme

Attention was drawn to operational research already at the second meeting of the Science Committee in July 1958, when the United States announced that it would pay the living costs and tuition fees for about thirty scientists from European NATO countries to attend an introductory course in the methods of operational research at the Massachusetts Institute of Technology. In August 1959, through the Military Weapons Development Team, the United States also supported a course on operational research techniques, given at Brussels by a team of American scientists.

The primary aim of the operational research programmes which were started in 1960 was to increase the capability of the operational research groups to generate interest in operational research by assisting in the spread of information and by increasing the background knowledge of the operational research scientists. The conference and symposia programme which started in 1960 has been continued and at present about four conferences or symposia are held each year. This programme has introduced a very useful forum where a large number of interesting topics, including many sophisticated yet practically useful papers given by world experts, has been brought to the attention of a large number of participants. The meetings have taken place in most European countries of the Alliance and have done much to stimulate national interest and to put individual operational research scientists in touch with their colleagues in other countries. Several thousand scientists have participated and a much larger audience has benefited from the publications from the conferences and symposia.

In 1968 the Study Visits and Visiting Expert programmes were introduced. Study Visit Awards are given to research scientists or post-graduate students in NATO countries who wish to make a short visit to a foreign country in order to receive information, advice or advanced instruction in some aspects of operational research or related disciplines. The Visiting Expert programme is designed to help develop new or newly-formed operational research groups which need advice or assistance from an expert in another country. It is envisaged that such an expert might devote several weeks at different times of the year, acting as a resident adviser, while maintaining contact with the group by correspondence during the intervening period.

Operational research is an exceedingly practical subject and an operational research team is successful only to the extent that the executives whom it serves are given sound advice. Accordingly, as the need for short courses decreased, the NATO consultant programme was dropped in 1962 in favour of a more extensive Graduate Apprenticeship Programme. Under this programme, young scientists may be assigned for 'on the job' training in operational research to a number of national or NATO centres. The normal assignment is for two years, subject to satisfactory completion of the first year, as this is the period of time considered necessary to give the average apprentice experience of adequate depth and variety. In 1973 this programme was changed to a Graduate Degree Apprenticeship Programme, a change in favour of more formal study at selected universities. About 100 apprentices have participated in this programme.

Since their inception, the programmes in operational research have done much to establish the day-to-day use of operational research in countries where it was formerly insufficiently developed. They have contributed to the speed up of information exchange in all countries and helped operational research scientists to meet and discuss problems of common interest. In 1973 the scientific area of this programme was enlarged to include the whole field of systems science under the guidance of a Special Programme Panel. The new Panel has modified the different programmes in line with the larger area of responsibility and also started new activities in their area of sponsored research and Advanced Research Institutes.

171

The Radiometeorology Programme

Important data on atmospheric structure can be derived from various techniques of radio and radar probing. These data include information on atmospheric turbulence, variation of humidity in space and time, and the structure of precipitation. On the other hand the atmospheric structure is not only important in weather forecasting, but is a decisive parameter for radio communication of certain wavelengths. In radio communication at frequencies above about 30 MHz and especially above 3 GHz, the understanding of the effect of scattering and absorption in the atmosphere is extremely important. Centimetric radar, beyond-the-horizon scatter links, microwave, terrestrial and space communication links are all greatly affected in various ways by meteorological factors. Thus radiometeorology is an important inter-disciplinary topic in relation to both radio communication and meteorological probing of the environment.

Radiometeorology is by its very nature particularly suited for international collaboration and in realization of this and the importance of the field as such, the Science Committee in 1961 established an Advisory Group on Radiometeorology. The Group was charged with the task of promoting radiometeorological research and development of interest to the member countries with particular emphasis on identification and stimulation of collaborative research projects, initiation of Advanced Study Institutes in the field, and to stimulate exchange of information between research groups. The Group has, accordingly, initiated, sponsored and supervised research projects and Advanced Study Institutes in the field of Radiometeorology. In 1973 the Group was changed to a Special Programme Panel, and the Panel has, in addition, to continue the work of the Group, prepared a list of organizations participating in Radiometeorological research, initiated the development of a high-resolution microwave refractometer cavity for use in turbulence studies and initiated and supported an Advanced Study Institute and a conference.

The Eco-Sciences Programme

Ecology – the study of the mutual relationship between life forms and their environment – was until recently only a little-noticed, esoteric discipline of chiefly academic interest. But in the last part of the 1960s, the perspective of the ecologists, who look at the 'ecosystem' as a whole, has been absorbed by other scientists, city planners, politicians and public administrators, and projected on to a world-wide plane.

The degradation of the environment is an international problem which requires multinational efforts for the winds, the oceans and many rivers which spread the pollutants, know no national boundaries. The world-wide ecological crisis has gradually been recognized by the governments and the general public. Public concern for the environmental issue has mounted more rapidly among the industrial nations, most of whom are members of NATO, than in other parts of the world. The NATO Science Committee has for some years sponsored Advanced Study Institutes and awarded Research Grants in the fields of eco-sciences. However, NATO's first major decision to take an active part in combatting environmental problems came in 1969 when the Council decided to establish the Committee on the Challenges of Modern Society (CCMS). CCMS has been very successful in encouraging practical efforts to solve specific environmental problems by the 'pilot nation study' approach, but does not sponsor scientific studies. The Science Committee, having long been aware of the need for scientific studies in the eco-sciences, decided in 1971 to establish an Advisory Panel on Eco-Sciences.

The eco-science field is extremely wide with a multitude of areas which need special attention. To be able to determine in which way and in which area of eco-sciences the limited funds available could be best utilized in order to produce a catalytic effect, the Panel decided to survey some areas before any definite programmes were established. It was thus decided that a Sub-Panel of Experts on Toxicology should be established to study the action of the toxic substances moving through an entire eco-system, paying particular attention to the transformation of the substances which take place within the food chain and participating organisms, leading eventually to unsuspected effects. The Sub-Panel was specifically asked to look at the sub-lethal, long-term and genetic effects and to formulate plans for further action. It was further decided to survey the fields of 'Toxonomy in an Ecological Framework' and 'Pollution Indicator Organisms'. The results of these efforts have been followed up, and the Panel has planned and supported conferences, awarded research grants and fellowships with main emphasis in the areas of sub-lethal Toxicology, Toxonomy, Pollution Indicator Organisms and Environmental Data Management. In 1973 the Panel was changed to a Special Programme Panel.

The Air-Sea Interaction Programme

Very little is known about the important and complex air-sea interaction science, and very few measurements have been taken. Except for weather stations on some of the outlying islands and a few weather ships, there are no weather stations in all the vast oceanic regions of the world. And while it is relatively easy to measure all the physical properties of the atmosphere over the land, even down to the last cubic millimetre between the blade of grass, it is quite a different task to make measurements between the wave crests at sea in the middle of an Atlantic storm. This task is indeed so difficult that only very recent advances in the design of instruments have given promise of eventual success, still far from our reach.

The Air-Sea Interaction Programme was started in 1973. However,

173

significant contributions in the air-sea interaction area had already been made under the Oceanographic Research and Meteorology Programmes. The objective of the Programme is to accelerate progress towards a fuller understanding of the complex interaction between the atmosphere and the sea. The Panel has started research grants, research associateships and visiting lectureships programmes, and has also planned and sponsored one Advanced Study Institute.

The Stress Corrosion Cracking Programme

Stress corrosion cracking is a phenomenon which is of interest to a wide range of metal users. When it occurs under service conditions, often without any prior indication of impending failure, its effects may be catastrophic. Despite the expenditure of large sums of money on research during the last 25 years, stress corrosion cracking is still a relatively little understood phenomenon about which there is considerable ambiguity and argument.

Within NATO the engineering aspects of stress corrosion have been examined periodically by AGARD,[1] but the first attempt to provide a situation in which scientists within the Alliance who are concerned with the fundamental theories of stress corrosion cracking could meet was the Science Committee Conference on the Theory of Stress Corrosion Cracking in Alloys, held in March-April 1971. The recommendations from this conference were discussed by the Science Committee and resulted in the creation of the Special Programme Panel on Stress Corrosion Cracking in 1973. The Panel has considered many areas for possible support and has concentrated its main support for research grants in four specified areas. The Panel has also initiated and supported the work on a Directory of Stress Corrosion Cracking Research and an Advanced Study Institute.

Science policy and international co-operation

Science policy

In addition to establishing scientific programmes designed to overcome the more immediate deficiencies, the Science Committee has concerned itself with studying the long-term aspects of scientific development in the Western World. In early 1959, the Committee proposed an independent study of this problem. The study was financed jointly by the Science Committee and the Ford Foundation, and carried out under the auspices of the Foundation Universitaire of Brussels. The Study Group, which was chaired by M. Louis Armand and included some of the most distinguished scientists in the NATO countries, examined the factors tend-

1. See page 232.

ing to retard the development of science in the Western World. The factors impeding science are often political and administrative, and they may result from a failure to appreciate the nature of science and of the conditions necessary for its growth. The Armand Report, published in 1960 under the title 'Increasing the Effectiveness of Western Science', addressed itself primarily to such matters. Many of its recommendations have been translated into general practice and it has also served a more general purpose of inducing governments to give serious thought to the problems discussed.

One of the Armand Group's recommendations was that the member countries should examine the idea of establishing an International Institute of Science and Technology. The Science Committee acted promptly on this recommendation and the Secretary General of NATO, in 1961, appointed a Working Group under the Chairmanship of Dr. J. R. Killian, Jr., USA, to study this idea. The report of the Killian Group, published in 1962, proposed that the Western countries should establish an International Institute of Science and Technology in Europe, based on the concept of a group of interdisciplinary centres devoted to research and education at the post-graduate level. Though institutions on the scale of the Massachusetts Institute of Technology and the California Institute of Technology might be beyond the resources of most European countries, it was considered that they could be supported on a co-operative basis. The report of the Killian Group has had a salutary influence in persuading European universities to adopt an interdisciplinary approach to the teaching of science. The report was released by the Council so that countries outside the Alliance might have an opportunity to study the proposal.

Computer Science

One of the subjects in which the Science Committee has taken a special interest is that of Computer Science. The Committee recognized at an early stage that electronic computers were bound to become a tool for application across the whole spectrum of human activity and that computer science would be of the greatest importance both in its direct impact on society and in its effect on advanced engineering. This interest was first shown by the support of a number of Advanced Study Institutes, with topics ranging from fundamental computer systems designed to specific computer application areas, and later also in two Science Committee Conferences in 1968 and 1969. To intensify its consideration of the subject, the Science Committee established a Study Group on Computer Science at the end of 1967. The Study Group, composed of international experts, was asked to survey the subject of computer science and select specific areas where international co-operation could be expected to stimulate progress.

The Study Group recognized the necessity of concentrating its efforts on subjects of a basic nature which are common to the largest possible class of computer applications. It also noted that limitations in the application of computers are due not to shortcomings in the technology of the machines themselves but rather to the complexity of their control and use. The Study Group, in reporting its conclusions to the Science Committee in May 1968, identified one subject in particular, software engineering, which it considered could benefit from international action. It recommended that an International Institute for Computer Science be established, specializing initially in the field of software engineering.

The recommendations of the Study Group were accepted by the Science Committee. However, since the Science Committee has no aspirations of establishing or operating international institutes, a multinational Planning Board within NATO was established to consider further details of the scientific work programme, the form of organization which the institute might take, and its links with national efforts. The plans were aimed at pooling European resources for a continuous effort in this new area of software engineering for the purpose of more efficient use of big computers. When the deliberations among the interested countries had advanced so far that it was found possible for the Group to proceed with the further planning on its own, independent of the Science Committee and the NATO Secretariat, France undertook the responsibility for further leading the work, and several countries from outside NATO were invited to participate. The work led by France is still proceeding and preparations are underway which will hopefully lead not only to co-operation between European computer institutes which, as a matter of fact has already been the result of the work started by the Science Committee, but also to the establishment of a central co-ordinating institute.

The von Karman Institute for Fluid Dynamics

The establishing of the von Karman Institute for Fluid Dynamics was mainly due to the foresight of Prof. von Karman, who already in 1954 approached the Belgian Government and suggested that the Aerodynamic laboratory built at Rhode-Saint-Génèse, might in some way be put at the disposal of the NATO countries through the Advisory Group for Aerospace Research and Development (AGARD). A Working Party of experts in aerodynamics from several NATO countries and AGARD with Prof. von Karman as chairman, decided unanimously in favour of the scheme, suggested various necessary additions to the laboratory and formulated a plan of organization and development and outlined curricula. As a result a bilateral agreement was drawn up between Belgium and the United States and the first students entered in 1956. In 1960 a new funding arrangement was established including the majority of the NATO countries.

The institute has programmes for undergraduate, graduate and doctoral studies. In addition to the regular students a large number take part in a part-time training programme, short courses, seminars and specialists' meetings. The institute has in addition an extensive research and consulting programme. The von Karman Institute is an excellent example of an international institute devoted to education and research. It has shown that such an institute is both necessary and desirable for a variety of reasons but especially because it is in accordance with the growing international character of trade and industry and the associated need to correct the imbalance between nations. It has also shown that by a careful balance between teaching and research, the funding required can be kept modest by any standards in relation to the benefit achieved.

The Science committee was not involved in the establishment of the von Karman Institute but took at an early stage a strong interest in the institute and has provided research grants and fellowships for visiting professors. In 1965 the Committee sponsored a Study Group which laid long-term plans for the development of the Institute's curriculum and research programmes.

Defence research co-operation

The long-term aim of the Science Committee is the strengthening of the Alliance by means of scientific collaboration. While the Committee has not initiated many activities with an immediate impact on defence research, some of its programmes have an obvious bearing on this field. The Panels for Operational Research/Systems Science and Human Factors, for example, report not only to the Science Committee but also the Defence Research Group. This body, which succeeded the Committee of Defence Research Directors, in the creation of which the Science Committee took an active part in 1967, now has the main responsibility for defence research within NATO. The military branches of the Organization have their own research establishments, such as the SHAPE Technical Centre at The Hague, the SACLANT Anti-Submarine Warfare Research Centre at La Spezia, and the Advisory Group for Aerospace Research and Development in Paris. The Scientific Affairs Division has co-operated closely with AGARD and the latter has arranged a number of symposia suggested by the Division. This two-way co-operation was also demonstrated by the Science Committee's Support Evaluation Conference on Refractory Metals, which met a demand experienced by AGARD's Materials Panel, which assisted in the choice of subjects and participated in the meeting.

Science and security

The philosophy upon which the work of the Science Committee is based appears even more compelling now than in 1957. National and international strength and security are clearly directly related to progress in science and technology, which forms the basis of economic and military development. In conjunction with its role of advising the Council on scientific and technological questions of concern to the Alliance, the Committee will continue its financial support for different types of international collaboration.

CHAPTER 12

The Committee on the Challenges of Modern Society

Purpose of the CCMS

Since the establishment of the Committee on the Challenges of Modern Society (CCMS) on November 6, 1969, NATO has contributed to the search for a better life in member and non-member countries by giving increased impetus to national and international efforts to cope with urgent environmental problems. Complementing and reinforcing activities under way in other international forums during its first five years, the CCMS has speeded action in preventing ocean oil spills, improving road safety, and combatting air pollution. These specific objectives were achieved by the combination of the practical way in which the CCMS attacks each of the challenges to which it addresses itself and to the political impetus behind the North Atlantic Treaty Organization.

For example, as one outcome of the CCMS pilot study in Coastal Water Pollution, member countries committed themselves to cease all intentional oil spills into the sea if possible by 1975 but in any case no later than the end of this decade. As a result of this resolution adopted by the North Atlantic Council in January 1971 action was speeded by member countries to assure better control of oil spillage from nationally-registered ocean vessels, increased impetus was given to the global anti-pollution efforts of the Intergovernmental Maritime Consultative Organization (IMCO), and by means of annual follow-up reports implementation measures were reported to NATO by member nations.

The practical results of CCMS were made possible by the adoption of the proposal by the United States at the 20th anniversary meeting of NATO in Washington in April 1969 to give the Alliance a new 'social' dimension, specifically to deal with concern 'for the quality of life in this final third of the 20th century'. This new dimension implied both a special focus on problems besetting modern societies and the unique contribution which might be made by an Alliance having the political will to work collectively towards their solution.

It was only after careful exploration of the concept of CCMS that a final decision was taken by the Council of Permanent Representatives to create the Committee. Such a procedure was prompted by the concern that NATO avoid duplicating or competing with environmental activities already being carried on in other international and regional organizations. Thus it became clear early in the planning for CCMS that the objective would be not to tackle global problems nor to deal with the purely scientific, technical, economical or trade aspects of environmental issues. Rather it was to attack practical problems already under study at national level and by combining the expertise and technology available in a number of countries to arrive fairly rapidly at valid conclusions and action recommendations of benefit to all. This deliberate approach assured that the contribution by NATO to the resolution of urgent problems confronting modern, urban, industrial societies would be relevant and would not undesirably duplicate the activities of other organizations.

Co-operation in NATO towards the improvement of modern society evolved both from the terms of the North Atlantic Treaty and from the experience of the Alliance during its first 20 years. Article 2 of the Treaty provides that member countries would contribute towards the further development of peaceful and friendly international relations by promoting conditions of stability and well-being. This Article also served as the basis for the statement in the report of the Committee of Three in 1956 that 'from the very beginning of NATO . . . it was recognized that while defence co-operation was the first and most urgent requirement, this was not enough'. Specifically, the Three recommended that one area of special importance be that of science and technology. This led two years later to the creation of the NATO Science Committee[1] which undertook an active programme of scientific and technical co-operation. This provided an important precedent for the prospective work of the CCMS, especially in the interchange and practical application of technological and scientific information.

How does the CCMS work?

In creating the CCMS, the North Atlantic Council decided that the Committee would not itself engage in any research activities and that its work would be carried out on an entirely decentralized basis without building up a large bureaucracy within the NATO International Staff. Indeed, these

---

1. See Chapter 11, page 160, on the Science Committee.

objectives were assured due to the fact that no programme funds for CCMS activities were made available through the NATO budget. Accordingly, three concepts are pivotal to the work of the Committee.

The first is the pilot country concept: one country – often in collaboration with other countries as co-pilots – volunteers to be responsible for the planning, funding and execution of one of the studies which the Committee has decided to undertake.

The second concept is that efforts will not be directed towards long-term research but rather towards using the information and technology currently available to reach conclusions and make recommendations within a period of a few years rather than in terms of decades. The objective is to adopt action recommendations at Council level to alleviate an important problem which member countries would undertake to implement through national efforts and internationally.

Thirdly, the CCMS observes a policy of complete openness. Thus, at expert level, subject to a simple silent consent procedure, all CCMS meetings are open to observers from non-member countries and other international organizations. Furthermore, the results of completed studies are made freely available to all interested institutions, governments, and international organizations free of charge. The objective is to spread the results of the pilot studies as widely as possible so as to encourage broadest implementation.

The choice of subjects to be considered by the CCMS largely depends on the interest of a member country in leading a study in a particular field. One factor in this decision is the degree of activity in the field already taking place in other member countries. This makes for a highly practical approach in which only those countries interested in a subject would be prepared to commit their expert personnel and financial inputs to that line of work. For example, the Air Pollution pilot study, piloted by the United States included at the outset only the Federal Republic of Germany and Turkey as co-pilots. On the basis of the recognition of the significant results being achieved a number of other countries subsequently joined in, including Italy, the Netherlands, and Norway. This illustrates the flexibility and open-endedness of the pilot study approach.

Both in organizing and in completing pilot studies, there is a link with the NATO Council, thus assuring a political content. The CCMS first decides on the suitability of studies proposed by member countries and then seeks approval of the Council to go ahead. Upon completion of a pilot study, the CCMS receives and recommends approval of the final report, which is then submitted to the Council for its endorsement.

A useful exchange of expertise and immediate access to technology need not await completion of the pilot studies, which generally require three or four years to be carried out. There is in fact an immediate exchange of information and technology each time experts gather under the auspices of CCMS. Indeed, it is significant that approximately 2,000 experts meet annually to participate in various projects carried out under CCMS's auspices, and there is no cost to NATO for their participation.

What is the role of the International Staff?

The Secretary General of NATO is the Chairman of the CCMS. The Assistant Secretary General for Scientific and Environmental Affairs is the Acting Chairman and is responsible for organizing the Plenary Sessions and for administering the daily work of the Committee. He is assisted by the CCMS Projects Officer, who is responsible for monitoring and facilitating the progress of work within the pilot studies. The Committee is also served by a Secretary with responsibility not only for administering the usual Committee secretarial functions but also assisting in monitoring the activities of CCMS. This tiny staff operates as a team in carrying out International Staff responsibility for CCMS. The principal factor permitting such a small group to co-ordinate the programme is the vital role played by the pilot country from the time a pilot study has been agreed, the final report adopted and into the period when follow-up reports on implementation are submitted. Under a new procedure adopted at the beginning of 1975 increased flexibility was given to the follow-up reporting procedure which will enable both the pilot country and the Chairman of CCMS to evaluate more fully the effectiveness of implementation.

The pilot studies

As of early 1975, six CCMS projects had been completed and nine were under way. Those studies already completed included Ocean Oil Spills, Disaster Assistance, Environment and Regional Planning, Road Safety, Air Pollution, and Inland Water Pollution. Those on which work was continuing included Coastal Water Pollution, Advanced Health Care, Advanced Waste Water Treatment, Urban Transportation, Disposal of Hazardous Wastes, Solar Energy, Geothermal Energy, and Rational Use of Energy.

The following is a review of the completed CCMS pilot projects:

Ocean Oil Spills

As part of the Coastal Water Pollution pilot study led by Belgium, a colloquium was held in Brussels in December 1970 to consider the problem of Ocean Oil Spills. The colloquium was attended by more than 100 delegates representing all the maritime member countries of the Alliance. A number of resolutions were adopted dealing both with intentional and accidental spillage of oil into the oceans. The principal resolution stated that member countries agreed to cease all intentional oil spills into the sea if possible by 1975 but in any case no later than the end of the decade. This resolution as well as others recommending more specific operational and technical actions were subsequently adopted by the North Atlantic Council. In prescribing both national and multinational measures to implement these resolutions, CCMS gave increased impetus to the efforts of the Intergovernmental Maritime Consultative Organization, a United Nations' body, and other international organisms in preventing ocean pollution. Follow-up reports were submitted to the pilot country during the next four years which indicated a considerable degree of implementation of the NATO resolutions with a generally beneficial effect on both national and intergovernmental activity not only to stop spillage of oil into the oceans but also of controlling more widespread ocean pollution.

Disaster Assistance

Two of the major natural disaster problems confronting mankind involve earthquakes and floods. While it is recognized that preventive measures are often inadequate to cope with potential disasters, much can be done in pre-planning to mitigate the effects of floods and earthquakes. Furthermore, adequate preparations can permit speedier rescue and post-disaster rehabilitation. It was with these considerations in mind that a pilot study in Disaster Assistance was undertaken by the CCMS to be piloted by the United States and with Italy and Turkey as co-pilots. As a result of two international symposia sponsored by CCMS on flooding late in 1970 and on earthquake hazard reduction in Spring 1971, a number of recommendations were put forward. These called for national and multinational action to cope with earthquakes and floods through more effective member country preparedness and by improved co-ordination of international efforts. The recommendations called upon countries to improve their state of readiness through planning related to pre-disaster preparations, emergency measures to be taken during disasters, and steps to speed post-disaster reconstruction and rehabilitation. A special role was assigned to the NATO communications network which could during time of disaster be used to co-ordinate requests for and deliveries of relief supplies. Member countries were also requested to give complete support to the disaster relief activities of the United Nations. Follow-up reports were submitted to the pilot country for two years after completion of this pilot study in 1972 which indicated that a number of measures had been undertaken in member nations which would serve to implement the recommendations on Disaster Assistance approved by NATO.

Environment and Regional Planning

As interest in the environment gained momentum during the past decade, increased attention was given to the land-use planning process in member

countries. In this context, France undertook to pilot a study on Environment and Regional Planning, with the United Kingdom as co-pilot and
with the active participation of the United States. It was not intended that
there would thereby evolve a master blueprint for regional planning
through a centralized authority which might be applicable in all member
countries. Rather, it was contemplated that in sharing their national
experience, the participants in the CCMS study might contribute to better
understanding of the relationship between environmental quality and
regional development in a national context. Consequently, a series of case
studies of projects undertaken in France, the United Kingdom, and the
United States were contributed as key inputs. These served as the basis
for the enunciation in 1973 of nine recommended guidelines to serve as a
yardstick for improved interaction between national land-use planners, on
the one hand, and those concerned with environmental quality, on the
other. Specific ways of implementing these guidelines were left essentially
to the discretion of each member country depending upon its particular
problems and the national approach to their resolution. However, it was
anticipated that the multinational dialogue which had been launched
through this pilot study would strengthen and give encouragement to
continued international co-operation and flow of information with regard
to maintaining environmental quality and national land-use planning.

Road Safety

Of all the problems confronting modern, urban, industrial society, road
safety is one of the most urgent. This arises not only out of the tragic
number of fatalities on roads and highways each year, but also the considerable economic losses which result from road accidents. Accordingly,
the United States undertook to pilot a multi-faceted study in Road Safety
under CCMS aegis in which a large number of member countries joined in.
There were seven principal projects: Experimental Safety Vehicles
(United States); Pedestrian Safety (Belgium); Alcohol and Highway
Safety (Canada); Identification and Elimination of Road Hazards (France);
Motor Vehicle Inspection (Federal Republic of Germany); Emergency
Medical Services (Italy); and Accident Investigation (Netherlands). In
addition to the project leader countries enumerated, a number of other
nations, both NATO and non-NATO, participated. These included Denmark
and the United Kingdom, and Japan and Sweden. Perhaps the most
active project was that in Experimental Safety Vehicles (ESV), in which all
the major automobile-producing countries of the world participated. The
result was more urgent development of ESVs and their crash-testing on an
accelerated basis. As one outcome, important design and safety features
built into the ESVs could be translated into safer production model automobiles. Indeed, the work of all the Road Safety project areas contributed

184

to the adoption by the North Atlantic Council in November 1973 of the CCMS International Road Safety Resolution under which member countries resolved to use their best efforts to prevent any increase in the annual number of traffic deaths for each class of road user on their road networks over the next five-year period, and thereafter to reduce such number progressively. Considering the anticipated increase in the number of motor vehicles and continued highway construction during that period, important national efforts would be required to meet that objective. In addition, a follow-up procedure was agreed under which the work begun in CCMS would continue in other forums and a group of senior highway safety administrators would periodically review and report to CCMS on the extent to which the goal was being achieved.

Air Pollution

Of all the pollution problems confronting mankind none is more widespread than the fouling of the air around the globe. Whether the result of discharges of automobile fumes, industrial wastes, or heating smoke, ambient air has become unclean. It has also spread rapidly across national frontiers. Accordingly, the CCMS undertook to tackle this problem using the more modern technology and methodology available. The original participants in the study consisted of the United States as pilot country and the Federal Republic of Germany and Turkey as co-pilots. France, Italy, the Netherlands, and Norway later joined in the work as did Israel. A major accomplishment was publication of 19 technical reports on such topics as air pollution modelling, assessment of air quality, air quality criteria and control techniques for various pollutants, and Low Pollution Power Systems Development (cleaner vehicular engines). Of special significance was the work in air pollution modelling, which permitted development of highly sophisticated mathematical models of air pollution in major urban areas, including Frankfurt, Ankara, Saint Louis, Milan, Rotterdam, and Oslo. The Council adopted a resolution in 1972 under which member countries resolved to endeavour to use, where appropriate, the systems methodology generated by the CCMS pilot study for setting up national air quality management programmes. A number of countries including the Federal Republic of Germany drew upon the CCMS technical reports in drafting legislation for the control of air pollution in the Federal Republic. The UN World Health Organization (WHO) also made use of the results in its world-wide anti-air pollution programmes. Indeed, the pilot study was so well-regarded that following its completion in late 1974, a new pilot study in Air Pollution Assessment Methodology and Modelling was approved in early 1975. Work was also to continue in the development of cleaner vehicular engines through the Low Pollution Power Systems Development project.

185

Inland Water Pollution

Under the leadership of Canada, this pilot study was completed with publication of a final report in late 1974 which reflected effective sharing of trans-Atlantic experience in dealing with Inland Water Pollution. Canada focused its efforts on comprehensive river basin planning and management. As co-pilot countries, the United States was concerned with approaches to water quality objectives and standards in international basins; France concentrated on the use of indirect instruments in water management, and Belgium studied the role of models in management decision-making. These four subjects served as the central topics at workshops held in each of the four lead countries. Emerging from these workshops were detailed technical reports which contributed to the drafting of the pilot study final report. The latter was considered by the CCMS at its Plenary Session in October 1974 and was approved by the North Atlantic Council the following month. Member countries are expected to submit follow-up reports on implementation of the resolutions and recommendations during the two-year period 1975–76. As an additional element of this pilot study, it was anticipated that a volume of technical documentation on the detailed work done would be issued by the pilot country during the course of 1975.

On-going pilot study activity

Coastal Water Pollution

Belgium is the pilot country of the CCMS pilot study on Coastal Water Pollution, in which Canada, Portugal, and France serve as co-pilots. The principal focus of the study is a Mathematical Model of the North Sea, one objective of which is to provide a detailed description of the character, extent and derivation of North Sea pollution. Based upon current data and a projection of future trends, the mathematical model, if accurate, could predict the nature and extent of such pollution in future. The model might thus serve as a guide to promote co-operation among the North Sea riparian states on means whereby the level of pollution could be diminished through national action and international co-operation. Thus far, three interim reports have been issued by the pilot country on the progress of the work. Significant inputs have been provided by other participants, especially Canada. Drawing on these accomplishments, Belgium together with its CCMS co-pilot partners is expected to draft a final report in 1975 on the CCMS study, which will include conclusions and recommendations relevant to solving the urgent problem of North Sea pollution.

Advanced health care

The aim of this study, piloted by the United States, is to facilitate international co-operation in providing better quality health care to ever-increasing numbers of patients. The objective is not to duplicate the efforts of the WHO, which for the most part, is concerned with improving health care in developing countries but rather to supplement them by coping with medical problems arising in the more developed countries. Accordingly, four areas of activity were selected, each led by a pilot country: Systematic Assessment of Health Services (Canada); Organized Ambulatory Health Services (Federal Republic of Germany); Emergency Medical Services (Italy); and Automation of Clinical Laboratories (United Kingdom). The project led by Canada seeks to develop guidelines for the establishment and operation of systems to assess the quality of health care services while monitoring costs. The Federal Republic leads the work in comparing how health services for non-hospitalized patients can be organized and administered in the most effective way. Italy aims to collate data and experience from a number of countries on ways in which to organize and finance emergency medical services. The United Kingdom heads a project which is expected to include recommendations with respect to the use of standard reference methods in laboratory practice, improving information exchange through the identification of international keywords for computer retrieval of information; guidelines for commercial laboratory kits and reagents; and patient identification systems. All four of the above project areas were expected to complete their work during 1975 and thus pave the way for the drafting of a final report to the CCMS and the Council.

Advanced waste water treatment

The United Kingdom, as pilot country, is heading this study to explore a variety of techniques and equipment to purify waste water. A new plant constructed in the Coleshill area near Birmingham will be the site of a pilot project on use of the physical-chemical process. Meanwhile, a number of co-pilot countries will be testing alternative technologies, as follows: France is exploring the use of oxygen-enriched air in treating waste water, especially that resulting from dairy plant operations. The Federal Republic of Germany is testing the effectiveness of the oxygenation process in treatment of waste water, and, illustrating its activity, held a workshop and demonstration near Wuppertal in early 1973. Canada is giving principal attention to the process whereby phosphorous could be removed from waste sludge, and conducted a workshop and demonstration at the Canada Centre for Inland Water in February 1974. Stimulated by the Canadian demonstration, several other countries decided to take an active part in this pilot study, including Italy and Norway. The United States is also a co-pilot participant with a number of technologies being tested. The ultimate objective of the wide variety of project activity will be the drafting of a final report containing conclusions and recommendations regarding waste water treatment technology and methodology. This should provide a wide range of options from which countries may choose in order to meet their increased need for treatment plants.

Urban transportation

In order to cope with the problem of transportation in cities, the United States undertook to lead a pilot study in which four member countries took major roles. All five projects within the study, which got underway in late 1972, aimed at facilitating faster and more convenient travel for passengers and more efficient delivery of freight in metropolitan agglomerations. Implicit in the objectives was the expectation that the number of private automobiles using city streets would gradually diminish as public transportation improved and the costs of bringing a car into the centre of town, e.g., parking, would increase considerably. Belgium took responsibility for a project in Collection Systems Evaluation which aimed at improving the collection of suburban travellers at a central point (i.e. Waterloo) for rapid transit to another point (Brussels). This would involve some form of demand pick-up system which would be flexible and efficient as well as reasonably cost-effective. France led a project on Urban Goods Movement, the objective of which was to explore means whereby freight might be delivered more rapidly and with minimum impact on traffic volume. The Federal Republic of Germany agreed to lead a survey of all available short distance transport techniques for use in cities and to evaluate these. The United States, in addition to its pilot role consented to co-ordinate a project in Urban Travel Forecasting which would provide data concerning the need for public transit facilities in cities of the future. To assure that the recommendations in the pilot study final report would indeed facilitate action at the local and municipal levels of government, where urban transportation decisions are made, the pilot country requested special guidance from the Committee at its Plenary Session in October 1974. Guidance was especially sought on ways in which the pilot study recommendations agreed by national authorities could be most effectively implemented through decisions taken by local and municipal authorities.

Disposal of hazardous wastes

This pilot study, led by the Federal Republic of Germany, was approved by the Council in November 1973. Co-piloted by the United States, the principal objective was to deal with the ever burgeoning problem of how to dispose of industrial toxic wastes in the safest and least damaging manner. This will involve the testing of appropriate technologies for the disposal and recycling of these wastes as well as the establishment of effective planning instruments and organizational systems. It is anticipated that the study will ultimately result in action recommendations whereby member countries will be able to deal more effectively – both at the national and international levels – with the problem of hazardous wastes such as residual hardening salts, acidic resins, organic solvents, arsenic residues, mercury, lead and non-ferrous sludges. As an outcome of a meeting of experts in Munich in September 1974, a number of countries expressed interest in possible development of project activity along five lines: the United Kingdom contemplated the use of land-fill; Belgium expressed strong interest in the study of underground disposal of wastes in mines; the Netherlands considered the possibility of useful input by its national programme and legislation on classification of wastes; Denmark expressed special interest in evaluating experience in exchanges involving hazardous wastes; and France considered contributing inputs related to the chromium cycle on which work was already proceeding. In addition, the pilot country agreed to take the lead in a project to consider problems of the organization of hazardous waste disposal. The United States offered to lead an examination of the transportation of hazardous wastes and would help co-ordinate efforts to derive general guidelines and recommendations from the various project activities in the pilot study.

Solar energy

As a new departure for ccms pilot study activity, three energy studies were undertaken beginning in late 1973. Included among these was a study in Solar Energy piloted by the United States, and co-piloted by Denmark and France, which aimed at showing the possibilities of using solar energy to heat, cool, and provide hot water to buildings. Two possible benefits are seen as emerging from this study: the first would be development of a supplemental source of energy to help augment energy provided by fossil fuel and nuclear sources. Secondly, solar energy represents a source of power with very little, if any, polluting effects. The ultimate purpose of the study is to develop recommendations to permit incorporation of the most up-to-date technology and methodologies in drawing upon solar energy to meet some of the increasing demands for energy. A meeting of experts was held in Odeillo, France, in October 1974 attended by representatives from 12 member countries and 5 non-NATO countries – Australia, Brazil, Israel, Jamaica, and Saudi Arabia. This broad spectrum of representation indicated the scope of interest in greater use of solar energy as a supplemental source of power. Two main project areas were selected by the group for initial work: development of a 'zero-energy house', led by Denmark, which would use a variety of energy conservation and recycling technologies, as well as employ solar energy in generating power. The second involved development of a reporting format so that data can be exchanged on a comparable basis.

189

Geothermal Energy

The United States also undertook to lead a study in Geothermal Energy with Italy and Turkey as co-pilots. This subject attracted widespread interest and resulted in project activity involving both member and non-member countries on three continents: Asia, America, and Europe. In May 1974, the first geothermal implementation conference was held in New Zealand where the following projects were agreed: international geothermal information exchange; non-electrical uses; and multi-purpose utilization, processing, and disposal of geothermal brines. The New Zealand meeting was followed by a study tour on non-electrical uses of geothermal energy which included Japan. The study tour was continued through Italy, France, and Iceland in June in which representatives of five nations participated: France, Iceland, the Philippines, Turkey and the United States, culminating in discussion in Iceland of preparation of a state-of-the-art report. Another expert meeting was held in Los Alamos, New Mexico on Dry Hot Rock Exploitation in September where the United States offered to accommodate foreign experts interested in this technology at visits or on working assignments at the Los Alamos facility. Possible project activity is also envisaged regarding small geothermal power plants and a meeting of experts was planned in Europe for Spring 1975.

Rational Use of Energy

This study, piloted by the United States, attracted broad interest in 1974 in connection with project activity on three topics: Electric Utility Load Management, Development of an International Data Base, and Use of Energy in the Cement Industry. Expert meetings involving both government and industry representatives were held on Electric Utility Load Management in July in Paris and in Brussels four months later. In addition to member country representation, delegates were present representing the electric utility industries of Ireland and Switzerland. The objective was to draw on the experience on both sides of the Atlantic in determining how to achieve a better balance between the peak and off-peak use of electricity. By the sharing of experience and technology, it was anticipated that considerable improvement could be effected. At an expert meeting in November in Milan, four industries were selected for the initial compilation of information under the International Data Base project. These included steel, petroleum refining, plastics, and cement. It was projected that with respect to all these except cement (which would be dealt with separately), a considerable data base would be developed. Plans were made for a follow-up project meeting in Rome in late February 1975 to further develop the planning in this project. The Cement Industry project involved both government and industry representatives in meetings in Denmark in May and in Milan in December. As there appeared to be a special opportunity to use energy more efficiently in cement production, work will continue on this project with that objective. It is anticipated that a number of other potential areas on energy conservation will result in future project activity, for example in the use of heat pumps as a means of conserving and using energy more efficiently.

Other activities of CCMS

During its initial years the Committee on the Challenges of Modern Society also dealt with two other areas of concern: the problems of cities and of drug abuse. In the Spring of 1971, the CCMS participated in the sponsorship of an International Conference on Cities in Indianapolis which examined a wide range of urban problems. Although no overall pilot study proposal resulted from the Conference, the CCMS did undertake a number of studies of particular significance for urban residents, for example, Urban Transportation, Advanced Waste Water Treatment, Air Pollution, and Advanced Health Care.

The Committee considered the problem of the misuse of drugs at its plenary sessions during the period 1970–72, although no formal pilot study on the subject was initiated. It was instead agreed that international co-operation to cope with this problem would be strengthened and action through the United Nations' Commission on Dangerous Drugs be accelerated.

The CCMS organized a Fellowship Programme which was able to make grants to small numbers of scholars each year, numbering four in 1971, eight in 1972, and 11 each in 1973 and 1974. The programme had two principal aims: first, to encourage studies *not* in purely scientific or technological areas but rather in public policy as related to the natural or social environment. Secondly, to assist younger researchers in completing their studies or improving their training for future publicly-related work. A considerable number of grants have been awarded for research on topics which were socially oriented, such as a study of the adaptation of Portuguese workers to living and working in France and the Federal Republic of Germany. In order to strengthen the programme and permit a larger number of grants, the CCMS agreed in principle that beginning in 1976 the funds available would be increased beyond the two million Belgian francs available in 1975.

The CCMS has encouraged contacts with other international organizations concerned with environment in order to exchange information and help avoid undesirable duplication of effort. These contacts have been accomplished using three techniques: International Staff contacts, work of CCMS representatives in other international forums, and participation by national experts in projects in CCMS and in other multilateral agencies. At various levels, the International Staff is in contact either officially or unofficially with the secretariats of other inter-governmental organizations such as the United Nations Environment Programme, Organization for Economic Co-operation and Development, Commission of the European Communities, Council of Europe, and Economic Commission for Europe. These contacts permit a useful exchange of information and documentation. National representatives to the CCMS provide information on activities and programmes of other international bodies during the Round Table discussions held at each Plenary Session. These inputs are especially valuable as they reflect the direct experience of the CCMS representatives in these other forums. Finally, the national experts who participate in CCMS project activity are generally those who take part in similar programmes sponsored by other international bodies. Their expertise and multi-organizational participation provide a valuable safeguard against undesirable duplication of activities.

One extremely important point of contact for the CCMS is the North Atlantic Assembly. This group of parliamentarians representing all 15 NATO nations has through its Scientific and Technical Committee continuously given strong support to the activities of CCMS. That group has encouraged especially effective national implementation and follow-up of CCMS pilot study recommendations and resolutions. It has also appealed for better national information activities on CCMS and for pilot study proposals to replace completed studies. To demonstrate its active concern, the Scientific and Technical Committee set up a Sub-Committee on CCMS in November 1973, so that continuing attention could be given to the work of the Committee on the Challenges of Modern Society.

CHAPTER 13

Cultural co-operation

Co-heirs of the same civilization, the peoples of our countries have been for centuries part of one of the distinctive world cultures. A common culture contributes a powerful and enriching force to an Alliance which aspires 'to safeguard the common heritage and civilization' of its members and to foster their sense of belonging together. But, as the Committee of Three remarked in Chapter 4 of their Report this sense will exist only to the extent that peoples are made aware of the innate common values informing their habits of life and thought.

In this context, NATO has something unique to offer as an organization: it brings together not only the Northern and Western European cultures but allies them, through the Mediterranean peoples, to North America. No other international body is in a position to profit from these particular transatlantic links.

These simple facts were recognized by Governments during the early years of the Alliance. In considering the endowment of NATO with a programme of cultural activities the recurring theme was that the Alliance must constantly strengthen its transatlantic links by exchanging between Europe and North America people in many walks of life, techniques and ideas. In planning NATO's small programme in this field, account was taken of the participation by member countries in other international bodies dedicated to culture, as well as to the bilateral cultural agreements in existence between them. It was against this background that Governments encouraged NATO to launch two small programmes, one of research fellowships and the other of visiting university lectureships.

Fellowship Selection Committee
Established in 1955 to promote study of the Alliance in the widest sense,

some 297 fellowships have been awarded to post-graduate students in all fifteen member countries. An international panel of academic personalities, brought together annually by the Council, examines the applications and makes the awards which are announced each April 4th. About fifteen fellowships are granted each year. Originally restricted to university graduates, since 1974 the competition has been open to other applicants, provided they have the required qualification to carry out the proposed research. In addition to many pamphlets, articles and doctoral theses, several books have been published as the result of these fellowships – see end of this chapter for selected list. Full information about the Fellowships may be obtained by writing to the Cultural Relations Section, NATO Information Directorate, 1110, Brussels. Programmes and application forms for the Fellowships are available at NATO from September 1st each year and individual applications must be filed with national authorities before November 1st. The addresses of the national authorities are listed in the Programme.

Visiting Professorships Programme

Launched originally in 1958, the Visiting Professorships Programme, owing to other more urgent demands on the international budget of NATO, had to be cancelled as from the close of thc 1970/71 academic year. During the thirteen years of the programme's existence, over 100 university professors were enabled to lecture for a period of up to twenty weeks at a university in another NATO country on the opposite side of the Atlantic. Ten grants were available each academic year and the beneficiaries were required to lecture in fields of direct interest to the Alliance.

Other activities

NATO has also supported arrangements for seminars or lectures on questions of interest to the Alliance at universities in member countries. Within the limits set, and in view of their very nature, these activities cannot show rapid and spectacular results, nor is this the aim. The intention is rather to explain and justify the community feeling which is already discernable in public opinion of the countries of the Alliance, and on which, in the last resort, the unity of the free world depends.

Selected list of published works

Title	Author	Publisher
NATO and the European Union Movement	MARGARET BALL	Stevens & Sons, Ltd., London, 1959
Die Strategische Bedeutung des Ost-West Handels	M. VON BERG	A. W. Sijthoff, Atlantic Series No. 5, Leyden, 1966

Title	*Author*	*Publisher*
Developing Countries & NATO	M. W. J. M. BROEKMEIJER	A. W. Sijthoff, Atlantic Series No. 1, Leyden, 1963
Freedom of Speech in the West	Frede CASTBERG	Oslo University Press & George Allen & Unwin, London, 1960
Basic Values of Western Civilization	Shepard B. CLOUGH	Columbia University Press, New York, 1960
The Armed Attack (Der bewaffnete Angriff)	G. MEIER	Charlotte Schön, Munich, 1963
The Pressure on the Dollar	M. NEGREPONTI-DELIVANIS	A. W. Sijthoff, Atlantic Series No. 3, Leyden
Le Rôle de l'Opinion Publique dans la Communauté Atlantique	A. STERNBERG-MONTALDI	A. W. Sijthoff Atlantic, Series No. 2, Leyden 1963
Civilians and the NATO Status of Forces Agreement	G. I. A. D. DRAPER	A. W. Sijthoff, Atlantic Series No. 4, Leyden, 1966
The Committee System of the NATO Council	B. ERIKSEN	Oslo University Press, 1967
Atlantic Democracy	C. D'OLIVIER FARRAN	W. Green & Son, Ltd., Edinburgh, 1957
Panlibhonco e NATO	M. GABRIELE	A. Giuffré, Milan, 1961
International Regional Organizations	R. LAWSON	F. A. Praeger, New York, 1961
L'Italie	M. MARANINI	Pichon & Durand Auzias, Paris, 1961
L'Organisation des Transports dans le cadre de l'Europe des Six	André FISCHER	A. W. Sijthoff, Atlantic Series, No. 6, Leyden, 1968
Citizen Participation: Doomed to Extinction or Last Foothold of Democracy?	Gustave A. de COCQ	A. W. Sijthoff, Atlantic Series, No. 7, Leyden, 1969
L'Inquinamento Marino nel Diritto Internazionale	Guiseppe TESAURO	A. Giuffré, Milan, 1971
Das Völkerrecht und die militärische Nutzung des Meeresbodens	W. KÜHNE	A. W. Sijthoff, Atlantic Series No. 8, Leyden, 1975
Nuclear Weapons and International Behavior	Henry T. NASH	A. W. Sijthoff, Atlantic Series No. 9, Leyden, 1975

CHAPTER 14

Co-ordination of air traffic

Several thousand civil and military aircraft cruising, climbing and descending in all directions up to 60,000 feet at widely varying speeds are accommodated in the NATO European airspace. Close co-ordination of civil and military use of the airspace and control of air traffic is essential to ensure safety from collision and optimum freedom of movement. It is also necessary for the establishment and maintenance of a comprehensive picture of the air situation and identification of all aircraft – this in turn is a prerequisite for effective defence. NATO is concerned with these problems because of its responsibilities for air defence and for the training and operation of air forces in the area – and because civil aviation is of considerable economic importance to NATO member countries.

Airspace Co-ordination Committee

To achieve these aims, the Council established in April 1955 a Committee for European Airspace Co-ordination (CEAC).

The members of CEAC are high-ranking civil and military representatives of NATO countries. NATO military authorities are represented on the Committee, in particular the major Commands. The International Civil Aviation Organization,[1] the International Air Transport Association[2] and the European Organization for the Safety of Air Navigation[3] are invited to

1. ICAO is a UN specialized agency set up by the Convention on International Civil Aviation (signed at Chicago on December 7, 1944) which co-ordinates international civil aviation.

2. IATA includes most of the world airlines; it was set up in Havana in April 1945. Its aim is to promote safe and economical air transport, to provide means of co-ordination between air transport companies, and to co-operate with other international organizations such as ICAO.

3. EUROCONTROL is an Agency providing air traffic services for civil air traffic in the upper air spaces of Belgium, France, the Federal Republic of Germany, the Republic of Ireland, Luxembourg, the Netherlands and the United Kingdom.

attend as observers when subjects of concern to their organization are
being studied.

Committee studies have led to improved conditions for all users by
standardizing civil and military airspace organization and air traffic
control systems and procedures, by establishment of joint civil/military
control centres and by joint use of radars. Joint air/ground/air communications, navigational aid and associated frequency requirements have
been co-ordinated in one overall plan for the entire area.

Control during exercises

During large-scale NATO exercises, large numbers of sorties lead to
congested airspace and necessitate special arrangements in respect of airspace organization and control to ensure civil and military aircraft safe,
economic and flexible operation. It is, for example, necessary to redelineate
certain airways and restrict military operations in high density civil traffic
areas. CEAC has established methods and procedures to effect this co-
ordination and draws up an overall plan for the exercise, which describes
the area, date and time of the exercise as well as measures to be taken by
non-exercise aircraft to ensure safe and economic passage. This plan is
published by nations in Notices to Airmen in adequate time for all air-
crews to acquaint themselves with the conditions that will be encountered
and measures to be taken. These procedures have considerably improved
operating conditions for all users.

Joint use of facilities

As the employment of high-speed, high-flying jet aircraft for civil transport
has generated control requirements similar to military requirements and
as modern semi-automatic systems are costly to install and maintain, the
Committee studies include plans for joint civil/military use of equipment
and facilities on a progressively increasing scale.

CHAPTER 15

Press and information

The Report of the Committee of Three adopted unanimously by all 15 governments, devotes a special chapter (Chapter 5) to Information.[1] After stressing the need for the people of member countries 'to know about NATO if they are to support it' the report states that 'the important task of explaining and reporting NATO activities rests primarily on national Information Services', and each member country should designate an officer specifically charged with this work. The report adds, 'NATO can and should assist national governments in this work. The promotion of information about, and public understanding of, NATO and the Atlantic Community should, in fact, be a joint endeavour by the Organization and its members'.

The NATO Press and Information Services co-operate closely with the national information services as well as maintaining contact with non-official organizations, such as the Atlantic Treaty Associations and the North Atlantic Assembly. The activities of the NATO Press Service and the Information Service, which are organized as two separate parts of the International Staff, within the Political Division, are described below.

Press Service

The Head of the Press Service, as the official spokesman for the Organization, deals directly with the press on behalf of the Secretary General. He briefs the international press during Ministerial meetings, and also deals with daily press enquiries and is responsible for keeping the

1. See Appendix 5, page 308.

press informed of current NATO activities and such of the Council's discussions and decisions as may, by agreement, be made public.

In addition to this the Press Service has a second function: to ensure that the Secretariat is provided with the latest information through a daily press review and cuttings from a selection of the international press and news agency services.

Information Service

This is organized under the NATO Director of Information assisted by three Assistant Directors and an international staff. While the Press Service deals with current NATO news and announcements the Information Service is concerned with providing facts through all available media about the long-term aspects, such as why and how NATO was created, how it functions and the general lines of agreed long-term NATO policy. Media used include publications, films (including films for television), photographs, displays, seminars, group visits (including journalists) to NATO Headquarters for special briefings, the provision of visiting lecturers, as well as a library and documentation service. The Sections are organized as follows:

Audio-visual media

The TV/Films/Radio Section provides technical assistance to television companies making programmes on any aspect of NATO, and encourages production of such programmes. This is done by arranging suitable briefings for commentators, providing background material for scriptwriters, organizing interviews and providing ready-made filmed material, which can be incorporated in programmes at short notice. When required, special filming is done by the Films Service (e.g. in the security zone inaccessible to the Press) using NATO cameramen. A limited number of documentary films are made illustrating NATO activities not normally covered by national information services.

As with television, radio offers a wide medium for the diffusion of information on NATO and this Section arranges for interviews and discussions to be relayed through the networks of many NATO countries. It also produces a fortnightly taped programme 'Report from NATO'.

The Photo Section provides all sections of the world Press with both individual photographs of NATO subjects (including Ministerial meetings) and features covering various aspects of the Organization.

It also makes available for use by member countries small displays covering a wide range of NATO subjects.

199

Visiting groups

About 300 groups, totalling up to 10,000 people, visit NATO Headquarters each year. These range from two-day NATO-sponsored tours to short visits for two briefings in a morning or afternoon and are often combined with a visit to SHAPE. They cover all categories of visitor from parliamentarians and chief editors to trade unionists and university students, but priority is normally given to those in a position to pass on information to wider circles, such as journalists, teachers, etc.

Youth and other special audiences

To stimulate interest by the younger generation in NATO affairs many projects are carried out under NATO auspices in close co-operation with international and national Youth Movements. In this context, courses, seminars, and exchange programmes for youth leaders, students and young trade unionists are regularly organized in all NATO countries. Moreover, every year one country acts as host to an International Youth Seminar for studies on the Atlantic Alliance and related subjects.

Publications

A periodical magazine, the NATO Review, is published in English and French with editions in other NATO languages. It presents current topics and discusses subjects of interest to the Alliance. Distributed free throughout the world, the Review contains a documentation section giving the latest NATO published texts. Other publications and works of reference include this book, a volume of Final Communiques of the Council, DPC and NPG, a booklet containing NATO Basic Documents, a general purpose Handbook outlining the origins and organization of the Alliance, and a series of pamphlets on specific subjects.

Financing

The NATO Information activities are financed by a vote from the international budget and the programme is discussed each year by a conference of National Information Officials who lay down general lines. The detailed programme is then approved by the NATO Committee on Information and Cultural Relations. The scale of the programme is strictly limited by the funds available.

Work of the Atlantic Treaty Associations

Private societies in all NATO *countries second the activities engaged in by the Organization and by Governments in the cultural and information fields, particularly the national voluntary organizations affiliated to the Atlantic Treaty Association* (ATA).[1]

Created at a conference held at The Hague on June 18, 1954, to promote the loyal fulfilment of the North Atlantic Treaty, these citizens' associations or committees are working, generally with very meagre funds at their disposal, to create and to foster in their respective countries a current of opinion favourable to the Alliance and to NATO. *Their assistance is multiform : the distribution of printed matter, the arrangement of lectures, symposia, seminars, exhibitions, etc.*

Other activities of the ATA *and its national branches include summer camps for young people, Round Table Conferences to study particular themes, meetings of young Trade Unionists and very active work among the younger politicians in the member countries, who in 1963 formed the Atlantic Association of Young Political Leaders.*

Further information concerning the ATA *may be obtained from the Secretary General, Atlantic Treaty Association, 185 rue de la Pompe, Paris 75116.*

Arising out of a recommendation of the Teacher's Conference held at Strasbourg in 1962, the ATA *founded in 1963 an Atlantic Information Centre for Teachers* (AICT). *From its office in London this Centre publishes three times a year a folder entitled 'The World and the School' containing special articles, graphs and bibliography designed to assist teachers dealing with current international affairs. It also organizes conferences and seminars in member countries for teachers in secondary schools concerned with civics, history or geography.*

Inquiries about the Atlantic Information Centre for Teachers should be addressed to the Director, AICT, *37A High Street, Wimbledon, London SW19 5BY.*

1. For the list of national associations or committees affiliated to the ATA see Appendix 13, page 360.

Civil and military structure

The North Atlantic Council, the highest authority in NATO, provides a forum for wide political consultation and co-ordination between the Allies. Military policy is discussed in the Defence Planning Committee (DPC) composed of member countries participating in NATO's integrated defence system. The Council and the DPC assemble twice yearly in Ministerial meetings when member countries are represented by Foreign and Defence Ministers. In permanent session the Council/DPC meets at least once a week at the level of Ambassadors (Permanent Representatives). The Secretary General of NATO is chairman of the Council and the DPC and also heads the International Staff. In support of their roles, the Council and the DPC have established a number of Committees, the most important of which are shown in the diagram below. These Committees cover the whole range of NATO's activities and meet under the chairmanship of a member of the International Staff.

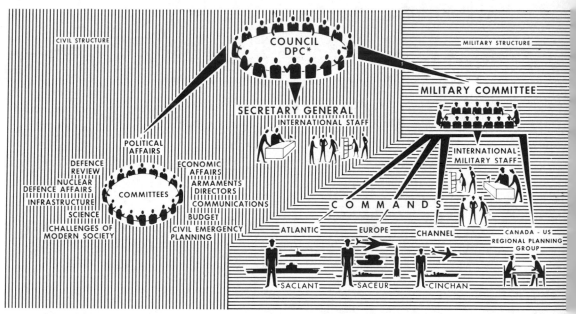

* DPC: The Defence Planning Committee, dealing with military policy, meets at the same levels as the Council.

The Military Committee, composed of the Chiefs-of-Staff of the member countries taking part in the NATO integrated military structure, is the senior military authority in the Alliance. It provides advice to the Council/DPC on military matters and gives guidance to the major NATO Commanders. Meeting at Chiefs-of-Staff level at least twice a year, the Committee in permanent session meets weekly at the level of national Military Representatives appointed by their Chiefs-of-Staff. The Chairman of the Military Committee is elected by the Chiefs-of-Staff for a period of 2–3 years. Implementation of the policies and decisions of the Military Committee is ensured by the International Military Staff (IMS) acting as executive agency. The NATO defence area is divided into three separate regional Commands – the Atlantic Ocean Command, the European Command and the Channel Command – and a Regional Planning Group for the North American area. Under the general guidance of the Military Committee the major NATO Commanders are responsible for planning the defence of their areas and for conducting NATO's land, sea and air exercises.

CHAPTER 16

Civil organization

What is the Council?

The North Atlantic Council, which was set up pursuant to Article 9 of the Treaty, provides a unique forum for confidential and constant inter-governmental consultation and represents the highest level of decision-making machinery within NATO. There is no supranational element in the Organization and all the fifteen sovereign member countries have an equal right to express their views around the Council table.

Each Government appoints a Permanent Representative of Ambassadorial rank supported by staffs which vary in size. The role of the Permanent Representatives is to act, under instructions from their capitals, as spokesmen for their Governments. In a reciprocal way they are also the spokesmen of the Council with their Governments. Permanent Representatives do not represent only their Foreign Minister but all Ministers concerned in the Alliance's business.

The Council may be compared to a standing committee of Governments or to a 'Diplomatic Workshop' (see diagram on page 94). To attain such a high degree of constant and timely consultation between the fifteen member nations by the customary method of bilateral political exchanges would be quite impracticable – in fact every time the Council meets it provides the equivalent of·over 100 bilateral exchanges. It is also significant that there is no other forum in which the two North American countries and thirteen European countries, including eight of the nine EEC nations, can meet at least once a week as members of one and the same institution to exchange views on current affairs.

The Council meets under the Chairmanship of the Secretary General and is serviced by the Executive Secretariat. To carry out its functions the

Principal Committees of the Council

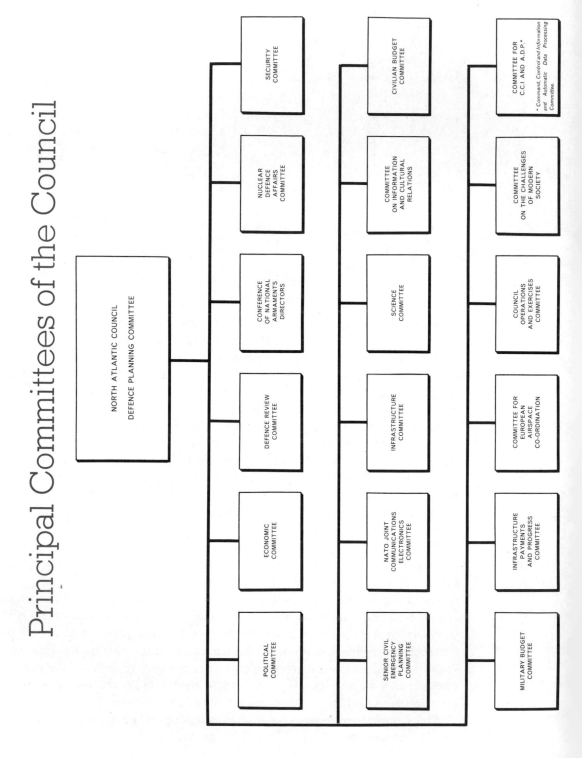

NORTH ATLANTIC COUNCIL
DEFENCE PLANNING COMMITTEE

POLITICAL COMMITTEE

ECONOMIC COMMITTEE

DEFENCE REVIEW COMMITTEE

CONFERENCE OF NATIONAL ARMAMENTS DIRECTORS

NUCLEAR DEFENCE AFFAIRS COMMITTEE

SECURITY COMMITTEE

SENIOR CIVIL EMERGENCY PLANNING COMMITTEE

NATO JOINT COMMUNICATIONS ELECTRONICS COMMITTEE

INFRASTRUCTURE COMMITTEE

SCIENCE COMMITTEE

COMMITTEE ON INFORMATION AND CULTURAL RELATIONS

CIVILIAN BUDGET COMMITTEE

MILITARY BUDGET COMMITTEE

INFRASTRUCTURE PAYMENTS AND PROGRESS COMMITTEE

COMMITTEE FOR EUROPEAN AIRSPACE CO-ORDINATION

COUNCIL OPERATIONS AND EXERCISES COMMITTEE

COMMITTEE ON THE CHALLENGES OF MODERN SOCIETY

COMMITTEE FOR C.C.I AND A.D.P.*

* Command, Control and Information and Automatic Data Processing Committee.

Council has set up a large number of subsidiary Committees which, at various levels, prepare the work of the Council or implement its directives. All these Committees, be they civil or military, act for and under the authority of the Council (see Chart on opposite page).

The Council at Ambassadorial level is known as the Council in Permanent Session. It also meets at Ministerial level where each nation is represented by its Foreign Minister, although Defence and Finance Ministers have also attended these meetings. On three occasions, in 1957, 1974 and 1975, it has met at Heads of Government level, when Prime Ministers and the President of the United States were present. At whatever level the Council meets, it remains the NATO Council and its decisions have equal validity.

Its Genesis

The structure of the Council has been modified in a number of ways since the institution of the Alliance. In September 1949 it was decided that the Council would be composed of the Foreign Ministers of member countries and would meet once a year in ordinary session and as often as required in extraordinary session. At the same date a Defence Committee composed of the Defence Ministers was also set up and it was agreed that it would also meet once a year. Then in November 1949, a Defence, Financial and Economic Committee composed of Finance Ministers was established.

This system proved too cumbersome to deal with day to day problems and it was decided in 1950 to institute the Council Deputies in London charged with the execution of the Council's directives and the co-ordination of the military and civil activities of the Alliance. Following the suppression in 1951 of the Defence Committee and of the Financial and Economic Committee, the role of the Council Deputies was enhanced and began to acquire some of the characteristics of the North Atlantic Council as it now exists. A further change was made at the Lisbon Ministerial Meeting in 1952. This change was of a more radical nature, directed at the creation of a genuinely permanent body, which, broadly speaking, has remained unchanged since that date.

How it works

As a general rule the Council in Permanent Session meets every Wednesday, but in practice it meets much more frequently; as often as four/five times a week when circumstances require it. In fact, the Council may be convened at any time of the day or night and on any day, weekends and holidays included. Arrangements have been made through a duty officers' system to enable the Council to meet at about two hours' notice.

Almost all Council meetings begin with the same item 'Political

NATO International Staff

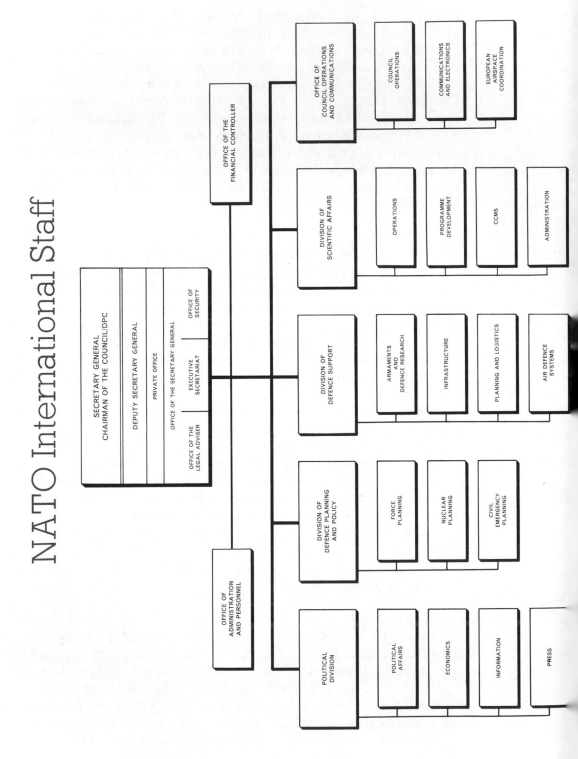

Subjects'. Under this item Permanent Representatives are able to raise and discuss in a restricted forum topical matters of interest to the Alliance; it is a practical feature of the political consultation process. No official records are kept of these discussions in order to foster free and uninhibited exchanges. Whenever necessary Private Meetings are held with an even more restricted attendance to allow for complete informality and confidentiality.

The other items which come up to the Council for discussion and decision cover all aspects of the Organization's activities and are based on documents prepared by the Council's subordinate Committees. These documents contain recommendations which are then adopted unchanged or modified by the Council itself to reconcile divergent views and arrive at unanimously agreed decisions. Agreement by common consent is the rule; there is no voting or majority decision. Council decisions, when adopted, become binding and can only be reversed by the Council itself.

Each year the Foreign Minister of a member state is elected President of the Council, the selection being made in English alphabetical order of countries.[1]

The Defence Planning Committee (DPC)

Defence matters are dealt with in the Defence Planning Committee, composed of representatives of the member nations participating in the NATO integrated defence system. Within the specialized field of defence the DPC has, for all practical purposes, the same functions and authority as the Council. Like the Council it meets regularly at Ambassadorial level and assembles twice yearly in Ministerial sessions when the nations are represented by their Defence Ministers.

The Secretary General

Chairman of the North Atlantic Council and the Defence Planning Committee[2] the Secretary General is also Chairman of the Nuclear Defence Affairs Committee[3] and the Nuclear Planning Group.[4] He also has responsibility for the direction of the International Staff. The Deputy Secretary General assists the Secretary General in the exercise of his functions, and replaces him in his absence. The work of the International Staff is organized as follows (see Chart on opposite page):

1. See Appendix 9, page 350, for list of Presidents of the NATO Council.
2. Composed of all nations participating in the integrated military structure of the Organization.
3. Composed of all NATO countries except France, Iceland and Luxembourg.
4. Composed of seven or eight nations selected from among the members of the NDAC.

The Office of the Secretary General

The Secretary General has under his direct control a 'Private Office' and 'The Office of the Secretary General' composed of the Executive Secretariat, the Office of Security, and the Office of the Legal Adviser.

The Private Office supports the Secretary General and the Deputy Secretary General in all phases of their work.

The Executive Secretary is Secretary to the Council, the Defence Planning Committee, the Nuclear Defence Affairs Committee and the Nuclear Planning Group. He is responsible for preparing the work of the Council/DPC and their Committees, recording the proceedings of meetings and following up decisions. The Executive Secretariat provides the secretaries for all the main Committees and Working Groups of the Organization, and thus ensures co-ordination between them.

The Office of Security is responsible for the overall co-ordination of security for NATO and for providing advice and guidance on NATO security matters.

The Office of the Legal Adviser provides advice on the legal aspects of all matters affecting NATO.

Political Affairs Division

Under the Assistant Secretary General for Political Affairs the Political Division is organized in three separate Directorates – Political Affairs, Economic Affairs, and Information – and a Press Service.

The Assistant Secretary General is Chairman of the Political Committee and of the Committee on Information and Cultural Relations.

– The Political Affairs Directorate has the following responsibilities:

a) Preparation of the political discussions of the Council and of the discussions of the Committee of Political Advisers;

b) Preparation of notes and reports on political subjects for the Secretary General and the Council;

c) Political liaison with the Delegations of member countries;

d) Liaison with other international organizations, both governmental and non-governmental.

– The Economic Directorate carries out similar functions with regard to all economic questions having political or defence implications of concern to NATO and maintains contacts with international economic organizations. The Director presides over the Economic Committee.

– The Information Directorate has the task of informing public opinion about the aims and achievements of the Atlantic Alliance. It assists member governments to widen public understanding of NATO activities

210

through the medium of periodicals, films, radio and TV programmes, publications and exhibitions. It also arranges for group visits to NATO Headquarters for briefings and participates in the organization of special courses and seminars on NATO matters for young people. The Directorate includes a Library and Documentation Service.

– The Press Service
The Head of the Press Service acts as the official spokesman for NATO in contacts with the Press. He is also responsible for daily press reviews and press cutting services to the International Staff.

Defence Planning and Policy Division

The Assistant Secretary General for Defence Planning and Policy is Chairman of the Defence Review Committee (DRC), Deputy Chairman of the Executive Working Group (EWG), and supervises the work of the Nuclear Planning Group (NPG) Staff Group, and the Civil Emergency Planning (CEP) Committee.

The Division is organized into three Directorates, viz:

a) Directorate of Force Planning and Policy – responsible for the preparation, in collaboration with national delegations, of all papers and business concerned with the NATO Defence Review, including the analysis of national defence programmes; for other matters of a politico-military and military/economic nature considered by the Defence Planning Committee; for the preparation of studies of general or particular aspects of NATO defence on behalf of the Executive Working Group; and for the maintenance of a computerized data base of information on NATO and Warsaw Pact forces.

b) Directorate of Nuclear Planning – responsible for co-ordination of work on the development of NATO defence policy in the nuclear field and with the preparation of business for the Nuclear Planning Group and Nuclear Defence Affairs Committee.

c) Directorate of Civil Emergency Planning – responsible for co-ordination of plans for the use of civil resources in support of the Alliance defence effort, and the rapid transition of peacetime economies to an emergency footing; and for the preparation of business in this field for the North Atlantic Council and other bodies.

The Assistant Secretary General for Defence Planning and Policy is responsible for providing advice to the Secretary General on all these matters, for maintaining liaison with national delegations, the Military Authorities and other Divisions of the International Staff, and with other organizations as appropriate.

211

Defence Support Division

The Assistant Secretary General heading the Defence Support Division has, through four different Directorates, the following responsibilities:

a) The promotion of the most efficient use of the resources of the Alliance for the equipment and support of its forces. This task especially involves:

- The encouragement of co-operation between nations in research, development and production and standardization of weapons and equipment and their supply and maintenance within the framework of the defence plans of the Alliance.
- The organization of exchanges of information which may lead to such equipment.
- The study of logistic problems including the operation of the NATO Pipeline System, the NATO Maintenance and Supply Organization, etc. . . .

b) To assure technical and financial supervision of the NATO Infrastructure programme.

c) Participation in the process of Defence Reviews on matters within the responsibility and competence of the Division.

Scientific Affairs Division

The Assistant Secretary General for Scientific and Environmental Affairs is the Chairman of the Science Committee, and has the following responsibilities:

a) To advise the Secretary General on scientific matters of interest to NATO.

b) To ensure liaison in the scientific field with the military and civil authorities of NATO, with agencies in the member countries responsible for implementation of science policies and with international organizations having scientific and environmental affiliations.

c) To direct the activities of the working groups created by the Science Committee, and in general to implement the decisions of the Science Committee and its working groups.

d) To serve as Acting Chairman of the Committee on the Challenges of Modern Society (CCMS), to provide secretariat services for that Committee, and liaison between the International Staff and the pilot projects.

Office of Council Operations and Communications

The Director of the Office of Council Operations and Communications is Chairman of the Council Operations and Exercise Co-ordination Working

Group, the NATO Joint Communications and Electronics Committee and Co-Chairman of the Working Group on NATO Alert Systems.

He is responsible to the Secretary General for the organization and function of the 'Machinery for Crisis Management' including the Situation Centre and the NATO-wide Communications System, described in Chapter 7.

The Office consists of:

- The Council Operations Directorate which provides for the co-ordination of all activities associated with the functioning of the Situation Centre and for the co-ordination and staff work connected with the planning and conduct of exercises in which the civil elements of NATO participate.
- The Communications and Electronics Directorate which is responsible for the staff work in connection with the Council's interest in overall NATO communication requirements·and operations.
- A section which provides technical advice to and performs the staff work for the Committee for European Airspace Co-ordination (CEAC).

Administration

The Director of Administration is responsible for the general administration of the International Staff and for the preparation and presentation of the annual budget. He heads the personnel services and provides co-ordinating personnel management and policy guidance for the civilian staffs throughout NATO.

The Office of Administration provides the conference linguistic services and is responsible for the translation and reproduction of documents, for the graphic service, for the registry and archives, and for the security and maintenance of the headquarters. The Statistics Service, which comes under the Director of Administration, is responsible for the organization and direction of all statistical studies and in particular those required to assess the NATO defence effort.

Financial Control

The Financial Controller is appointed by the Council and is responsible for the control of expenditures within the framework of the budgets – see Chapter 18 on Financial Control.

International Board of Auditors

The accounts of the various NATO bodies and the accounts relating to commonly financed NATO Infrastructure works are audited by the International Board of Auditors for NATO. See page 243 for details.

Special Agencies

Between 1957 and 1975 the Council created the following NATO Agencies to carry out specialized tasks:

- Central Europe Pipeline System (CEPS);
- NATO Maintenance and Supply Organization (NAMSO);
- NATO HAWK Production and Logistics Organization (NHPLO) (European Limited Improvement Programme started in 1974);
- NATO F-104G STARFIGHTER Production Organization[1]
- NATO SIDEWINDER Production and Logistics Organization[1]
- NATO BULLPUP Production Organization
- NATO Air Defence Ground Environment Organization (NADGE)[1];
- NATO Multi-Role Combat Aircraft Development and Production Management Organization (NAMMO);
- NATO Integrated Communication System Organization (NICSO).

The Council also created the following Steering Committees to co-ordinate the production of:

- NATO Maritime Patrol Aircraft (ATLANTIC);
- AS/30 Air to Surface Missile[2];
- M.72 (LAW) Light Anti-Tank Weapon[2];
- Mark 44 Torpedo Co-ordinating Committee[2].

In accordance with the new procedures for co-operation in research development and production of military equipment approved by the Council in May 1966,[3] the Conference of National Armaments Directors (CNAD) accepted as a NATO Project Steering Committee the following Committee set up by member countries participating in the JAGUAR project:

- NATO JAGUAR Steering Committee.

Proposals for further NATO Projects have been approved and the following NATO Steering Committees have been created:

- SEASPARROW Point Defence Missile System;
- AZORES Fixed Acoustic Range (AFAR);
- AN-USD-501 Surveillance System[2];

1. These agencies have completed their missions and have now been disbanded.
2. These Steering Committees have now been disbanded.
3. For details see page 140.

- FH-70 155 mm Towed Howitzer;
- SP70 Self-Propelled Howitzer;
- Acoustic Communication with Submarines;
- NATO PUMA, GAZELLE and LYNX Helicopters;
- Multi-Role Combat Aircraft (MRCA);
- ZENDA Cannon and Free Flight Rocket Launcher Locating Radar[1];
- Combat Vehicle Reconnaissance (Tracked) (CVR(T));
- NATO Mark 20 RH202 Rapid-Fire Gun and Anti-Aircraft Field Mount HS 669N;
- NATO MILAN Anti-Armour System;
- NATO FORACS (NATO Naval Forces Sensor and Weapon Accuracy Check Sites in Europe);
- NATO Frigate for the 1970s;
- NATO Patrol Boat Hydrofoil (Guided Missile).

1. This Steering Committee has now been disbanded.

NATO Military Structure

MILITARY COMMITTEE
MC

INTERNATIONAL MILITARY STAFF
IMS

Brussels

(1) See Chart on page 220
(2) See Chart on page 224
(3) See Chart on page 226
(4) ACSA : Allied Communications Security Agency (Brussels)
     ALLA : Allied Long Lines Agency (Brussels)
     ARFA : Allied Radio Frequency Agency (Brussels)
     ANCA : Allied Naval Communications Agency (London)
     ATCA : Allied Tactical Communications Agency (Brussels)

SUPREME ALLIED COMMANDER EUROPE
SACEUR
Shape   1   *Belgium*

SUPREME ALLIED COMMANDER ATLANTIC
SACLANT
Norfolk   2   *USA*

ALLIED COMMANDER-IN-CHIEF CHANNEL
CINCHAN
Northwood   3   *U.K.*

CANADA U.S. REGIONAL PLANNING GROUP
CUSRPG
Washington DC

SHAPE TECHNICAL CENTRE
STC
The Hague

SACLANT ANTI-SUBMARINE WARFARE RESEARCH CENTRE
SACLANTCEN
La Spezia   *Italy*

NATO DEFENCE COLLEGE
NDC
Rome

MILITARY AGENCY FOR STANDARDIZATION
MAS
Brussels

ADVISORY GROUP FOR AEROSPACE RESEARCH AND DEVELOPMENT
AGARD
Paris

ACSA
ALLA
ARFA
ANCA
ATCA
4

CHAPTER 17

Military organization

Forces in 1949

In 1949, the twelve founder members of NATO had less than 20 divisions, and their reserves of trained manpower were inadequately equipped and therefore ineffective. In Western Europe, there were fewer than 1,000 operational aircraft available, many of which were obsolete models from World War II. Airfields (less than 20 in all) were not equipped to handle jet aircraft and were situated in vulnerable forward areas. The greatest concentration of NATO air and ground support was located in Western Germany where it was deployed, not for defence against attack, but to carry out occupation and police duties. Supply lines ran from north to south instead of from west to east. The naval position was no better. Many warships had been scrapped, put in reserve, or converted for use as civilian transport. The West would have been incapable of putting up any serious resistance to an attack, and its total fighting forces were far from being strong enough to deter aggressive attempts.

Build-up of allied forces

The history of NATO since 1949 has witnessed the build-up of member countries' forces, and their progressive adaptation to new technological developments as well as the steady creation of an allied command structure.

The strategic area covered by the North Atlantic Treaty is divided among three Commands and a Regional Planning Group. This division is governed by both geographical and political factors and the authority exercised by the different Commands varies in form in relation to those factors and to the situation in peacetime or in wartime.

217

The forces of member countries include those assigned in peacetime to NATO Commands, those earmarked for these commands, and those remaining under national command. The NATO Commanders are responsible for the development of defence plans for their respective areas, for the determination of force requirements and for the deployment and exercise of the forces under their command. Their reports and recommendations regarding forces and their logistic support are referred to the NATO Military Committee.

Military Committee

The NATO Military Committee is the highest military authority in the North Atlantic Treaty Organization. It is composed of the Chief of Staff of each member nation except France. France is represented by a military mission to the Military Committee. Iceland, having no military forces, may be represented by a civilian. At the level of the Chiefs of Staff, the Committee meets at least twice a year or whenever it is deemed necessary. In order for the Committee to function on a continuous basis with effective powers of decision, each nation appoints a permanent Military Representative of their Chief of Staff as a member of the Military Committee in Permanent Session.

The Military Committee is charged by the North Atlantic Council with the peacetime task of recommending those measures considered necessary for the common defence of the NATO area. As NATO's highest military authority, the NATO Military Committee is the body to which the Supreme Allied Commander, Europe, the Supreme Allied Commander, Atlantic, the Commander-in-Chief, Channel, and the Canada-United States Regional Planning Group are responsible. In addition, fourteen NATO Military agencies serve under the authority of the Military Committee. Among these are the Military Agency for Standardization, in Brussels, the Advisory Group for Aerospace Research and Development, in Paris, and the NATO Defence College, in Rome, as well as several communications agencies.

The Presidency[1] of the Military Committee rotates among the nations annually in order of the English alphabet.

The Chairman[1] of the Military Committee presides over both the Chief-of-Staff and Permanent Sessions. He is elected by the Chiefs-of-Staff for a two year term which can be extended.

He directs the day-to-day business of the Committee and acts as its spokesman. The Chairman is assisted by the Deputy Chairman, who also is responsible for the co-ordination of nuclear matters and of the MBFR military aspects within the IMS.

1. See Appendix 11, page 356, for list of Presidents and Chairmen of the Military Committee.

History of the Military Committee

The history of the Military Committee began with the establishment of the Organization itself. Two days before the North Atlantic Treaty was signed on April 4, 1949, a working group began to formulate recommendations for the establishment of agencies the treaty organization would require for successful operation. The report of this group was approved by the NATO foreign ministers meeting as members of the North Atlantic Council at their first session on September 7, 1949. The working group recommended 'the military organization should include a Military Committee (composed of one military representative of each country, preferably a Chief-of-Staff) . . .'. During its first session, the North Atlantic Council created a Defence Committee to consist of the NATO defence ministers and charged that committee with establishing the required military organization. The Defence Committee convened on October 5, 1949, and promptly established the NATO Military Committee. The first meeting of the Committee was held on October 6, 1949, in Washington, D.C.

Standing Group

To assist the Military Committee in performing its tasks, an executive agency, the NATO Standing Group was created to function in continuous session. This gave the Military Committee a day-to-day channel for the exchange of national viewpoints and the orderly flow of military plans, studies and recommendations. France, the United Kingdom and the United States provided permanent representatives to the Standing Group in addition to the necessary technical and staff support. Each of the remaining NATO nations with military forces appointed an 'accredited national representative in permanent liaison to the Standing Group'. In 1950 this liaison group was officially designated as the 'Military Representatives' Committee' and re-named 'Military Committee in Permanent Session' in 1957. This action generally corresponded to the creation of the North Atlantic Council in Permanent Session.

Also in 1957, the Standing Group staff was expanded by inviting each non-Standing Group nation to provide one staff planner in order to secure the input of national guidance on a working level. In 1963 the Military Committee in Chiefs-of-Staff Session agreed to modify the Standing Group further by establishing an International Planning Staff made up of members from both Standing Group and non-Standing Group nations.

The Standing Group continued to support the Military Committee until France withdrew from integrated defence arrangements of the Alliance in 1966, clearly making the concept of a three-nation executive agency invalid. The North Atlantic Council directed that on July 1, 1966, the Standing Group and International Planning Staff be disestablished and

Allied Command Europe

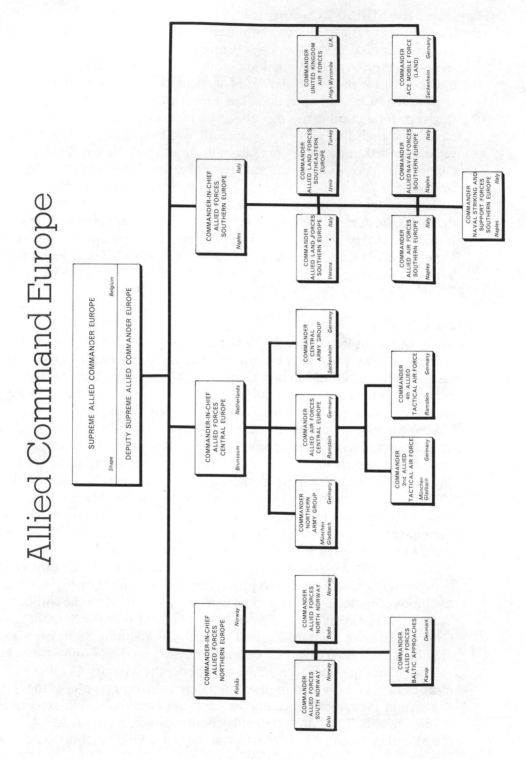

their authority be transferred to the Military Committee. An International Military Staff, composed of officers of the NATO nations who contribute to the integrated military forces of the treaty organization, was established on February 10, 1967.

International Military Staff

The International Military Staff which comprises about 150 officers, 150 enlisted men and 70 civilian employees, is headed by a Director of three star rank,[1] who is nominated by the member nations and is selected by the Military Committee. He may be from any one of the member nations, but he must be of a different nationality than the Chairman of the Military Committee. The Director is assisted by seven flag or general officers; six Assistant Directors and the Secretary of the IMS. There are six divisions: Intelligence; Plans and Policy; Operations; Management and Logistics; Communications and Electronics; and Command, Control and Information Systems. In addition there is a Secretariat and a support branch for administration and personnel matters.

As the executive agent of the Military Committee, the International Military Staff is tasked with ensuring that the policies and decisions of the Military Committee are implemented as directed. In addition, the International Military Staff prepares plans, initiates studies and recommends policy on matters of a military nature referred to NATO or the Military Committee by various national or NATO authorities, commanders or agencies.

The Military Committee in Permanent Session meets regularly at NATO Headquarters in Brussels, Belgium. The members of the Military Committee in Permanent Session have their offices in the Headquarters complex with those of the Chairman and the International Military Staff. The meetings of the Military Committee in Chiefs-of-Staff Session may be held at NATO Headquarters or in any one of the member countries.

Allied Command Europe

Allied Command Europe covers the land area extending from the North Cape to North Africa and from the Atlantic to the eastern border of Turkey, excluding the United Kingdom and Portugal whose defence does not fall under the responsibility of any single major NATO Command. The present Supreme Allied Commander in Europe (SACEUR) is General Alexander M. Haig Jr. (United States Army).[2] The mission of the

1. The following General Officers have served as Director IMS:
Lt. General Ezio Pistotti (Italy) 1967–68;
Lt. General N. G. Palaiologopoulos (Greece) 1969–71;
Lt. General Sir John Read (United Kingdom) 1971–74;
Lt. General Gerhard Schmückle (Germany) 1974–
2. See Appendix 12, page 358, for list of Supreme Allied Commanders Europe.

Supreme Allied Commander Europe is to ensure the security of Western Europe by unifying Allied defence plans, strengthening Allied military forces in peacetime and planning for their most advantageous use in time of war.

Functions of SACEUR

SACEUR is responsible, under the general direction of the Military Committee, for the defence of Allied countries situated within his Command area against any attack. In time of war, he would control all land, sea and air operations in this area. Internal defence and defence of coastal waters remain the responsibility of the national authorities concerned, but the Supreme Commander would have full authority to carry out such operations as he considered necessary for the defence of any part of the area under his Command.

SACEUR's peacetime functions include organizing, training and equipping the North Atlantic forces assigned and earmarked to his Command so as to ensure that they are knit together into one unified force; preparing and finalizing defence plans; and making recommendations to the Military Committee about such matters as the instruction, training, equipping and support of his forces, and indeed on any military questions which affect his ability to carry out his responsibilities in peace or war. While the Supreme Commander receives direction from the Military Committee he nevertheless has right to direct access to the Chiefs-of-Staff of any of the powers and, in certain circumstances, to Defence Ministers and Heads of Government. In addition, all the North Atlantic countries, with the exception of France and Iceland, maintain a National Military Representative (NMR) at SHAPE, who is responsible for liaison with his Chief-of-Staff. France is represented by a military mission. Iceland has no armed forces. SHAPE which was originally located in Rocquencourt near Paris, now occupies a new headquarters complex near Mons, Belgium.

To control the vast areas covered by Allied Command Europe there are three subordinate Commands directly responsible to SACEUR:

The Northern European Command comprises – Allied Forces North Norway; Allied Forces South Norway; and Allied Forces Baltic Approaches.

The Central European Command comprises – Northern Army Group; Central Army Group; and Allied Air Forces Central Europe.

The Southern European Command comprises – Allied Land Forces Southern Europe; Allied Land Forces South Eastern Europe; Allied Air Forces Southern Europe; Allied Naval Forces Southern Europe; and Naval Striking and Support Forces Southern Europe.

In addition, two other Commanders are directly subordinate to SACEUR, the Commander Allied Command Europe Mobile Force (Land

Component), and the Commander-in-Chief United Kingdom Air Forces. (See Chart on page 220.)

Allied Command Atlantic

Allied Command Atlantic extends from the North Pole to the Tropic of Cancer and from the coastal waters of North America to those of Europe and Africa, including Portugal, but not including the Channel and the British Isles. The Supreme Allied Commander Atlantic (SACLANT) is Admiral Isaac C. Kidd (United States Navy),[1] who, like the Supreme Allied Commander Europe, receives his direction from the Military Committee. The mission of the Supreme Allied Commander, Atlantic, is to develop defence plans in the North Atlantic area. He also organizes and conducts combined training exercises. In wartime, his main duty would be to assure that the communication lines of the Atlantic Ocean are maintained intact, to conduct conventional and nuclear operations against enemy naval bases and airfields and to support operations carried out by SACEUR.

Functions of SACLANT

SACLANT's peacetime responsibilities are defined as preparing and finalizing defence plans; conducting joint and combined training exercises; laying down training standards and determining the establishment of units; and supplying the NATO authorities with information on his strategic requirements.

The primary task in wartime of the Allied Command Atlantic would be to ensure security in the whole Atlantic area by guarding the sea lanes and denying their use to an enemy. SACLANT has responsibility for islands in this area, such as the Faeroes and the Azores. His authority in the event of war covers, in particular, the determination of the composition and deployment of forces, overall direction of operations; and assignment of forces.

SACLANT's responsibilities are almost entirely operational. NATO's Standing Naval Force Atlantic (STANAVFORLANT), the first to be formed on a permanent basis in peacetime, is an international squadron composed of ships from NATO countries which normally operate their naval forces in the Atlantic. STANAVFORLANT is under the command of the Supreme Allied Commander Atlantic, but control will be delegated to Commander-in-Chief Eastern Atlantic when the force is operating in European waters. Furthermore, additional forces have been earmarked for assignment to SACLANT for training and in the event of war.

Like SACEUR, SACLANT has the right of direct access to the Chiefs-of-

---

1. See Appendix 12, page 358, for list of Supreme Allied Commanders Atlantic.

Allied Command Atlantic

SUPREME ALLIED COMMANDER ATLANTIC	U.S.A.
Norfolk	
DEPUTY SUPREME ALLIED COMMANDER ATLANTIC	

COMMANDER-IN-CHIEF WESTERN ATLANTIC AREA — U.S.A. — *Norfolk*

COMMANDER SUBMARINES ALLIED COMMAND ATLANTIC — U.S.A. — *Norfolk*

COMMANDER-IN-CHIEF EASTERN ATLANTIC AREA — U.K. — *Northwood*

COMMANDER STANDING NAVAL FORCE ATLANTIC — *Afloat*

COMMANDER IBERIAN ATLANTIC AREA — *Lisbon* — Portugal

COMMANDER STRIKING FLEET ATLANTIC — *Afloat*

COMMANDER SUBMARINE FORCES WESTERN ATLANTIC AREA — U.S.A. — *Norfolk*

COMMANDER OCEAN SUB-AREA — U.S.A. — *Norfolk*

COMMANDER CANADIAN ATLANTIC SUB-AREA — Canada — *Halifax*

ISLAND COMMANDER BERMUDA — Bermuda — *Hamilton*

ISLAND COMMANDER GREENLAND — Greenland — *Gronnedal*

ISLAND COMMANDER AZORES — Azores — *San Miguel*

COMMANDER SUBMARINE FORCES EASTERN ATLANTIC AREA — U.K. — *Gosport*

COMMANDER★ BAY OF BISCAY SUB-AREA — U.K. — *Northwood*

ISLAND COMMANDER ICELAND — Iceland — *Keflavik*

ISLAND COMMANDER FAROES — Faroes — *Thorshavn*

STRIKING FLEET AND SPECIAL TASK FORCES (when assigned)

COMMANDER MARITIME AIR EASTERN ATLANTIC AREA — U.K. — *Northwood*

COMMANDER NORTHERN SUB-AREA — U.K. — *Rosyth*

COMMANDER MARITIME AIR NORTHERN SUB-AREA — U.K. — *Rosyth*

COMMANDER CENTRAL SUB-AREA — U.K. — *Plymouth*

COMMANDER MARITIME AIR CENTRAL SUB-AREA — U.K. — *Plymouth*

ISLAND COMMANDER MADEIRA — Madeira — *Funchal*

COMMANDER CARRIER STRIKING FORCE — *Afloat*

COMMANDER CARRIER STRIKING GROUP ONE — *Afloat*

COMMANDER CARRIER STRIKING GROUP TWO — *Afloat*

★ Currently, Cinceastlant holds direct responsibility for this area

▨▨▨ Co-ordination and Planning

▪▪▪ Maritime air chain of command

▬▬ Operational Control

Staff and, as occasion demands, to the appropriate Defence Ministers and Heads of Government.

There are six subordinate commands directly responsible to SACLANT:

The Western Atlantic Command comprises – a Submarine Force Western Atlantic Area Command; an Ocean Sub-Area Command; a Canadian Atlantic Sub-Area Command; and the Bermuda, Azores and Greenland Island Commands.

The Eastern Atlantic Command comprises – Maritime Air Eastern Atlantic Area; Northern Sub-Area; Maritime Air Northern Sub-Area; Central Sub-Area; Maritime Air Central Sub-Area; Submarine Forces Eastern Atlantic Area; Bay of Biscay Sub-Area; and the Island Commanders of Iceland and the Faeroes.

The Standing Naval Force Atlantic.

The Striking Fleet Atlantic Command comprises – a Carrier Striking Force, and the Carrier Striking Groups One and Two.

The Submarines Allied Command Atlantic

The Iberian Atlantic Command comprising – the Island Command of Madeira. (See Chart on opposite page.)

Channel Command

The Channel Command extends from the Southern North Sea through the English Channel. The Allied Commander-in-Chief, Channel (CINCHAN) is Admiral Sir John Treacher (Royal Navy).[1] CINCHAN Headquarters are located at Northwood, England. The primary mission of the Channel Command is to control and protect merchant shipping and contribute to the deterrence of all forms of aggression in the ACCHAN area. Should aggression occur, CINCHAN would endeavour to establish and maintain control of the area and support operations in adjacent commands, co-operating with SACEUR in the air defence of the Channel. CINCHAN has no forces permanently attached to his command in peacetime. The forces earmarked to CINCHAN in an emergency are predominantely naval, but include maritime air forces.

CINCHAN's subordinate commanders include Commander Allied Maritime Air Force, Channel; Commander North Sub-Area Channel; Commander Plymouth Sub-Area Channel; and Commander Benelux Sub-area Channel. In addition there are Commanders for the Maritime Air Forces in the Nore Sub-Area and the Plymouth Sub-Area.

CINCHAN has also under his orders the NATO Standing Naval Force

1. See Appendix 12, page 358, for list of Allied Commanders-in-Chief, Channel.

Allied Command Channel

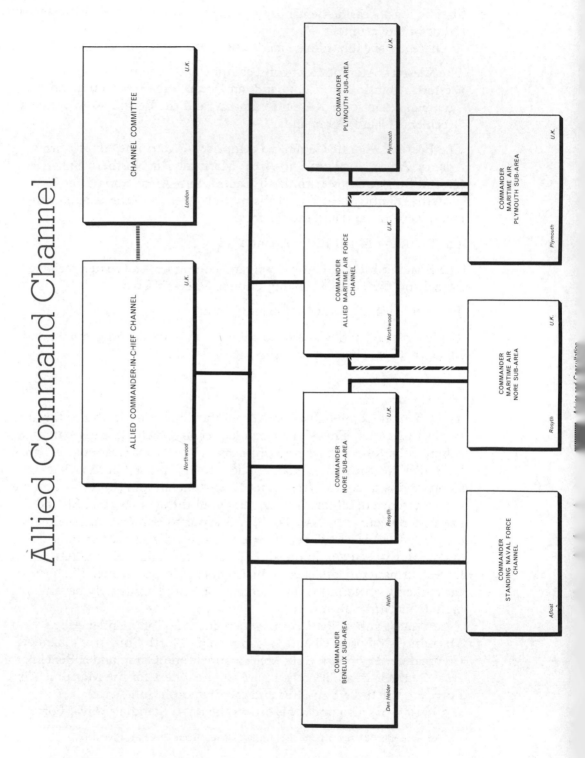

CHANNEL COMMITTEE — *London* — U.K.

ALLIED COMMANDER-IN-CHIEF CHANNEL — *Northwood* — U.K.

COMMANDER PLYMOUTH SUB-AREA — *Plymouth* — U.K.

COMMANDER ALLIED MARITIME AIR FORCE CHANNEL — *Northwood* — U.K.

COMMANDER NORE SUB-AREA — *Rosyth* — U.K.

COMMANDER BENELUX SUB-AREA — *Den Helder* — Neth.

COMMANDER MARITIME AIR PLYMOUTH SUB-AREA — *Plymouth* — U.K.

COMMANDER MARITIME AIR NORE SUB-AREA — *Rosyth* — U.K.

COMMANDER STANDING NAVAL FORCE CHANNEL — *Afloat*

Channel (STANAVFORCHAN) which is a permanent force comprising mine counter measures vessels of Belgium, the Netherlands and the United Kingdom.

A Channel Committee composed of the Naval Chiefs-of-Staff of Belgium, the Netherlands and the United Kingdom serves as an advisory and consultative body to the Commander-in-Chief, Channel. (See Chart on opposite page.)

Both SACLANT and SACEUR have official representatives at NATO Head-quarters in Brussels. These representatives provide liaison with the NATO and national authorities and with the various staffs. SACLANTREPEUR also acts as representative for CINCHAN when directed.

Canada-US Regional Planning Group

The Canada-US Regional Planning Group, which covers the North American area, develops and recommends to the Military Committee plans for the defence of the Canada-United States region. It meets alternately in Washington and Ottawa.

NATO exercises

To increase the effectiveness and combat value of the NATO armed forces and to further the spirit of co-operation amongst the different nationalities, international exercises are organized periodically by the Supreme Allied Commanders Europe and Atlantic, or by the Commander-in-Chief Channel, in conjunction with member governments. They are planned a long time in advance in order to prevent overlapping, to ensure that the necessary forces will be available and to give member governments an opportunity to co-ordinate national exercises with NATO exercises. They fall into two main categories: those in which no forces take part, which are called Command Post Exercises, and those in which actual forces participate.

The aims of Command Post Exercises (military abbreviation CPX) are to familiarize commanders and staff officers with wartime problems; to test and evaluate plans and executive bodies; to study tactical and other questions; and to test communications facilities. The object of a CPX is to define, examine and solve military defence problems. It may consist of a series of group discussions in which the 'Exercise Director' describes the problems chosen for study and the different commanders and their staffs present their views; or of a staff exercise, undertaken at any or all levels, in which tactics and procedures are acted out without the use of actual troops.

Live exercises (those in which forces take part) are carried out either in a limited area, in which case they are organized by Supreme or Subordinate Commanders, or on a NATO-wide scale when they are jointly conducted by the Supreme Allied Commanders and the Commander-in-Chief Channel.

There are different types of exercises each of which is given a specific name, and the number of forces participating varies considerably. The general purpose is to increase co-operation between the forces of various member countries and to test plans or study strategic problems. International manoeuvres have increased in scale with additions to the strength of forces assigned to NATO Commands.

Military Agencies

In addition to its other responsibilities the Military Committee is charged with the direction of several NATO Military Agencies and Organizations.

Among these are the Military Agency for Standardization (MAS), several Communications Agencies, the Advisory Group for Aerospace Research and Development (AGARD), and the NATO Defence College (NADEFCOL).

MAS

Organized in London in 1951, MAS is the principal agency for standardization within NATO. In January 1970, the agency moved to Brussels. The purpose of MAS is to facilitate military standardization both procedural and material, among member nations to enable the NATO forces to operate together in the most effective manner. Co-operation between the international technical expert groups and the agency in regard to defence equipment is effected by liaison with the International Staff. See Chapter 10, for details concerning the problems of standardization.

Communications Agencies

Five specialized multinational communications agencies provide the Military Committee with expert technical advice on all military matters within their own field of competence.

These are:

Allied Radio Frequency Agency (ARFA)
Allied Long Lines Agency (ALLA)
Allied Communications Security Agency (ACSA)
Allied Naval Communications Agency (ANCA)
Allied Tactical Communications Agency (ATCA)

The permanent staff of ARFA, ALLA, ACSA and ATCA are drawn from the NATO International Military Staff and are co-located in Brussels.

The ANCA staff is located in London.

AGARD

This Group was established in Paris in 1952. The mission of AGARD is to provide scientific and technical advice to the Military Committee, to improve the co-operation of member nations in aerospace research and development, to facilitate exchange of scientific/technical information, and to provide assistance to member nations for the purpose of increasing their scientific and technical potential in the aerospace field. (See pages 232–235 for full description of the functions of AGARD.)

NADEFCOL
See pages 235–241 for full details of the NATO Defence College.

SHAPE Technical Centre
The SHAPE Technical Centre was conceived as early as 1954 when General Gruenther, then Supreme Allied Commander Europe, expressed concern about the relative weakness of air defence within the NATO defence system. To remedy this, he suggested that air defence be studied as a whole and organized internationally according to a general plan, each country of the Alliance putting into effect the part which concerned it.

However, the creation of such an integrated air defence system, whose operation must cut across national boundaries, entailed the solution of political, tactical and technical problems, which in turn had to be considered from the viewpoint of all the NATO countries. The political and military authorities of the Alliance, therefore, authorized SHAPE, as the executive command for the integrated air defence system, to secure the assistance of a technical and scientific air defence centre composed of experts to be drawn from all the member countries.

In view of the time inevitably required to agree on the organization, structure, method of financing, and site of such a Centre, the United States Government agreed to bear the costs until NATO could take over, providing, naturally, that the Centre had proved its worth. After exhaustive enquiries, the United States Government decided to entrust the establishment and control of this Centre to a non-profit making Dutch Scientific Research Agency, RVO-TNO (Rijksverdedigings Organisatie-Toegepast Natuurkundig Onderzoek). A contract was signed between the United States and Netherlands Governments on December 14, 1954, setting up at The Hague the SHAPE Air Defence Technical Centre, to be administered by RVO-TNO.

Tasks of the Centre
Established as a Netherlands non-profit making organization operating under the policy guidance of SHAPE, the Centre continued to be funded by the United States Government until July 1, 1960, when, following a decision taken by the NATO Council on February 24, 1960, it became eligible for international financing under the Military Budget Committee. This did not affect the way in which the Centre was organized. The Netherlands Government renewed, with respect to NATO, the under-

takings it had given to the United States Government in 1954. On March 1, 1963, following a Council decision, the Centre was established as an international military organization in its own right under the policy direction of the Supreme Allied Commander Europe.

The SHAPE Technical Centre's mission is to provide scientific and technical advice and assistance to SHAPE. The Centre is required to undertake research, studies, investigations, development projects and operational tests for Allied Command Europe. As a subsidiary function the Centre may, without prejudice to its main task, render similar scientific and technical assistance, within the approved programme, to NATO nations requesting such aid. Initially the mission was limited to air defence problems, in the broadest sense of the phrase, but on October 23, 1963, the Council approved a widening of its scope to cover all offensive and defensive matters pertaining to Allied Command Europe.

At that time the name of the Centre was changed to SHAPE Technical Centre.

Work of the Centre

The focal point of the Centre's work has changed to keep pace with SHAPE's problems. In the beginning it was occupied in assessing the effectiveness and compatibility of early warning systems and communication facilities provided by member nations for integration into a NATO system, and to propose new and better means. Later, new tasks were added, including the evaluation of effectiveness and survivability of air defence weapon systems against aircraft and missile attack, taking into account the constraints imposed by the sites; the evaluation of exercises; assistance in planning NADGE; war headquarter operations and survivability; command and control; and force structure analysis.

The Centre's scientific staff has grown to an authorized complement of 98 scientists plus management (4), supported by technicians and the necessary administration. The facilities grew accordingly. A general purpose digital computer was acquired at the end of 1961 to help solve mathematical problems, to process data collected in exercises, and to assist in war games. In 1965, a high speed, high capacity type CDC 3600 computer was rented and is in use at the Centre. The growth of the Centre is reflected also in the buildings occupied. STC has now moved into a new building which re-assembles the staff under one roof and offers a suitable growth capability for the future.

When international funding was introduced, a new Board was established, the Scientific Committee of National Representatives. This makes possible the easy flow of information between nations and the Centre, avoids duplication of work and stimulates the work of the Centre.

SACLANT ASW Research Centre

The SACLANT Anti Submarine Warfare Research Centre was commissioned in May 1959 at La Spezia, Italy. Nine NATO nations participated: Canada, Denmark, France, Germany, Italy, Netherlands, Norway, United Kingdom and United States. Financial support for the Centre was initially provided by the United States until such time as NATO could take over.

Discussions leading to a NATO charter for the Centre began in July 1962 with the formation of a working group, authorized by the Council, with representatives from interested NATO countries and permanent military commands. The working group examined the future status of both the SACLANT Centre and the SHAPE Technical Centre. NATO charters and appropriate transition plans were worked out for both centres.

The NATO charter, which resulted from discussions carried out in Paris during the summer and autumn of 1962, was adopted by the Council on October 20. Its provisions were based on the reorganization of the Centre as a NATO international military organization under the continuing policy direction of SACLANT. The transfer to NATO was completed on July 1, 1963.

Mission of the Centre

The mission of the Centre is to provide scientific and technical advice and assistance to SACLANT in the field of anti-submarine warfare, and to be in all respects responsive through SACLANT to the requirements of NATO naval forces in this field. The Centre may also, without prejudice to its main task, render scientific and technical assistance within the approved programme to NATO nations requesting aid on ASW problems.

The Centre carries out research and limited development (but not engineering or manufacture) in the field of anti-submarine warfare, including oceanography, operational research and analysis; advisory and consultant work; exploratory research and other related tasks as necessary. It is organized by a Director, assisted by a Deputy Director and a Naval Adviser appointed by SACLANT. The broad scientific direction of the Centre is carried out by a Scientific Committee of national representatives, to which any NATO nation may appoint a member. The scientific work is conducted, under the supervision of the Director, by a staff of scientists, engineers, and technicians from the participating nations.

The headquarters and shore-based laboratories occupy buildings made available by the Italian Government in the naval base at La Spezia. Floating facilities consist of a chartered merchant ship modified as a research vessel, some small craft for local use, and an equipment-calibration barge on a local lake. Its staff of over two hundred includes scientists, engineers, technicians and administrators.

The scientific programme is divided into the following main categories;

231

the detection, location, and classification of submarines; the physical properties of the ocean, as related to anti-submarine warfare; analysis of the effectiveness of anti-submarine warfare tactics, training and hardware.

About 40 scientific reports per year are distributed to NATO governments and to interested NATO commands.

AGARD

The Advisory Group for Aerospace Research and Development (AGARD) was formed in 1952 as a result of recommendations made by a conference of Aeronautical Research Directors from NATO countries organized a year earlier by Dr. Theodore von Karman. The NATO Standing Group agreed to the formation of AGARD on a trial basis of two years. At the end of this period, the experiment was considered sufficiently successful to warrant a permanent establishment for AGARD and it was designated as a Standing Group Agency, financed from NATO funds. In 1966, when the Standing Group was disbanded, it became an Agency under the Military Committee which approved the Charter under which AGARD operates.

The first General Assembly of AGARD was held in Paris in 1952. This was followed by subsequent General Assemblies, held annually until 1964. The Assemblies were rotated through the entire list of the participating countries and consisted of a meeting of the National Delegates Board together with meetings of a number of technical panels.

From 1965 onwards, the General Assemblies have been replaced by Annual Meetings, which are on a smaller scale but which retain the principle of rotation through the NATO nations. They have been held up to the present in France (1965), Netherlands (1966), Italy (1967), UK (1968), Germany (1969), US (1970), Norway (1971), Brussels (1972) to celebrate the 20th Anniversary of AGARD, Greece (1973), again in France (1974) and in Canada in 1975.

According to its Charter, the mission of AGARD is to bring together the leading personalities of NATO nations in the fields of science and technology relating to aerospace in order to:

– Exchange scientific and technical information.

– Continuously stimulate advances in the aerospace sciences relevant to strengthening the common defence posture.

– Improve the co-operation among member nations in aerospace research and development.

– Provide scientific and technical advice and assistance to the NATO Military Committee in the field of aerospace research and development.

– Render scientific and technical assistance, as requested, to other NATO bodies and to member nations in connection with research and development problems in the aerospace field.

– Provide assistance to member nations for the purpose of increasing their scientific and technical potential.

– Recommend effective ways for member nations to use their research and development capabilities for the common benefit of the NATO community.

AGARD organization

The highest authority within AGARD is the National Delegates Board composed of from one to three officially appointed representatives from each member nation. Dr. von Karman served as the Chairman of AGARD until his death in 1963 and since then the Chairman has been elected from among the National Delegates. The AGARD Headquarters is located in Neuilly-sur-Seine, near Paris. It has a technical and administrative staff of approximately 40 and is headed by a Director who is a full-time NATO official appointed on the recommendation of the National Delegates Board.

AGARD accomplishes its mission through the Panel Programmes, the Consultant and Exchange Programme, and the Military Committee Studies Programme. The Panel programmes are conducted at meetings which are organized as conferences, symposia, specialists meetings, working group meetings, and planned at business meetings. The Consultant and Exchange Programme organizes Lecture Series and Short Courses as well as providing individual consultants to the nations and AGARD Programmes. The Military Committee Studies Programme organizes and participates in Technology Studies and Aerospace Applications Studies requested by or through the NATO Military Committee.

AGARD Panels

There are nine permanent Panels in AGARD, with a total of over 350 members:

– Aerospace Medical Panel

– Avionics Panels

– Electromagnetic Wave Propagation Panel

– Flight Mechanics Panel

– Fluid Dynamics Panel

– Guidance and Control Panel

– Propulsion and Energetics Panel

– Structures and Materials Panel

– Technical Information Panel

Each Panel elects from among its members a Chairman and Deputy Chairman and such committees as are necessary and these Panel Officers are assisted by a Panel Executive from the AGARD staff. Each Panel normally holds two main meetings each year.

The Consultant and Exchange Programme and the Lecture Series are designed to supplement the activities of the Panels in cases where the task proposed is not appropriate for the Panel operation. Upon invitation from National Delegates, individual consultants can be made available either to give lectures on specific subjects or to give advice and assistance with particular problems.

Lecture Series and Short Courses are given by groups of consultants, frequently in several different countries in succession. They are normally designed to present an up-to-the-minute, state-of-the-art review. In addition, the Consultant and Exchange Programme arranges for interchange of scientists or technologists between various NATO nations.

The major element concerned with the planning and conduct of studies for the Military Committee is the AGARD Steering Committee. It was set up in 1964 to ensure that the activities of AGARD are directed towards ends most useful to the NATO Military Authorities.

In the process of identifying areas of research and development of particular significance to military applications, the Steering Committee differentiate between technology items identifiable with the areas of interest of the individual Panels, and those items of a systems nature which cross the boundaries of the disciplines of several Panels. The latter are referred for investigation to the Aerospace Applications Studies Committee, established in 1971 to provide an effective mechanism for organization, management, and review of systems studies.

Although NATO provides administrative and staff support, and funds for consultants and the preparation and printing of publications, the main support for AGARD is derived directly from the member nations, which make available their own nationals to contribute to the work of AGARD and act as hosts to meetings. AGARD organizes usually about 40 major meetings a year.

AGARD publications

The end-product of most of the Panel and other activities of AGARD take the form of published documents. The AGARD series of publications fall into the following groups:

– *AGARDographs* are normally specially commissioned by one of the Panels, and are monographs or coherent collections on a single subject.

– *Reports* are short publications on a limited subject frequently related to a specific item of research work.
– *Advisory Reports* are generally similar to Reports but addressed to a specific audience, normally the NATO Military Committee.
– *Conference Proceedings* are reports of the Panels' technical meetings, generally including both the papers that were presented at the meeting and the discussions that followed. Conference Pre-prints are normally published before each meeting.
– *Lecture Series* publications consist of the full texts of the lectures given in the Lecture Series.
– Miscellaneous publications are produced by AGARD Headquarters and are of an administrative nature like the AGARD Bulletins, Annual Reports, Calendars of Meetings, Membership Lists and Handbooks.

All AGARD publications are distributed through National Distribution Centres in each NATO country. These Centres do not form part of AGARD but are national institutions (in most cases the national aerospace information unit).

AGARD publishes an Index of its publications, which are also listed in the official abstract and accession journals published by many of the NATO nations.

NATO Defence College

The idea of a NATO Defence College began when General D. Eisenhower was prompt to realize in 1951 that the common defence in peacetime of a group of countries stretching over vast regions could only be conducted to a good end by means of a framework of individuals perfectly adapted to this new environment.

Such men were required as could see beyond the horizons of the national interests to which, up till then, they had been limited, in order to grasp rapidly the essential features of military, political, economic and social problems within the Alliance. It was necessary for them not only to be competent in their own particular fields but also to be inspired by the spirit of co-operation and collaboration that is essential for any alliance. In a message which even today, many years later, has lost none of its value, the first Supreme Allied Commander in Europe said: 'it is highly desirable to establish in the near future a NATO Defence College for the training of individuals who will be needed to serve in key capacities in NATO organizations. It should be under the general direction of the Standing Group[1] or of the Council Deputies, or of both. Its students

1. It will be remembered that the Standing Group was disbanded in 1966.

should consist of carefully selected officers of the military services probably of the grade of colonel or equivalent, who are considered of suitable calibre for later assignment to key NATO military posts, and also of selected national civil servants who may later be made available to serve in key NATO posts. The course might include a study of military, political and economic factors which influence our NATO defence efforts, as well as a consideration of specific problems in both the military and the political fields for which satisfactory solutions may not yet have been found'. SACEUR's conclusions were accepted by the Council and Admiral Lemonnier was appointed as the first Commandant of the College.

The French government made available the Artillery wing of the Ecole Militaire at the southern end of the Champ-de-Mars and on November 19, 1951, the College, which is one of the most novel achievements ever seen in the realm of international teaching, opened for its first course. Since that date, over 100 graduates a year emerge from the College to fill key posts, not only on high-level NATO staffs but also in their respective national ministries.

An important change in the history of the College, occurred in the spring of 1966 when the French Government decided to cease its participation in the activities of the College and request its transfer from French territory. The 29th Course, the last to be held in the Ecole Militaire, came to an end on July 23, 1966, and the College began preparations to move. At the Ministerial Meeting in Brussels in June 1966, the Council extended a unanimous invitation to Italy to provide a new site for the College and on September 12, 1966, the Italian Government acquired new quarters for the College in the EUR District of Rome.[1]

Move to Rome

The EUR is a large suburb on the southern edge of Rome, chosen to be the site of a Roman Universal Exhibition planned for 1942. Now it is a garden city of Rome and a centre of international activities, to which the College, located in one of the newly constructed buildings of advanced Italian architecture will certainly contribute.

In the autumn of 1966, the College moved to Rome and prepared for the start of the next course at the beginning of 1967.

How could the academic programme be conceived so that it would satisfy the essential aims of the Atlantic Alliance and, at the same time, be flexible enough to allow a study of world events that were sometimes un-foreseeable and always in a state of flux?

Yet again, what could be done to prepare the members for their new responsibilities after leaving the College? Finally, how might the studies of

---

1. The address of the NATO Defence College is: Viale della Civilta del Lavoro 38, 00144 Roma. Telephone number: Rome 59.37.41.

this rather special insitution be given the particular style called for by the composition of its staff and members?

Planning of courses

Some experience in this field was already available. On the national level there were the examples of the National War College in Washington, the Imperial Defence College in London and the Institut des Hautes Etudes de Défense Nationale in Paris. These establishments already combined the study of strictly military problems with that of social, political and economic matters, the whole conducted in a broad national spirit and in the manner of the old Western universities. The first basic elements of the mission that the College was to assume were inspired by these examples. This mission was thus to give members of the armed forces, the NATO staffs and, by extension of the experiment, the national armed forces and ministries, the occasion to study, in common and thoroughly, the following aspects:

a. The aim and policies of the Alliance, its Strategic Concept, Organizations and Functions.

b. The geographical, political and military characteristics including special defence problems and technological and economic potential of member nations.

c. The developments outside of the NATO area and their effect on the Alliance.

d. Defence management orientations.

e. Practice in English and French languages.

Organized on a military basis, the College, which comes directly under the Military Committee, is commanded by a field officer of the rank equivalent or superior to Lieutenant General.[1] The appointment is normally for a two year period.

1. The following have held the post of Commandant of the NATO Defence College:
Admiral Lemonnier (France) November 1951–November 1953;
Air Vice Marshal Darval (UK) November 1953–November 1955;
Lieutenant General Byers (USA) November 1955–July 1957;
Lieutenant General de Renzi (Italy) July 1957–January 1958;
Major General Estcourt (UK) (temporarily in charge) January 1958–May 1958;
Lieutenant General Ariburun (Turkey) May 1958–May 1959;
Major General Sizaire (France) May 1959–September 1959;
Lieutenant General Harteon (Belgium) September 1959–August 1961;
General De Martino (Italy) September 1961–August 1963;
Lieutenant General Wolf Graf von Baudissin (Federal Republic of Germany) August 1963–April 1965;
Lieutenant General Duilio Fanali (Italy) April 1965–March 1966;
Lieutenant General E. Tufte Johnsen (Norway) March 1966–February 1968;
Lieutenant General Sefik Erensü (Turkey) February 1968–July 1970;
Vice Admiral J. C. O'Brien (Canada) July 1970–July 1973;
Lieutenant General E. H. Wolff (Denmark) July 1973–July 1975,
and since July 1975 Lieutenant General R. J. W. Heslinga (Netherlands).

The Commandant is assisted by a Faculty comprised of three military deputies (an army deputy, a naval deputy and an air deputy), a civilian deputy and 12 Faculty Advisers, one-third of whom are civilians: they are selected by virtue of their special competence and their knowledge of the problems to be studied at the College. Indeed their task is less to teach, in the strict sense of the word, than to assist the members who come from all the countries of the Alliance in the study of the latter's problems and to help them to visualize solutions to these problems by a work of research undertaken in common in a spirit of intellectual freedom and objectivity.

This working formula and the liberal atmosphere that prevails at the College are a direct consequence of the community of spirit and methods, which are employed there. More than 2,400 members (including four ladies) have emerged from the College since its creation and there is no doubt that the NATO spirit with which these are fired when they leave the College has always shown itself in their subsequent assignments. In addition, where human relations are concerned, their stay at the College has allowed them to form lasting friendships and the annual reunion, during which political and military events of a topical nature are examined, is a happy prolongation of the period of study previously completed at the College.

Academic Advisory Board

In April 1970, an independent Advisory Board of highly qualified men of different NATO countries was established to advise the Commandant, individually and collectively, on the continuing improvement of the academic activities of the College. The NATO Defence College Academic Advisory Board consists of a chairman (the Chairman of the Military Committee) and up to six members appointed for a period of two years.

The academic programme

The academic programme is divided into Study Periods covering the main aspects of the College mission. Study Periods are devoted to the examination of the various factors affecting the security and the defence of the Alliance. The content of the programme is continuously reviewed.

The first Group of Study Periods is devoted to the 'Basic factors of NATO' and the study of 'Communism'. Members, who, before joining the College are expected to acquire a knowledge of the basic elements of the Organization, go more deeply into the study of the military and political organization of the Alliance and of the economic institutions of the Western world. They come to grips with the principles that today govern the three Services. They also examine the latest state of preparation of Western defence in the face of an opponent whose structures and development are explained to them.

The second Group of Study Periods is directed towards an analysis of the 'External factors of the Alliance' to include: the relations within the non-Communist Developed World, the situation in the Third World and the current technological issues. This is, in fact, a first contact with the very essence of the major problems affecting the world outside the geographical limits of the North Atlantic Treaty. These studies are given a measure of flexibility as day to day events must be taken into account. It is in this Group that the Members come into contact with the developing continents and their continually evolving ideologies.

The third Group of Study Periods relates to 'The Way Ahead' and focuses the attention on some of the problems which are likely to confront us in the foreseeable future. Here the personal experience of members is called upon: they are asked to make an effort of synthesis and imagination to forecast what will happen in the years to come.

Academic Activities

The academic activities of the College are mainly in the form of lectures and discussions (in Committee or at full meetings of the course), in team studies, in examining and attempting to solve designated problems, and in instructional tours.

The role of the College consists of organizing these various methods of instruction.

Lectures are the linchpin of the course. They normally take place each morning. Lecturers are selected from among the most competent and highly qualified men in the fields of politics, command, strategy, government, economy and social sciences.

Each lecture is followed by a discussion period during which the lecturer replies to Members' questions. This period enables the lecturer to expand some aspects of his subject and often takes the form of a Round Table which stimulates the lecturer and from which everybody benefits. This discussion is frequently as valuable as the lecture itself.

Committee Work is the most valuable work of all, however, and takes place in Committee Meetings. Course Members are grouped in Committees, each of which has a Faculty Adviser. Committees are changed during the course to allow Members to have the opportunity of working with as many of their colleagues as possible. In this way various personal and national points of view are brought out and the particular views of the various services and ministries from which the Members come, can be examined. Committees usually meet for an hour each morning before the lecture and again nearly every afternoon.

As the Members have no command or administrative responsibilities they are not tied by political or other considerations, thus there are virtually no limits to their freedom of expression. Furthermore, each

Committee includes officers of different services and different nationalities with varying traditions and each benefits from the knowledge and experience of his partners and the pooling of their intellectual ability. Thus remarkable analyses are produced which are well worthy of attention.

Committees are also invited to produce solutions, in writing, to certain complex problems affecting the Atlantic Alliance. Those studies are presented and discussed in a full meeting of the course. Committee solutions are kept in the College Documentation Centre.

Instructional Tours and Visits are also scheduled and are an essential part of the course. Each course goes to the United States and Canada during its North American Tour and to most of the European member countries of the Atlantic Alliance during its European Tour. When on tour, the Course Members visit major NATO Headquarters and military and industrial installations in these countries. In addition, short visits are organized in Italy.

During these tours and visits, on the spot briefings are given by high national authorities and important personalities in the fields of industry, economics, etc. Tours are so arranged that Course Members have a chance to familiarize themselves with the various member nations thus increasing their knowledge and understanding of their Allies. It is only by breathing the atmosphere of a country and by making contact with its people that a true opinion of it may be formed. It is this which makes the College instructional tours of fundamental and lasting benefit to all participants.

National Representatives of those countries which cannot be visited during a particular course come to the College to give their National Presentations.

The military and civilian representatives of the countries of the Alliance are thus given the opportunity of working together during a period of over five months within a determined setting. The choice of the members, about 25% of whom are civilians, is left entirely to the Governments whose task it is to make a selection on the basis of past experience and training. It is also up to the Governments to employ these same officers in suitable future appointments which make the best use of the instruction received at the College.

Desirable qualifications

On this point, it can be said that the first quality required of a member appointed to the College is that he should be thoroughly competent in his own field and have a breadth of vision such as will allow him to grasp the points of view of other members within the context of the Alliance. It is also highly desirable that prospective members should have a very thorough knowledge of one of the two official languages of the Alliance. In this way, the College gives to those who are appointed there by their governments the unique opportunity of acquiring the basic notions of strategy and diplomacy within the framework of an Atlantic institution. For some, this will mean increasing their knowledge of problems which are often difficult to understand because of their international implications. Others will acquire the idea put forward by a military thinker who said that 'Politicians must know the instrument they will use'.

Finally, for the Governments which will, in fact, be represented at the College by their nationals, the institution will be the instrument that will allow them to enhance still further the high qualities of their best men under the most favourable conditions possible.

CHAPTER 18

Financial control

The operating expenditures of the International Staff, the International Military Staff, the military headquarters and the various specialized agencies are paid for by means of contributions from member countries. Naturally there has to be strict and effective control of monies placed at the disposal of the Organization by member governments. Since the funds are international, control machinery must be operated in such a way as to satisfy member countries that they are being managed correctly and economically.

The Civil and Military Budget Committees

Responsibility for NATO finances is assumed by the highest authority of the Alliance, the Council. That body is assisted in its task of financial control by the Military and Civil Budget Committees and by the International Board of Auditors.

The operating expenses of the Organization are covered by budgets adopted by the Council on the basis of reports by its Budget Committees. The Civil Budget Committee examines the budget estimates of the International Staff. The Military Budget Committee examines those of the International Military Staff, SACEUR, SACLANT and CINCHAN, as well as the various subordinate headquarters and specialized agencies.

The NATO Financial Regulations approved by the Council cover every step in the process of commitment and expenditure of funds contributed by member countries to ensure that they are properly used for the purpose for which they were authorized.

Financial control

Competitive bidding procedures are followed for works and supply contracts, thus ensuring economy and at the same time offering contractors and suppliers in all member countries a chance to submit bids. There is an established system for the clearance and payment of accounts, and a set of appropriate rules is applied to the maintenance of accounting records. Effective measures to streamline the general financial administration have likewise been introduced.

The responsibility for ensuring strict compliance with the Financial Regulations and for the day-to-day control of the various budgetary and financial operations devolves upon Financial Controllers who are independent of the administrative services and combine these functions with that of Treasurers. There is a Financial Controller for the International Staff and the International Military Staff and one for each of the Supreme Commands – SACEUR, SACLANT and CINCHAN. Their appointment is subject to approval by the Council. At subordinate headquarters, local Controllers are responsible to the Financial Controllers of the respective Supreme Commands.

It is also the responsibility of Financial Controllers to obtain the contributions due from member countries, payable in three instalments in the course of the year and in principle equivalent to the total amounts voted in the annual budgets. Each nation's contribution is calculated on the basis of an agreed cost-sharing formula.

Infrastructure financing

When infrastructure works are carried out on their territory, the NATO countries incur expenditures which are financed jointly by all the members of the Alliance. This common funding is based on a cost-sharing formula approved by all countries. No project is eligible for common funding unless the work has been authorized beforehand by the Infrastructure Payments and Progress Committee, which estimates the cost entailed. Throughout the execution of a project the host country – that is the country in which the work is being done – sends in reports to the International Staff on the expenditure incurred.

After these half-yearly financial reports have been analysed by the International Staff, the Payments and Progress Committee authorizes payment by contributing countries to the host country of their share of the expenditures incurred by the latter. Settlement of the sums due is made directly from country to country, the amounts being calculated by the International Staff, which sets off against the amounts owing by individual countries the sums due to them in respect of work carried out on their territory.

International Board of Auditors

The accounts of the International Staff, the International Military Staff, the military headquarters and agencies, and the accounts relating to commonly funded infrastructure works, are audited by the International Board of Auditors for NATO. The members of the Board are high-ranking government officials belonging to audit bodies in member countries or having a thorough knowledge of official auditing procedures. They are selected and remunerated by their respective countries and appointed by the Council, have independent status, and are responsible only to the Council and have assistants who are members of the International Staff.

Correct use of common funds

The primary function of the Board is to enable the Council and, through their Permanent Council Representatives, the governments of member countries, to satisfy themselves that common funds have been properly used for authorized purposes. It ensures that expenditures are within the relevant budgetary authorizations and that they have been carried out, in compliance with the financial regulations in force, as economically as possible. The Board establishes its own audit procedures, following the most modern methods.

The Board prepares, for approval by the Council, annual reports on the various audits it has performed. It may include in these reports whatever recommendations it deems appropriate concerning the efficiency of NATO procedures for financial control and the financial implications of administrative practices, drawing special attention to the need for adequate justification and economy.

The financial organization of NATO, therefore, has been developed along modern lines, thus ensuring that the funds entrusted to the Organization are protected by the same guarantees and subject to the same auditing processes as in national administrations.

PART 4

Chronology

Statistics

Appendices

Alphabetical Index

Chronology

1945

26 June
The United Nations Charter is signed at San Francisco.

6 August
Explosion of the Hiroshima atom bomb.

1946

16 March
Winston Churchill's 'Iron Curtain' speech at Fulton, Missouri.

1947

19 January
Elections in Poland. The Soviet-sponsored communist 'Lublin-Committee' monopolizes power.

4 March
France and the United Kingdom sign a 50-year Treaty of Alliance and Mutual Assistance at Dunkirk.

12 March
President Truman delivers his message to Congress urging the United States of America 'to support free peoples who are resisting attempted subjugation by armed minorities or by outside pressure' (Truman Doctrine) and requesting the appropriation of direct financial aid to Greece and Turkey.

247

1947 cont.

5 June

General of the Army George C. Marshall, United States Secretary of State, speaking at Harvard, announces a plan for the economic rehabilitation of Europe. This speech initiated the action which led to the European Recovery Programme and the formation of the OEEC.

2 July

Soviet bloc turns down Marshall Aid.

5 October

Cominform, the organization for the ideological unity of the Soviet bloc, established.

1948

22 January

Mr. Ernest Bevin, United Kingdom Secretary of State for Foreign Affairs, speaking in the House of Commons, proposes a form of Western Union.

22 February

The Communist Party of Czechoslovakia gains control of the government in Prague through a *coup d'état*.

17 March

The Brussels Treaty – a 50-year treaty of economic, social and cultural collaboration and collective self-defence – is signed by the Foreign Ministers of Belgium, France, Luxembourg, the Netherlands and the United Kingdom.

11 April

Secretary of State Marshall and Under Secretary Robert A. Lovett begin exploratory conversations with Senator Arthur H. Vandenberg and Senator Tom Connally on security problems of the North Atlantic area.

16 April

The Convention for European Co-operation is signed by the Foreign Ministers of sixteen European countries and by the Commanders-in-Chief of the Western Zones of Occupation in Germany. The OEEC was set up under Article 1 of the Convention.

11 June

The United States Senate adopts Resolution 239, known as the 'Vandenberg Resolution'.

24 June

Start of the Berlin blockade by the Russians.

28 June

Yugoslavia's expulsion from Cominform officially announced.

6 July

Mr. Lovett and the Ambassadors in Washington of the Brussels Treaty Powers and of Canada begin discussions about North Atlantic defence.

1 September

West German Constituent Assembly convened.

27–28 September

The Defence Ministers of the Brussels Treaty Powers decide to create a Western Union Defence Organization.

25–26 October

The Consultative Council of the Brussels Treaty Powers announces 'complete agreement on the principle of a defensive pact for the North Atlantic and on the next steps to be taken in this direction'.

10 December

Negotiations on the drafting of the North Atlantic Treaty open in Washington between the representatives of the Brussels Treaty Powers, Canada and the United States.

1949

15 March

The negotiating Powers invite Denmark, Iceland, Italy, Norway and Portugal to adhere to the North Atlantic Treaty.

18 March

The text of the North Atlantic Treaty is published.

31 March

The Soviet Government presents a memorandum to the twelve prospective signatories claiming that the Treaty is contrary to the United Nations Charter and to the decisions of the Council of Foreign Ministers.

1949 cont.

2 April

The twelve governments repudiate the Soviet assertions in a common note.

4 April

The North Atlantic Treaty is signed in Washington by the Foreign Ministers of Belgium, Canada, Denmark, France, Iceland, Italy, Luxembourg, the Netherlands, Norway, Portugal, the United Kingdom and the United States.

8 April

Texts published of requests by the Brussels Treaty Powers, Denmark, Italy and Norway for United States military and financial assistance.

5 May

The London 10-Power Agreement sets up the Council of Europe.

9 May

The Berlin blockade is lifted.

10 August

The Council of Europe's inaugural session at Strasbourg.

24 August

The North Atlantic Treaty enters into effect upon the deposit in Washington of the final instruments of ratification.

17 September

North Atlantic Council, first session, Washington.

20 September

German Federal Republic constituted.

22 September

Anglo-American-Canadian announcement that an atomic explosion has taken place in the USSR.

6 October

Mutual Defence Assistance Act of 1949 is signed by President Truman.

18 November

North Atlantic Council, second session, Washington.

1950

6 January

North Atlantic Council, third session, Washington.

27 January

President Truman approves the plan for the integrated defence of the North Atlantic area, thus releasing $900,000,000 of military aid funds.

9 May

The French Government proposes the creation of a single authority to control the production of steel and coal in France and Germany, open for membership to other countries (Schuman Plan).

15–18 May

North Atlantic Council, fourth session, London.

25 June

North Korean forces attack the Republic of South Korea.

25 July

Council Deputies, first meeting, London, Ambassador Charles M. Spofford, United States Deputy Representative to the North Atlantic Council, is elected Permanent Chairman.

1 August

Announcement is made in Ankara that the Turkish Government has decided to make formal application for Turkey's adhesion to the North Atlantic Treaty,

15–18 September

North Atlantic Council, fifth session, New York.

26 September

North Atlantic Council, fifth session, New York (continued).

2 October

Turkey accepts Council invitation to be associated with the military agencies of NATO in Mediterranean defence planning.

5 October

Greece accepts Council invitation to be associated with Mediterranean defence planning.

24 October

French Prime Minister, M. René Pleven, outlines to the National Assembly his plan for a European unified army, including German contingents, within the framework of NATO (Pleven Plan).

28–31 October

The NATO Defence Committee discusses the methods by which Germany might participate in the defence of Western Europe, and refers the political and military aspects of the problem to the Council Deputies and Military Committee respectively for further study.

251

1950 cont.

18–19 December

North Atlantic Council, sixth session, Brussels.

19 December

The Council appoints General Dwight D. Eisenhower (United States) Supreme Allied Commander Europe.

19 December

The Foreign Ministers of France, the United Kingdom and the United States, acting on the invitation of the North Atlantic Council at its sixth session, authorize the Allied High Commissioners in Western Germany to open discussions with the Federal Republic on a possible German contribution to the defence of Western Europe (Petersberg negotiations).

20 December

The Consultative Council of the Brussels Treaty Powers decides to merge the military organization of the Western Union into the North Atlantic Treaty Organization.

1951

24 January

The French Government announces it will convene a Conference to discuss the European Army Plan.

15 February

Conference on the setting up of a European Army opens in Paris.

2 April

General Eisenhower issues General Order No. 1 activating Allied Command Europe, and the Supreme Headquarters, Allied Powers Europe (SHAPE).

18 April

Representatives of Belgium, France, Italy, Luxembourg, the Netherlands and the Federal Republic of Germany sign a joint declaration formally setting up the European Coal and Steel Community.

3 May

The Council Deputies announce important changes in the top structure of NATO, namely the incorporation by the North Atlantic Council of the Defence Committee and the Defence Financial and Economic Committee. The Council thus becomes the sole Ministerial body of the Organization.

19 June

An agreement between the Parties to the North Atlantic Treaty on the Status of their Forces (Military Status Agreement) is signed in London by the Council Deputies on behalf of their governments.

8 July

The Petersberg negotiations are suspended.

24 July

The Paris Conference approves an interim report to governments, recommending the creation of a European Army. General Eisenhower agrees to co-operate in working out the military problems.

1 September

Australia, New Zealand and the USA sign the Pacific Defence (ANZUS) Pact.

15–20 September

North Atlantic Council, seventh session, Ottawa.

20 September

Agreement signed in Ottawa on the Status of NATO, National Representatives and International Staff (Civilian Status Agreement).

9–11 October

Temporary Council Committee (TCC), first session, Paris. Executive Bureau (Three Wise Men) established.

17–22 October

Protocol to the North Atlantic Treaty on the accession of Greece and Turkey is signed in London by the Council Deputies acting on behalf of their governments.

19 November

Inauguration of the NATO Defence College, Paris.

24–28 November

North Atlantic Council, eighth session, Rome.

1952

30 January

Council Deputies, acting on behalf of the Council, appoint Vice-Admiral Lynde D. McCormick (United States) Supreme Allied Commander Atlantic (SACLANT).

18 February

Greece and Turkey accede to the North Atlantic Treaty.

1952 cont.

20–25 February

North Atlantic Council, ninth session, Lisbon. The Council reorganizes the structure of the Alliance and NATO becomes a permanent organization with its headquarters in Paris.

21 February

The Council decides to establish a Channel Command and appoints Admiral Sir Arthur John Power Commander-in-Chief.

12 March

Announcement is made of the appointment of Lord Ismay, the United Kingdom Secretary of State for Commonwealth Relations, as Vice-Chairman of the North Atlantic Council, and Secretary General of the North Atlantic Treaty Organization.

4 April

Third anniversary of the signing of the Treaty. Lord Ismay takes office and the North Atlantic Council assumes responsibility for the tasks hitherto performed by the Council Deputies, the Defence Production Board and the Economic and Financial Board. The international staffs serving those agencies are amalgamated into one organization with headquarters in Paris.

10 April

Activation of Headquarters, Supreme Allied Commander Atlantic (SACLANT).

16 April

NATO opens its provisional Headquarters at the Palais de Chaillot, Paris.

28 April

The North Atlantic Council, now in permanent session, holds its first meeting in Paris. Appoints General Matthew B. Ridgway (United States) Supreme Allied Commander Europe, to succeed General Eisenhower.

25 May

United States detonates first thermonuclear device at Eniwetok atoll.

26 May

Signing in Bonn of the Convention on Relations between the Three Powers and the Federal Republic of Germany and the appended Conventions.

27 May

The Foreign Ministers of Belgium, France, Italy, Luxembourg, the Netherlands and the German Federal Republic sign in Paris the Treaty setting up the European Defence Community. Representatives of the

North Atlantic Treaty governments sign a Protocol to the Treaty on Guarantees given by the Parties to the North Atlantic Treaty to the members of the European Defence Community.

6 June

Admiral Sir John Edelsten succeeds Admiral Sir Arthur John Power as Commander-in-Chief, Channel Command.

4 November

General Eisenhower elected President of the USA.

15–18 December

North Atlantic Council meets in Ministerial session in Paris.

1953

28 February

A Treaty of 'friendship and collaboration' is signed in Ankara between Greece, Turkey and Yugoslavia.

5 March

The death of Stalin.

23–25 April

North Atlantic Council meets in Ministerial session in Paris.

28 May

Soviet recognition of the so-called German Democratic Republic.

17 June

Riots in the Soviet sector of Berlin and the Soviet occupied zone of Germany.

10 July

The North Atlantic Council appoints General Alfred M. Gruenther (United States) to succeed General Ridgway as Supreme Allied Commander Europe.

23 July

Korean Armistice signed at Panmunjon.

8 August

USSR announces its possession of the hydrogen bomb.

5 December

Lord Ismay attends the Bermuda Conference (France, the United Kingdom and the United States) as observer for NATO.

14–16 December

The North Atlantic Council meets in Ministerial session in Paris.

23 December

The announcement of Beria's execution.

1954

25 January–18 February

Big Four Foreign Ministers' abortive Conference in Berlin on German re-unification.

17 February

North Atlantic Council appoints Admiral Jerauld Wright (United States) to succeed Admiral McCormick as Supreme Allied Commander Atlantic.

23 April

North Atlantic Council meets in Ministerial session in Paris.

26 April

Opening of Geneva Conference convened by France, the United Kingdom, the Soviet Union and the United States for the purpose of reaching a settlement of the Korean problem and of considering the question of the re-establishment of peace in Indo-China.

7 May

In their reply to a Soviet note of March 31, France, the United Kingdom and the United States reject the USSR's bid to join the North Atlantic Treaty Organization.

17–18 June

Meeting at The Hague of the Constituent Conference of the Atlantic Treaty Association sponsored by the International Atlantic Committee (representing pro-NATO voluntary organizations). The constitution of the Association is agreed upon.

21 July

Geneva Armistice Agreements and Declarations on Indo-China.

29 August

The French National Assembly refuses to ratify the European Defence Community (EDC) project.

2 September

Admiral Sir George Creasy replaces Admiral Sir John Edelsten as Allied Commander-in-Chief Channel.

6 September

Opening of Manilla Conference which culminates in the signing of the treaties setting up SEATO (South-East Asia Treaty Organization).

28 September

Meeting in London of the Conference of Nine to seek an alternative to the EDC. Participating countries: Belgium, Canada, France, Federal Republic of Germany, Italy, Luxembourg, Netherlands, United Kingdom and United States.

3 October

Close of London Conference; it is decided to invite Italy and the German Federal Republic to accede to the Brussels Treaty.

5 October

Agreement embodying the settlement of the Trieste dispute signed.

20–22 October

Four-Power Conference in Paris attended by France, Federal Republic of Germany, United Kingdom and United States. The decisions of the Conference of Nine are endorsed and a protocol adopted terminating the occupation regime in the Federal Republic.

23 October

Signing of the Paris Agreements. The North Atlantic Council endorses the decisions taken at both the London and Paris Conferences and invites the Federal Republic of Germany to join NATO. Italy and the Federal Republic of Germany also accede to the Western European Union (WEU) set up under the terms of the Paris Agreements.

17–18 December

Ministerial Meeting of the North Atlantic Council in Paris.

1955

26 January

The USSR ends the state of war with Germany.

3–9 February

Supreme Soviet meets; Malenkov resigns; Bulganin appointed Chairman of the Council of Ministers.

24 February

Signing of Baghdad Pact (Turkey, Pakistan, Iran, Iraq and the United Kingdom).

5 March

President Eisenhower undertakes publicly to maintain United States Forces in Europe for as long as is necessary.

6 April

Sir Anthony Eden succeeds Sir Winston Churchill as UK Prime Minister.

1955 cont.

17 April

Opening at Bandoeng of the first conference of the 'uncommitted' countries of Asia and Africa.

5 May

The Federal Republic of Germany officially becomes a member of NATO.

7 May

The USSR denounces the Franco-Soviet and Anglo-Soviet Treaties.

9–11 May

Ministerial Meeting of the North Atlantic Council. A public ceremony marks the entry into NATO of the German Federal Republic.

14 May

The USSR concludes the Warsaw Pact with its European satellites by way of reply to the accession of the Federal Republic of Germany to the North Atlantic Treaty.

15 May

Signing of Austrian State Treaty ending the Four-Power occupation régime.

26 May

Bulganin and Khrushchev on a state visit to Tito in Belgrade, express their sincere regret for Soviet-Yugoslav tensions since 1948 and their Government's determination 'to sweep away all the bitterness of that period'.

7 June

The Governments of France, the United Kingdom and the United States invite the USSR to take part in a Four-Power Conference in Geneva from 18 to 21 July.

16 July

Ministerial Meeting of the North Atlantic Council to enable the Allies to exchange views before the Geneva Conference.

18–21 July

The so-called Summit Meeting at Geneva. No agreement is reached but a 'directive' is given to the Foreign Ministers on the continued examination of the outstanding questions.

18–23 July

First Conference of NATO Parliamentarians in Paris.

8 August

Opening in Geneva of the first conference on the peaceful uses of atomic energy.

8 September
Chancellor Adenauer visits Moscow.

25 October
Ministerial Meeting of the North Atlantic Council. The Foreign Ministers of France, the United Kingdom and the United States submit to their colleagues proposals they intend to make at the Foreign Ministers' Conference in Geneva on the 27th October.

27 October–11 November
Four-Power Meeting of Foreign Ministers in Geneva. Abortive.

15–16 December
Ministerial Meeting of the North Atlantic Council. The Council decides to equip the Atlantic forces with the most advanced weapons, i.e. atomic weapons, and adopts the principle of strengthening air defence by achieving closer co-operation between the European NATO countries in this field.

30 December
The USSR signs a treaty with the Pankow régime of the Soviet occupied zone of Germany, granting it the prerogatives of a State.

1956

27 January
The Soviet occupied zone of Germany is admitted to the Warsaw Pact.

14 February
Opening of the Twentieth Congress of the Soviet Communist Party: commencement of 'de-Stalinization'.

18 April
Pravda announces the dissolution of Cominform.

4–5 May
Ministerial Meeting of the North Atlantic Council. Mr. Gaetano Martino (Italy), Mr. Halvard Lange (Norway), and Mr. Lester B. Pearson (Canada) are instructed to submit recommendations to the Council on how to improve and extend co-operation between the NATO countries in non-military fields and to develop greater unity within the Atlantic Community.

28 June
Riots at Poznan, in Poland.

1956 cont.

26 July

The Egyptian Government nationalizes the Suez Canal.

17 August

The Communist Party is banned in the Federal Republic of Germany.

29 September

Franco-German Agreements on the Saar.

21 October

Wladyslaw Gomulka defeats the Stalinist old guard and is appointed First Secretary of the Polish United Workers' (Communist) Party.

23 October

People's rebellion in Hungary starts.

29 October

Beginning of the Israeli Sinai campaign.

29 October

Soviet Marshal Rokossovsky ceases to be Defence Minister of Poland.

31 October

Franco-British intervention in the Suez Canal area.

4 November

Soviet troops crush the Hungarian People's rebellion.

6 November

President Eisenhower re-elected President of the United States.

9 November

General Gruenther, Supreme Allied Commander Europe, bids farewell to the Council.

19–23 November

Second Conference of NATO Parliamentarians in Paris.

20 November

General Lauris Norstad, new Supreme Allied Commander Europe, takes command.

11–14 December

Ministerial Meeting of the North Atlantic Council. The Council approves the recommendations contained in the Report of the Committee of Three. Lord Ismay, NATO Secretary General, announces his wish to retire in the Spring of 1957. The Council appoints Mr. Paul-Henri Spaak, Belgian Foreign Minister, to succeed him.

12 December

Announcement of the United States plan of aid to Middle East.

1957

1 January

Political integration of the Saar with the Federal Republic of Germany.

10 January

Mr. Harold Macmillan succeeds Mr. Anthony Eden as United Kingdom Prime Minister.

6 February

General Speidel is appointed Commander-in-Chief Land Forces Central Europe.

23 March

The United States accedes to the Baghdad Pact.

24 March

Signature of the Rome Treaties setting up Euratom and the European Common Market.

8 April

Reopening of the Suez Canal.

2–3 May

Ministerial Meeting of the North Atlantic Council in Bonn. The Council says goodbye to Lord Ismay and decides to intensify its efforts in favour of German reunification by means of free elections.

7 May

Admiral Sir Guy Grantham succeeds Admiral Sir George Creasy as Commander-in-Chief Channel.

16 May

Mr. Paul-Henri Spaak takes up his post as Secretary General of NATO.

3 July

Malenkov, Molotov and Kaganovitch fail to oust Khrushchev; they are in turn expelled from the Party's Praesidium and Central Committee and deprived of all their political functions.

29 July

Signing in Berlin of a declaration by the Governments of France, the Federal Republic of Germany, the United Kingdom and the United States, affirming the identity of their policies with regard to the reunification of Germany and to European security.

2 August

Unification of the Air Defence Commands of the United States and Canada. Installation of an integrated Headquarters at Colorado Springs (NORAD).

1957 cont.

29 August

Proposals approved by all the NATO countries are submitted to the Disarmament Sub-Committee in London.

14 September

The General Assembly of UN condemns the Soviet intervention in Hungary.

27 September

Mr. Hammarskjoeld is re-elected Secretary General of the United Nations for five years.

4 October

The first Soviet Sputnik is launched.

7 October

Creation of the International Atomic Energy Agency with headquarters in Vienna.

14 October

Mr. Lester B. Pearson, one of the 'Wise Men' of the Committee of Three, is awarded the Nobel Peace Prize.

23–25 October

President Eisenhower and Mr. Harold Macmillan, joined later by Mr. Paul-Henri Spaak, meet in Washington. A declaration of common purpose is issued by the President of the United States and the Prime Minister of the United Kingdom, underlining the interdependence of the countries of the free world. It is decided that the Atlantic Council will meet at the level of Heads of Government.

11–16 November

Third Conference of NATO Parliamentarians in Paris.

16–19 December

Meeting of Heads of Government in Paris. A solemn declaration reaffirms the principles and purposes of the Atlantic Alliance. The Council decides to arm NATO with the most effective weapons. It also decides to promote closer co-operation in the political and economic fields and to increase scientific and military co-operation.

1958

31 January

The first United States satellite 'Explorer I' is launched.

19 March

First meeting in Strasbourg of the European Parliamentary Assembly.

27 March

Mr. Khrushchev replaces Marshal Bulganin at the head of the Soviet Government.

15–17 April

In compliance with decisions taken by the Heads of Government in December, 1957, the Defence Ministers of the NATO countries meet in Paris. They reaffirm the defensive character of NATO strategy.

5–7 May

Ministerial Meeting of the North Atlantic Council in Copenhagen. The Council declares that it is in favour of negotiations with the Eastern Bloc provided they are properly prepared and offer prospects of a settlement of the outstanding questions.

13 May

The Algerian French rebel against the Metropolitan Government and form a 'Committee of Public Safety'.

1 June

General de Gaulle invited to head the Government of France.

7 August

The atomic submarine 'Nautilus' establishes the first link between the Atlantic and the Pacific passing beneath the North Pole.

10 November

Mr. Khrushchev announces that the USSR wishes to terminate the Four-Power agreement on the Status of Berlin.

17–21 November

Fourth Conference of NATO Parliamentarians in Paris.

27 November

The Soviet Government confirms Mr. Khrushchev's position on Berlin.

16–19 December

Ministerial Meeting of the North Atlantic Council. The Council associates itself fully with the views expressed by the Governments of France, the United Kingdom and the United States on Berlin and on the right of the Western Powers to remain there.

21 December

General de Gaulle elected President of the French Republic.

31 December

The Western Powers reject Mr. Khrushchev's plan for Berlin.

1959

1 January

Entry into force of the European Common Market (the EEC).

13 February

Vice-Admiral Sir Manley Power is appointed Commander-in-Chief Channel in replacement of Admiral Sir Guy Grantham.

19 February

An Anglo-Greco-Turkish Conference decides that Cyprus shall become independent on November 19, 1960.

21 February–3 March

Mr. Macmillan visits the USSR.

26 February

President Eisenhower issues proclamation on the occasion of the forth-coming 10th anniversary of the signing of the North Atlantic Treaty.

24 March

Iraq withdraws from the Baghdad Pact.

2–4 April

Ministerial Meeting of the North Atlantic Council in Washington, arranged to coincide with the Tenth anniversary of the signing of the North Atlantic Treaty, and observed in all the NATO countries.

15 April

Resignation of Mr. John Foster Dulles, United States Secretary of State.

11 May

Four-Power Meeting of Foreign Ministers (France, the United Kingdom, the United States and the USSR) on the German question opens in Geneva.

4–10 June

An Atlantic Congress is held in London organized by the Conference of NATO Parliamentarians; attended by 700 delegates, the conference is opened by Her Majesty, Queen Elizabeth II. The Congress, in particular, recommends the creation of the Atlantic Institute.

19 June

The Geneva Conference is adjourned.

13 July

Resumption of the Geneva Conference.

25 July–2 August

Mr. Richard Nixon, Vice President of the United States, visits the USSR.

5 August

Second adjournment of the Geneva Conference; the four Ministers issue a statement on disarmament.

9 August

The Baghdad Pact becomes CENTO (Turkey, Pakistan, Iran, the United Kingdom and the United States). Its Headquarters is set up in Ankara.

15–23 September

Mr. Khrushchev visits the United States. There are conversations between the President of the United States and his Soviet guests at Camp David.

15 November

Fifth Conference of NATO Parliamentarians in Washington.

20 November

Austria, Denmark, Norway, Portugal, Sweden, Switzerland and the United Kingdom initial the Stockholm Convention establishing the European Free Trade Association (EFTA).

4 December

President Eisenhower, on a trip to Europe, pays a visit to the North Atlantic Council.

15–22 December

Ministerial Meeting of the North Atlantic Council. The meeting marked the inauguration of the new NATO Headquarters at the Porte Dauphine in Paris; it was largely devoted to discussing East/West negotiations, in preparation for a new Summit Meeting.

1960

29 February

Admiral Robert L. Dennison (US) succeeds Admiral Jerauld Wright as Supreme Allied Commander Atlantic.

15 March

The United Nations Ten Power Disarmament Committee starts negotiations in Geneva.

23 March

Start of a visit to France by Mr. Khrushchev at the invitation of the French Government.

1 May

American U2 aircraft is shot down over Soviet territory.

1960 cont.

2–4 May

Ministerial Meeting of the North Atlantic Council in Istanbul. The member countries review the situation prior to the Summit Meeting.

3 May

EFTA ratification instruments deposited.

7 May

In connection with the shooting down of a U2 airplane, Khrushchev announces that a Soviet Rocket Force Command had been established under Marshal Nedelin.

16 May

Abortive Summit Meeting in Paris (France, the United Kingdom, the United States and the USSR).

19 May

French, United Kingdom and United States Foreign Ministers report to the Atlantic Council on the breakdown of the Summit talks.

27 June

The Communist delegates to the Geneva Conference walk out.

16 August

Cyprus becomes an independent republic.

23 September

Mr. Khrushchev attends the General Assembly of the United Nations in New York and indulges in demonstrations.

8 November

Mr. John Kennedy is elected President of the United States.

10 November

Summit Meeting in Moscow of the Communist leaders of 81 countries. Approval of Mr. Khrushchev's concept of peaceful co-existence.

21–26 November

Sixth Conference of NATO Parliamentarians in Paris.

14 December

The OEEC becomes the OECD, with the United States and Canada among its membership.

16–18 December

Ministerial Meeting of the North Atlantic Council. The Council confirms its declaration of December 16, 1958, on Berlin.

1961

1 January

Inception of the Atlantic Institute with provisional Headquarters set up in Milan.

1 February

Mr. Paul-Henri Spaak, NATO Secretary General, informs the Council of his decision to resume active participation in the political life of his country. The Council accepts his resignation.

17 February

In a note to the Federal Republic of Germany, the Soviet Union reverts to the Berlin question.

5 March

Mr. Spaak leaves his post of Secretary General. Mr. Alberto Casardi, Deputy Secretary General, replaces him provisionally.

12 April

Soviet Major Yuri Gagarin first man orbited in extra-terrestrial space.

14–15 April

The abortive landing of Cuban exiles in the Bay of Pigs.

18 April

The North Atlantic Council offers the post of Secretary General of NATO to Mr. Dirk U. Stikker, Permanent Representative of the Netherlands on the North Atlantic Council.

21 April

Mr. Dirk U. Stikker takes up his appointment as Secretary General of NATO.

8–10 May

Ministerial Meeting of the North Atlantic Council in Oslo. The Council once more confirms its position on Germany, as expressed in its declaration of December, 1958. The Council also decides to consider ways and means of helping Greece and Turkey to expedite implementation of their development programmes.

1 June

President Kennedy visits NATO Headquarters in Paris.

2–3 June

Meeting of Mr. Kennedy and Mr. Khrushchev in Vienna. Aim: personal contact and general exchange of views.

1961 cont.

13 August

The 'Vopos' seal off the Eastern sector of Berlin. The Allied Powers send a note of protest against the building of the 'Wall of Shame'.

31 August

The USSR resumes nuclear tests.

30 September

The OECD Convention comes into force.

17 October

Opening of the Twenty-Second Congress of the Soviet Communist Party. Mr. Khrushchev waives the end-of-year time-limit for settlement of the Berlin question. De-Stalinization is intensified.

26 October

Admiral Sir Alexander Bingley succeeds Admiral Sir Manley Power as Commander-in-Chief Channel.

30 October

The USSR detonates a bomb of over 50 megatons.

8 November

Mr. Cabot Lodge is appointed Director General of the Atlantic Institute. The permanent Headquarters of the Institute is set up in Paris.

13–15 November

Seventh Conference of NATO Parliamentarians.

13–15 December

Ministerial Meeting of the North Atlantic Council in Paris. The Council reaffirms its position on Berlin, strongly condemning the building of the wall, and approves the renewal of diplomatic contacts with the Soviet Union to determine whether a basis for negotiation can be found. It also announces the establishment of a mobile task force.

1962

19 January

The 'Atlantic Convention' of the NATO countries meets from January 8 to 20, and endorses the 'Declaration of Paris' in favour of strengthening the Alliance and Atlantic Community.

20 February

Lt.-Col. John Glenn launched as first American astronaut and carries out 3 orbits around the earth in his 'Friendship' capsule.

14 March

The 17-Nation disarmament conference opens in Geneva.

18 March

The Evian Agreements establish an independent Algeria.

29 March

Signing of the Convention for the establishment of a European Organization for the Development and Construction of Space Vehicle Launchers (ELDO) – member countries: Australia, Belgium, Federal Republic of Germany, France, Italy, Netherlands, and United Kingdom.

10 April

In a joint statement Mr. Macmillan and President Kennedy appeal to Mr. Khrushchev for agreement on a test ban treaty.

18 April

The French people approve of Algerian independence by referendum.

4–6 May

Ministerial Meeting of the North Atlantic Council in Athens. The Foreign Ministers and Defence Ministers review the circumstances in which the Alliance might be compelled to have recourse to nuclear weapons.

14 June

Signing of the Convention for the establishment of a European Space Research Organization (ESRO) – member countries: Belgium, Denmark, France, Federal Republic of Germany, Italy, Netherlands, Spain, Sweden, Switzerland and United Kingdom.

25 July

The Atlantic Council approves the appointment of General Lyman L. Lemnitzer as Supreme Allied Commander Europe, to succeed General Norstad who is to retire.

5 August

The Soviet Union starts a series of atmospheric nuclear tests.

20 October

China attacks India.

22 October

President Kennedy reveals the building of missile bases in Cuba and orders a partial blockade of the island.

28 October

Mr. Khrushchev agrees to dismantle the missile bases in Cuba.

1962 cont.

12–16 November
Eighth Conference of NATO Parliamentarians.

20 November
The partial blockade of Cuba is lifted, Mr. Khrushchev having agreed to withdraw Soviet bombers.

11 December
US Defence Secretary MacNamara announces in London the cancelling of the 'Skybolt' air-to-ground nuclear missile.

13–15 December
Ministerial Meeting of the North Atlantic Council in Paris. The Council closely examines the implications of the Cuban affair and approves the action taken by the United States. It also reaffirms its position on Berlin and disarmament.

18–20 December
President Kennedy and Prime Minister Macmillan confer at Nassau, Bahamas. They agree to contribute part of their strategic nuclear forces to NATO.

1963

2 January
General L. Norstad hands over his command to General L. Lemnitzer.

14 January
President de Gaulle voices his opposition to Great Britain's entry into the European Economic Community.

16 January
After a statement from the French Representative, the Council notes that insofar as the former Algerian Departments of France are concerned, the relevant clauses of the North Atlantic Treaty became inapplicable as of July 3, 1962.

21–22 January
Chancellor Adenauer visits Paris and a Franco-German Treaty of Co-operation is signed.

28 January
The negotiations in Brussels for United Kingdom entry into the Common Market are broken off.

1 February

Admiral Sir Wilfrid Woods (UK) takes over command as Allied Commander-in-Chief Channel.

5 April

The Soviet Union agrees to the establishment of a 'hot line' between Washington and Moscow.

30 April

Admiral Harold Page Smith succeeds Admiral Dennison as Supreme Allied Commander Atlantic.

22–24 May

The Ministerial Meeting of the North Atlantic Council in Ottawa is devoted largely to defence problems. The British V-bomber force and three American Polaris submarines are assigned to SACEUR who is to appoint a Deputy responsible to him for nuclear affairs.

10 June

President Kennedy announces that representatives of the United States, United Kingdom and Russia will meet in Moscow in July to discuss a nuclear test ban treaty.

20 June

An agreement on a 'hot line' between Washington and Moscow is signed in Geneva by the United States and Russia.

21 June

The Geneva disarmament conference is adjourned to July 30.

25 June

On a visit to Europe, President Kennedy solemnly reaffirms America's guarantee to defend Europe and the principle of equal partnership within the Alliance.

15–25 July

Talks in Moscow between the United States, United Kingdom and Russia lead to the initialing of an agreement banning nuclear tests in the atmosphere, in outer space and under water.

29 July

General de Gaulle announces at a press conference that France will not sign the Moscow treaty.

21 September

The Soviet Union criticizes China's intention to possess atomic weapons and announces that there have been more than 5,000 violations of the Russian border by the Chinese.

271

1963 cont.

10 October

The Moscow treaty on the partial nuclear test ban comes into force.

11 October

Dr. Konrad Adenauer resigns from the office of Chancellor of the Federal Republic of Germany.

17 October

Professor Ludwig Erhard sworn in.

22–23 October

Operation 'Big Lift': 14,500 American soldiers are flown from the United States to Germany in record time to demonstrate that the United States is able to reinforce NATO forces in Europe in an emergency.

4–9 November

Ninth Conference of NATO Parliamentarians.

22 November

President Kennedy is assassinated in Dallas, Texas. Vice President Lyndon Johnson becomes President of the United States.

25 November

Extraordinary meeting of the North Atlantic Council to pay tribute to the memory of President John F. Kennedy.

16–17 December

Ministerial Meeting of the North Atlantic Council in Paris. In a message to the Council President Johnson renews America's pledges of 'steadfast resolve' to NATO. The Ministers reaffirm their common policies and express the hope that a genuine and fundamental improvement in East-West relations can be achieved.

1964

7 January

France recognizes the Peking Government.

23 April

Mr. Dirk Stikker announces to the North Atlantic Council his intention of retiring from the Secretary-Generalship during the summer of 1964.

12–14 May

Ministerial Meeting of the North Atlantic Council at The Hague in the Netherlands. The Ministers reaffirm their position on the major international problems as well as their full support for the United Nations in its action to restore law and order in Cyprus. The Council pays tribute to Mr. Stikker and invites Mr. Manlio Brosio, former Italian Minister and present Italian Ambassador in Paris, to succeed Mr. Stikker as from August 1, 1964.

4 June

The North Atlantic Council authorizes the implementation, beginning July 1, 1964, of the reorganization of the planning staff of the Standing Group. This reorganization, decided by the Military Committee, is designed to allow a broader participation on the part of officers from non-Standing Group nations in the preparation of NATO military plans and policies.

30 June

Mr. Ismet Inonu, Prime Minister of Turkey, visits NATO Headquarters.

29 July

Mr. Dirk Stikker takes leave of the North Atlantic Council.

1 August

Mr. Manlio Brosio takes up his post as Secretary General of NATO.

18 September

M. Paul-Henri Spaak, Belgian Foreign Minister, becomes President of the North Atlantic Council.

8–9 October

First meeting of the Defence Research Directors Committee. The main function of this Committee, created in the spring of 1964, is to advise the Alliance on the applications of science in strengthening its defences, especially those aspects which call for international scientific co-operation.

15 October

The Labour party wins the general election in the United Kingdom. Mr. Harold Wilson becomes Prime Minister.

15 October

Mr. Khrushchev is removed from office. He is replaced by Mr. Alexei Kosygin as Prime Minister, and by Mr. Leonid Brezhnev as party leader.

16 October

Communist China explodes its first atomic bomb.

3 November

Mr. Lyndon B. Johnson is elected President of the United States.

16–21 November

Tenth Conference of NATO Parliamentarians.

273

1964 cont.

15–17 December

Ministerial Meeting in Paris of the North Atlantic Council. The ministers review the international situation taking into consideration recent developments in the Soviet Union and China. They reaffirm their basic policies as well as the need for continued vigilance, and examine the problem confronting the Alliance in the field of conventional and nuclear weapons. The Council decides to hold its next meeting in London in May, 1965.

1965

24 January

Death of Sir Winston Churchill in London

6 April

World's first commercial satellite, 'Early Bird' launched into orbit by United States. Successfully tested as first in global communications system for telephone, TV, and telegraphic communications.

7 April

Soviet and East German authorities block land access to Berlin at intervals for one week when West German Parliament holds plenary session in West Berlin's Congress Hall. Session declared illegal by Soviets on ground that West Berlin is not a part of West Germany.

23 April

Soviet Union launches first communications satellite.

30 April

Admiral Thomas H. Moorer (US) succeeds Admiral Harold Page Smith (US) as Supreme Allied Commander Atlantic in Norfolk, Virginia.

11–12 May

The Ministerial Meeting of the North Atlantic Council in London associates itself with the Declaration issued by the Governments of France, the UK and the USA on May 12, 1965, which considered that in the absence of a real solution of the German problem, based on the exercise in the two parts of Germany of the right of self-determination, the situation in Europe as a whole would remain unsettled.

14 May

Communist China explodes its second atomic bomb.

31 May–1 June

Meeting of the NATO Defence Ministers in Paris pay special attention to the defence problems of Greece and Turkey and agree that further consideration should be given to a proposal for ways in which consultation might be improved and participation by interested Allied countries extended in the planning of nuclear forces.

1 July

France breaks off discussions in Brussels on the Agricultural Fund of EEC; a 6-month boycott of the Communities by France begins.

24 August

Admiral Sir Varyl Begg (UK) relieves Admiral Sir Wilfred Woods (UK) as Allied Commander-in-Chief Channel.

9 September

At his Press Conference General de Gaulle announces that as far as France is concerned military integration within NATO would have to come to an end, at the latest by 1969.

4–9 October

NATO Parliamentarians 11th Conference in New York.

20 October

The North Atlantic Council approves the revised missions of the major NATO Commanders and the Canada-US Regional Planning Group.

27 November

Special Committee of NATO Defence Ministers meets to initiate year-long study to explore ways of improving Allied participation in nuclear planning.

5–19 December

General de Gaulle re-elected, in two rounds, by universal suffrage, as President of the French Republic.

14–16 December

The North Atlantic Council meets in Ministerial Session in Paris. The Ministers accept in principle the new procedures designed to improve the annual process of reviewing the defence efforts of member countries and agreeing upon their force contributions.

1966

21 January

Admiral Sir John Frewen (UK), Commander-in-Chief, Eastern Atlantic Area assumes additional responsibilities of Allied Commander-in-Chief Channel from Admiral Sir Varyl Begg (UK).

1966 cont.

7 March

President de Gaulle writes to President Johnson stating French intention to cease participation in NATO integrated military commands.

10 March

French Government forwards Aide Memoire to 14 other NATO nations proposing to end assignment of French forces. France proposes simultaneous withdrawal from French territory of Allied military forces and the Headquarters of SHAPE and AFCENT.

29 March

Referring to 10th March Aide Memoire, the French Government announces that French force assignments will end July 1, 1966, and declares that the withdrawal of French elements entails the transfer of Allied facilities out of France by April 1, 1967.

9 May

First Chinese thermo-nuclear weapon (3rd test) detonated.

7–8 June

Ministerial Session of the North Atlantic Council in Brussels. Ministers agree to examine the problems raised by the French Memoranda of March 1966, to transfer the military headquarters of NATO from France.

16 June

The North Atlantic Council decides, inter alia, the Standing Group should end its function on July 1, 1966, and invites the Military Committee to submit proposals for the reorganization of a new common-funded, integrated International Military Staff.

21 June

The Belgian Chamber of Representatives approves the transfer of SHAPE to Belgium.

25 July

Defence Ministers meet in Paris. They adopt a NATO force plan for the period up to and including 1970, and lay down guide-lines for further improvement in the years following 1970. Ministers underline the importance of the defence of the flank regions.

13 September

The decision is made to transfer SHAPE to Casteau near Mons, Belgium.

13 September

The North Atlantic Council notes that the Channel Committee should be reorganized into an advisory and consultative body and that henceforth CINCHAN would be responsible directly to the Military Committee.

10 October

The NATO Defence College moves to its new headquarters in Rome.

10 October

Decision made to transfer AFCENT to Brunssum, Holland.

26 October

The North Atlantic Council decides to move the NATO political headquarters to Brussels, Belgium.

27 October

China announces its first guided missile nuclear weapon test (its 4th
atomic experiment).

10 November

The NATO Defence Planning Committee (or DPC, in which representatives
of member countries participating in NATO's integrated defence system
meet to discuss defence questions) invites the Military Committee to
move from Washington to Brussels.

14 November

Mr. Harold Wilson, UK Prime Minister, announces his Government's
determination to take Britain into the EEC.

14–18 November

NATO Parliamentarians' 12th annual Conference.

1 December

After Professor Erhard's resignation a 'grand coalition' Government of
the German Federal Republic is formed with Dr. Kurt-Georg Kiesinger
as Chancellor (Christian Democrat), and Herr Willy Brandt (Social
Democrat) as Vice-Chancellor and Foreign Minister.

5 December

The DPC approves the activation of the Iberlant Command which will be
the first NATO Command in Portugal.

8 December

Agreement reached at United Nations on the first international treaty
governing space exploration.

9 December

The DPC approves a revision of the overall organization of the integrated
NATO forces and a revised strategy.

14–16 December

The Ministerial Meeting of the North Atlantic Council in Paris
emphasizes willingness to explore ways of developing co-operation with
the Soviet Union and the States of Eastern Europe. The Council adopted

1966 cont.

2 Resolutions: one on technological co-operation and the second on undertaking an analysis of international developments since the signature of the Treaty to determine the influence of these on the Alliance with the view of identifying the tasks which lie before it. Acting on recommendations of the Special Committee of NATO Defence Ministers, the DPC decides to establish two permanent bodies for nuclear planning, the Nuclear Defence Affairs Committee and the Nuclear Planning Group. The DPC also approves other arrangements to facilitate consultation.

20 December

The DPC notes the organization of the integrated International Military Staff as the executive agency of the Military Committee.

27 December

Fifth Chinese atomic guided-missile test.

1967

18 January

NATO Defence College officially opened in Rome.

30 March

Final flag-lowering ceremony at SHAPE in France.

31 March

Official opening ceremony of SHAPE in Belgium. Headquarters becomes officially operational.

6–7 April

The Nuclear Planning Group meets in Washington.

1 June

AFCENT officially opened at Brunssum, Holland.

5 June

AFMED is disestablished and on the same date NAVSOUTH is established at Malta as a principal subordinate Command under the Commander-in-Chief Allied Forces, Southern Europe.

14 June

The North Atlantic Council meeting in Ministerial Session in Luxembourg, reviews the Middle East situation following the hostilities between Israel and its Arab neighbours. A Resolution adopted by the Ministers invites the Council in Permanent Session to pursue its studies of the role which the Alliance could play in the field of technology.

17 June

China detonates successfully its first thermo-nuclear 'hydrogen' bomb – the sixth in its atomic series.

26 June

Admiral Ephraim P. Holmes (US) succeeds Admiral Thomas H. Moorer (US) as Supreme Allied Commander Atlantic in Norfolk, Virginia.

7 July

Marshal Ivan Yakubovsky of the USSR appointed Commander-in-Chief of the Warsaw Pact forces in succession to Marshal Grechko.

28–29 September

The Nuclear Planning Group meet in Ankara.

6 October

Admiral Sir John Bush (UK) relieves Admiral Sir John Frewen (UK) as Allied Commander-in-Chief Channel and Commander-in-Chief, Eastern Atlantic Area.

16 October

Official opening of new NATO Headquarters in Brussels.

20–25 November

The North Atlantic Assembly, new title of NATO Parliamentarian Conference, holds its 13th annual Conference in Brussels.

12 December

The Nuclear Defence Affairs Committee hold a meeting in Brussels to examine the Report of the Nuclear Planning Group on the year's work concerning Strategic Nuclear Forces, anti-ballistic missiles, the tactical use of nuclear weapons, and national participation in nuclear planning.

13–14 December

The first Ministerial Meeting of the North Atlantic Council to be held at the new Brussels Headquarters approves the Harmel Report on the Future Tasks of the Alliance. Sitting as the Defence Planning Committee (with the exception of France which did not associate itself with the corresponding decisions) the Ministers adopt NATO's new strategic concept submitted to them by the Military Committee following its first comprehensive review of NATO strategy since 1956. This concept is based on a flexible and balanced range of appropriate responses, conventional and nuclear, to all levels of aggression or threats of aggression. The Council also approves the establishment of a Standing Naval Force Atlantic (STANAVFORLANT).

1968

13 January

STANAVFORLANT is commissioned at Portland, England. Ships from the Netherlands, Norway, the United Kingdom and the United States participate in the activation ceremonies.

19 January

The United States and the Soviet Union agree on a complete draft of the nuclear non-proliferation treaty and table this at the Geneva disarmament conference.

18–19 April

The Nuclear Planning Group meets in The Hague.

10 May

The Ministerial Session of the DPC held in Brussels reaffirms the need for the Alliance to assure a balance of forces between NATO and the Warsaw Pact. Ministers adopt a series of force goals for the period 1969–1973 and endorse the view put forward by the Nuclear Defence Affairs Committee that present circumstances do not justify the development of an anti-ballistic missile system in Europe.

24–25 June

Ministerial Meeting of the North Atlantic Council in Reykjavik, Iceland. The Ministers review the current problems of the Alliance including the situation created by current measures affecting access routes to Berlin, and issue a Declaration on Mutual and Balanced Force Reductions, published as an annex to the communique.

20–21 August

Soviet, Polish, East German, Bulgarian and Hungarian troops invade Czechoslovakia. Party leader Dubcek is arrested.

21 August

The North Atlantic Council meets to discuss the crisis created by this intervention.

22 August

An open-ended working Group is created under the authority of the North Atlantic Council to proceed with consultations and discussions concerning relations with Malta.

23 August

General Svoboda, President of the Popular Republic of Czechoslovakia goes to Moscow and begins negotiations with the Soviets.

26 August

The Soviet-Czechoslovak talks in Moscow end with a joint communiqué announcing agreement on the terms of the withdrawal of the Warsaw Pact troops from Czech territory 'as the situation in Czechoslovakia normalizes'.

27 August

Return to Prague of President Svoboda, Mr. Dubcek and other Czech personalities.

10–11 October

The Nuclear Planning Group meets in Bonn.

17 October

Signature in Prague of legal agreement authorizing temporary stationing of Soviet troops in Czechoslovakia.

5 November

Mr. Richard Nixon is elected President of the United States.

10–15 November

Fourteenth annual Conference of the North Atlantic Assembly held in Brussels.

14–16 November

Ministerial Meeting of the Council in Brussels. The Ministers denounce Soviet actions in Czechoslovakia as contrary to the basic principles of the United Nations Charter and give a warning to the USSR. They decide to improve the state of NATO defence forces, confirm they will continue to study possibilities of détente, and reaffirm the indispensable necessity of the Atlantic Alliance.

21 November

Activation of MARAIRMED at Naples to improve NATO surveillance of the Mediterranean area.

13 December

Announcement of the appointment of Mr. Osman Olcay (Turkey) as Deputy Secretary General of NATO in January 1969 in replacement of Mr. James A. Roberts (Canada).

1969

16 January

Ministerial Session of the Defence Planning Committee. Ministers adopt NATO force plans for the period 1969–73.

1969 cont.

24 February
President Nixon visits NATO Headquarters and addresses the Council.

10–11 April
Spring Ministerial meeting in Washington includes commemorative session to celebrate the 20th Anniversary of the signing of the North Atlantic Treaty. President Nixon proposes that NATO should study environmental problems. Ministers offer to examine with the USSR and other Eastern European countries which concrete issues best lend themselves to fruitful negotiations.

28 May
Ministerial Meeting of the Defence Planning Committee: discussion of procedures for consultation concerning Canadian forces in Europe. Approval for creation of naval on-call force in the Mediterranean.

29–30 May
The Nuclear Planning Group meets in London.

1 July
General Andrew J. Goodpaster (US) succeeds General Lyman L. Lemnitzer as Supreme Allied Commander Europe (SACEUR).

6 November
The Council approves the setting up of a Committee on the Challenges of Modern Society to study the problems of human environment.

11–12 November
Meeting of Nuclear Planning Group in Warrington, Virginia.

3–5 December
Ministerial Meeting in Brussels. The Council issues a Declaration on East/West Relations. Ministers endorse a number of remedial measures necessary to maintain adequate forces in Central Europe. Acting on the recommendation of the Nuclear Defence Affairs Committee, the Defence Planning Committee approves general guidelines for nuclear consultation procedures and for the possible tactical use of nuclear weapons in defence of the Treaty area.

1970

27 February
Admiral Sir William O'Brien (UK) relieves Admiral Sir John Bush as Allied Commander-in-Chief Channel (CINCHAN)

5 March

Non-Proliferation Treaty on Nuclear weapons comes into force.

20 March

NATO Communications satellite launched from Cape Kennedy.

16 April

Opening in Vienna of US-USSR negotiations on strategic arms limitation (SALT)

26–27 May

Ministerial meeting in Rome. Ministers issue a Declaration on Mutual and Balanced Force Reductions and request Italy to transmit it with the Final Communiqué to all interested governments.

11 June

The Defence Planning Committee in Ministerial Session discuss the continuing expansion of the Soviet presence in the Mediterranean and welcome the activation of the Naval On-Call-Force-Mediterranean.

12 August

Signing in Moscow of a Non-Aggression Treaty between the Federal Republic of Germany and the USSR.

1 October

Admiral Charles K. Duncan (US) succeeds Admiral Ephraim P. Holmes as Supreme Allied Commander Atlantic (SACLANT).

29–30 October

Nuclear Planning Group meets at Ottawa.

2 November

Second session of US/USSR SALT negotiations at Helsinki.

2–4 December

Ministerial Meetings of the Council and Defence Planning Committee (DPC) in Brussels. Ministers welcome President Nixon's pledge that given similar approach by other Allies, US will maintain and improve their forces in Europe and not reduce them except in context of reciprocal East–West action. DPC adopts study of 'Alliance Defence for the 70s'. Ten European countries adopt special European Defence Improvement Programme to improve certain aspects of Alliance defence capability. DPC adopts policy documents on role of NATO nuclear forces and political guidelines for possible defensive use of atomic demolition munitions.

7 December

Signing in Warsaw of a Treaty on Normalization of relations between the Federal Republic of Germany and Poland.

1971

27 January

Second NATO Communications satellite launched from Cape Kennedy.

1 April

General Johannes Steinhoff (Federal Republic of Germany) succeeds Admiral Sir Nigel Henderson as Chairman of the Military Committee.

26 May

Nuclear Planning Group meets at Mittenwald, Germany, Ministers discuss methods of supporting the strategy of flexible response by use of nuclear weapons.

28 May

Defence Planning Committee Ministerial meeting in Brussels. Ministers confirm important conclusions made at their last session.

3–4 June

Ministerial Meeting of the Council in Lisbon. Ministers renew study of Berlin problem and note with interest first Soviet reactions regarding mutual and balanced force reductions. They invite Mr. Joseph Luns, Netherlands Foreign Minister, to succeed M. Manlio Brosio as Secretary General of NATO on October 1. Ministers pay tribute to M. Brosio for his long and successful stewardship.

29 June

Announcement of the appointment of Mr. P. Pansa Cedronio (Italy) as Deputy Secretary General of NATO in replacement of Mr. Osman Olcay (Turkey).

20 August

The Defence Planning Committee directs that NAVSOUTH be transferred from Malta to Naples.

3 September

Signing of first stage of Four Power Agreement on Berlin.

17 September

Admiral Sir Edward Ashmore (UK) relieves Admiral Sir William O'Brien as Allied Commander-in-Chief Channel (CINCHAN).

5–6 October

Council meeting attended by Deputy Foreign Ministers. Mr. Brosio appointed to conduct exploratory talks on MBFR with Soviet and other interested Governments.

8–10 December

Ministerial Meetings of the Council and the Defence Planning Committee in Brussels. Ministers reaffirm readiness to begin multilateral exploration of European security and co-operation as soon as Berlin negotiations are successfully concluded.

1972

21 February

President Nixon arrives in Peking.

22 May

Arrival of President Nixon in Moscow.

24 May

Defence Planning Committee Ministerial Meeting in Brussels. Ministers note increased Soviet nuclear and conventional capabilities and review progress of Eurogroup members.

26 May

Signature in Moscow of interim agreement on strategic arms limitations (SALT).

30–31 May

Ministerial Meeting of the Council in Bonn. Ministers welcome favourable progress in East–West relations following signature of several bilateral agreements and agree to start multinational preparatory talks for a Conference on Security and Co-operation in Europe (CSCE). The Fourteen propose multilateral explorations on mutual and balanced force reductions (MBFR).

3 June

Four-Power Agreement on Berlin signed by Foreign Ministers of France, UK, USA and USSR.

31 October

Admiral Ralph W. Cousins (US) succeeds Admiral Charles K. Duncan as Supreme Allied Commander Atlantic (SACLANT).

7 November

Richard Nixon re-elected President of the United States.

19–24 November

18th Annual Session in Bonn of the North Atlantic Assembly.

21 November

Opening of SALT II in Geneva.

285

1972 cont.

22 November

Opening in Helsinki of multilateral preparatory talks on a CSCE.

7–8 December

Ministerial meeting in Brussels. Ministers review Western objectives at Helsinki and express resolve to maintain Alliance defences in face of increased Warsaw Pact forces.

21 December

Signature in East Berlin of the 'Basic Treaty' between the two States of Germany.

1973

1 January

Denmark, Eire and the UK join the EEC.

31 January

Multilateral exploratory talks on MBFR inaugurated in Vienna.

11 May

Inauguration of a permanent mine counter measures force within the Channel Command (STANAVFORCHAN).

16 May

13th Ministerial Meeting in Ankara of the Nuclear Planning Group.

14–15 June

Ministerial Council meeting in Copenhagen. Ministers consider outcome of CSCE preparatory talks and express willingness to enter first phase at Helsinki on July 3. The Fourteen reaffirm importance they attach to MBFR talks due to start in October in Vienna.

19 June

Start of Brezhnev/Nixon talks in Washington.

25 June

Announcement of US-USSR agreement on the prevention of nuclear war.

29 June

End of MBFR exploratory talks in Vienna.

30 June

The Permanent Representatives to the North Atlantic Council meet President Nixon at San Clemente, California.

3 July

First phase of CSCE opens in Helsinki.

18 September

Second phase of CSCE starts in Geneva.

21–27 October

19th Annual Session in Ankara of the North Atlantic Assembly.

30 October

Conference on mutual reduction of forces and armaments (MBFR) opens in Vienna.

7 December

Defence Planning Committee Ministerial Meeting in Brussels. Ministers consider budgetary and balance of payments problems arising from stationing of US troops in Europe and US share in NATO civil and military programmes.

10–11 December

Ministerial meeting in Brussels. Ministers review world developments and on-going negotiations and recognize a common Alliance effort is required to maintain US forces in Europe at present level.

20 December

Admiral Sir Terence Lewin (UK) relieves Admiral Sir Edward Ashmore as Allied Commander-in-Chief Channel (CINCHAN).

23 December

OPEC (Organization of Petroleum Exporting Countries) announces doubling of the price of crude oil sold by the six Persian Gulf members.

1974

11–13 February

Energy conference in Washington (USA, Canada, Japan, Norway and the EEC Nine).

28 February

Following elections in UK Mr. Harold Wilson forms a minority Government.

25 April

Military *coup d'Etat* in Portugal.

7 May

Helmut Schmidt becomes Chancellor of the FRG.

1974 cont.

15 May

General Spinola appointed President of the Portuguese Republic.

16 May

Marshal Tito elected life President of Yugoslavia.

19 May

M. Giscard d'Estaing elected President of France.

14 June

Defence Planning Committee Ministerial Meeting in Brussels. Ministers note continued expansion of Warsaw Pact forces, review progress of the European Defence Improvement Programme (EDIP) and reaffirm importance of standardization and specialization of defence tasks.

18–19 June

Ministerial Meeting of the Council in Ottawa observes 25th Anniversary Year of the Alliance. Ministers adopt and publish a Declaration on Atlantic Relations reaffirming commitment of all members to the Treaty.

26 June

Meeting of Heads of Government for consultation in Brussels. President Nixon and the Heads of Government, accompanied by their Foreign Ministers, sign the Declaration on Atlantic Relations.

15 July

Military *coup d'Etat* in Cyprus followed by landing of Turkish troops. Resignation of the military regime in Athens.

24 July

Mr. Karamanlis, returning from exile, is named Greek Prime Minister. All restrictions on civil liberties are removed.

8 August

Resignation of President Nixon. Mr. Gerald Ford becomes 38th President of the US.

16 September

Appointment of General Alexander M. Haig as SACEUR.

30 September

General Costa Gomes replaces General Spinola as President of the Portuguese Republic.

10 October

Following elections in the UK the Labour Party obtain a majority vote in Parliament.

17 November

Elections in Greece. Mr. Karamanlis gains support of 220 out of 300 seats in Parliament.

23–24 November

President Ford and Mr. Brezhnev, meeting in Vladivostok, reach agreement on limitation of US/USSR strategic nuclear arms.

10–11 December

Ministerial Meeting in Brussels of Defence Planning Committee. Ministers note strengthening of Warsaw Pact forces, review improvements to NATO conventional forces in 1974 and discuss impact of inflation on defence costs.

12–13 December

Council Ministerial Meeting in Brussels. Ministers review East-West relations and progress of CSCE and MBFR, discuss economic developments, and reaffirm importance of maintaining peace in the Middle East.

1975

23 May

Ministerial Meeting in Brussels of Defence Planning Committee. Ministers review the strategic situation in the Mediterranean, the activities of the Eurogroup, and issue 'guidelines' for future defence planning.

29–30 May

Ministerial Meeting of Heads of Government in Brussels. The Allies reaffirm their resolve to maintain the solidarity of the Alliance, safeguard the security of its members and to strive towards a durable and lasting peace.

30 May

Admiral Isaac C. Kidd (US) succeeds Admiral Ralph W. Cousins as Supreme Allied Commander Atlantic (SACLANT).

16–17 June

17th half-yearly meeting of the Nuclear Planning Group (NPG) in Monterey, California.

24–27 June

First civil defence seminar sponsored by NATO held in Battle Creek, Michigan. Attended by Belgium, Canada, Denmark, Federal Republic of Germany, Iceland, Italy, Netherlands, Norway, UK and US.

21 July

Ending of second phase of CSCE in Geneva.

1975 cont.

31 July–1 August

Final phase of CSCE in Helsinki. The Heads of State and Government sign the Final Act of the Conference.

9–10 December

DPC Ministerial Meeting in Brussels. Ministers note continued increase in Warsaw Pact strength and capabilities, reaffirm importance of maintaining and strengthening NATO forces, and review current efforts to improve standardization and compatibility of military equipment within the Alliance.

11–12 December

Ministerial session of the Council in Brussels. Ministers review status of East–West relations and reaffirm importance of maintaining solidarity and the defensive strength of the Alliance. The representatives of Governments taking part in the MBFR negotiations reaffirm their importance and approve additional proposals for presentation in Vienna.

Statistics

Area of NATO countries

Country	Area (Square miles)
Belgium	11,781
Canada	3,851,807
Denmark	16,629
France	211,208
Federal Republic of Germany	95,976
Greece	50,944
Iceland	39,769
Italy	116,304
Luxembourg	998
Netherlands	15,770
Norway	125,182
Portugal	35,553
Turkey	301,381
United Kingdom	94,227
United States	3,615,121
NATO Europe	1,115,722
NATO North America	7,466,928
TOTAL NATO	8,582,650

Population of NATO countries
(mid-year)

Unit: Thousands

Country	1949	1950	1951	1952	1953	1954	1955	1956	1957	
(0)	*(1)*	*(2)*	*(3)*	*(4)*	*(5)*	*(6)*	*(7)*	*(8)*	*(9)*	
Belgium	8,614	8,639	8,678	8,730	8,778	8,820	8,869	8,924	8,989	
Canada	13,447	13,712	14,009	14,459	14,845	15,287	15,698	16,123	16,677	1
Denmark	4,231	4,270	4,304	4,334	4,369	4,406	4,439	4,466	4,488	
France	41,400	41,736	42,056	42,360	42,652	43,057	43,428	43,843	44,311	
Federal Republic of Germany (a)	46,164	46,904	47,416	47,717	48,180	48,701	49,176	49,774	50,415	
Greece	7,483	7,566	7,646	7,733	7,817	7,893	7,966	8,031	8,096	
Iceland	140	143	145	148	151	154	158	161	165	
Italy	46,399	46,769	47,092	47,345	47,604	47,899	48,200	48,469	49,182	
Luxembourg	294	296	297	299	301	303	305	307	308	
Netherlands	9,955	10,114	10,264	10,382	10,493	10,616	10,751	10,888	11,026	
Norway	3,234	3,265	3,296	3,328	3,362	3,395	3,429	3,462	3,494	
Portugal	8,333	8,405	8,477	8,496	8,534	8,570	8,610	8,647	8,680	
Turkey	20,497	20,800	21,634	22,219	22,818	23,433	24,065	24,771	25,252	
United Kingdom	50,111	50,363	50,574	50,737	50,880	51,066	51,221	51,430	51,657	
United States	149,767	152,271	154,878	157,553	160,184	163,026	165,931	168,903	171,984	1
Total Europe (a)	246,855	249,270	251,879	253,828	255,939	258,313	260,617	263,173	266,063	2
Total North America	163,214	165,983	168,887	172,012	175,029	178,313	181,629	185,026	188,661	1
Total NATO (a)	410,069	415,253	420,766	425,840	430,968	436,626	442,246	448,199	454,724	4

(e) Estimate. (a) From 1960 onwards, including Saar and West Berlin. *Source :* United Nations and OECD.

292

959 (11)	1960 (12)	1961 (13)	1962 (14)	1963 (15)	1964 (16)	1965 (17)	1966 (18)	1967 (19)	1968 (20)	1969 (21)	1970 (22)	1971 (23)	1972 (24)	1973 (25)	1974(e) (26)
,104	9,153	9,184	9.218	9,283	9,367	9,448	9,508	9,557	9,590	9,613	9,638	9,673	9,711	9,742	9,771
,522	17,909	18,269	18,615	18,965	19,325	19,678	20,048	20,412	20,729	21,028	21,324	21,595	21,848	22,125	22,435
,547	4,581	4,612	4,647	4,684	4,720	4,757	4,797	4,839	4,867	4,890	4,929	4,963	4,992	5,027	5,057
,240	45,684	46,163	46,998	47,816	48,310	48,758	49,164	49,548	49,915	50,315	50,768	51,250	51,700	52,177	52,647
,628	55,433	56,175	56,837	57,389	57,971	58,619	59,148	59,286	59,500	60,067	60,651	61,302	61,669	61,967	62,100
,258	8,327	8,398	8,448	8,480	8,510	8,550	8,614	8,716	8,741	8,773	8,793	8,831	8,889	8,972	9,008
172	176	179	182	185	189	192	196	199	201	203	205	206	209	212	214
,832	50,198	50,524	50,844	51,199	51,601	51,988	52,332	52,667	52,987	53,317	53,661	54,005	54,411	54,888	55,272
312	314	317	321	324	328	332	334	335	336	338	340	342	347	350	352
,348	11,486	11,639	11,806	11,966	12,127	12,292	12,455	12,597	12,725	12,873	13,032	13,194	13,330	13,438	13,586
,556	3,585	3,615	3,639	3,667	3,694	3,723	3,753	3,785	3,819	3,851	3,877	3,903	3,933	3,961	3,993
,776	8,865	8,924	8,947	8,970	8,993	9,106	8,968	8,926	8,896	8,830	8,723	8,632	8,590	8,564	8,495
,735	27,509	28,233	28,933	29,655	30,394	31,151	31,934	32,750	33,585	34,442	35,321	36,221	37,010	37,930	38,878
,157	52,559	52,956	53,414	53,691	54,033	54,377	54,653	54,933	55,157	55,372	55,522	55,712	55,882	56,026	56,194
830	180,671	183,691	186,538	189,242	191,889	194,303	196,560	198,712	200,706	202,677	204,879	207,045	208,842	210,404	212,508
,665	277,870	280,919	284,234	287,309	290,237	293,203	295,856	298,138	300,319	302,884	305,460	308,234	310,673	313,254	315,567
,352	198,580	201,960	205,153	208,207	211,214	213,981	216,608	219,124	221,435	223,705	226,203	228,640	230,690	232,529	234,943
017	476,450	482,879	489,387	495,516	501,451	507,184	512,464	517,262	521,754	526,589	531,663	536,874	541,363	545,783	550,510

Defence expenditure of NATO countries expressed as a percentage of gross national product

(GNP at factor cost – current prices)

Country (0)	1949 (1)	1950 (2)	1951 (3)	1952 (4)	1953 (5)	1954 (6)	1955 (7)	1956 (8)
Belgium	2.8	2.8	3.9	5.7	5.5	5.3	4.3	4.0
Canada	2.4	2.9	6.2	8.5	8.5	7.7	7.2	6.7
Denmark	2.1	1.8	2.3	3.0	3.8	3.6	3.6	3.4
France	6.2	6.3	8.2	10.0	10.6	8.5	7.4	8.8
Federal Republic of Germany (a)	..	..	..	..	4.9	4.7	4.8	4.2
Greece	6.4	6.6	6.9	7.0	5.6	6.0	5.6	6.4
Italy	3.9	4.2	4.7	5.0	4.2	4.5	4.1	4.0
Luxembourg	1.0	1.5	1.7	2.6	3.2	3.6	3.6	2.1
Netherlands	4.5	5.4	5.6	6.3	6.3	6.7	6.3	6.4
Norway	2.9	2.6	3.4	4.5	5.7	5.6	4.4	4.0
Portugal	3.9	4.1	3.8	4.1	4.5	4.7	4.7	4.3
Turkey	6.9	6.9	6.2	6.0	5.9	6.5	6.3	5.8
United Kingdom	7.0	7.3	8.9	11.2	11.2	9.9	9.2	8.8
United States	5.1	5.5	10.8	14.9	14.7	12.7	11.0	10.7
Total Europe	5.6	5.8	7.1	8.6	8.0	7.1	6.5	6.6
Total North America	5.0	5.3	10.5	14.5	14.3	12.4	10.7	10.5
Total NATO	5.1	5.4	9.7	13.0	12.4	10.7	9.4	9.2

(e) = Estimation.   .. = Not available.

(a) These percentages have been calculated without taking into account the expenditures on Berlin (see note Table 'Total Defence Expenditures'); if these expenditures were included, the percentage would be 4.9% ir

Source : GNP : OECD.   Defence Expenditures : NATO Press Releases.

8	1959 (11)	1960 (12)	1961 (13)	1962 (14)	1963 (15)	1964 (16)	1965 (17)	1966 (18)	1967 (19)	1968 (20)	1969 (21)	1970 (22)	1971 (23)	1972 (24)	1973 (25)	1974(e) (26)
	4.1	3.9	3.8	3.9	3.8	3.8	3.5	3.5	3.5	3.5	3.3	3.3	3.2	3.1	3.0	3.1
	5.1	4.9	5.0	4.9	4.3	4.2	3.5	3.3	3.4	3.1	2.8	2.8	2.7	2.5	2.4	2.4
	3.0	3.1	2.9	3.5	3.5	3.3	3.3	3.2	3.1	3.3	3.0	2.8	3.0	2.8	2.5	2.6
	7.7	7.4	7.3	7.1	6.5	6.3	6.1	5.9	5.9	5.5	4.9	4.6	4.5	4.3	4.2	4.1
	5.0	4.6	4.6	5.5	6.0	5.4	5.0	4.7	5.0	4.1	4.1	3.7	3.8	3.9	3.9	4.1
	5.3	5.4	4.7	4.5	4.3	4.0	4.0	4.1	5.0	5.5	5.7	5.6	5.5	5.2	4.6	4.7
	3.7	3.7	3.5	3.6	3.7	3.7	3.7	3.8	3.5	3.3	3.0	3.0	3.3	3.4	3.3	3.0
	1.9	1.2	1.1	1.5	1.4	1.6	1.5	1.5	1.3	1.0	1.0	0.9	0.9	1.0	1.0	0.9
	4.3	4.5	4.9	5.0	4.9	4.8	4.4	4.1	4.3	4.0	4.0	3.8	3.9	3.8	3.6	3.8
	4.1	3.7	3.8	4.1	4.0	3.9	4.3	4.0	4.0	4.0	4.1	4.1	4.0	3.9	3.8	3.8
	4.6	4.5	7.0	7.6	7.0	7.3	6.8	6.9	8.0	8.2	7.6	7.9	8.3	8.0	6.9	6.4
	5.4	5.7	6.0	5.7	5.2	5.3	5.5	4.8	5.1	5.1	4.8	4.7	4.9	4.7	4.5	4.1
	7.4	7.3	7.0	8.0	6.9	6.8	6.6	6.5	6.5	6.2	5.8	5.6	5.8	5.9	5.6	5.8
	10.3	9.9	10.0	10.2	9.7	8.9	8.3	9.2	10.3	10.2	9.6	8.7	7.7	7.3	6.6	6.6
	5.9	5.7	5.6	6.0	5.7	5.5	5.3	5.1	5.2	4.8	4.5	4.2	4.3	4.3	4.1	4.1
	9.9	9.5	9.7	9.9	9.4	8.5	7.9	8.8	9.9	9.7	9.1	8.2	7.4	6.9	6.3	6.3
	8.6	8.2	8.3	8.5	8.0	7.4	7.0	7.5	8.2	8.0	7.4	6.7	6.2	5.9	5.3	5.3

295

Total defence expenditure of NATO countries

(current prices) 1949–1974

Country (0)	Currency Unit (1)	1949 (2)	1950 (3)	1951 (4)	1952 (5)	1953 (6)	1954 (7)	1955 (8)	1956 (9)
Belgium	Million Belgian Francs	8,273	8,914	14,095	20,735	20,589	20,707	17,857	17,887
Canada	Million Canadian $	372	495	1,220	1,875	1,970	1,771	1,819	1,888
Denmark	Million Danish Kroner	360	359	475	676	889	885	920	936
France	Million Francs	4,787	5,591	8,811	12,531	13,865	11,710	11,020	14,690
Fed. Rep. of Germany (a)	Million DM	..	..	..	..	6,195	6,287	7,383	7,211
Greece	Million Drachmae	1,630	1,971	2,515	2,655	2,767	3,428	3,688	4,939
Italy	Milliard Lire	301	353	457	521	480	543	551	584
Luxembourg	Million Luxembourg Francs	112	170	264	436	488	565	614	395
Netherlands	Million Guilders	680	901	1,060	1,253	1,330	1,583	1,699	1,854
Norway	Million Norwegian Kroner	370	357	572	831	1,067	1,141	953	967
Portugal	Million Escudos	1,419	1,516	1,553	1,691	1,975	2,100	2,224	2,297
Turkey	Million Liras	556	599	652	725	827	934	1,077	1,159
United Kingdom	Million £s Sterling	779	849	1,149	1,561	1,684	1,569	1,565	1,615
United States	Million US $	13,503	14,307	33,059	47,598	49,377	42,786	40,371	41,513
Area									
Total Europe (b)	Million US $	4,838	5,458	7,642	10,248	12,426	11,756	11,838	13,154
Total North America	Million US $	13,875	14,802	34,279	49,473	51,347	44,557	42,215	43,432
Total NATO (b)	Million US $	18,713	20,260	41,921	59,721	63,773	56,313	54,053	56,586

.. = Not available.

(a) Before it acceded to the North Atlantic Treaty Organization (May 1955), the Federal Republic of Germany contribut[ed] the defence budgets of certain NATO countries by the payment of occupation costs; moreover, it bore certain other costs wh[ich] also fall within the NATO definition of defence expenditures. In addition to defence expenditures (NATO definition), the Ger[man] Authorities are obliged to incur large annual expenditures for Berlin owing to the exceptional situation of this city and the [...] in the interests of the defence of the free world, to ensure its viability. These expenditures, which are not included in the f[igures] given above since they do not come within the NATO definition, are forecast to be 7,405 million DM in 1974.

																Forecast
'58	1959	1960	1961	1962	1963	1964	1965	1966	1967	1968	1969	1970	1971	1972	1973	1974
1)	(12)	(13)	(14)	(15)	(16)	(17)	(18)	(19)	(20)	(21)	(22)	(23)	(24)	(25)	(26)	(27)
254	19,658	20,209	20,641	22,341	23,596	26,241	26,606	28,169	30,396	32,676	33,892	37,502	39,670	44,140	48,941	57,315
740	1,642	1,654	1,716	1,810	1,712	1,813	1,659	1,766	1,965	1,927	1,899	2,061	2,131	2,238	2,405	2,770
988	986	1,113	1,180	1,551	1,651	1,764	1,974	2,080	2,249	2,591	2,640	2,757	3,195	3,386	3,520	4,343
569	17,926	19,162	20,395	22,184	22,849	24,280	25,300	26,732	28,912	30,264	30,696	32,672	34,907	37,992	42,284	47,570
853	11,087	12,115	13,175	17,233	19,924	19,553	19,915	20,254	21,408	19,310	21,577	22,573	25,450	28,720	31,908	35,964
469	4,735	5,110	5,034	5,102	5,385	5,647	6,290	7,168	9,390	11,003	12,762	14,208	15,480	17,211	19,866	24,126
547	667	710	749	861	1,031	1,118	1,212	1,342	1,359	1,403	1,412	1,562	1,852	2,162	2,392	2,676
429	402	263	290	355	348	462	477	497	413	374	391	416	442	517	601	677
556	1,505	1,728	2,013	2,186	2,307	2,661	2,714	2,790	3,200	3,280	3,682	3,968	4,466	4,974	5,465	6,347
24	1,107	1,058	1,179	1,371	1,465	1,570	1,897	1,947	2,097	2,300	2,502	2,774	3,022	3,239	3,505	4,081
485	2,820	3,023	4,922	5,744	5,724	6,451	6,680	7,393	9,575	10,692	10,779	12,538	14,699	16,046	16,736	20,910
470	2,153	2,410	2,718	2,980	3,157	3,443	3,821	3,996	4,596	5,159	5,395	6,237	8,487	9,961	12,192	15,831
93	1,595	1,657	1,709	1,814	1,870	2,000	2,091	2,153	2,276	2,332	2,303	2,444	2,815	3,258	3,505	4,148
96	45,833	45,380	47,808	52,398	52,295	51,213	51,827	63,572	75,448	80,732	81,443	77,854	74,862	77,639	78,473	84,332
47	13,924	14,466	15,335	17,433	18,784	19,733	20,606	21,512	22,925	22,346	22,999	24,482	28,028	33,606	40,678	45,167
89	47,545	47,085	49,501	54,089	53,879	52,890	53,362	65,205	77,265	82,515	83,199	79,821	76,973	79,898	80,876	87,176
36	61,469	61,551	64,836	71,522	72,663	72,623	73,968	86,717	100,190	104,861	106,198	104,303	105,001	113,504	121,554	132,343

) The totals for Europe and for NATO do not include defence expenditures of the Federal Republic of Germany for the period prior to , and for this reason they are not directly comparable to the totals for the following years. Moreover, these totals have been established e basis of the current exchange rates during the years under review; this being so, the changes in them, to some extent, reflect the ct of monetary events and a certain amount of caution should be exercised in making comparisons.

ce : NATO Press Releases.

Aid from NATO countries to developing countries expressed as a percentage of donor countries gross national product

(GNP at factor cost-current prices)

A. Total aid (a)

Country	1960	1961	1962	1963	1964	1965	1966	1967	1968	1969	1970 (b)	1971 (b)	1972 (b)
(0)	(1)	(2)	(3)	(4)	(5)	(6)	(7)	(8)	(9)	(10)	(11)	(12)	(13)
Belgium	1.77	1.52	1.02	1.42	1.19	1.46	1.11	0.95	1.32	1.25	1.35	1.23	1.26
Canada	0.42	0.26	0.32	0.35	0.35	0.38	0.54	0.51	0.53	0.57	0.90	1.16	1.13
Denmark	0.73	0.57	0.23	0.16	0.41	0.17	0.22	0.24	0.79	1.27	0.66	0.95	0.68
France	2.54	2.47	2.19	1.74	1.73	1.54	1.43	1.34	1.55	1.42	1.45	1.15	1.22
Federal Republic of Germany	1.01	1.19	0.78	0.75	0.77	0.73	0.74	1.07	1.40	1.52	0.90	1.00	0.77
Italy	0.96	0.75	1.01	0.72	0.49	0.51	1.11	0.46	0.81	1.13	0.82	0.95	0.64
Netherlands	2.35	1.79	0.95	1.02	0.76	1.39	1.37	1.12	0.82	1.50	1.50	1.29	1.78
Norway	0.25	0.62	0.15	0.43	0.41	0.61	0.25	0.41	0.74	0.88	0.70	0.60	0.44
Portugal	1.59	1.79	1.56	1.80	2.01	0.90	1.07	1.90	1.06	1.98	1.29	2.40	3.01
United Kingdom	1.38	1.32	1.18	0.95	1.11	1.17	0.98	0.83	0.93	1.20	1.18	1.20	1.09
United States	0.83	0.96	0.84	0.84	0.91	0.85	0.71	0.79	0.76	0.57	0.69	0.71	0.71
Total NATO donor Countries	1.03	1.10	0.95	0.89	0.94	0.90	0.82	0.84	0.90	0.84	0.85	0.88	0.85

(a) Net flow of total official and private financial resources.   (b) Including grants by voluntary agencies

B. Aid from the public sector

Country	1960	1961	1962	1963	1964	1965	1966	1967	1968	1969	1970	1971	1972
(0)	(1)	(2)	(3)	(4)	(5)	(6)	(7)	(8)	(9)	(10)	(11)	(12)	(13)
Belgium	0.98	0.85	0.61	0.65	0.51	0.67	0.50	0.58	0.57	0.58	0.53	0.57	0.64
Canada	0.22	0.18	0.16	0.26	0.32	0.28	0.43	0.40	0.37	0.47	0.57	0.57	0.68
Denmark	0.12	0.14	0.11	0.15	0.14	0.15	0.27	0.27	0.28	0.46	0.43	0.53	0.56
France	1.63	1.66	1.54	1.19	1.09	0.93	0.83	0.84	0.79	0.79	0.79	0.80	0.78
Federal Republic of Germany	0.57	0.87	0.60	0.52	0.46	0.47	0.45	0.51	0.50	0.40	0.44	0.47	0.42
Italy	0.34	0.23	0.29	0.18	0.08	0.18	0.20	0.25	0.22	0.18	0.21	0.33	0.23
Netherlands	0.34	0.50	0.54	0.29	0.32	0.41	0.51	0.56	0.60	0.59	0.74	0.64	0.77
Norway	0.25	0.21	0.15	0.41	0.30	0.19	0.19	0.22	0.30	0.45	0.39	0.40	0.52
Portugal	1.59	1.79	1.56	1.80	2.01	0.61	0.64	1.15	0.77	1.62	1.00	1.93	2.80
United Kingdom	0.64	0.67	0.67	0.54	0.60	0.55	0.55	0.49	0.48	0.45	0.43	0.48	0.45
United States	0.60	0.72	0.68	0.68	0.59	0.55	0.49	0.50	0.45	0.38	0.36	0.36	0.33
Total NATO donor Countries	0.65	0.75	0.69	0.64	0.57	0.54	0.50	0.51	0.47	0.43	0.42	0.44	0.43

Source : OECD.

Appendices

APPENDIX 1

Article 51 of the Charter of the United Nations

October 24, 1945

Nothing in the present Charter shall impair the inherent right of individual or collective self-defence if an armed attack occurs against a Member of the United Nations, until the Security Council has taken measures necessary to maintain international peace and security. Measures taken by Members in the exercise of this right of self-defence shall be immediately reported to the Security Council and shall not in any way affect the authority and responsibility of the Security Council under the present Charter to take at any time such action as it deems necessary in order to maintain or restore international peace and security.

The North Atlantic Treaty

Washington D.C., April 4, 1949

The Parties to this Treaty reaffirm their faith in the purposes and principles of the Charter of the United Nations and their desire to live in peace with all peoples and all governments.

They are determined to safeguard the freedom, common heritage and civilization of their peoples, founded on the principles of democracy, individual liberty and the rule of law.

They seek to promote stability and well-being in the North Atlantic area.

They are resolved to unite their efforts for collective defence and for the preservation of peace and security.

They therefore agree to this North Atlantic Treaty:

Article 1

The Parties undertake, as set forth in the Charter of the United Nations, to settle any international dispute in which they may be involved by peaceful means in such a manner that international peace and security and justice are not endangered, and to refrain in their international relations from the threat or use of force in any manner inconsistent with the purposes of the United Nations.

Article 2

The Parties will contribute toward the further development of peaceful and friendly international relations by strengthening their free institutions, by bringing about a better understanding of the principles upon which these institutions are founded, and by promoting conditions of stability and well-being. They will seek to eliminate conflict in their international economic policies and will encourage economic collaboration between any or all of them.

Article 3

In order more effectively to achieve the objectives of this Treaty, the Parties, separately and jointly, by means of continuous and effective self-help and mutual aid, will maintain and develop their individual and collective capacity to resist armed attack.

Article 4

The Parties will consult together whenever, in the opinion of any of them, the territorial integrity, political independence or security of any of the Parties is threatened.

Article 5

The Parties agree that an armed attack against one or more of them in Europe or North America shall be considered an attack against them all and consequently they agree that, if such an armed attack occurs, each of them, in exercise of the right of individual or collective self-defence recognized by Article 51 of the Charter of the United Nations, will assist the Party or Parties so attacked by taking forthwith, individually and in concert with the other Parties, such action as it deems necessary, including the use of armed force, to restore and maintain the security of the North Atlantic area.

Any such armed attack and all measures taken as a result thereof shall immediately be reported to the Security Council. Such measures shall be terminated when the Security Council has taken the measures necessary to restore and maintain international peace and security.

Article 6[1]

For the purpose of Article V an armed attack on one or more of the Parties is deemed to include an armed attack on the territory of any of the Parties in Europe or North America, on the Algerian Departments of France,[2] on the occupation forces of any Party in Europe, on the islands under the

1. The definition of the territories to which Article V applies has been revised by Article II of the Protocol to the North Atlantic Treaty on the accession of Greece and Turkey (see Appendix 3).

2. On January 16, 1963, the North Atlantic Council has heard a declaration by the French Representative who recalled that by the vote on self-determination on July 1, 1962, the Algerian people had pronounced itself in favour of the independence of Algeria in co-operation with France. In consequence, the President of the French Republic had on July 3, 1962, formally recognized the independence of Algeria. The result was that the 'Algerian departments of France' no longer existed as such, and that at the same time the fact that they were mentioned in the North Atlantic Treaty had no longer any bearing.

Following this statement the Council noted that insofar as the former Algerian Departments of France were concerned, the relevant clauses of this Treaty had become inapplicable as from July 3, 1962.

301

jurisdiction of any Party in the North Atlantic area north of the Tropic of Cancer or on the vessels or aircraft in this area of any of the Parties.

Article 7

This Treaty does not affect, and shall not be interpreted as affecting, in any way the rights and obligations under the Charter of the Parties which are members of the United Nations, or the primary responsibility of the Security Council for the maintenance of international peace and security.

Article 8

Each Party declares that none of the international engagements now in force between it and any other of the Parties or any third State is in conflict with the provisions of this Treaty, and undertakes not to enter into any international engagement in conflict with this Treaty.

Article 9

The Parties hereby establish a Council, on which each of them shall be represented, to consider matters concerning the implementation of this Treaty. The Council shall be so organized as to be able to meet promptly at any time. The Council shall set up such subsidiary bodies as may be necessary; in particular it shall establish immediately a defence committee which shall recommend measures for the implementation of Articles III and V.

Article 10

The Parties may, by unanimous agreement, invite any other European State in a position to further the principles of this Treaty and to contribute to the security of the North Atlantic area to accede to this Treaty. Any State so invited may become a Party to the Treaty by depositing its instrument of accession with the Government of the United States of America. The Government of the United States of America will inform each of the Parties of the deposit of each such instrument of accession.

Article 11

This Treaty shall be ratified and its provisions carried out by the Parties in accordance with their respective constitutional processes. The instruments of ratification shall be deposited as soon as possible with the Government of the United States of America, which will notify all the other signatories of each deposit. The Treaty shall enter into force between the States which have ratified it as soon as the ratifications of the majority of the signatories, including the ratifications of Belgium, Canada, France, Luxembourg, the Netherlands, the United Kingdom and the United States, have been deposited and shall come into effect with respect to other States on the date of the deposit of their ratifications.

Article 12

After the Treaty has been in force for ten years, or at any time thereafter, the Parties shall, if any of them so requests, consult together for the purpose of reviewing the Treaty, having regard for the factors then affecting peace and security in the North Atlantic area, including the development of universal as well as regional arrangements under the Charter of the United Nations for the maintenance of international peace and security.

Article 13

After the Treaty has been in force for twenty years, any Party may cease to be a Party one year after its notice of denunciation has been given to the Government of the United States of America, which will inform the Governments of the other Parties of the deposit of each notice of denunciation.

Article 14

This Treaty, of which the English and French texts are equally authentic, shall be deposited in the archives of the Government of the United States of America. Duly certified copies will be transmitted by that Government to the Governments of other signatories.

Protocol to the North Atlantic Treaty on the accession of Greece and Turkey

London, October 22, 1951

The Parties to the North Atlantic Treaty, signed at Washington on April 4, 1949,

Being satisfied that the security of the North Atlantic area will be enhanced by the accession of the Kingdom of Greece and the Republic of Turkey to that Treaty,

Agree as follows:

Article 1

Upon the entry into force of this Protocol, the Government of the United States of America shall, on behalf of all the Parties, communicate to the Government of the Kingdom of Greece and the Government of the Republic of Turkey an invitation to accede to the North Atlantic Treaty, as it may be modified by Article II of the present Protocol. Thereafter the Kingdom of Greece and the Republic of Turkey shall each become a Party on the date when it deposits its instruments of accession with the Government of the United States of America in accordance with Article X of the Treaty.

Article 2

If the Republic of Turkey becomes a Party to the North Atlantic Treaty, Article VI of the Treaty shall, as from the date of the deposit by the Government of the Republic of Turkey of its instruments of accession with the Government of the United States of America, be modified to read as follows:

'For the purpose of Article 5, an armed attack on one or more of the Parties is deemed to include an armed attack:

    i. on the territory of any of the Parties in Europe or North America, on the Algerian Departments of France, on the territory of Turkey or on the islands under the jurisdiction of any of the Parties in the North Atlantic area north of the Tropic of Cancer;

    ii. on the forces, vessels, or aircraft of any of the Parties, when in or over these territories or any other area in Europe in which occupation forces of any of the Parties were stationed on the date when the Treaty entered into force or the Mediterranean Sea or the North Atlantic area north of the Tropic of Cancer.'

Article 3

The present Protocol shall enter into force when each of the Parties to the North Atlantic Treaty has notified the Government of the United States of America of its acceptance thereof. The Government of the United States of America shall inform all the Parties to the North Atlantic Treaty of the date of the receipt of each such notification and of the date of the entry into force of the present Protocol.

Article 4

The present Protocol, of which the English and French texts are equally authentic, shall be deposited in the Archives of the Government of the United States of America. Duly certified copies thereof shall be transmitted by that Government to the Governments of all the Parties to the North Atlantic Treaty.

Protocol to the North Atlantic Treaty on the accession of the Federal Republic of Germany

Paris, October 23, 1954

The Parties to the North Atlantic Treaty signed at Washington on April 4, 1949,

Being satisfied that the security of the North Atlantic area will be enhanced by the accession of the Federal Republic of Germany to that Treaty, and

Having noted that the Federal Republic of Germany has, by a declaration dated October 3, 1954, accepted the obligations set forth in Article 2 of the Charter of the United Nations and has undertaken upon its accession to the North Atlantic Treaty to refrain from any action inconsistent with the strictly defensive character of that Treaty, and

Having further noted that all member governments have associated themselves with the declaration also made on October 3, 1954, by the Governments of the United States of America, the United Kingdom of Great Britain and Northern Ireland and the French Republic in connection with the aforesaid declaration of the Federal Republic of Germany,

Agree as follows:

Article 1

Upon the entry into force of the present Protocol, the Government of the United States of America shall on behalf of all the Parties communicate to the Government of the Federal Republic of Germany an invitation to accede to the North Atlantic Treaty. Thereafter the Federal Republic of Germany shall become a Party to that Treaty on the date when it deposits its instruments of accession with the Government of the United States of America in accordance with Article 10 of the Treaty.

Article 2

The present Protocol shall enter into force, when (a) each of the Parties to the North Atlantic Treaty has notified to the Government of the United States of America its acceptance thereof, (b) all instruments of ratification of the Protocol modifying and completing the Brussels Treaty have been deposited with the Belgian Government, and (c) all instruments of ratification or approval of the Convention on the Presence of Foreign Forces in the Federal Republic of Germany have been deposited with the Government of the Federal Republic of Germany. The Government of the United States of America shall inform the other Parties to the North Atlantic Treaty of the date of the receipt of each notification of acceptance of the present Protocol and of the date of the entry into force of the present Protocol.

Article 3

The present Protocol, of which the English and French texts are equally authentic, shall be deposited in the Archives of the Government of the United States of America. Duly certified copies thereof shall be transmitted by that Government to the Governments of the other Parties to the North Atlantic Treaty.

Text of the report of the Committee of Three on non-military co-operation in NATO

CHAPTER I

General introduction

The Committee on Non-Military Co-operation, set up by the North Atlantic Council at its session of May 1956, was requested: 'to advise the Council on ways and means to improve and extend NATO co-operation in non-military fields and to develop greater unity within the Atlantic Community'.

2. The Committee has interpreted these terms of reference as requiring it (1) to examine and re-define the objectives and needs of the Alliance, especially in the light of current international developments; and (2) to make recommendations for strengthening its internal solidarity, cohesion and unity.

3. The Committee hopes that the report and recommendations which it now submits will make NATO's purely defensive and constructive purposes better understood in non-NATO countries, thereby facilitating and encouraging steps to lessen international tension. The events of the last few months have increased this tension and reduced hopes, which had been raised since Stalin's death, of finding a secure and honourable basis for competitive and ultimately for co-operative co-existence with the Communist world. The effort to this end, however, must go on.

4. Inter-Allied relations have also undergone severe strains. The substance of this report was prepared by the Committee of Three in the course of its meetings and inter-governmental consultations last September. Subsequent events have reinforced the Committee's conviction that the Atlantic Community can develop greater unity only by working constantly to achieve common policies by full and timely consultation on issues of common concern. Unless this is done, the very framework of co-operation in NATO, which has contributed so greatly to the cause of freedom, and which is so vital to its advancement in the future, will be endangered.

5. The foundation of NATO, on which alone a strong superstructure can be built, is the political obligation that its members have taken for collective defence: to consider that an attack on one is an attack on all which will be met by the collective action of all. There is a tendency at times to overlook the far-reaching importance of this commitment, especially during those periods when the danger of having to invoke it may seem to recede.

6. With this political commitment for collective defence as the cornerstone of the foreign and defence policies of its members, NATO has a solid basis for existence. It is true, of course, that the ways and means by which the obligation is to be discharged may alter as political or strategic conditions alter, as the threat to peace changes its character or its direction. However, any variations in plans and strategic policies which may be required need not weaken NATO or the confidence of its members in NATO and in each other; providing, and the proviso is decisive, that each member retains its will and its capacity to play its full part in discharging the political commitment for collective action against aggression which it undertook when it signed the Pact; providing also – and recent events have shown that this is equally important – that any changes in national strategy or policy which affect the coalition are made only after collective consideration.

7. The first essential, then, of a healthy and developing NATO lies in the whole-hearted acceptance by all its members of the political commitment for collective defence, and in the confidence which each has in the will and ability of the others to honour that commitment if aggression should take place.

8. This is our best present deterrent against military aggression, and consequently the best assurance that the commitment undertaken will not be engaged.

9. However, this deterrent role of NATO, based on solidarity and strength, can be discharged only if the political and economic relations between its members are co-operative and close. An Alliance in which the members ignore each other's interests or engage in political or economic conflict, or harbour suspicions of each other, cannot be effective either for deterrence or defence. Recent experience makes this clearer than ever before.

10. It is useful, in searching for ways and means of strengthening NATO unity and understanding, to recall the origin and the aims of the Organization.

11. The Treaty which was signed in Washington in 1949 was a collective response – we had learned that a purely national response was insufficient for security – to the fear of military aggression by the forces of the USSR and its allies. These forces were of overwhelming strength. The threat to Greece, the capture of Czechoslovakia, the blockade of Berlin, and the pressure against Yugoslavia showed that they were also aggressive.

12. While fear may have been the main urge for the creation of NATO, there was also the realization – conscious or instinctive – that in a shrinking nuclear world it was wise and timely to bring about a closer association of kindred Atlantic and Western European nations for other than defence purposes alone; that a partial pooling of sovereignty for mutual protection should also promote progress and co-operation generally. There was a feeling among the government and peoples concerned that this close unity was both natural and desirable; that the common cultural traditions, free institutions and democratic concepts which were being challenged, and were marked for destruction by those who challenged them, were things which should also bring the NATO nations closer together, not only for their defence but for their development. There was, in short, a sense of Atlantic Community, alongside the realization of an immediate common danger.

13. Any such feeling was certainly not the decisive, or even the main impulse in the creation of NATO. Nevertheless, it gave birth to the hope that NATO would grow beyond and above the emergency which brought it into being.

14. The expression of this hope is found in the Preamble and in Articles II and IV of the Treaty. These two Articles, limited in their terms but with at least the promise of the grand design of an Atlantic Community, were included because of this insistent feeling that NATO must become more than a military alliance. They reflected the very real anxiety that if NATO failed to meet this test, it would disappear with the immediate crisis which produced it, even though the need for it might be as great as ever.

15. From the very beginning of NATO, then, it was recognized that while defence co-operation was the first and most urgent requirement, this was not enough. It has also become increasingly realized since the Treaty was signed that security is today far more than a military matter. The strengthening of political consultation and economic co-operation, the development of resources, progress in education and public understanding, all these can be as important, or even more important, for the protection of the security of a nation, or an alliance, as the building of a battleship or the equipping of an army.

16. These two aspects of security – civil and military – can no longer safely be considered in watertight compartments, either within or between nations. Perhaps NATO has not yet fully recognized their essential inter-relationship, or done enough to bring about that close and continuous contact between its civil and military sides which is essential if it is to be strong and enduring.

17. North Atlantic political and economic co-operation, however, let alone unity, will not be brought about in a day or by a declaration, but by creating over the years and through a whole series of national acts and policies, the habits and traditions and precedents for such co-operation and unity. The process will be a slow and gradual one at best; slower than we might wish. We can be satisfied if it is steady and sure. This will not be the case, however, unless the member governments – especially the more powerful ones – are willing to work, to a much greater extent than hither-to, with and through NATO for more than purposes of collective military defence.

18. While the members of NATO have already developed various forms of non-military co-operation between themselves and have been among the most active and constructive participants in various international organiza-tions, NATO as such has been hesitant in entering this field, particularly in regard to economic matters. Its members have been rightly concerned to avoid duplication and to do, through other existing international organiza-tions, the things which can best be done in that way.

19. Recently, however, the members of NATO have been examining and re-examining the purposes and the needs of the Organization in the light of certain changes in Soviet tactics and policies which have taken place since the death of Stalin, and of the effect of the present turmoil in Eastern Europe on this development.

20. These changes have not diminished the need for collective military defence but they have faced NATO with an additional challenge in which the

311

emphasis is largely non-military in character. NATO must recognize the real nature of the developments which have taken place. An important aspect of the new Soviet policies of competitive co-existence is an attempt to respond to positive initiatives of the Western nations aimed at improving, in an atmosphere of freedom, the lot of the economically less-developed countries, and at establishing a just and mutually beneficial trading system in which all countries can prosper. The Soviet Union is now apparently veering towards policies designed to ensnare these countries by economic means and by political subversion, and to fasten on them the same shackles of Communism from which certain members of the Soviet *bloc* are now striving to release themselves. The members of NATO must maintain their vigilance in dealing with this form of penetration.

21. Meanwhile some of the immediate fears of large-scale all-out military aggression against Western Europe have lessened. This process has been facilitated by evidence that the Soviet Government have realized that any such all-out aggression would be met by a sure, swift and devastating retaliation, and that there could be no victory in a war of this kind with nuclear weapons on both sides. With an increased Soviet emphasis on non-military or paramilitary methods, a review is needed of NATO's ability to meet effectively the challenge of penetration under the guise of co-existence, with its emphasis on conflict without catastrophe.

22. Certain questions now take on a new urgency. Have NATO's needs and objectives changed, or should they be changed? Is the Organization operating satisfactorily in the altered circumstances of 1956? If not what can be done about it? There is the even more far-reaching question: 'Can a loose association of sovereign states hold together at all without the common binding force of fear?'

23. The Committee has been examining these questions in the light of its firm conviction that the objectives which governments had in mind when the Pact was signed remain valid; that NATO is as important now to its member states as it was at that time.

24. The first of these objectives – as has already been pointed out – is security, based on collective action with adequate armed forces both for deterrence and defence.

25. Certainly NATO unity and strength in the pursuit of this objective remain as essential as they were in 1949. Soviet tactics may have changed; but Soviet armed might and ultimate objectives remain unchanged. More-over, recent events in Eastern Europe show that the Soviet Union will not hesitate in certain circumstances to use force and the threat of force. Therefore the military strength of NATO must not be reduced, though its character and capabilities should be constantly adapted to changing circumstances. Strengthening the political and economic side of NATO is an essential complement to – not a substitute for – continuous co-operation in defence.

26. In spite of these recent events Soviet leaders may place greater emphasis on political, economic and propaganda action. There is no evidence, however, that this will be permitted to prejudice in any way the maintenance of a high level of military power in its most modern form as a base for Soviet activity in these other fields.

27. We should welcome changes in Soviet policies if they were genuinely designed to ease international tensions. But we must remember that the weakening and eventual dissolution of NATO remains a major Communist goal. We must therefore remain on guard so long as Soviet leaders persist in their determination to maintain a preponderance of military power for the achievement of their own political objectives and those of their allies.

28. This brings us again to the second and long-term aim of NATO: the development of an Atlantic Community whose roots are deeper even than the necessity for common defence. This implies nothing less than the permanent association of the free Atlantic peoples for the promotion of their greater unity and the protection and the advancement of the interests which, as free democracies, they have in common.

29. If we are to secure this long-term aim, we must prevent the centrifugal forces of opposition or indifference from weakening the Alliance. NATO has not been destroyed, or even weakened, by the threats or attacks of its enemies. It has faltered at times through the lethargy or complacency of its members: through dissension or division between them; by putting narrow national considerations above the collective interest. It could be destroyed by these forces, if they were allowed to subsist. To combat these tendencies, NATO must be used by its members, far more than it has been used, for sincere and genuine consultation and co-operation on questions of common concern. For this purpose, resolution is more important than resolutions; will than words.

30. The problem, however, goes deeper than this. NATO countries are faced by a political as well as a military threat. It comes from the revolutionary doctrines of Communism which have by careful design of the Communist leaders over many years been sowing seeds of falsehood concerning our free and democratic way of life. The best answer to such falsehoods is a continuing demonstration of the superiority of our own institutions over Communist ones. We can show by word and deed that we welcome political progress, economic advancement and orderly social change and that the real reactionaries of this day are these Communist regimes which, adhering to an inflexible pattern of economic and political doctrine, have been more successful in destroying freedom than in promoting it.

31. We must, however, realize that falsehoods concerning our institutions have sometimes been accepted at face value and that there are those, even in the non-Communist world, who under the systematic influence of Communist propaganda do not accept our own analysis of NATO's aims and values. They believe that while NATO may have served a useful defensive deterrent role in the Stalinist era, it is no longer necessary even for the security of its members; that it is tending now to become an agency for the pooling of the strength and resources of the 'colonial' powers in defence of imperial privileges, racial superiority, and Atlantic hegemony under the leadership of the United States. The fact that we know these views to be false and unjustified does not mean that NATO and its governments should not do everything they can to correct and counteract them.

32. NATO should not forget that the influence and interests of its members are not confined to the area covered by the Treaty, and that common interests of the Atlantic Community can be seriously affected by developments outside the Treaty area. Therefore, while striving to improve their relations with each other, and to strengthen and deepen their own unity, they should also be concerned with harmonizing their policies in relation to other areas, taking into account the broader interests of the whole international community; particularly in working through the United Nations and elsewhere for the maintenance of international peace and security and for the solution of the problems that now divide the world.

33. In following this course, NATO can show that it is more than a defence organization acting and reacting to the ebb and flow of the fears and dangers arising out of Soviet policy. It can prove its desire to co-operate fully with other members of the international community in bringing to reality the principles of the Charter of the United Nations. It can show that it is not merely concerned with preventing the cold war from deteriorating into a shooting one; or with defending itself if such a tragedy should take place, but that it is even more concerned with seizing the political and moral initiative to enable all countries to develop in freedom, and to bring about a secure peace for all nations.

34. Our caution in accepting without question the pacific character of any Soviet moves, our refusal to dismantle our defences before we are convinced that conditions of international confidence have been restored, will, particularly after the events in Hungary, be understood by all people of sincerity and good-will. What would not be understood is any unwillingness on our part to seek ways and means of breaking down the barriers with a view to establishing such confidence.

35. The coming together of the Atlantic nations for good and constructive purposes – which is the basic principle and ideal underlying the NATO concept – must rest on and grow from deeper and more permanent factors than the divisions and dangers of the last ten years. It is a historical, rather than a contemporary, development, and if it is to achieve its real purpose, it must be considered in that light and the necessary conclusions drawn. A short-range view will not suffice.

36. The fundamental historical fact underlying development is that the nation state, by itself and relying exclusively on national policy and national power, is inadequate for progress or even for survival in the nuclear age. As the founders of the North Atlantic Treaty foresaw, the growing interdependence of states, politically and economically as well as militarily, calls for an ever-increasing measure of international cohesion and co-operation. Some states may be able to enjoy a degree of political and economic independence when things are going well. No state, however powerful, can guarantee its security and its welfare by national action alone.

37. This basic fact underlies our report and the recommendations contained therein which appear in the subsequent chapters.

38. It has not been difficult to make these recommendations. It will be far more difficult for the member governments to carry them into effect. This will require, on their part, the firm conviction that the transformation of the Atlantic Community into a vital and vigorous political reality is as important as any purely national purpose. It will require, above all, the will to carry this conviction into the realm of practical governmental policy.

CHAPTER II

Political co-operation

1. Introduction

39. If there is to be vitality and growth in the concept of the Atlantic Community, the relations between the members of NATO must rest on a solid basis of confidence and understanding. Without this there cannot be constructive or solid political co-operation.

40. The deepening and strengthening of this political co-operation does not imply the weakening of the ties of NATO members with other friendly countries or with other international associations, particularly the United Nations. Adherence to NATO is not exclusive or restrictive. Nor should the evolution of the Atlantic Community through NATO prevent the formation of even closer relationships among some of its members, for instance within groups of European countries. The moves toward Atlantic co-operation and European unity should be parallel and complementary, not competitive or conflicting.

41. Effective and constructive international co-operation requires a resolve to work together for the solution of common problems. There are special ties between NATO members, special incentives and security interests, which should make this task easier than it otherwise would be. But its successful accomplishment will depend largely on the extent to which member governments, in their own policies and actions, take into consideration the interests of the Alliance. This requires not only the acceptance of the obligation of consultation and co-operation whenever necessary, but also the development of practices by which the discharge of this obligation becomes a normal part of governmental activity.

42. It is easy to profess devotion to the principle of political – or economic – consultation in NATO. It is difficult and has in fact been shown to be impossible, if the proper conviction is lacking, to convert the profession into practice. Consultation within an alliance means more than exchange of information, though that is necessary. It means more than letting the NATO Council know about national decisions that have already been taken; or trying to enlist support for those decisions. It means the discussion of problems collectively, in the early stages of policy formation, and before national positions become fixed. At best, this will result in collective decisions on matters of common interest affecting the Alliance. At the least, it will ensure that no action is taken by one member without a knowledge of the views of the others.

II. Consultation on foreign policies

A. SCOPE AND CHARACTER OF POLITICAL CONSULTATION

43. The essential role of consultation in fostering political co-operation was clearly defined by an earlier NATO Committee on the North Atlantic Community in 1951:

'. . . The achievement of a closer degree of co-ordination of the foreign policies of the members of the North Atlantic Treaty, through the development of the 'habit of consultation' on matters of common concern, would greatly strengthen the solidarity of the North Atlantic Community and increase the individual and collective capacity of its members to serve the peaceful purposes for which NATO was established. . . . In the political field, this means that while each North Atlantic government retains full freedom of action and decision with respect to its own policy, the aim should be to achieve, through exchanging information and views, as wide an area of agreement as possible in the formulation of policies as a whole'.

'Special attention must be paid, as explicitly recognized in Article IV of the Treaty, to matters of urgent and immediate importance to the members of NATO, and to 'emergency' situations where it may be necessary to consult closely on national lines of conduct affecting the interests of members of NATO as a whole. There is a continuing need, however, for effective consultation at an early stage on current problems, in order that national policies may be developed and action taken on the basis of a full awareness of the attitudes and interests of all the members of NATO. While all members of NATO have a responsibility to consult with their partners on appropriate matters, a large share of responsibility for such consultation necessarily rests on the more powerful members of the Community'.

44. These words were written five years ago. They hold true now more than ever before. If we can say that they have not been ignored by NATO we must also recognize that the practice of consulting has not so developed in the NATO Council as to meet the demands of political changes and world trends. The present need, therefore, is more than simply broadening the scope and deepening the character of consultation. There is a pressing requirement for all members to make consultation in NATO an integral part of the making of national policy. Without this the very existence of the North Atlantic Community may be in jeopardy.

45. It should, however, be remembered that collective discussion is not an end in itself, but a means to the end of harmonizing policies. Where common interests of the Atlantic Community are at stake consultation should always seek to arrive at timely agreement on common lines of policy and action.

46. Such agreement, even with the closest possible co-operation and consultation, is not easy to secure. But it is essential to the Atlantic Alliance that a steady and continuous effort be made to bring it about. There cannot be unity in defence and disunity in foreign policy.

47. There are, of course, certain practical limitations to consultation in this field. They are sufficiently obvious in fact to make it unnecessary to emphasize them in words. Indeed the danger is less that they will be minimized or evaded than that they will be exaggerated and used to justify practices which unnecessarily ignore the common interest.

48. One of these limitations is the hard fact that ultimate responsibility for decision and action still rests on national governments. It is conceivable that a situation of extreme emergency may arise where action must be taken by one government before consultation is possible with the others.

49. Another limitation is the difficulty, and indeed the unwisdom, of trying to specify in advance all the subjects and all the situations where consultation is necessary; to separate by area or by subject the matters of NATO concern from those of purely national concern; to define in detail the obligations and duties of consultations. These things have to work themselves out in practice. In this process, experience is a better guide than dogma.

50. The essential thing is that on all occasions and in all circumstances member governments, before acting or even before pronouncing, should keep the interests and the requirements of the Alliance in mind. If they have not the desire and the will to do this, no resolutions or recommendations or declarations by the Council or any Committee of the Council will be of any great value.

51. On the assumption, however, that this will and this desire do exist, the following principles and practices in the field of political consultation are recommended:

a. members should inform the Council of any development which significantly affects the Alliance. They should do this, not merely as a formality but as a preliminary to effective political consultation;

b. both individual member governments and the Secretary General should have the right to raise for discussion in the Council any subject which is of common NATO interest and not of a purely domestic character;

c. a member government should not, without adequate advance consultation, adopt firm policies or make major political pronouncements on matters which significantly affect the Alliance or any of its members, unless circumstances make such prior consultation obviously and demonstrably impossible;

d. in developing their national policies, members should take into consideration the interest and views of other governments, particularly those most directly concerned, as expressed in NATO consultation, even where no community of views or consensus has been reached in the Council;

e. where a consensus has been reached, it should be reflected in the formation of national policies. When for national reasons the consensus is not followed, the government concerned should offer an explanation to the Council. It is even more important that where an agreed and formal recommendation has emerged from the Council's discussions, governments should give it full weight in any national actions or policies related to the subject of that recommendation.

B. ANNUAL POLITICAL APPRAISAL

52. To strengthen the process of consultation, it is recommended that Foreign Ministers, at each Spring meeting, should make an appraisal of the political progress of the Alliance and consider the lines along which it should advance.

53. To prepare for this discussion, the Secretary General should submit an annual report:

a. analysing the major political problems of the Alliance;

b. reviewing the extent to which member governments have consulted and co-operated on such problems;

c. indicating the problems and possible developments which may require future consultation, so that difficulties might be resolved and positive and constructive initiative taken.

54. Member governments, through their Permanent Representatives, should give the Secretary General such information and assistance, including that of technical experts, as he may require in preparing his report.

C. PREPARATION FOR POLITICAL CONSULTATION

55. Effective consultation also requires careful planning and preparation of the agenda for meetings of the Council both in Ministerial and permanent session. Political questions coming up for discussion in the Council should so far as practicable be previously reviewed and discussed, so that representatives may have background information on the thinking both of their own and of other governments. When appropriate, drafts of resolutions should be prepared in advance as a basis for discussion. Additional preparatory work will also be required for the annual political appraisal referred to in the preceding section.

56. To assist the Permanent Representatives and the Secretary General in discharging their responsibilities for political consultation, there should be constituted under the Council a Committee of Political Advisers from each delegation, aided when necessary by specialists from the capitals. It would meet under the chairmanship of a member of the International Staff appointed by the Secretary General, and would include among its responsibilities current studies such as those on trends of Soviet policy.

III. Peaceful settlement of inter-member disputes

57. In the development of effective political co-operation in NATO, it is of crucial importance to avoid serious inter-member disputes and to settle them quickly and satisfactorily when they occur. The settlement of such disputes is in the first place the direct responsibility of the member governments concerned, under both the Charter of the United Nations (Article XXXIII) and the North Atlantic Treaty (Article I). To clarify NATO's responsibilities in dealing with disputes which have not proved capable of settlement directly and to enable NATO, if necessary, to help in the settlement of such disputes, the Committee recommends that the Council adopt a resolution under Article I of the Treaty on the following lines:

a. re-affirming the obligation of members to settle by peaceful means any disputes between themselves;

b. declaring their intention to submit any such disputes, which have not proved capable of settlement directly, to good offices procedures within the NATO framework before resorting to any other international agency; except for disputes of a legal character appropriate for submission to a judicial tribunal, and those disputes of an economic character for which attempts at settlement might best be made initially in the appropriate specialized economic organization;

c. recognizing the right and duty of member governments and of the Secretary General to bring to the attention of the Council matters which in their opinion may threaten the solidarity or effectiveness of the Alliance;

d. empowering the Secretary General to offer his good offices informally at any time to the parties in dispute, and with their consent to initiate or facilitate procedures of enquiry, mediation, conciliation, or arbitration; and

e. empowering the Secretary General, where he deems it appropriate for the purpose outlined in d. above, to use the assistance of not more than three Permanent Representatives chosen by him in each instance.

IV. Parliamentary Associations and the Parliamentary Conference

58. Among the best supporters of NATO and its purposes are those Members of Parliament who have had a chance at first hand to see some of its activities and to learn of its problems, and to exchange views with their colleagues from other parliaments. In particular, the formation of national Parliamentary Associations and the activities of the Conference of Members of Parliament from NATO countries have contributed to the development of public support for NATO and solidarity among its members.

59. In order to maintain a close relationship of Parliamentarians with NATO, the following arrangements are recommended:

a. that the Secretary General continue to place the facilities of NATO Headquarters at the disposal of Parliamentary Conferences and give all possible help with arrangements for their meetings;

b. that invited representatives of member governments and the Secretary General and other senior NATO civil and military officers attend certain of these meetings. In this way the Parliamentarians would be informed on the state of the Alliance and the problems before it, and the value of their discussions would be increased.

CHAPTER III

Economic co-operation

I. Introduction

60. Political co-operation and economic conflict are not reconcilable. Therefore, in the economic as well as in the political field there must be a genuine desire among the members to work together and a readiness to consult on questions of common concern based on the recognition of common interests.

61. These common economic interests shared by the members of NATO call for:

a. co-operative and national action to achieve healthy and expanding economies, both to promote the well-being and self-confidence of the Atlantic peoples and to serve as the essential support for an adequate defence effort;

b. the greatest possible freedom in trade and payments and in the movement of manpower and long-term capital;

c. assistance to economically underdeveloped areas for reasons of enlightened self-interest and to promote better relations among peoples; and

d. policies which will demonstrate, under conditions of competitive co-existence, the superiority of free institutions in promoting human welfare and economic progress.

62. A recognition of these common NATO interests, and collective and individual efforts to promote them, need not in any way prejudice close economic relations with non-NATO countries. Economic, like political co-operation, is and must remain wider than NATO. At the same time, the NATO countries have an interest in any arrangements for especially close economic co-operation among groups of European member nations. It should be possible – as it is desirable – for such special arrangements to promote rather than conflict with the wider objectives of Article II of our Treaty, which are of basic importance to the stability and well-being, not only of the North Atlantic area, but of the whole non-Communist world.

II. NATO and other organizations

63. While the purposes and principles of Article II are of vital importance, it is not necessary that member countries pursue them only through action in NATO itself. It would not serve the interests of the Atlantic Community for NATO to duplicate the operating functions of other international organizations designed for various forms of economic co-operation.[1] NATO members play a major part in all these agencies, whose membership is generally well adapted to the purposes they serve.

64. Nor do there now appear to be significant new areas for collective economic action requiring execution by NATO itself. In fact, the common

1. The outstanding instances are the Organization for European Co-operation and Development (OECD) (which includes all NATO countries and four others); the General Agreement on Tariffs and Trade (GATT); the International Monetary Fund (IMF); the International Bank for Reconstruction and Development (IBRD); the International Finance Corporation (IFC); and the various other United Nations agencies including the Economic Commission for Europe. Several NATO members participate actively in the Colombo Plan for promoting economic development in Asia. Most members are taking an active part in technical assistance programmes and are also participating in discussions of proposals for the creation of a Special United Nations Fund for Economic Development (SUNFED).

economic concern of the member nations will often best be fostered by continued and increased collaboration both bilaterally and through organizations other than NATO. This collaboration should be reinforced, however, by NATO consultation whenever economic issues of special interest to the Alliance are involved, particularly those which have political or defence implications or affect the economic health of the Atlantic Community as a whole. This, in turn, requires a substantial expansion of exchange of information and views in NATO in the economic as well as in the political field. Such economic consultation should seek to secure a common approach on the part of member governments where the questions are clearly related to the political and security interests of the Alliance. Action resulting from such a common approach, however, should normally be taken by governments either directly or through other international organizations.

65. NATO, as such, should not seek to establish formal relations with these other organizations, and the harmonizing of attitudes and actions should be left to the representatives of the NATO governments therein. Nor is it necessary or desirable for NATO members to form a 'bloc' in such organizations. This would only alienate other friendly governments. There should, however, be consultation in NATO when economic issues of special political or strategic importance to NATO arise in other organizations and in particular before meetings at which there may be attempts to divide or weaken the Atlantic Alliance, or prejudice its interests.

III. Conflicts in economic policies of NATO countries

66. NATO has a positive interest in the resolution of economic disputes which may have political or strategic repercussions damaging to the Alliance. These are to be distinguished from disagreements on economic policy which are normally dealt with through direct negotiations or by multilateral discussions in other organizations. Nothing would be gained by merely having repeated in NATO the same arguments made in other and more technically qualified organizations. It should, however, be open to any member or to the Secretary General to raise in NATO issues on which they feel that consideration elsewhere is not making adequate progress and that NATO consultation might facilitate solutions contributing to the objectives of the Atlantic Community. The procedures for peaceful settlement of political disputes discussed in the previous chapter should also be available for major disputes of an economic character which are appropriate for NATO consideration.

IV. Scientific and technical co-operation

67. One area of special importance to the Atlantic Community is that of science and technology. During the last decade, it has become ever clearer that progress in this field can be decisive in determining the security of nations and their position in world affairs. Such progress is also vital if the Western world is to play its proper role in relation to economically under-developed areas.

68. Within the general field of science and technology, there is an especially urgent need to improve the quality and to increase the supply of scientists, engineers and technicians. Responsibility for recruitment, training and utilization of scientific and technical personnel is primarily a national rather than an international matter. Nor is it a responsibility solely of national governments. In the member countries with federal systems, state and provincial governments play the major part, and many of the universities and institutes of higher learning in the Atlantic area are independent institutions free from detailed control by governments. At the same time, properly designed measures of international co-operation could stimulate individual member countries to adopt more positive policies and, in some cases, help guide them in the most constructive directions.

69. Certain activities in this connection are already being carried out by other organizations. Progress in this field, however, is so crucial to the future of the Atlantic Community that NATO members should ensure that every possibility of fruitful co-operation is examined. As a first concrete step, therefore, it is recommended that a conference be convened composed of one or at the most two outstanding authorities, private or governmental, from each country in order:

a. to exchange information and views concerning the most urgent problems in the recruitment, training and utilization of scientists, engineers and technicians, and the best means, both long-term and short-term, of solving those problems;

b. to foster closer relations among the participants with a view to continued interchange of experience and stimulation of constructive work in member countries; and

c. to propose specific measures for future international co-operation in this field, through NATO or other international organizations.

V. Consultation on economic problems

70. It is agreed that the Atlantic Community has a positive concern with healthy and accelerated development in economically underdeveloped areas, both inside and outside the NATO area. The Committee feels, however, that NATO is not an appropriate agency for administering programmes of assistance for economic development, or even for systematically concerting the relevant policies of member nations. What member countries can and should do is to keep each other and the Organization informed of their programmes and policies in this field. When required, NATO should review the adequacy of existing action in relation to the interests of the Alliance.

71. The economic interests of the Atlantic Community cannot be considered in isolation from the activities and policies of the Soviet bloc. The Soviets are resorting all too often to the use of economic measures designed to weaken the Western Alliance, or to create in other areas a high degree of dependence on the Soviet world. In this situation it is more than ever important that NATO countries actively develop their own constructive commercial and financial policies. In particular, they should avoid creating situations of which the Soviet *bloc* countries might take advantage to the detriment of the Atlantic Community and of other non-Communist countries. In this whole field of competitive economic co-existence member countries should consult together more fully in order to determine their course deliberately and with the fullest possible knowledge.

72. There has been a considerable evolution in NATO's arrangements for regular economic consultation. In addition, a number of economic matters have been brought before the Council for consideration on an *ad hoc* basis. No substantial new machinery in this field is called for. However, in view of the extended range of topics for regular exchange of information and consultation described above, there should be established under the Council a Committee of Economic Advisers. This group should be entrusted with preliminary discussion, on a systematic basis, of the matters outlined above, together with such tasks as may be assigned by the Council or approved by the Council at the Committee's request. It would absorb any continuing function of the Committee of Technical Advisers. Since its duties would not be full-time, member governments could be represented normally by officials mainly concerned with the work of other international economic organizations. Membership, however, should be flexible, the Committee being composed, when appropriate, of specialists from the capitals on particular topics under consideration.

CHAPTER IV

Cultural co-operation

73. A sense of community must bind the people as well as the institutions of the Atlantic nations. This will exist only to the extent that there is a realization of their common cultural heritage and of the values of their free way of life and thought. It is important, therefore, for the NATO countries to promote cultural co-operation among their peoples by all practical means in order to strengthen their unity and develop maximum support for the Alliance. It is particularly important that this cultural co-operation should be wider than continental. This, however, does not preclude particular governments from acting on a more limited multilateral or even bilateral basis to strengthen their own cultural relations within the broader Atlantic framework. The Committee welcomes the measures for cultural co-operation within the Atlantic Community which have been initiated by private individuals and non-governmental groups. These should be encouraged and increased.

74. To further cultural collaboration, the Committee suggests that member governments be guided by the following general principles:

a. government activities in this field should not duplicate but should support and supplement private efforts;

b. member governments should give priority to those projects which require joint NATO action, and thus contribute to a developing sense of community;

c. in developing new activities in the cultural field, NATO can most fruitfully place the main emphasis on inspiring and promoting transatlantic contacts;

d. there should be a realistic appreciation of the financial implications of cultural projects.

75. In order to develop public awareness and understanding of NATO and the Atlantic Community, the Council should work out arrangements for NATO courses and seminars for teachers.

76. NATO and its member governments should broaden their support of other educational and related activities such as the NATO Fellowship and Scholarship Programme; creation of university chairs of Atlantic studies; visiting professorships; government-sponsored programmes for the exchange of persons, especially on a transatlantic basis; use of NATO information materials in schools; and establishment of special NATO awards for students.

77. Governments should actively promote closer relations between NATO and youth organizations and a specialist should be added to the International Staff in this connection. Conferences under NATO auspices of representatives of youth organizations such as that of July, 1956, should be held from time to time.

78. In the interests of promoting easier and more frequent contacts among the NATO peoples, governments should review and, if possible, revise their foreign exchange and other policies which restrict travel.

79. In view of the importance of promoting better understanding and goodwill between NATO service personnel, it would be desirable, in co-operation with the military authorities, to extend exchanges of such personnel beyond the limits of normal training programmes. Such exchanges might, at first step, be developed by governments on a bilateral basis. In addition, member governments should seek the assistance of the Atlantic Treaty Association and other voluntary organizations in the further development of such exchanges.

80. Cultural projects which have a common benefit should be commonly financed. Agreed cultural projects initiated by a single member government or a private organization, such as the recent seminar held at Oxford or the Study Conference sponsored by the Atlantic Treaty Association on 'The Role of the School in the Atlantic Community', should receive financial support from NATO where that is necessary to supplement national resources.

CHAPTER V
Co-operation in the information field

81. The people of the member countries must know about NATO if they are to support it. Therefore they must be informed not only of NATO's aspirations, but of its achievements. There must be substance for an effective NATO information programme and resources to carry it out. The public should be informed to the greatest possible extent of significant results achieved through NATO consultation.

82. NATO information activities should be directed primarily to public opinion in the NATO area. At the same time an understanding outside the NATO area of the objectives and accomplishments of the Organization is necessary if it is to be viewed sympathetically, and if its activities are not to be misinterpreted.

83. The important task of explaining and reporting NATO activities rests primarily on national information services. They cannot discharge this task if member governments do not make adequate provisions in their national programmes for that purpose. It is essential, therefore, that such provision be made. NATO can and should assist national governments in this work. The promotion of information about, and public understanding of NATO and the Atlantic Community should, in fact, be a joint endeavour by the Organization and its members.

84. One of NATO's functions should be to co-ordinate the work of national information services in fields of common interest. Governments should pool their experiences and views in NATO to avoid differences in evaluation and emphasis. This is particularly important in the dissemination of information about NATO to other countries. Co-ordinated policy should underline the defensive character of our Alliance and the importance of its non-military aspects. It should cover also replies to anti-NATO propaganda and the analysis of Communist moves and statements which affect NATO.

85. In its turn, the NATO Information Division must be given the resources by governments as well as their support, without which it could not discharge these new tasks – and should not be asked to do so.

86. In order to facilitate co-operation between the NATO Information Division and national information services, the following specific measures are recommended:

a. an Officer should be designated by each national information service to maintain liaison with NATO and to be responsible for the dissemination of NATO information material;

b. governments should submit to NATO the relevant information programmes which they plan to implement, for discussion in the Committee on Information and Cultural Relations. Representatives of national information services should take part in these discussions;

c. within the NATO Information Division budget, provision should be made for a translation fund so that NATO information material can be translated into the non-official languages of the Alliance, according to reasonable requirements of the member governments;

d. NATO should, on request, provide national services with special studies on matters of common interest.

87. The journalists' tours sponsored by NATO should be broadened to include others in a position to influence public opinion, such as trade and youth leaders, teachers and lecturers. Closer relations between private organizations supporting NATO and the NATO Information Division should also be encouraged.

CHAPTER VI

Organization and functions

88. The Committee considers that NATO in its present form is capable of discharging the non-military functions required of it. Structural changes are not needed. The machine is basically satisfactory. It is for governments to make use of it.

89. At the same time, certain improvements in the procedures and functioning of the Organization will be required if the recommendations of this report are to be fully implemented. The proposals in this Chapter are submitted for this purpose.

A. MEETINGS OF THE COUNCIL

90. More time should be allowed for Ministerial Meetings. Experience has shown that, without more time, important issues on the agenda cannot be adequately considered. Decisions concerning some of them will not be reached at all, or will be reached only in an unclear form.

91. Efforts should be made to encourage discussion rather than simply declarations of policy prepared in advance. Arrangements for meetings should be made with this aim in view. For most sessions, the numbers present should be sharply restricted. In order to facilitate free discussion, when Ministers wish to speak in a language other than French or English, consecutive translation into one of these official languages should be provided by interpreters from their own delegations.

92. Meetings of Foreign Ministers should be held whenever required, and occasionally in locations other than NATO Headquarters. Ministers might also participate more frequently in regular Council meetings, even though not all of them may find it possible to attend such meetings at the same time. The Council of Permanent Representatives has powers of effective decision: in other words, the authority of the Council as such is the same whether governments are represented by Ministers or by their Permanent Representatives. Thus there should be no firm or formal line between Ministerial and other meetings of the Council.

B. STRENGTHENING THE LINKS BETWEEN THE COUNCIL AND
MEMBER GOVERNMENTS

93. It is indispensable to the kind of consultations envisaged in this report that Permanent Representatives should be in a position to speak authoritatively and to reflect the current thinking of their governments. Differences in location and in constitutional organization make impossible any uniform arrangements in all member governments. In some cases it might be desirable to designate a high official in the national capital to be concerned primarily with NATO affairs. The purpose would be to help both in fostering NATO consultations whenever national policies impinge on the common interest of the Atlantic Community, and in translating the results of such consultation into effective action within the national governments.

94. To ensure the closest possible connection between current thinking in the governments and consultations in the Council, there might be occasional Council Meetings with the participation of specially designated officials or the permanent heads of foreign ministries.

C. PREPARATION FOR COUNCIL MEETINGS

95. Items on the agenda of Ministerial Meetings should be thoroughly examined by Permanent Representatives and relevant proposals prepared before Ministers meet. For this purpose it may be found desirable for governments to send senior experts to consult on agenda items before the meetings take place.

96. The preparation of questions for discussion in the Council should be assisted by appropriate use of the Council's Committees of Political and Economic Advisers. (Recommendations on the establishment of these Committees are set forth in Chapter 2, paragraph 56, and Chapter 3, paragraph 72.)

97. In the case of consultations on special subjects, more use should be made of senior experts from national capitals to assist permanent delegations by calling them, on an *ad hoc* basis, to do preparatory work. Informal discussions among specialists with corresponding responsibilities are a particularly valuable means of concerting governmental attitudes in the early stages of policy formation.

98. Member governments should make available to one another through NATO 'basic position material' for background information. This would help the Alliance as a whole in the consideration of problems of common concern and would assist individual governments to understand more fully the reasons for the position adopted by any member country on a particular issue which might be its special concern, but which might also affect in varying degrees other members of NATO.

D. THE SECRETARY GENERAL AND THE INTERNATIONAL STAFF

99. To enable the Organization to make its full contribution, the role of the Secretary General and the International Staff needs to be enhanced.

100. It is recommended that the Secretary General preside over meetings of the Council in Ministerial, as he does now in other sessions. Such a change with respect to the conduct of the Council's business would follow naturally from the new responsibilities of the Secretary General, arising out of the recommendations of this report. It is also warranted by the Secretary General's unique opportunities for becoming familiar with the problems and the activities of the Alliance as a whole.

101. It would, however, still be desirable to have one Minister chosen each year as President of the Council in accordance with the present practice of alphabetical rotation. This Minister, as President, would continue to have especially close contact with the Secretary General during and between Ministerial Meetings, and would, as at present, act as the spokesman of the Council on all formal occasions. He would also preside at the formal opening and closing of Ministerial sessions of the Council.

102. In addition:

a. the Secretary General should be encouraged to propose items for NATO consultation in the fields covered by this report and should be responsible for promoting and directing the process of consultation;

b. in view of these responsibilities member governments should undertake to keep the Secretary General fully and currently informed through their permanent delegations of their governments' thinking on questions of common concern to the Alliance;

c. attention is also called to the additional responsibilities of the Secretary General, recommended in connection with the annual political appraisal (Chapter II, paragraph 52), and the peaceful settlement of disputes (Chapter II, paragraph 57).

103. The effective functioning of NATO depends in large measure on the efficiency, devotion and morale of its Secretariat. Acceptance of the recommendations in this report would impose on the Secretariat new duties and reponsibilities. Governments must, therefore, be prepared to give the International Staff all necessary support, both in finance and personnel. If this is not done, the recommendations of the report, even if accepted by governments, will not be satisfactorily carried out.

ANNEX I

Committee of Three: Formal record of proceedings

The Committee of Three, consisting of Dr. Gaetano Martino (Italy), Mr. Halvard Lange (Norway), and Mr. Lester M. Pearson (Canada), was established by the North Atlantic Council in Ministerial Session on May 5, 1956, with the following terms of reference:

'. . . to advise the Council on ways and means to improve and extend NATO co-operation in non-military fields and to develop greater unity within the Atlantic Community.'

2. The Committee held its first meetings June 20 to 22, 1956, at NATO Headquarters in Paris. During these discussions, the procedure to be followed by the Committee was established, and it was decided to send a Questionnaire to each NATO member government in order to obtain its views on a number of specific problems with respect to co-operation in the political, economic, cultural and information fields and regarding the organization and functions of NATO. In addition, the Committee issued a memorandum containing explanatory notes and guidance to assist countries in the preparation of their replies to the Questionnaire. The Questionnaire was circulated on June 28, 1956, and governments were requested to submit their replies by August 20.

3. The Committee reassembled in Paris on September 10, 1956, and held a series of meetings lasting until the 22nd of that month. After having examined and analysed the replies to the Questionnaire, the Committee held consultations with each member country individually. The purpose of these consultations was to clarify, where necessary, the position taken by governments in their replies, and to discuss with the representatives of other governments in a preliminary way certain views of the Committee.

4. The consultations took place in the following order:

Wednesday, September 12:
    a.m. Iceland (represented by Mr. H. G. Andersen, Permanent Representative of Iceland to the North Atlantic Council).
    p.m. Turkey (represented by Mr. N. Birgi, Secretary General of the Ministry of Foreign Affairs).

Thursday, September 13:
    a.m. The Netherlands (represented by Mr. J. W. Beyen, Minister for Foreign Affairs).
    p.m. Greece (represented by Mr. E. Averof, Minister for Foreign Affairs).

Friday, September 14:

a.m. Belgium (represented by Mr. P.-H. Spaak, Minister for Foreign Affairs).

p.m. Germany (represented by Professor Hallstein, Secretary of State for Foreign Affairs).

Monday, September 17:

a.m. Luxembourg (represented by Mr. M. J. Bech, Prime Minister and Minister for Foreign Affairs).

a.m. France (represented by Mr. C. Pineau, Minister for Foreign Affairs).

p.m. United States (represented by Senator George, special representative of President Eisenhower).

p.m. Portugal (represented by Mr. P. Cunha, Minister for Foreign Affairs).

Tuesday, September 18:

a.m. Denmark (represented by Mr. Ernst Christiansen, Deputy Foreign Minister).

p.m. United Kingdom (represented by Mr. Anthony Nutting, Minister of State for Foreign Affairs).

5. In addition the Committee met the following groups:

a. On Wednesday, September 12, meeting with the Standing Committee of the Conference of Members of Parliament from NATO countries, consisting of the following persons:

Belgium:	Mr. Frans Van Cauwelaert, Mr. A. de Meeler.
Canada:	Senator, The Hon. Wishart McL. Robertson, P.C.
France:	Mr. Maurice Schumann.
Germany:	Herr. F. Berendsen, Dr. Richard Jeager.
Netherlands:	Mr. J. J. Fens, Mr. J. L. Kranenburg, Mr. E. A. Vermeer.
Turkey:	Colonel Seyfi Kurtbeck.
United Kingdom:	Colonel Walter Elliott, CH., MC., M.P.
United States:	Congressman Wayne L. Hays, M.C.

b. On Saturday, September 15, meeting with the Atlantic Treaty Association, represented by:

Count Morra, Chairman;

Dr. Nord, Vice-Chairman;

Dr. Flynt, Vice-Chairman, and Mr. John Eppstein, Secretary General, and a number of delegates from national member organizations.

c. On Tuesday, September 18, meeting with General Billotte and Mr. Barton, representing the Signatories of the Declaration of Atlantic Unity.

333

6. As a result of these consultations a draft report to the Council was prepared. In this work the Committee benefited from the expert advice of three special consultants. They were Professor Lincoln Gordon (Harvard University), Professor Guido Carli (Rome) and Mr. Robert Major (Oslo).

7. The Committee met again in New York on November 14 and re-examined the report in the light of the important world events which occurred in the interval since its September meeting. The Committee, after approving the report, furnished the other Foreign Ministers with an advance copy, preparatory to consideration of the report by the North Atlantic Council.

ANNEX II

Council Resolutions

1. Resolution on the peaceful settlement of disputes and differences between members of the North Atlantic Treaty Organization

Whereas the parties to the North Atlantic Treaty, under Article I of that treaty, have undertaken 'to settle any international disputes in which they may be involved by peaceful means in such a manner that international peace and security and justice are not endangered';

Whereas the parties have further undertaken to seek to eliminate conflicts in their international economics and will encourage economic collaboration between any or all of them;

Whereas NATO unity and strength in the pursuit of these objectives remain essential for continuous co-operation in military and non-military fields;

THE NORTH ATLANTIC COUNCIL:

Reaffirms the obligations of all its members, under Article I of the Treaty, to settle by peaceful means any dispute between themselves;

Decides that such disputes which have not proved capable of settlement directly be submitted to good offices procedures within the NATO framework before member governments resort to any other international agency except for disputes of a legal character appropriate for submission to a judicial tribunal and those disputes of an economic character for which attempts at settlement might best be made initially in the appropriate specialized economic organizations;

Recognizes the right and duty of member governments and of the Secretary General to bring to its attention matters which in their opinion may threaten the solidarity or effectiveness of the Alliance;

Empowers the Secretary General to offer his good offices informally at any time to member governments involved in a dispute and with their consent to initiate or facilitate procedures of enquiry, mediation, conciliation, or arbitration;

Authorizes the Secretary General where he deems it appropriate for the purpose outlined in the preceding paragraph to use the assistance of not more than three permanent representatives chosen by him in each instance.

2. Resolution on the report of the Committee of Three on non-military co-operation in NATO

Whereas the North Atlantic Council at its meeting in Paris on May 5th established a Committee composed of the Foreign Ministers of Italy, Canada and Norway to advise the Council on ways and means to improve and extend NATO co-operation in non-military fields and to develop greater unity within the Atlantic Community;

Whereas the Committee of Three has now reported on the task assigned to it and has submitted to the Council a number of recommendations on such ways and means to improve and extend NATO co-operation in non-military fields;

THE NORTH ATLANTIC COUNCIL:

Takes note of the Report of the Committee of Three; and

Approves its recommendations; and

Invites the Council in Permanent Session to implement in the light of the comments made by governments the principles and recommendations contained in the Report; and

Invites the Secretary General to draw up for consideration by the Council such further specific proposals as may be required for the implementation of these recommendations and to report periodically on the compliance with these recommendations by governments.

Authorizes the Committee of Three to publish their report.

APPENDIX 6

The Future Tasks of the Alliance

Report of the Council
Annex to the final communique of the
ministerial meeting

December, 1967

1. A year ago, on the initiative of the Foreign Minister of Belgium, the governments of the fifteen nations of the Alliance resolved to 'study the future tasks which face the Alliance, and its procedures for fulfilling them in order to strengthen the Alliance as a factor for durable peace'. The present report sets forth the general tenor and main principles emerging from this examination of the future tasks of the Alliance.

2, Studies were undertaken by Messrs. Schütz, Watson, Spaak, Kohler and Patijn. The Council wishes to express its appreciation and thanks to these eminent personalities for their efforts and for the analyses they produced.

3. The exercise has shown that the Alliance is a dynamic and vigorous organization which is constantly adapting itself to changing conditions. It also has shown that its future tasks can be handled within the terms of the Treaty by building on the methods and procedures which have proved their value over many years.

4. Since the North Atlantic Treaty was signed in 1949 the international situation has changed significantly and the political tasks of the Alliance have assumed a new dimension. Amongst other developments, the Alliance has played a major part in stopping Communist expansion in Europe; the USSR has become one of the two world super powers but the Communist world is no longer monolithic; the Soviet doctrine of 'peaceful co-existence' has changed the nature of the confrontation with the West but not the basic problems. Although the disparity between the power of the United States and that of the European states remains, Europe has

336

recovered and is on its way towards unity. The process of decolonization has transformed European relations with the rest of the world; at the same time, major problems have arisen in the relations between developed and developing countries.

5. The Atlantic Alliance has two main functions. Its first function is to maintain adequate military strength and political solidarity to deter aggression and other forms of pressure and to defend the territory of member countries if aggression should occur. Since its inception, the Alliance has successfully fulfilled this task. But the possibility of a crisis cannot be excluded as long as the central political issues in Europe, first and foremost the German Question, remain unsolved. Moreover, the situation of instability and uncertainty still precludes a balanced reduction of military forces. Under these conditions, the Allies will maintain as necessary, a suitable military capability to assure the balance of forces, thereby creating a climate of stability, security and confidence.

In this climate the Alliance can carry out its second function, to pursue the search for progress towards a more stable relationship in which the underlying political issues can be solved. Military security and a policy of détente are not contradictory but complementary. Collective defence is a stabilizing factor in world politics. It is the necessary condition for effective policies directed towards a greater relaxation of tensions. The way to peace and stability in Europe rests in particular on the use of the Alliance constructively in the interest of détente. The participation of the USSR and the USA will be necessary to achieve a settlement of the political problems of Europe.

6. From the beginning the Atlantic Alliance has been a co-operative grouping of states sharing the same ideals and with a high degree of common interest. Their cohesion and solidarity provide an element of stability within the Atlantic area.

7. As sovereign states the Allies are not obliged to subordinate their policies to collective decision. The Alliance affords an effective forum and clearing house for the exchange of information and views; thus, each Ally can decide its policy in the light of close knowledge of the problems and objectives of the others. To this end the practice of frank and timely consultations needs to be deepened and improved. Each Ally should play its full part in promoting an improvement in relations with the Soviet Union and the countries of Eastern Europe, bearing in mind that the pursuit of détente must not be allowed to split the Alliance. The chances of success will clearly be greater if the Allies remain on parallel courses, especially in matters of close concern to them all; their actions will thus be all the more effective.

8. No peaceful order in Europe is possible without a major effort by all concerned. The evolution of Soviet and East European policies gives ground for hope that those governments may eventually come to recognize the advantages to them of collaborating in working towards a peaceful settlement. But no final and stable settlement in Europe is possible without a solution of the German question which lies at the heart of present tensions in Europe. Any such settlement must end the unnatural barriers between Eastern and Western Europe, which are most clearly and cruelly manifested in the division of Germany.

9. Accordingly the Allies are resolved to direct their energies to this purpose by realistic measures designed to further a détente in East–West relations. The relaxation of tensions is not the final goal but is part of a long-term process to promote better relations and to foster a European settlement. The ultimate political purpose of the Alliance is to achieve a just and lasting peaceful order in Europe accompanied by appropriate security guarantees.

10. Currently, the development of contacts between the countries of Western and Eastern Europe is mainly on a bilateral basis. Certain subjects, of course, require by their very nature a multilateral solution.

11. The problem of German reunification and its relationship to a European settlement has normally been dealt with in exchanges between the Soviet Union and the three Western powers having special responsibilities in this field. In the preparation of such exchanges the Federal Republic of Germany has regularly joined the three Western powers in order to reach a common position. The other Allies will continue to have their views considered in timely discussions among the Allies about Western policy on this subject, without in any way impairing the special responsibilities in question.

12. The Allies will examine and review suitable policies designed to achieve a just and stable order in Europe, to overcome the division of Germany and to foster European security. This will be part of a process of active and constant preparation for the time when fruitful discussions of these complex questions may be possible bilaterally or multilaterally between Eastern and Western nations.

13. The Allies are studying disarmament and practical arms control measures, including the possibility of balanced force reductions. These studies will be intensified. Their active pursuit reflects the will of the Allies to work for an effective détente with the East.

14. The Allies will examine with particular attention the defence problems of the exposed areas, e.g. the South-Eastern flank. In this respect the present situation in the Mediterranean presents special problems, bearing in mind that the current crisis in the Middle East falls within the responsibilities of the United Nations.

15. The North Atlantic Treaty area cannot be treated in isolation from the rest of the world. Crises and conflicts arising outside the area may impair its security either directly or by affecting the global balance. Allied countries contribute individually within the United Nations and other international organizations to the maintenance of international peace and security and to the solution of important international problems. In accordance with established usage the Allies, or such of them as wish to do so, will also continue to consult on such problems without commitment and as the case may demand.

16. In the light of these findings, the Ministers directed the Council in permanent session to carry out, in the years ahead, the detailed follow-up resulting from this study. This will be done either by intensifying work already in hand or by activating highly specialized studies by more systematic use of experts and officials sent from capitals.

17. Ministers found that the study by the Special Group confirmed the importance of the role which the Alliance is called upon to play during the coming years in the promotion of détente and the strengthening of peace. Since significant problems have not yet been examined in all their aspects, and other problems of no less significance which have arisen from the latest political and strategic developments have still to be examined, the Ministers have directed the Permanent Representatives to put in hand the study of these problems without delay, following such procedures as shall be deemed most appropriate by the Council in permanent session, in order to enable further reports to be subsequently submitted to the Council in Ministerial Session.

Declaration on Atlantic relations

This declaration was approved and published by the North Atlantic Council in Ottawa on June 19, 1974 and signed by Heads of NATO Governments in Brussels on June 26, 1974.

1. The members of the North Atlantic Alliance declare that the Treaty signed 25 years ago to protect their freedom and independence has confirmed their common destiny. Under the shield of the Treaty, the Allies have maintained their security, permitting them to preserve the values which are the heritage of their civilization and enabling Western Europe to rebuild from its ruins and lay the foundations of its unity.

2. The members of the Alliance reaffirm their conviction that the North Atlantic Treaty provides the indispensable basis for their security, thus making possible the pursuit of détente. They welcome the progress that has been achieved on the road towards détente and harmony among nations, and the fact that a Conference of 35 countries of Europe and North America is now seeking to lay down guidelines designed to increase security and co-operation in Europe. They believe that until circumstances permit the introduction of general, complete and controlled disarmament, which alone could provide genuine security for all, the ties uniting them must be maintained. The Allies share a common desire to reduce the burden of arms expenditure on their peoples. But States that wish to preserve peace have never achieved this aim by neglecting their own security.

3. The members of the Alliance reaffirm that their common defence is one and indivisible. An attack on one or more of them in the area of application of the Treaty shall be considered an attack against them all. The common aim is to prevent any attempt by a foreign power to threaten the independence or integrity of a member of the Alliance. Such an attempt would not only put in jeopardy the security of all members of the Alliance but also threaten the foundations of world peace.

4. At the same time they realize that the circumstances affecting their common defence have profoundly changed in the last ten years: the strategic relationship between the United States and the Soviet Union has reached a point of near equilibrium. Consequently, although all the countries of the Alliance remain vulnerable to attack, the nature of the danger to which they are exposed has changed. The Alliance's problems in the defence of Europe have thus assumed a different and more distinct character.

5. However, the essential elements in the situation which gave rise to the Treaty have not changed. While the commitment of all the Allies to the common defence reduces the risk of external aggression, the contribution to the security of the entire Alliance provided by the nuclear forces of the United States based in the United States as well as in Europe and by the presence of North American forces in Europe remains indispensable.

6. Nevertheless, the Alliance must pay careful attention to the dangers to which it is exposed in the European region, and must adopt all measures necessary to avert them. The European members who provide three-quarters of the conventional strength of the Alliance in Europe, and two of whom possess nuclear forces capable of playing a deterrent role of their own, contributing to the overall strengthening of the deterrence of the Alliance, undertake to make the necessary contribution to maintain the common defence at a level capable of deterring and if necessary repelling all actions directed against the independence and territorial integrity of the members of the Alliance.

7. The United States, for its part, reaffirms its determination not to accept any situation which would expose its Allies to external political or military pressure likely to deprive them of their freedom, and states its resolve, together with its Allies, to maintain forces in Europe at the level required to sustain the credibility of the strategy of deterrence and to maintain the capacity to defend the North Atlantic area should deterrence fail.

8. In this connection the member states of the Alliance affirm that as the ultimate purpose of any defence policy is to deny to a potential adversary the objectives he seeks to attain through an armed conflict, all necessary forces would be used for this purpose. Therefore, while reaffirming that a major aim of their policies is to seek agreements that will reduce the risk of war, they also state that such agreements will not limit their freedom to use all forces at their disposal for the common defence in case of attack. Indeed, they are convinced that their determination to do so continues to be the best assurance that war in all its forms will be prevented.

9. All members of the Alliance agree that the continued presence of Canadian and substantial US forces in Europe plays an irreplaceable role in the defence of North America as well as of Europe. Similarly the substantial forces of the European Allies serve to defend Europe and North America as well. It is also recognized that the further progress towards unity, which the member states of the European Community are determined to make, should in due course have a beneficial effect on the contribution to the common defence of the Alliance of those of them who belong to it. Moreover, the contributions made by members of the Alliance to the preservation of international security and world peace are recognized to be of great importance.

10. The members of the Alliance consider that the will to combine their efforts to ensure their common defence obliges them to maintain and improve the efficiency of their forces and that each should undertake, according to the role that it has assumed in the structure of the Alliance, its proper share of the burden of maintaining the security of all. Conversely, they take the view that in the course of current or future negotiations nothing must be accepted which could diminish this security.

11. The Allies are convinced that the fulfilment of their common aims requires the maintenance of close consultation, co-operation and mutual trust, thus fostering the conditions necessary for defence and favourable for détente, which are complementary. In the spirit of the friendship, equality and solidarity which characterize their relationship, they are firmly resolved to keep each other fully informed and to strengthen the practice of frank and timely consultations by all means which may be appropriate on matters relating to their common interests as members of the Alliance, bearing in mind that these interests can be affected by events in other areas of the world. They wish also to ensure that their essential security relationship is supported by harmonious political and economic relations. In particular they will work to remove sources of conflict between their economic policies and to encourage economic co-operation with one another.

12. They recall that they have proclaimed their dedication to the principles of democracy, respect for human rights, justice and social progress, which are the fruits of their shared spiritual heritage and they declare their intention to develop and deepen the application of these principles in their countries. Since these principles, by their very nature, forbid any recourse to methods incompatible with the promotion of world peace, they reaffirm that the efforts which they make to preserve their independence, to maintain their security and to improve the living standards of their peoples exclude all forms of aggression against anyone, are not directed against any other country, and are designed to bring about the general improvement of international relations. In Europe, their objective continues to be the pursuit of understanding and co-operation with every European country. In the world at large, each Allied country recognizes the duty to help the developing countries. It is in the interest of all that every country benefit from technical and economic progress in an open and equitable world system.

13. They recognize that the cohesion of the Alliance has found expression not only in co-operation among their governments, but also in the free exchange of views among the elected representatives of the peoples of the Alliance. Accordingly, they declare their support for the strengthening of links among Parliamentarians.

14. The members of the Alliance rededicate themselves to the aims and ideals of the North Atlantic Treaty during this year of the twenty-fifth Anniversary of its signature. The member nations look to the future, confident that the vitality and creativity of their peoples are commensurate with the challenges which confront them. They declare their conviction that the North Atlantic Alliance continues to serve as an essential element in the lasting structure of peace they are determined to build.

Adopted and published in   Signed in Brussels
Ottawa on June 19, 1974   on June 26, 1974

Alliance Defence Policy— Ministerial Guidance 1975

Annex to Final Communique
DPC Ministerial Meeting — May 1975

Introduction

1. NATO procedures call for Ministers to give guidance for defence planning every two years. The guidance reflects the political, economic, technological and military factors which could affect the development of NATO forces during the next planning period. The guidance, being a major policy document endorsed by Ministers, provides a reference point and directive for all defence planning activities, at both the national and international level, in NATO.

Long-range defence concept

2. Previous editions of Ministerial Guidance have covered the seven-year period of the NATO Defence Planning Cycle. However, lengthened time-scales for the development and deployment of sophisticated weapon systems together with increased costs of military manpower and equipment now make it necessary to establish a more comprehensive framework for defence planning. To take account of these factors a Long-Range Defence Concept has been adopted, which places increased emphasis on co-operative measures within the Alliance and on the establishment of rigorous priorities.

3. The current international security situation and trends for the future underline the inescapable necessity for NATO to maintain a capability to deter aggression or the threat of it, and if deterrence fails, to restore and maintain the security of the North Atlantic area. The members of NATO are seeking improvements in relations with the East and the reduction of forces on a mutual and balanced basis, but negotiations are slow. Meanwhile the military capabilities of the Warsaw Pact nations continue to expand. Continued maintenance of NATO's defensive strength will furnish a secure basis from which to negotiate in addition to providing a bar to aggression or threats of aggression.

4. The long-range defence concept supports agreed NATO strategy by calling for a balanced force structure of interdependent strategic nuclear, theatre nuclear and conventional force capabilities. Each element of this Triad performs a unique rôle; in combination they provide mutual support and reinforcement. No single element of the Triad can substitute for another. The concept also calls for the modernization of both strategic and theatre nuclear capabilities; however, major emphasis is placed on maintaining and improving Alliance conventional forces. NATO has already achieved a large measure of success in this regard. NATO has fielded the basic ingredients for a stalwart conventional defence. However, disparities between NATO and the Warsaw Pact conventional forces remain. The Allies must reduce these disparities and provide a stable, long-term basis for attaining and maintaining adequate conventional forces.

5. The essence of the long-range defence concept is that NATO can provide an adequate force structure for deterrence and defence if the Allies maintain the forces already in existence (or foreseen in plans currently declared to NATO) and continue to modernize and improve these forces and their supporting facilities. This will require some modest annual increase in real terms in defence expenditures; the actual increase for each country will vary in accordance with its current force contribution, its present efforts and its economic strength. It also requires the optimum use of resources available for defence through the rigorous setting of priorities and a greater degree of co-operation between national forces within the Alliance.

6. This long-range defence concept will help to provide a more comprehensive basis for NATO planning with both the flexibility to absorb effects of political, economic and technological changes, and with the stability in national defence programmes to prevent sudden and uneconomic fluctuations.

The need for defence

7. The Allied governments have successfully engaged the Soviet Union and Warsaw Pact countries in discussions and negotiations on several issues of defence and security, e.g. on the limitation of strategic arms (SALT) and on

Mutual and Balanced Force Reductions. But although the atmosphere in East–West relations has improved over the last decade, it remains a fact that the Warsaw Pact continues to maintain a military capability much greater than that needed for self-defence. In the strategic nuclear field the Soviet Union, having already attained rough parity with the United States, now seems to be seeking to attain a strategic advantage through the development of more sophisticated and powerful missiles. Improvements are also being made in the quality and quantity of Warsaw Pact conventional forces, particularly in the offensive capabilities of aircraft, tanks, artillery and missiles. At sea the expansion of Soviet maritime forces over the past decade and their world-wide deployment have added a new dimension to their capabilities which are now such that, independently of a land/air attack on NATO territory, Soviet maritime forces could be used against NATO forces at sea or against our maritime lines of communication in order to interfere with the economies and vital supplies of NATO nations.

8. The basis of the North Atlantic Treaty is that the common defence of the Alliance is one and indivisible. The Allies would consider an attack on one or more of them an attack against all. The essential solidarity of the Alliance depends upon the political resolve of individual nations and the scale of effort they are prepared to devote to the common defence. Should weaknesses in either cause the Warsaw Pact countries to doubt our readiness to withstand political pressure or our determination to defend ourselves by all the means at our disposal against aggression, they might come to believe that they could use their military power against us for political or military ends without undue risk; accordingly the defence posture of NATO should be so constructed as to take into account the deployment, capabilities and possible objectives of the Warsaw Pact forces.

NATO strategy

9. The aim of NATO's strategy and military planning is to ensure security through deterrence. The primary aim is to deter an attack before it is launched, by making it clear to any aggressor that any attack on NATO would be met by a strong defence and might initiate a sequence of events which cannot be calculated in advance, involving risks to the aggressor out of all proportion to any advantages he might hope to gain. In an era of broad strategic nuclear parity deterrence to all forms of aggression cannot be based upon strategic nuclear forces alone; it must be provided by the overall capabilities of all NATO forces. The Alliance must be able to respond in an appropriate manner to aggression of any kind; the response must be effective in relation to the level of force used by the aggressor and must at the same time make him recognize the dangers of escalation to a higher level.

10. Should aggression occur, the military aim is to preserve or restore the integrity and security of the NATO area by employing such forces as may be necessary within the concept of forward defence and flexibility in response. NATO forces must be prepared to use any capabilities at their disposal (including nuclear weapons) for this purpose. This determination must be evident to the aggressor.

NATO forces

11. In order to implement this strategy of deterrence and defence NATO needs conventional land, sea and air forces, a capability for the effective use of nuclear weapons for tactical purposes, and strategic nuclear forces. These elements of NATO forces should each possess a credibility of their own, and should combine to produce an interlocking system of deterrence and defence. Specifically:

a) the conventional forces should be strong enough to resist and repel a conventional attack on a limited scale, and to deter larger scale conventional attacks through the prospect of an expansion of the area, scale and intensity of hostilities which could lead to the use of nuclear weapons. Nevertheless, should large-scale conventional aggression occur, these forces should be capable of sustaining a conventional defence in the forward areas sufficient to inflict serious losses on the aggressor and convince him of the risks of continuing his aggression;

b) the purpose of the tactical nuclear capability is to enhance the deterrent and defensive affect of NATO's forces against large-scale conventional attack, and to provide a deterrent against the expansion of limited conventional attacks and the possible use of tactical nuclear weapons by the aggressor. Its aim is to convince the aggressor that any form of attack on NATO could result in very serious damage to his own forces, and to emphasize the dangers implicit in the continuance of a conflict by presenting him with the risk that such a situation could escalate beyond his control up to all-out nuclear war. Conversely, this capability should be of such a nature that control of the situation would remain in NATO hands;

c) it is the function of the strategic nuclear forces to strengthen flexible response options, to provide the capability of extending deterrence across a wide range of contingencies, and to provide an ultimate sanction for the overall strategy.

347

These principles of deterrence and defence apply to aggression at sea as well as on land.

Resources

12. Until there is a downward trend in Warsaw Pact force levels, possibly as a result of MBFR negotiations, NATO's present force capabilities vis-à-vis the Warsaw Pact will at least have to be maintained. This implies the maintenance of the levels of forces already in existence (or foreseen in plans currently declared to NATO) and the regular replacement and modernization of major equipments. This is the basic principle which should determine the annual and long-term allocation of resources for defence purposes in all countries. Defence budgets should therefore compensate in full for necessary or unavoidable increases in operating and maintenance costs, including costs of personnel, e.g. those caused by inflation; moreover, in most countries the proportion of expenditure devoted to the provision of major new equipment needs to be substantially increased.

13. It is essential for the solidarity of the Alliance that each member nation should be seen to be making a contribution to the common defence which is commensurate with the rôle it has assumed in the structure of the Alliance and its economic strength.

Alliance co-operation

14. NATO defence programmes are organized for the most part on a strictly national basis. The existence of sovereign governments and national systems of finance are bound to place limits on the degree to which integration of common programmes can be achieved; nevertheless there are a number of possibilities for co-operative effort where a more active approach is now urgently required, e.g.:

a) Rationalization. This means the adjustment of tasks and functions both within national force structures and as between nations; such adjustments must not involve any diminution of the overall capabilities of NATO forces or any reduction in national defence efforts.

b) Flexibility. This requires the elimination of all obstacles to the optimum employment of all forces available.

c) Standardization. The standardization (or interoperability) of equipment makes it easier for forces of different nations to operate effectively together. It simplifies training and logistic support.

d) Co-operation in the development and production of military equipment is a particular form of standardization which can exploit the benefits of scale and reduce unit costs. Co-operation between North America and Europe in this field should become a two-way street.

15. The fullest use should be made of existing civil assets in support of military plans. Detailed planning is also needed in the civil sector to prepare for a rapid transition of national economies to an emergency footing.

Guidance

16. In light of the above considerations, Ministers established guidance on the levels and characteristics of forces, the scale of resources, the nature of the co-operative efforts, and the criteria for the determination of priorities to be used in all defence planning in NATO both national and international, for the future.

Presidents of the North Atlantic Council

Chairmen of the North Atlantic Council

1949–1950	Mr. Dean G. Acheson	(United States)
1950–1951	M. Paul van Zeeland	(Belgium)
1951–1952	Mr. Lester B. Pearson	(Canada)
1952–1953	Mr. Ole Bjorn Kraft	(Denmark)
1953–1954	M. Georges Bidault	(France)
	M. Pierre Mendes-France	(France)
1954–1955	M. Stephanos Stephanopoulos	(Greece)
1955–1956	Mr. Kristinn Gudmunsson	(Iceland)
	Mr. Gudmundur I. Gudmunsson	(Iceland)
1956	M. Gaetano Martino	(Italy)

Presidents of the North Atlantic Council[1]

1957	M. Gaetano Martino	(Italy)
	M. Giuseppe Pella	(Italy)
1957–1958	M. Joseph Bech	(Luxemburg)
1958–1959	Mr. Joseph M. A. H. Luns	(Netherlands)
1959–1960	Mr. Halvard M. Lange	(Norway)
1960–1961	M. Marcelo Mathias	(Portugal)
	M. Franco Nogueira	(Portugal)
1961–1962	M. Selim Sarper	(Turkey)
	M. Feredun Cemal Erkin	(Turkey)

1. In accordance with the recommendations of the Committee of Three, it was decided that each year a Foreign Minister of one of the member countries would become President of the North Atlantic Council, and that the Secretary General would be Chairman at all working sessions of the Council.

1962–1963	Lord Home	(United Kingdom)
1963–1964	Mr. Dean Rusk	(United States)
1964–1965	Mr. Paul-Henri Spaak	(Belgium)
1965–1966	M. Paul Martin	(Canada)
1966–1967	M. Jens Otto Krag	(Denmark)
1967–1968	M. Maurice Couve de Murville	(France)
	M. Michel Debré	(France)
1968–1969	M. Willy Brandt	(Germany)
1969–1970	M. Emil Jonsson	(Iceland)
1970–1971	M. Aldo Moro	(Italy)
1971–1972	M. Gaston Thorn	(Luxembourg)
1972–1973	Mr. W. K. N. Schmelzer	(Netherlands)
	Mr. M. van der Stoel	(Netherlands)
1974–1974	Sir Alec Douglas-Home	(United Kingdom)
	Mr. James Callaghan	(United Kingdom)
1974–1975	M. Dimitri S. Bitsios	(Greece)
1975–1976	Mr. Knut Frydenlund	(Norway)

Permanent Representatives to the North Atlantic Council

Belgium

1952–1975	M. André de Staercke
1976	M. Constant Schuurmans

Canada

1952–1953	Mr. Arnold D. Neeney
1953–1958	Mr. L. Dana Wilgress
1958–1962	Mr. Jules Léger
1962–1966	Mr. Georges Ignatieff
1966–1967	Mr. Charles Ritchie
1967–1972	Mr. Ross Campbell
1972	Mr. Arthur R. Menzies

Denmark

1952–1954	Mr. V. Steensen-Leth
1954–1956	Mr. J. A. Vestbirk
1956–1961	Mr. A. Wassard
1961–1966	Mr. E. Schram-Nielsen
1966–1973	Mr. H. Hjorth-Nielsen
1973	Mr. A. Svart

France

1952–1954	M. Hervé Alphand
1954–1955	M. Maurice Couve de Murville
1955–1956	M. Alexandre Parodi
1957–1958	M. Etienne de Crouy-Chanel
1958–1959	M. Geoffroy Chodron de Courcel

1959–1962   M. Pierre Leusse
1962–1965   M. François Seydoux de Clausonne
1968–1970   M. Jacques Kosciusko-Morizet
1970–1975   M. François de Tricornot de Rose
1975   M. Jacques Tiné

Federal Republic of Germany
1955–1958   Mr. Herbert Adolph Blankenhorn
1958–1962   Dr. Gebhardt von Walther
1962–1971   Prof. Dr. Wilhelm Grewe
1971   Mr. Franz Krapf

Greece
1952   M. Panayotis Pipinelis
1952–1956   M. Georges Exindaris
1956–1962   M. Michel Melas
1962–1967   M. Christos Palamas
1967–1972   M. Phaedon-Anninos Cavalieratos
1972–1974   M. Anghelos Chorafas
1974   M. Byron Theodoropoulos

Iceland
1952–1954   Mr. Gunnlaugur Pétursson
1954–1962   Mr. Hans G. Andersen
1962–1965   Mr. Pétur Thorsteinsson
1965–1967   Mr. Henrik S. V. Björnsson
1967–1971   Mr. Niels P. Sigurdsson
1971   Mr. Tómas A. Tomasson

Italy
1952–1954   M. Alberto Rossi Longhi
1954–1958   M. Adolfo Alessandrini
1958–1959   M. Umberto Grazzi
1959–1967   M. Adolfo Alessandrini
1967–1971   M. Carlo Ferrariis Salzano
1971   M. Felice Catalano di Melilli

Luxembourg
1952–1958   M. Nicolas Hommel
1958–1967   M. Paul Reuter
1967–1973   M. Lambert Schaus
1973   M. Marcel Fischbach

Netherlands

1952–1956	Mr. A. W. L. Tjarda van Starkenborgh Stachouwer
1956–1958	Mr. E. N. van Kleffens
1958–1961	Mr. Dirk U. Stikker
1961–1970	Mr. H. N. Boon
1970–1973	Mr. D. P. Spierenburg
1973	Mr. A. F. K. Hartogh

Norway

1952–1955	Mr. Arne Skaug
1955–1963	Mr. Jens Boyesen
1963–1967	Mr. Georg Kristiansen
1967–1971	Mr. Knut Aars
1971	Mr. Rolf Busch

Portugal

1952–1957	Count de Tovar
1958–1961	M. Antonio de Faria
1961–1970	M. Vasco da Cunha
1970–1974	M. Albano Nogueira
1974	M. João de Freitas-Cruz

Turkey

1952–1954	M. Fatin Rüştü Zorlu
1954–1957	M. Mehmet Ali Tiney
1957–1960	M. Selim Sarper
1960	M. Haydar Görk
1960–1972	M. Muharrem Nuri Birgi
1972	M. Orhan Eralp

United Kingdom

1952–1953	Sir Frederick Hoyer-Miller
1953–1957	Sir Christopher Steel
1957–1960	Sir Frank Roberts
1960–1962	Sir Paul Mason
1962–1966	Sir Evelyn Shuckburgh
1966–1970	Sir Bernard Burrows
1970–1975	Sir Edward Peck
1975	Sir John Killick

United States

1952	Mr. Charles M. Spofford
1952–1953	Mr. William H. Draper Jr.

1953–1955	Mr. John C. Hughes
1955–1957	Mr. George W. Perkins
1957–1961	Mr. W. Randolph Burgess
1961–1965	Mr. Thomas K. Finletter
1965–1969	Mr. Harlan Cleveland
1969–1971	Mr. Robert Ellsworth
1971–1973	Mr. David M. Kennedy
1973–1974	Mr. Donald Rumsfeld
1974–1976	Mr. David K. E. Bruce
1976	Mr. Robert Strausz-Hupé

Presidents and Chairmen of the Military Committee

Chairmen of the NATO Military Committee in Chiefs-of-Staff Session

1949–1950	General Omar N. Bradley	(United States)
1951–1952	Lt. General Etienne Baele	(Belgium)
1952–1953	Lt. General Charles Foulkes	(Canada)
1953–1954	Admiral E. J. C. Quistgaard	(Denmark)
1954–1955	General Augustin Guillaume	(France)
1955–1956	Lt. General Stylianos Pallis	(Greece)
1956–1957	General Guiseppe Mancinelli	(Italy)
1957–1958	General B. R. P. F. Hasselman	(Netherlands)
1958–1959	Lt. General Bjarne Øen	(Norway)
1959–1960	General J. A. Beleza Ferras	(Portugal)
1960	General Rustu Erdelhun	(Turkey)
1960–1961	Admiral of the Fleet Earl Mountbatten of Burma	(United Kingdom)
1961–1962	General Lyman L. Lemnitzer	(United States)
1962–1963	Lt. General C. P. de Cumont	(Belgium)

Chairmen of the NATO Military Committee in Permanent Session

1958–1961	General B. R. P. F. Hasselman	(Netherlands)
1961–1963	General Adolf Heusinger	(Germany)

Presidents of the NATO Military Committee[1]

1963–1964	Air Chief Marshal Frank R. Miller	(Canada)
1964–1965	General Kurt Ramberg	(Denmark)
1965–1966	General Charles Ailleret	(France)
1966–1967	General Ulrich de Maizière	(Germany)
1967	Vice Admiral Spyros Avgheris	(Greece)
1967–1968	Lt. General Odysseus Angelis	(Greece)
1968–1969	General Guido Vedovato	(Italy)
1969–1970	Admiral H. M. van den Wall Bake	(Netherlands)
1970–1971	Admiral F. H. Johannessen	(Norway)
1971–1972	General Venancio Deslandes	(Portugal)
1972	General Memdu Tagmaç	(Turkey)
1972–1973	General Faruk Gurler	(Turkey)
1973	General Semih Sançar	(Turkey)
1973	Admiral of the Fleet Sir Peter Hill-Norton	(United Kingdom)
1973–1974	Field Marshal Sir Michael Carver	(United Kingdom)
1974–1975	General George S. Brown	(United States)

Chairmen of the NATO Military Committee[2]

1963–1964	General Adolf Heusinger	(Germany)
1964–1968	Lt. General C. P. de Cumont	(Belgium)
1968–1971	Admiral Sir Nigel Henderson	(United Kingdom)
1971–1974	General Johannes Steinhoff	(Germany)
1974	Admiral of the Fleet Sir Peter Hill-Norton	(United Kingdom)

1. On December 11, 1963, the Council approved the introduction of a President of the Military Committee, rotating annually among the nations.
2. In addition to the introduction of a post of President, Military Committee, in December 1963 the Chairman of the Military Committee in Permanent Session also became Chairman of the Military Committee in Chiefs-of-Staff Session.

Major NATO Commanders

Supreme Allied Commanders Europe

Since the departure of General Dwight D. Eisenhower (US) in May, 1952, the post of Supreme Allied Commander Europe has been held as follows:

General Mathew B. Ridgway (US) – appointed May, 1952
General Alfred B. Gruenther (US) – appointed July, 1953
General Lauris Norstad (US) – appointed November, 1956
General Lyman L. Lemnitzer (US) – appointed January, 1963
General Andrew J. Goodpaster (US) – appointed July, 1969
General Alexander M. Haig, Jr. (US) – appointed December, 1974.

Supreme Allied Commanders Atlantic

The first Supreme Allied Commander Atlantic, was the late Admiral Lynde D. McCormick (US)

The following officers have succeeded Admiral McCormick as SACLANT:

Admiral Jerault Wright (US) – appointed April, 1954
Admiral Robert L. Dennison (US) – appointed December, 1959
Admiral H. P. Smith (US) – appointed April, 1963
Admiral Thomas H. Moorer (US) – appointed May, 1955
Admiral Ephraim P. Holmes (US) – appointed June, 1967
Admiral Charles K. Duncan (US) – appointed October, 1970
Admiral Ralph W. Cousins (US) – appointed October, 1972
Admiral Isaac C. Kidd (US) – appointed May, 1975.

Allied Commanders-in-Chief Channel

The first Allied Commander-in-Chief Channel was Admiral of the Fleet Sir Arthur J. Power (UK) – appointed in February, 1952.

Since then the post of CINCHAN has been held by the following RN officers:

Admiral Sir John H. Edelsten – appointed June, 1952

Admiral of the Fleet Sir George E. Creasey – appointed September, 1954

Admiral Sir Guy Grantham – appointed May, 1957

Admiral Sir Manley L. Power – appointed February, 1959

Admiral Sir Alexander N. C. Bingley – appointed October, 1961

Admiral Sir Wilfrid J. Woods – appointed February, 1963

Admiral Sir Varyl C. Begg – appointed August, 1965

Admiral Sir John B. Frewen – appointed January, 1966

Admiral Sir John Bush – appointed October, 1967

Admiral Sir William O'Brien – appointed February, 1970

Admiral Sir Edward Ashmore – appointed September, 1971

Admiral Sir Terence Lewin – appointed December, 1973

Admiral Sir John Treacher – appointed October, 1975.

National voluntary organizations belonging to the Atlantic Treaty Association

185, rue de la Pompe, 75116 Paris.

BELGIUM:
The Belgian Atlantic Association
12, rue des Taxandres
1040 – Bruxelles

CANADA:
The Atlantic Council of Canada
31, Wellesley Street East,
Toronto 5, Ontario

DENMARK:
Danish Atlantic Association
H.C. Andersens Blvd 11,
1553 Copenhagen V.

FRANCE:
French Association for the
Atlantic Community
185, rue de la Pompe
75116 Paris

FEDERAL REPUBLIC OF
GERMANY
The German Atlantic Society
Meckenheimer Strasse 62
53 Bonn

GREECE:
Hellenic Atlantic Association
18, Sina Street
Athens, 135

ICELAND:
Association of Western Co-operation
Box 28
Reykjavik

ITALY:
Italian Atlantic Committee
Piazza di Firenze 27
00186 Rome

LUXEMBOURG:
Luxembourg Atlantic Association
20bis, rue de Louvigny
Luxembourg

MALTA:
Malta Atlantic Association,
16, Britannia Street,
Valletta

NETHERLANDS:
Netherlands Atlantic Committee
Raamweg 44
The Hague

NORWAY:
Norwegian Atlantic Committee
Akersgaten 57
Oslo 1

PORTUGAL:
Portuguese Atlantic Committee
Rua das Portas de Santo Antao, 89,
Lisbon 2

TURKEY:
Türk Atlantik Andlasmasi Dernegi
Vali Dr. Resit Caddesi 35/6
Çankaya – Ankara

UNITED KINGDOM:
The British Atlantic Committee
Benjamin Franklin House
36, Craven Street
London WC2N 5NG

UNITED STATES:
The Atlantic Council of the
United States,
1616 H Street, N.W.
Washington D.C. 20006

Abbreviations in common use

ABM	Anti-Ballistic Missile
ACCHAN	Allied Command Channel
ACE	Allied Command Europe
ACLANT	Allied Command Atlantic
ACSA	Allied Communications Security Agency
ADM	Atomic Demolition Munition(s)
AFCENT	Allied Forces Central Europe
AFNORTH	Allied Forces Northern Europe
AFSOUTH	Allied Forces Southern Europe
AGARD	Advisory Group for Aerospace, Research and Development
ALLA	Allied Long Lines Agency
AMF	ACE Mobile Force
ANCA	Allied Naval Communications Agency
ARFA	Allied Radio Frequency Agency
ATA	Atlantic Treaty Association
ATCA	Allied Tactical Communications Agency
BMEWS	Ballistic Missile Early Warning System
CCMS	Committee on Challenges of Modern Society
CEAC	Committee for European Airspace Co-ordination
CEOA	Central Europe Operating Agency
CEPS	Central Europe Pipeline System
CSCE	Conference on Security and Co-operation in Europe
CHANCOM	Channel Committee
CINCEASTLANT	Commander-in-Chief Eastern Atlantic Area
CINCENT	Commander-in-Chief Allied Forces Central Europe

CINCHAN	Commander-in-Chief Channel and Southern North Sea
CINCIBERLANT	Commander-in-Chief Iberian Atlantic Area
CINCNORTH	Commander-in-Chief Allied Forces Northern Europe
CINCSOUTH	Commander-in-Chief Allied Forces Southern Europe
CINCWESTLANT	Commander-in-Chief Western Atlantic Area
CNAD	Conference of National Armaments Directors
CUSRPG	Canada-US Regional Planning Group
DPC	Defence Planning Committee
ECSC	European Coal and Steel Community
EDC	European Defence Community
EDIP	European Defence Improvement Programme
EEC	European Economic Community
ELDO	European Launcher Development Organization
ESRO	European Space Research Organization
IATA	International Air Transport Association
IBERLANT	Iberian Atlantic Area
ICAO	International Civil Aviation Organization
ICBM	Intercontinental Ballistic Missile
IMS	International Military Staff
IRBM	Intermediate Range Ballistic Missile
MARAIRMED	Maritime Air Forces Mediterranean
MAS	Military Agency for Standardization
MBFR	Mutual and Balanced Force Reductions
MC	Military Committee
MILREP	Military Representative (to MC)
MLF	Multilateral Force
NAA	North Atlantic Assembly
NAC	North Atlantic Council
NADEEC	NATO Air Defence Electronic Environment Committee
NADEFCOL	NATO Defence College
NADGE	NATO Air Defence Ground Environment System
NAMFI	NATO Missile Firing Installation
NAMMO	NATO Multi-Role Combat Aircraft Development and Production Management Organization
NAMSA	NATO Maintenance and Supply Agency
NAMSO	NATO Maintenance and Supply Organization
NATO	North Atlantic Treaty Organization
NDAC	Nuclear Defence Affairs Committee
NIAG	NATO Industrial Advisory Group
NICS	NATO Integrated Communication System
NMR	National Military Representative (to SHAPE)
NORAD	North American Air Defence System
NPG	Nuclear Planning Group

NPLO	NATO Production and Logistics Organization
NSC	NATO Supply Centre
OECD	Organization for Economic Co-operation and Development
SAC	Strategic Air Command
SACEUR	Supreme Allied Commander Europe
SACLANT	Supreme Allied Commander Atlantic
SACLANTCEN	SACLANT (Anti-Submarine Warfare Research) Centre
SALT	Strategic Arms Limitation Talks
SATCOM	Satellite Communications
SHAPE	Supreme Headquarters Allied Powers Europe
STANAVFORCHAN	Standing Naval Force Channel
STANAVFORLANT	Standing Naval Force Atlantic
STC	SHAPE Technical Centre
TCC	Temporary Council Committee
WEU	Western European Union

Alphabetical index

(In order to balance the index,
many entries starting with N, NA, and NATO, are listed under the second word: thus:
NATO Maintenance and Supply Agency will be found under the letter 'M'.)

365